Foucault, Management and Organization Theory

Foucault, Management and Organization Theory

From Panopticon to Technologies of Self

edited by

Alan McKinlay and Ken Starkey

SAGE Publications
London • Thousand Oaks • New Delhi

First published 1998

SAGE Publications Ltd
6 Bonhill Street
London EC2A 4PU

SAGE Publications Inc.
2455 Teller Road
Thousand Oaks, California 91320

SAGE Publications India Pvt Ltd
32, M-Block Market
Greater Kailash – I
New Delhi 110 048

British Library Cataloguing in Publication data

A catalogue record for this book is available from the British
Library

ISBN 0 8039 7546 5
ISBN 0 8039 7547 3 (pbk)

Library of Congress catalog card number 97–061884

Typeset by Photoprint, Torquay, Devon
Printed in Great Britain by Biddles Ltd, Guildford, Surrey

Contents

Notes on Contributors

Pippa Carter is a senior lecturer in the Department of Management Systems and Sciences at the University of Hull, UK. Her research interests are the ontological and epistemological conditions of organization, the function of management and the nature of work. These research interests are informed by the radical critique of organization theory. Her current research is concerned with the potential contribution to organization theory of post-structuralism and of the modernist/postmodernist debate.

Stewart Clegg is Professor of Management at the University of Technology, Sydney, Australia. His many books include *Frameworks of Power* (1989), *Organization Theory and Class Analysis* (1989) and *Modern Organizations: Organization Studies in the Postmodern World* (1990).

Stanley Deetz is President of the International Communication Association and Professor of Communication at the University of Colorado, Boulder, Colorado, USA. He is the author of many books, including *Transforming Communications, Transforming Business* (1995), *Democracy in an Age of Corporate Colonization* (1992). In 1994, he was a Senior Fulbright Scholar in the Företagsekonomiska Institutionen, Göteborgs Universitet, Sweden, lecturing and conducting research on knowledge-intensive workplaces.

Patricia Findlay is Lecturer in Organization Studies at the University of Edinburgh, UK. Her research interests include management strategy and employment relationships in the microelectronics industry and gender issues in labour process theory. She is currently researching workplace innovation in mature branded goods sectors.

Trevor Hopper is the KPMG Professor of Management Accounting at the University of Manchester, UK. He has co-edited three books: *Critical Accounts, Debating Coal Closures* and *Issues in Management Accounting*. He is currently interested in management accounting change in the context of globalization with empirical reference to the advanced economies of Japan, Germany and the UK and the developing zones of Bangladesh and Sri Lanka.

Keith Hoskin is Professor of Accounting in the Manchester School of Management, UMIST, UK. He has written extensively on the relation between practices and the genesis of forms of knowledge/power, including the development of modern forms of accounting, accountability and managerialism. He is currently writing a book with Richard Macve on this theme.

Norman Jackson is a senior lecturer in the Department of Management Studies of the University of Newcastle upon Tyne, UK. After a number of years in engineering management, he gained an MA in Organizational Psychology at the University of Lancaster and a PhD from Aston University, having also studied at Manchester Business School. His research contributes to the radical critique of organization theory and he is particularly interested in the possibility of non-surplus repressive organization. He is currently researching the contribution of the modernist/postmodernist debate to this possibility.

Norman Macintosh is a Professor of Accounting at Queen's University, Kingston, Canada. He researches and publishes in the area of the behavioural, organizational, sociological and poststructural aspects of management accounting and control systems. He has been a visiting professor at universities around the globe, is a member of the editorial board of several accounting journals, and has served as an executive officer of the American Accounting Association for many years.

Alan McKinlay is Professor of Management at St Andrews University, UK. He has published extensively on business and labour history. He is currently researching a Foucauldian history of the factory and the dynamics of workplace trade unionism in British heavy industries.

Tim Newton is a lecturer in Organization Studies, Birkbeck College, University of London, UK. With a background in industrial psychology he is author of *'Managing' Stress; Emotion and Power at Work* (1995). His current research includes the application and development of actor network theory; subjectivity; and organizations and the natural environment.

Mike Savage is Professor of Sociology at Manchester University, UK. His interests lie in the study of social inequality, urban sociology and social theory. Recent books include *Gender, Careers and Organisations* (with Susan Halford and Anne Witz, 1997) and *Social Change and the Middle Classes* (edited with Tim Butler, 1995).

Ken Starkey is Professor of Management at Nottingham University, UK. His interests span corporate strategy, organization studies and critical social theory. His many books include *Time, Work and Organization* (1989) and, with Alan McKinlay, *Strategy and the Human Resource: Ford's Search for Competitive Advantage* (1993).

Philip Taylor is a lecturer in Industrial Relations at the University of Stirling, UK. Current research interests include 'The Employment Relationship in Call Centres', 'Sick Building Syndrome and the Politics of Occupational Ill-Health', 'Flexible Work Patterns and Part-time Employment' and 'HRM and Worker Resistance in the Scottish Electronics Industry'.

Barbara Townley is Professor of Organizational Analysis, University of Alberta, Edmonton, Canada. She has written on the implications of Michel Foucault's work for the governance of organizations. Her publications include *Reframing Human Resource Management: Power, Ethics and the Subject at Work* (1994).

1

Managing Foucault: Foucault, Management and Organization Theory

Alan McKinlay and Ken Starkey

Foucault's *oeuvre* examines the birth of modernism, the caesura of the Enlightenment. There has been growing interest in the contribution of the work of Michel Foucault to our understanding of organizations, accounting and the control of work. In part this reflects the influence of postmodernism on organization theory and the social sciences in general. Postmodernism presents us with a different agenda than modernism, where the concern was with the steady evolution of 'progress' and 'reason'. In modernist theory, organization is viewed as a social tool and an extension of human rationality, 'the expression of planned thought and calculative action', while in postmodernism, organization is a 'defensive reaction to forces . . . which constantly threaten the stability of organized life' (Cooper and Burrell, 1988: 91). These themes run through the essays contained in this volume.

Foucault's work is complex and multifaceted, at once playful and profound, historical and philosophical. Here our concern is primarily with the later Foucault, where his key concerns were the relationship between power and knowledge and the 'genealogy' of 'organizations (as) social machines which produce elaborate discourses of information/knowledge in which human subjects are a necessary part of the material flow on which the discourses are inscribed' (Cooper and Burrell, 1988: 105). Genealogy has its roots in Nietzsche's *Genealogy of Morals*, where the origins of morality are traced to the will to power. Foucault's seminal work *Discipline and Punish* (1977) examines punishment as a technique for the exercise of power. It also examines how the tactics of power translate into knowledge that defines particular moments in the evolution of thought about social relations. To follow Foucault is to look for the roots of knowledge in power relations and for the tactics of power immanent in various forms of discourse (Foucault, 1979: 70). Discipline, crucially, is conceptualized not as the expression of already existing power but constitutive of it. Given the inherently contingent nature of power this is why knowledge of institutions becomes so vital.

Truth and knowledge, from the Foucauldian perspective, are weapons by which a society manages itself. Norms cannot be divorced from techniques of normalization which structure thought and discourse into mutually exclusive categories such as correct–incorrect and desirable–undesirable

(Cooper and Burrell, 1988: 106). 'Truth' is conditional upon a 'tight web of constraint' (Eribon, 1990: 219–21). 'Rationality' is normative, not transcendental or emancipatory. Foucault analyses the emergence and the constitution of formal organization and its foundation in processes of normalization at the beginning of the modern age. What he reveals is that behind the facade of efficiency, equity, or humanity which surrounds formal organizations of all kinds lie distinct concentrations of power and knowledge.

Crucial to Foucault's views on normalization is the notion of visibility in a disciplinary society. For Foucault, the Panopticon provides the image of the disciplinary society's aspirations. This was an architectural innovation conceived by the utilitarian philosopher Jeremy Bentham. The Panopticon consisted of a twelve-sided polygon with a central tower through which the superintendent could observe the behaviour of institutional inmates. Initially conceived for the observation of convicts and paupers, Bentham saw the structure as a solution to the control problems arising from managing students, asylum inmates and workers. 'Prisons resemble factories, schools, barracks, hospitals, which all resemble prisons' (Foucault, 1977: 83).

Panopticon was the architectural representation of the 'will to power' of modernity. Its aim is

> to induce in the inmate a state of conscious and permanent visibility that assures the automatic functioning of power. So to arrange things that the surveillance is permanent in its effects, even if it is discontinuous in its action; that the perfection of power should tend to render its actual exercise unnecessary; that this architectural apparatus should be a machine for creating and sustaining a power relation independent of the person who exercises it; in short, that the inmates should be caught up in a power situation of which they are themselves the bearers. . . . Bentham laid down the principle that power should be visible and unverifiable. Visible: the inmate will constantly have before his eyes the tall outline of the central tower from which he is spied upon. Unverifiable: the inmate must never know whether he is being looked at any one moment; but he must be sure that he may always be so. (Foucault, 1977: 201)

For Bentham the Panopticon promised a panoply of benefits: 'morals reformed – health preserved – industry invigorated – instruction diffused – public burdens lightened . . . its aim is to strengthen the social forces – to increase production, to develop the economy, spread education, raise the level of public morality; to increase and multiply' (Foucault, 1977: 207–8). Over time, the threat of constant observation leads to internalization and reduces the need for discipline so that, finally, 'discipline, regulation and surveillance are taken for granted' (Zuboff, 1988: 319).

> A real subjection is born from a fictitious relation. So it is not necessary to use force to constrain the convict to good behaviour, the madman to calm, the patient to the observation of the regulations. Bentham was surprised that panoptic institutions could be so light . . . no more bars, no more chains, no more heavy locks. . . . He who is subjected to a field of visibility, and who knows it, assumes responsibility for the constraints of power; he makes them play spontaneously upon himself; he inscribes in himself the power relation in which he simultaneously plays both roles; he becomes the principle of his own subjection. (Foucault, 1977: 202–3)

We no longer need to look for the 'headquarters' of power externally (Foucault 1979: 95). In Lyotard's (1986: 62) phrase, administrative procedures work best when they 'make individuals "want" what the system needs in order to perform well'. It is the central principle of 'continuous observation made possible by technical arrangements' (Zuboff, 1988: 322) which is Foucault's major contribution to organizational analysis. The Panopticon is, as Gibson Burrell puts it, 'the metaphor for the disciplinary mode of domination'. Its image of organization (Morgan, 1986) in which all is visible to the managerial gaze serves as a prototype of all those 'mechanisms that analyse distributions, gaps, series, combinations, and which use instruments that render visible, record, differentiate and compare (Foucault, 1977: 208). Unlike the asylum, clinic and prison, the factory is not an institution which holds its inhabitants captive. But, in common with such total institutions, the creation of the factory in the early nineteenth century represented a clear, if protracted, break with pre-industrial production regimes. Just as the crumbling walls and open commerce of the early nineteenth-century prison gave way to corporal confinement and moral improvement, so the factory gradually became the site of new forms of power and knowledge (Ignatieff, 1978; Marglin, 1974). The essays in this volume all attempt to apply Foucauldian categories and procedures to throw fresh light on the history of the factory, management and the modern corporation.

Situating Foucault

Within organization theory Foucault is conventionally associated with Jeremy Bentham's utilitarian scheme for the construction of the Panopticon penitentiary, the ideal prison: an efficient, humane, punitive form of moral rehabilitation. However, for Bentham, Panopticism was a set of principles applicable to all forms of social governance. The prison was but the simplest institution in which to apply these principles and one, moreover, where the near collapse of the English prison system opened up the prospect – ultimately elusive – of his vision becoming reality (Semple, 1993). Foucault can be properly criticized for his cavalier disregard for the realities of nineteenth-century English penal practice and his highly selective use of Bentham's monumental writings (Semple, 1992). But Foucault is surely correct to regard the Panopticon as the very emblem of modern power in Bentham's writings. As a jurist and as a political philosopher, Bentham's utilitarianism focused on the governance of individuals and society. The law was a system of social control directed towards guiding individuals towards self-control. Prison walls and manacles were restraints and rehabilitators of last resort, but for Bentham the primary site of social control was a legally regulated civil society (Lyons, 1991: 131). Nor was Panopticism solely intended for the reform of rogues and the improvement of already virtuous citizens. For Bentham, Panoptic institutions were essential foundations of democracy: the scrutiny of legislators and rulers by the ruled through accountability and public inspection was fundamental to the nascent democratic state (Rosen, 1983: 82–112). Bentham extended the principles of Panopticism to the emerging capitalist enterprise of the industrial revolution. Management, Bentham advised his brother Samuel who superintended a naval dockyard, was a matter of planning, vigilance, inspection and correction (Hume, 1970, 1981). There are clear overlaps between Bentham and other progressive managers of the industrial revolution and twentieth-century management thinkers such as F.W. Taylor. In this sense, then, we are correct to regard Panopticism as the defining feature of Bentham's moral and political universe which, in turn, legitimizes Foucault's dramatic use of the Panopticon prison as *the* metaphor for the utilitarian remaking of knowledge and institutions in the modern era.

But perhaps the drama of the slow execution of Damiens, the deadly spectacle of monarchic power, contrasted with Bentham's unrealized vision of the Panopticon as the perfect machine of disciplinary power has clouded our reading of Foucault. For Miller,

> The prison was not the only site for the exercise of disciplinary power. The whole of society down to its smallest details offered a site for its deployment. There was always the danger that such a notion be interpreted in too zealous a fashion. A disciplin*ary* society would be mistaken for a disciplin*ed* society. The distinction was between a society in which all individuals obediently conformed to the demands placed upon them, and a society in which individuals constantly escape, evade and subvert the functioning of discipline. The latter was clearly the conception Foucault had intended. (1987: 196; original emphasis)

In both imagery and intent Foucault recalls Weber – Weber's image of the 'iron cage' of rationality which simultaneously materially enriches Western civilization and spiritually impoverishes the captive individual. By examining the behavioural and corporeal politics of rational administration inside the limit institutions of the clinic, asylum and prison, Foucault both extends and complements Weber's formal definition of bureaucratic rationality (O'Neill, 1986). Foucault traces the genesis of new forms of administrative rationality not as a series of abstract ideal-types but as spheres of power/ knowledge centred on specific institutions and discourses. Nor is this a neutral process of unfolding rationality but the construction and refinement of new forms of power and powerlessness.

To speak of power is to speak of politics. But, as Stanley Deetz (1992) reminds us, for critical theory to rely exclusively on images of power derived from political science is far too narrow. Political science is the analysis of power in the public sphere, of the election and the legislature, not in the hidden assumptions of administrative routines (Deetz, 1992: 37):

> Disciplinary power resides in every perception, every judgement, every act. . . . Rather than analysing power in the organization as if it were a sovereign state, the conception of power has to be reformed to take account of this more massive and invisible structure of control. Administration has to be seen in relation to order and discipline if its power is to be understood. . . . It is not just the rule and routine which becomes internalized, but a complex set of practices which provide common-sense, self-evident experience and personal identity.

And it is on this level, the level of the everyday, of 'common-sense' assumptions about formal organizations and their genesis, that Foucault has most to offer, for Foucault's approach, his use of jarring, shocking images of torture juxtaposed with administrative processes of mind-numbing detail, all combine to force us 'to see the ordinary with a fresh vision'. Foucault compels us to confront 'the strangeness of the familiar' (Cooper and Burrell, 1988: 101). The proliferation of 'normalizing gazes', of professional disciplines whose very purpose is to establish the parameters of the acceptable and so isolate the deviant for correction, is found in all manner of unlikely settings. For Gibson Burrell, Foucault's attention to the sheer range of disciplinary practices and their drive to establish standards and control of even the most intimate aspects of our lives is his most significant contribution to organization theory. One of the greatest difficulties in approaching Foucault is that each theoretical position was a way station rather than a final destination. Contradiction, wilful obscurantism and a determination to avoid totalizing theories marked each phase of Foucault's writings. Burrell's opening chapter offers a periodization of Foucault's work and suggestions as to how insights from each phase can be brought to bear on contemporary issues in organization theory.

The idea of the historicity of disciplinary power – the central theme of Foucault's work – is considered by Stewart Clegg. Foucault, Marx and the labour process school, Clegg reminds us, share a common focus on control and resistance in the capitalist workplace. The major distinction is that control through discipline is pioneered not in the factory but in a variety of state institutions. And that the objective of disciplinary power – the construction of obedient bodies – initially reflects the purpose of the superintendents of total institutions rather than the factory master. Indeed, Foucault points to the interplay between capitalists and learned and reforming societies in the construction of a range of specific disciplinary powers through the nineteenth century. Disciplinary power is most potent and efficient when it operates through administrative rules rather than *force majeure*. The existence of rules, in other words, presupposes agency and discretion. Similarly, to analyse any particular complex of power/knowledge is necessarily to confront resistance, a resistance which, in turn, legitimizes disciplinary power itself. It is to the historicity and temporary nature of any form of power/knowledge that Foucault alerts us, *not* to the inevitability of an inescapable 'iron cage'. The tension between what Foucault terms 'governmentality' – the cluster of apparatuses, practices and knowledge which operates at the macro level – and the local control of populations is the issue considered by Norman Jackson and Pippa Carter. In particular, Jackson and Carter unpick the layers of meaning in the term 'dressage', one of the three functions of labour identified by Foucault. For Foucault, labour is both productive and symbolic but he also adds the less familiar term, dressage, which refers to work which is exclusively to confirm the docility, obedience and control of the governed. Indeed, the defining activity of twentieth-century management is not coordination but control. By drawing

attention to managed work as dressage, as discipline, taming and performance, Jackson and Carter highlight aspects of the managerial control of work
which escape conventional labour process analysis.

Accounting for Foucault

Perhaps Foucault's greatest impact on our understanding of management and
organization has been on critical studies of accounting. Seen through the
prism of Foucault's concept of power/knowledge, accounting becomes a set
of practices and a discourse which aims to disaggregate the organization and
lay the actions of all its members open to critical scrutiny, comparison and
modification. The development of standard costing in the first decades of the
twentieth century was a critical innovation in the formation of the modern
managerial bureaucracy. Standard costing held the promise of opening the
mind of the executive as well as the shopfloor worker to objective scrutiny.
Standard costing allied to scientific management made everyone within the
organization visible and governable in a new and much more intimate
way.

> With this step the possibility of a knowledge of every individual within the
> enterprise was established. A visibility and an allocation of responsibility could be
> attached to the individual. The person's activities were at last rendered knowable
> according to prescribed standards and deviations from the norm. Standard costing
> and budgeting made possible a pinpointing of responsibilities for preventable
> inefficiencies at the level of the very individual from whom they derived. The
> human element in production, and most importantly the individual person, could
> now be known according to their contribution to the efficiency of the enterprise.
> (Miller and O'Leary, 1987: 242)

Management accounting is at the centre of modern management, it is the
set of practices which makes individuals knowable, divisional performances
comparable, and organizations governable. Keith Hoskin's examination of
accounting seeks to invert unproblematic discussions of the 'economic'.
Hoskin begins his essay by misquoting Foucault. This misquotation is
deliberate, for Hoskin is drawing attention to the centrality of education and
the examination to Foucault's reflections on governmentality, a central
theme of his later work. In particular, Hoskin highlights the importance of
tracing the history of modern accounting, planning and bureaucratic coordination as practices well before the advent of the modern managerial
enterprise. The examination of American military cadets in the first decade
of the nineteenth century was the conduit for the set of human accounting
practices which eventually formed the basic principles of the managerial
enterprise. Only by tracing specific practices, then, can one develop a
genealogy of modern management conventions which looks beyond the
'economic'.

   The importance of sophisticated accounting controls in making the
modern corporation both knowable and governable cannot be overstated. As
Alfred Chandler (1977: 8, 12) famously put it 'when the volume of

economic activities reached a level that made administrative coordination more efficient and more profitable than market coordination' so 'the visible hand of management replaced the invisible hand of market forces'. Standard costing was vital to the coordination and control of business and worker behaviour inside the large-scale managerial enterprise (Hoskin and Macve, 1988). But, contrary to Chandler's argument that the development of the modern corporation was driven by the pursuit of greater efficiency, McKinlay and Starkey point to the managerial enterprise as a structure for the more thorough surveillance of corporate managers. If Henry Ford's assembly line pioneered a new form of shopfloor discipline then Alfred Sloan's design of General Motors' organizational structure extended the principle of surveillance to managerial employees. Managing managers through continuous surveillance and comparison, the intensification of the normalizing gaze, was the defining objective of Sloan's organizational architecture. Hierarchy and bureaucratic control were the defining character-istics of the giant American enterprise for over 50 years. But, as McKinlay and Starkey point out, the last two decades have witnessed the emergence of new forms of processual controls over managerial performance as important tasks are increasingly delegated to project teams which exist, often uneasily, alongside bureaucratic structures.

The interweaving of the biography of Harold Geneen and the develop-ment of standard cost accounting regimes as vehicles for intimate corporate control is discussed in the chapter by Trevor Hopper and Norman McIntosh. Geneen, the archetypal cold, desiccated accountant, designed a detailed management information system to oversee ITT. Geneen's professional code was that 'the drudgery of numbers will make you free', a code which extended into his management of his personal life. Being a disciplined disciplinarian was not just a business creed but a moral imperative through-out one's entire life. We hear echoes of this ascetic principle in other mid-twentieth-century American corporate organization men. For Robert McNamara, a seminal figure in American corporate and political life, his pursuit of rational control inside Ford Motor Company was paralleled by his relentless search for logic, order and control over his personal life (Shapley, 1993).

The bureaucratic career was first developed as a disciplinary device, not by mid-twentieth-century American corporations but, as Mike Savage dem-onstrates, in the great nineteenth-century railway companies. A geograph-ically dispersed workforce made the elaborate rule books and stringent penalities of these new managerial bureaucracies extraordinarily difficult to enforce. It was the inadequacies of managerial control rather than a drive for technical coordination which stimulated the rise of the career as an alternative form of disciplining the railway workforce. This was registered in the decline of fines and suspensions as punishment for infringing railway rules and the use of promotion through job ladders as reward for self-control. The late-nineteenth-century career and not the punitive discipline of the factories of the industrial revolution was, argues Savage, the first truly 'modern' attempt to solve the problem of industrial discipline. Whatever their initial debt to military models of discipline, it was the failure of visual inspection and exemplary punishment which stimulated the organizational innovation of control through managerial monitoring of individual career paths. Through his pathbreaking analysis of the career as a control device in the nascent railway bureaucracies, Savage has raised fundamental questions about bodily regulation and the discipline of the soul which demand detailed historical analysis in other industrial and commercial settings.

But for writers such as Neimark (1990) and Armstrong (1994) the assimilation of the Panopticon metaphor into critical accounting research to counter claims of objectivity and neutrality has gone too far. Armstrong (1994: 31) contends that Foucauldian studies have almost exclusively focused on 'managerial intention, rather than the actual effect on subjects'. As soon as one accepts the possibility of resistance, the bleak image of a disciplinary dystopia is dispelled. Accounting simply becomes but one element in a complex of disciplinary structures and processes – all of which are contested – rather than the *deus ex machina* of hegemonic control. There is something in this criticism. As several essays in this collection note – and Foucault himself conceded – resistance is much more important than his studies of the prison and the asylum allow. That said, similar criticisms were levelled against Harry Braverman's seminal *Labor and Monopoly Capitalism* (1974) which portrayed the routinization of work and the deskilling of workers as an unstoppable trend throughout the twentieth century. Subsequent work in the labour process tradition has done much to enrich – and correct – Braverman's original thesis; we suspect something similar will happen to Foucault's legacy to organization studies.

Current developments in new managerial technologies aim both to broaden the scope and deepen the intensity of the managerial gaze. The emergence of activity-based costing in the last decade offers corporate managers a new way of understanding not just the internal workings of the corporation but its relationship to suppliers and consumers. Standard costing focuses on allocating costs to particular operations and neglects the necessary interdependencies in complex multi-product enterprises. More than this, however, activity-based accounting allows the managerial gaze to roam over supplier networks and calculates the costs and profits derived from particular market segments (Cooper and Kaplan, 1991). The extension of just-in-time supplier relationships accelerates the concentration, widens the scope and the speed of corporate knowledge acquisition. And this is knowledge combined with economic power which is not reciprocal: there is no parallel gaze by consumers or supplier companies into the internal transaction costs of the corporation. Similarly, the use of electronic trading devices to track streams of purchases by narrowly defined consumer segments deepens the intimacy of corporate knowledge of consumption. Again, the danger is that the aspirations of target marketing rekindle fears of all-seeing 'hidden persuaders' building new forms of power/knowledge and deny the autonomy of reflexive consumption which makes – and remakes – the signs of commodities.

Working with Foucault

The critical literature on the social history of twentieth-century work has been dominated by evaluations of the impact of F.W. Taylor's 'scientific management'. As Taylor himself acknowledged, 'scientific management' was associated with the piecemeal introduction of time and motion studies or bonus systems. But Taylor was as strident in his denunciation of such partial managerial innovations as he was about the opposition of craft workers. His was a total system for improving the operations of any factory or office and could not be judged on isolated efficiency measures. For the principles of 'scientific management' to succeed was dependent upon both managers and managed undergoing nothing less than a 'complete mental revolution': a surrender of craft control over the pace of work, and managers surrendering their personal, monarchic authority in the face of rational bureaucracy (Nelson, 1992).

The refinement of Taylorist principles through, for example, operations research remains uncharted territory for critical theory. But operations research was both an extension of Taylorism and a rejection of its impact in fragmenting the organization. Equally significant was the development of new ways of managing managers. Drawing on his personal experience inside Alfred Sloan's General Motors, the prototypical managerial enterprise, Drucker developed 'management by objectives' as an alternative method of managing managers and technocrats. For corporate executives, 'management by objectives' held the promise of legitimizing corporate goals whilst fulfilling individual needs. In organizational terms, the 'management by objectives' contract struck between the corporation and the individual combined 'the advantages of subcontracting with those of bureaucracy' (Waring, 1991: 91):

> The negotiation process would atomise workers and get each to contract to individual goals. . . . the negotiations assumed that managerial power was legitimate, conflict would be transformed from quarrels over controls to disagreements over goals. And since managers could better control their new skilled workers without directly controlling their work, they could benefit from contract and control, entrepreneurship and employeeship.

'Management by objectives' was predicated on the transparency and measurement of individual performance: results were fed back to the individual who would then seek to improve performance. By forging a new type of renewable psychological contract, organizational goals were transformed into personal goals; self-control supplemented – or replaced – organizational control.

Current understanding of the articulation of personnel psychology has also drawn heavily on Foucault's concepts of power/knowledge and disciplinary power. In its attempt to progressively displace intuitive judgements with scientific assessment, personnel psychology claims to offer an objective normalizing gaze (Newton, 1994). The array of assessment and selection techniques now wielded by employers is an example of the development of 'disciplinary' rather than 'monarchic' power/knowledge.

Analyses of human resource management are, maintains Barbara Townley, bedevilled by restrictive binary divisions which take idealized taxonomies as their starting point for empirical research. Rather, Townley argues, we should begin by examining how actual practices structure social relations. In this respect, Foucault offers the most fruitful methodology to produce a detailed topography of labour regulation. This is particularly so when we are confronting new managerial technologies whose targets include rendering the individual knowable, calculable and comparable. Such analyses would replace flat binary analyses of conventional 'critical' approaches to human resource management with rich relief maps of practice and discourse. Counselling and appraisal, the articulation of the individual's motivations and corporate objectives, lie at the heart of all appraisal systems. But Tricia Findlay and Tim Newton caution against reading the existence of individual appraisal systems as *necessarily* part of a rational, disciplinary form of organizational power. Rather, the appraisal process *can* be a vehicle for the sustaining of monarchic, highly personalized forms of managerial power. Contrary to Foucault, monarchic power was not totally displaced during the Enlightenment. Monarchic and disciplinary power continues to co-exist in an uneasy, shifting relationship in the late twentieth century. On this at least, Findlay and Newton agree with Townley on the need for more thick anthropological studies of actual appraisal processes, not just the thoughts of managerial ideologues. Just as Mike Savage's reconstruction of the changing nature of disciplinary power in nineteenth-century railways pointed to the need for long-run historical analysis, so Foucault's project – and its limits – demands much more extensive research into the history of the factory and the office.

Foucault's concept of disciplinary power has an immediate, almost intuitive, resonance when we discuss the modern managerial bureaucracy. But can one argue that disciplinary power is embedded in the emerging, knowledge-intensive workplaces whether they be software houses, consultancies, or group-based production lines? Such organizations are surely 'organic' rather than 'mechanistic', and and their creativity is reliant on the absence of disciplinary power? This view is challenged in the essays by Stanley Deetz and by Alan McKinlay and Phil Taylor. For Deetz, the cultural or normative controls which operate as alternatives to bureaucratic rules and direct supervision are new techologies of power developed within knowledge-intensive organizations. The mobility and extensive exposure of such workers to a range of cross-cutting professional obligations coupled with the uncertainty and ambiguity of their tasks makes such control fragmented and contingent. Drawing on the work of Michael Burawoy (1989), Deetz contends that normative control is effective only in so far as it is sustained by the practices and discourses of daily organizational life.

Normative control seeps into the unspoken codes of the workplace, the dress code, acceptable behaviour towards colleagues and clients and so forth. For knowledge professionals, there is a more or less explicit trade-off between the self-subordination inherent in normative control and the job security and personal development opportunities open to them in knowledge-intensive organizations. A quite different kind of workplace is analysed by McKinlay and Taylor. Their study of a greenfield microelectronics plant examines the impact of teamworking on employee attitudes to discipline, supervision and resistance. In one important sense, teamworking regimes have been designed to be the opposite of Taylorist labour processes. By making line workers responsible for both the planning and execution of their tasks, teamworking seeks to overcome the radical division between 'thinking' and 'doing' inherent in Taylorism. Surveillance and control in this factory hinged not on the diligence of supervisors but on mutual control by the workers them-selves. The tension between self-control and collective resistance, so important yet underdeveloped in Foucault's historical writing, is the central issue considered by McKinlay and Taylor. Resistance in this teamworking regime took the form of a collective subversion, or, rather, an inversion of panopticism. The carceral gaze was turned not on colleagues who deviated from corporate objectives but on those team-mates who persisted in their application of managerial standards of behaviour on the shopfloor.

In the afterword, Starkey and McKinlay link the issue of discipline to the increasing attention Foucault paid to desire in his final works. One of the issues Foucault struggled with was how to explain the apparent 'willing' involvement of subjects in systems of power that could be regarded as working against their own best interests. Starkey and McKinlay suggest that we need to work on a deconstructive reading of Foucault, particularly of the later work, that accommodates the tension between discipline and desire. In short, what they suggest is that a 'final' reading of Foucault – which is, of course, impossible – a reading that does ultimate justice to the complexity of the issues he was wrestling with in his later work, will focus upon more than the disciplinary concerns of his 'middle' period centred on his prison book. A fruitful approach here is one that deconstructs the concern with discipline using the prism of its opposite, desire. Kilduff (1993: 15), drawing upon the work of Derrida (1978), captures the essence of the deconstructive gesture:

> A deconstructive reading opens up the text to renewed debate concerning the limits of the text and the relationship between the explicit and hidden textual levels. In investigating the limits of the text, the critic asks: . . . Why are certain themes never questioned, whereas other themes are condemned? Why, given a set of premises, are certain conclusions not reached? The aim of such questions is not to point out textual errors but to help the reader to understand the extent to which the text's objectivity and persuasiveness depend on a set of strategic exclusions.

'Subjectification' in Foucault's final works embraces a dual phenomenon: individuals lose themselves in regimes of power but, paradoxically, they are created as subjects/other-selves by these same regimes. We would hope that future work using a Foucauldian perspective can advance our understanding of this process.

References

Armstrong, P. (1994) 'The influence of Michel Foucault on accounting research', *Critical Perspectives on Accounting*, 5: 25–55.

Braverman, H. (1974) *Labor and Monopoly Capitalism: The Degradation of Work in the Twentieth Century*. New York: Monthly Review Press.

Burawoy, M. (1989) *The Politics of Production: Factory Regimes under Capitalism and Socialism*. London: Sage.

Chandler, A. (1977) *The Visible Hand: The Managerial Revolution in American Business*. Cambridge, MA: Belknap.

Cooper, R. and Burrell, G. (1988) 'Modernism, postmodernism and organizational analysis', *Organization Studies*, 9 (1): 91–112.

Cooper, R. and Kaplan, R. (1991) 'Profit priorities from activity-based costing', *Harvard Business Review*, May–June: 130–5.

Deetz, S. (1992) 'Disciplinary power in the modern corporation', in M. Alvesson and H. Willmott (eds), *Critical Management Studies*. London: Sage. pp. 21–45.

Derrida, J. (1978) *Writing and Difference*. Chicago: University of Chicago Press.

Eribon, M. (1990) *Michel Foucault*. Cambridge, MA: Harvard University Press.

Foucault, M. (1977) *Discipline and Punish: The Birth of the Prison*. Harmondsworth: Penguin.

Foucault, M. (1979) *The History of Sexuality, Volume 1*. Harmondsworth: Penguin.

Hoskin, K. and Macve, R. (1988) 'The genesis of accountability: the West Point connections', *Accounting, Organizations and Society*, 13 (1): 37–73.

Hume, L.J. (1970) 'Jeremy Bentham on industrial management', *Yorkshire Bulletin of Economic and Social Research*, xxii: 3–15.

Hume, L.J. (1981) *Bentham and Bureaucracy*. Cambridge: Cambridge University Press.

Ignatieff, M. (1978) *A Just Measure of Pain: The Penitentiary in the Industrial Revolution*. London: Macmillan.

Kilduff, M. (1993) 'Deconstructing *Organization*', *Academy of Management Review*, 18 (1): 13–31.

Lyons, D. (1991) *In the Interest of the Governed: A Study in Bentham's Philosophy of Utility and Law*. Oxford: Clarendon.

Lyotard, J.F. (1986) *The Postmodern Condition*. Manchester: Manchester University Press.

Marglin, S. (1974) 'What do bosses do? The origins and functions of hierarchy in capitalist production', *Review of Radical Political Economics*, 6: 60–112.

Miller, P. (1987) *Domination and Power*. London: Routledge and Kegan Paul.

Miller, P. and O'Leary, T. (1987) 'Accounting and the construction of the governable person', *Accounting, Organizations and Society*, 12 (3): 235–65.

Morgan, G. (1986) *Images of Organization*. London: Sage.

Neimark, M. (1990) 'The King is dead – Long live the King!', *Critical Perspectives on Accounting*, 1 (1): 103–14.

Nelson, D. (ed.) (1992) *A Mental Revolution: Scientific Management since Taylor*. Columbus, OH: Ohio State University Press.

Newton, T.J. (1994) 'Discourse and agency: the example of personnel psychology and "assessment centres"', *Organization Studies*, 15 (6): 879–902.

O'Neill, J. (1986) 'The disciplinary society: from Weber to Foucault', *British Journal of Sociology*, xxxviii (1): 42–60.

Rosen, F. (1983) *Jeremy Bentham and Representative Democracy: A Study of the Constitutional Code*. Oxford: Clarendon.

Rosenblum, N. (1978) *Bentham's Theory of the State*, Cambridge MA: Harvard University Press.

Semple, J. (1992) 'Foucault and Bentham: a defence of panopticism', *Utilitas*, 4 (1): 105–20.

Semple, J. (1993) *Bentham's Prison: A Study of the Panopticon Penitentiary.* Oxford: Clarendon.

Shapley, D. (1993) *Promise and Power: The Life and Times of Robert McNamara.* Boston: Little, Brown.

Townley, B. (1994) *Reframing Human Resource Management: Power, Ethics and the Subject.* London: Sage.

Waring, S.P. (1991) *Taylorism Transformed: Management Theory since 1945.* Chapel Hill, NC: University of North Carolina Press.

Zuboff, S. (1988) *In the Age of the Smart Machine: The Future of Work and Power.* Oxford: Heinemann.

I
FOUCAULT AND ORGANIZATION THEORY

2

Modernism, Postmodernism and Organizational Analysis: The Contribution of Michel Foucault

Gibson Burrell

Michel Foucault's untimely death in 1984, at the age of 57, put to an end a steady stream of scholarship which has a direct, though poorly recognized, relevance for the study of organizations. In this paper, an attempt will be made to briefly explicate the role played by Foucault's work in the postmodernism debate and, in the light of this contribution, to show its possible beneficial impact upon contemporary organizational analysis.

As we have seen (Cooper and Burrell, 1988), the modernism–postmodernism debate is multi-faceted, but in some ways it is characterized by Habermas's defence of the modernist position against a line of French thinkers leading 'from Bataille via Foucault to Derrida' (Habermas, 1981: 13). Foucault and Habermas met in 1983 and 1984, but this merely continued a debate in which they had been engaged for several years. It was unlikely that this exchange ever would have led to a dialogue, because the protagonists defined 'modernity' in incompatible ways (Dreyfus and Rabinow, 1982: 109), and perceived the Enlightenment in particular (and Kant's role within it) in very different lights. As a result, Habermas saw Foucault as producing a failed critique of modernism because the latter supposedly provided outdated and well-worn attacks on the development of human rationality, no explanation of why the present *should* be condemned, and a reactionary political message. Foucault, for his part, was reluctant to accept the epithet of postmodernism as a description of his work – although, as we shall see, he rejected most labels that critics attempted to attach to his books. Nevertheless, Foucault's critique of modernism is important but is open to a wide variety of interpretation, and so what follows is but one path through his *oeuvres*.

Michel Foucault was Professor of the History of Systems of Thought in Paris from 1970, publishing a series of texts (Foucault, 1973, 1975, 1977a, 1977b, 1977c, 1979) in which a number of common themes are discernible, but which were not designed to produce, in any programmatic way, a grand theoretical edifice. Rather, through the medium of a mass of detailed analysis, Foucault was often keen to confront and reject received opinion. In the place of widely held views, he substituted tentative hypotheses which invite, indeed beg for, heated discussion and debate. He was an iconoclast who suggested alternative modes of thinking. His style is ornate and like a thicket, often impenetrable – but deliberately and consciously so. It should not be assumed that Foucault's writings are fully coherent to the Anglo-American eye. They are the product of a long European tradition in which philosophical idealism is strongly represented, the epistemology of empiricism is seen as suspect and where a complex, convoluted writing style is self-consciously adopted to escape from what is seen as the limitations and constraints of 'clear prose'. Since his work does not contain a fixed set of theoretical propositions in the conventional sense, it is merely suggestive of alternative ways of approaching problems and ordering material. Furthermore, it is important to note that Foucault's iconoclasm takes him into positions which are not readily defensible, and his refusal to retain one position for longer than the period between his last book and the next is certainly problematic. For the sake of exposition, however, let us assume a wide three-fold periodization in his work.

The archaeological period

Foucault's earlier work (published in English, 1975, 1977a, 1977b) deals provocatively with psychiatry, medicine and the human sciences and the ways in which respectively 'sanity', 'health' and 'knowledge' are perceived, classified and distributed with Western culture.

In *Madness and Civilization* (1977a), which is based upon Foucault's doctoral dissertation, the author presents a 'history of madness in the Age of Reason' in which before – and after – snapshots are presented to demonstrate the presence of a 'target divide' in Western thought. In the mid-seventeenth century 'the great exclusion' had taken place in which deviants had been incarcerated in the newly built lunatic asylums, there to look after themselves. However, psychiatric knowledge developed at the end of the eighteenth century as a new way to deal with the insane. The brain came to be seen as a different 'organ' over a brief 25-year period, as a new brand of experts came to the fore, who saw madness as their object of study. The history of 'madness' then, is a history with a great break or rupture in it between 1780 and the turn of that century.

Similarly, the development in this period of 'la clinique' – both the clinical lecture and the institution – is the topic of Foucault's *The Birth of the Clinic* (1975). This book is also about a self-constituted class of experts who, through their talk, can establish truth or falsehood. The method of analysis used in writing this kind of history is termed 'archaeology' by Foucault, who develops it much more as a methodology in *The Order of Things* (1973). The project in this text was to write a history of the 'immature sciences', in which the rules of formation *common* to the (apparently unrelated) sciences of natural history, economics and grammar were shown to exist and were described. These anonymous rules of formation concern the discursive practices through which statements are formed and produced. They differ markedly in each period of thought (or episteme) and do not map onto each other. By the nineteenth century, the key concepts have become life, labour and language and are the provinces of biology, economics and linguistics, respectively. These form new objects for thought, new discourses which have to be seen as independent of the speaker. The autonomy of discourse is maintained by Foucault at this point to such an extent that the knowing subject disappears and is replaced by a concern for discourse alone.

The Archaeology of Knowledge (1977b) represents the long and cryptic methodological summation of this early period. Rather than accept the 'History of Ideas' in which truth is taken to be the accurate representation of reality in an ever-expanding body of statements made by great figures in science, archaeology sees truth as the production of sets of statements and their regulation within discrete systems of discourse independent of the conscious speaker. Thus the archaeological method presupposes discontinuities in the forms of discourse adopted; its key aim is to constitute discursive series and to see where they begin and end. It seeks primarily to understand the 'archive' – the diversity of autonomous and sometimes amorphous discourses.

The early works, then, consist of an overriding concern with the literary and the discursive as they relate to the human sciences, particularly those concerned with discourses on madness and disease. The human sciences are not seen as developing after the Enlightenment unilinearly but are held to be fragmented into discrete periods which need to be understood through the notions of 'episteme' and 'archive'. The subject is decentred in this early work since it is not a question of who speaks a discourse, but of what discourse is spoken. In Foucault, there is no unity of history, no unity of the subject, no sense of progress, no acceptance of the History of Ideas.

On the basis of this work, the early Foucault is often assumed to be a 'structuralist', although he explicitly rejected such a label himself (White, 1979; Dreyfus and Rabinow, 1982). Nevertheless Foucault is structuralist enough to wish to displace the subject and consciousness from the centre of theoretical concern, and, because of this process of 'decentring the subject' (Lemert, 1979), human beings appear in his writings as mere objects. Moreover, the search for common features in a variety of discourses suggests a concern for 'the same in the different', a desire to point to underlying commonalities in a wide range of discursive practices; discourses, whether scientific or not, must be analysed with literary tools and concepts. White, in his discussion of Foucault's structuralism (White, 1979) goes so far as to maintain that underpinning 'the archaeological method' of Foucault's early work is a theory of tropes (Morgan, 1980; Bourgeois and Pinder, 1982) in which analogies and differences are the key focus of attention.

One does not find other features associated with structuralist thought, however. For example, there is no easy acceptance of the geological metaphor (Clegg, 1981), nor of a realist ontology nor of Marxian analytical categories (Sheridan, 1980; Smart, 1983). Indeed, the differences between Foucault and his one-time structuralist colleague and teacher, Althusser (Althusser, 1969), are somewhat fundamental and are located in precisely this kind of terrain. Certainly, Foucault's early advocacy of an 'archaeological analysis' stands against Althusser's views on both history and scientific practice. Nevertheless, the archaeological period in the late 1960s can be characterized with some validity as being quasi-structuralist (Hoy, 1986: 4) and therefore as not at all in sympathy with the modernist projects of Habermas and other humanists. Interestingly, Foucault himself lost sympathy with this quasi-structuralism, as a whole series of interviews demonstrates (Rabinow, 1984). In place of the archaeological method with its emphasis on discourse, Foucault turned to the non-discursive realm, and particularly to the issue of power as understood from the point of view of genealogy.

Genealogical period

For a while, Foucault attempted to supplement this archaeological theory with genealogy, but, in the later works, the separation between these approaches grows and archaeology assumes a very minor role. The genealogist is a diagnostician who is interested in power, knowledge and the body and how these interrelate. In relation to archaeology, practice now becomes much more important than theory (Dreyfus and Rabinow, 1982); moreover, practices become viewed from the inside rather than from the viewpoint of the detached observer. In developing this new stance, Foucault was greatly influenced by his understanding of Nietzsche. For both, the claim of objectivity masks subjective motivations, high-sounding stories hide the lowest of motives, accidents and lies lie behind the march of history. Thus, genealogy is opposed to traditional history and the search for underlying laws and finalities. Like archaeology, it stands against continuity and for discontinuities, but inverts the earlier position in that it seeks to avoid the search for depth. Genealogy is interested in the superficial and the unexpected. Reality does not cover up some hidden underlying essences. It is as it appears. Our knowledge of reality, however, is enmeshed in a power field. Indeed, the petty malices of those who seek to dominate mean that knowledge itself is increasingly part of the play of domination. Thus, the issues of power, knowledge and the body are intertwined as the focus of the genealogist.

Whilst little attention has been paid here to the substance of Foucault's earlier texts, in this section I wish to consider in some detail the work of the genealogical period, for it is here that Foucault's relevance to organization studies is most important. Thus, it is *Discipline and Punish* (1977c) and *The History of Sexuality, Volume I* (1979) to which attention will now be given. Throughout all of Foucault's writing there is a stress on the importance of an historical understanding, stemming not from an interest in the past, but from a deep commitment to understanding the present. He maintains that he is concerned with *genealogy* and with locating traces of the present in the past, not with the reconstruction of the past (Foucault, 1979; Weeks, 1981). Historically, two modes of domination are recognized by Foucault as characterizing the Western world; these are the 'traditional' and the 'disciplinary' and are to be sharply contrasted. *Discipline and Punish* begins with a horrific description of the execution of the regicide, Damiens, on 2 March 1757. His death was to take the following form.

> The flesh will be torn from his breasts, arms, thighs and calves with red-hot pincers, his right hand, holding the knife with which he commited the said parricide, burnt with sulphur and on those places where the flesh will be torn away, poured molten lead, boiling oil, burning resin, wax and sulphur melted together and then his body drawn and quartered by four horses and his limbs and body consumed by fire . . . (Foucault, 1977c: 3)

Some 80 years later rules 'for the House of Young Prisoners in Paris' were drawn up. These include

> at half past seven in summer, half past eight in winter, the prisoners must be back in their cells after the washing of hands and the inspection of clothes in the courtyard; at the first drum-roll they must undress and at the second get into bed. (Foucault, 1977c: 7)

In these two contrasting descriptions – one of an execution, the other of a timetable – we see the contrast between traditional and disciplinary modes of domination. The disciplinary mode replaced the traditional in less than a century as public taste for physical punishment and 'the spectacle' declined. Punishment began, slowly and in one or two isolated places at first, to become directed towards the 'soul', the mind, the will. Extremes of violence inflicted on the body speedily diminished and, in some cases, even disappeared, but were replaced, according to Foucault, by complex, subtle forms of correction and training. It is his belief that our own contemporary society is not maintained by a visible state apparatus of national guards and state police, less still by shared value systems, but by the hidden techniques of discipline always at work in 'carceral' institutions.

The development of such 'complete and austere' organizations is well described by Foucault. For him, the techniques of discipline and close observation incorporated in the new prisons of eighteenth-century Pennsylvania and Tuscany, France and Prussia derived from three centuries of practices in other spheres, notably education and the military (Sunesson, 1985). But there is an astonishing resemblance between the new prisons and other organizations of the disciplinary age: hospitals, factories, housing estates, schools and barracks. Jeremy Bentham's design for the Panopticon – a circular building with central observation tower from which inmates (or workers or prisoners) could be surveyed at work or sleep without being able to observe their observers – becomes for Foucault *the* metaphor for the disciplinary mode of domination. The implication is that, built into the architecture and geometry of disciplinary organizations is the distinctive arrangement of observation and close surveillance.

The eighteenth century also witnessed great attention being paid to the body as an object or target for manipulation and training. Once the human body became conceptualized as a machine, it was thereafter opened up to mechanical rearrangement and tuning. This discovery allows the development of 'political anatomy' where 'power seeps into the very grain of individuals, reaches right into their bodies, permeates their gestures, their posture, what they say, how they learn to live and work with other people' (Foucault, 1977c: 28). The minutest features of life become subject to detailed analysis and investigation: regulations become meticulous, inspections fussy, supervision extremely close. Great attention is paid to the posture of school children and the marching steps of soldiers. Whatever the organization, discipline revolves around the minute details of the lives of those subjected to it. Discipline soon comes to require a cellular system of locating and concentrating individuals in space, a timetable for activity, manuals for the correct movement of the body and a precise economical system of command. Individuals become 'cases' who are measured, described, evaluated, examined and compared. Real lives are converted into written case notes. In short, the body loses its mystery.

Similarly, the development of bio-power (Foucault, 1979: 140–4) is marked by an explosion of numerous and diverse techniques for achieving the subjugation of bodies and the control of populations. This set of techniques focus their attention upon sexuality, for this is the pivot of two axes. One axis is the life of the body and control over it; the other axis is the life of the species and its regulation and domination. Sexuality becomes the prime target for control within disciplinary society and therefore the subject of a steady proliferation of discourses concerning sex. In the nineteenth century, sexuality was increasingly analysed, classified, specified and examined. Four basic categories of target were recognized. Action was taken against 'the hysterical woman', 'the masturbating child', 'the Malthusian couple' and 'the perverse adult' (Foucault, 1979). Many attempts to 'normalize' the behaviour of the population were made as individuals became seen as part of a homogeneous social body (Foucault, 1977c: 184). To be sure, specific differences between human beings were recognized, but only in so far as they deviated from the Norm. The Norm was established by a variety of 'professional' groupings – anatomists, doctors, health workers, demographers, priests, teachers and so on, who focused their gaze upon the body and the soul of the population (Melossi and Pavarini, 1981).

Bio-power was taken from existing organizations, notably the army, and was transplanted into a social setting which was becoming organizational.

Political anatomy and bio-power provided the basis for the growth of hospitals, prisons, asylums, housing estates, universities and schools. In turn, these organizations drew support from the establishment and proliferation of the many 'professions' which serviced these carceral institutions. Today, a 'normalizing' function is performed by a whole series of subsidiary authorities who swarm around the 'disciplines'. For example, educationalists, psychiatrists, psychological experts, members of the prison service and magistrates all form parallel judgements of the 'cases' coming before them. Foucault maintains that

> The judges of normality are present everywhere. We are in the society of the teacher-judge, the doctor-judge, the educator-judge, the social worker-judge. It is on them that the universal reign of the normative is based; and each individual, wherever he may find himself, subjects to it his body, his gestures, his behaviour, his aptitudes, his achievements. (Foucault, 1977c: 304)

Thus, the prison is only 'the extreme form' of what Foucault calls disciplinary power, for its boundaries extend well beyond the walls of the penitentiary. Within the whole range of organizations found in contemporary society, one finds not a plurality of powers but a unified power field encapsulated within the bureaucratic, military and administrative apparatus. For Foucault, power does not reside in things, but in a network of relationships which are systematically interconnected. Disciplinary power should not be viewed as negative power. It is not a series of prohibitions delimiting, proscribing and discouraging activities of lower-order organizational members. Power should be seen in a positive sense as actively directed towards the body and its possibilities, converting it into something both useful and docile. Moreover, organizational superordinates do not create discipline through their actions or strategies. On the contrary, they are as much disciplined as their subordinates. Disciplinary power is invested in, transmitted by and reproduced through all human beings in their day-to-day existence. It is discrete, regular, generalized and uninterrupted. It does not come from outside the organization but it is built into the very processes of education, therapy, house building and manufacture (Donzelot, 1980). Thus, the body of the individual is 'directly involved in a political field: power relations have an immediate hold upon it; they invest it, mark it, train it, force it to carry out tasks, to perform ceremonies, to emit signs' (Foucault, 1977c: 27).

Foucault sees the predominant perspective on power as essentially flawed, for within it power is seen as residing in the state and as filtering down to lower levels such as the school, the courts and so on. He characterizes this position as 'juridic consciousness'. In contrast, Foucault wishes to conceptualize power as located in the 'micro-physics' of social life in the 'depths' of society. Here, minute and diffuse power relations exist, always in tension, always in action. But it is from this level and from such small beginnings, that 'a global unity of domination' arises or 'the globality of discipline'. So deeply entrenched is the disciplinary mode of domination, so pervasive is it in its operation, and so ubiquitous is it in its location, that changing any part of the power field leaves the basic form untouched. Discipline cannot be simply removed by challenging and overturning the state; it is part and parcel of the everyday life of the body of the individual and of the body politic.

Such a view does not lend itself to optimism, since the prospects for an early end to disciplinary power evaporate in its wake. This is particularly so given the nature of 'resistance'. A number of commentators have pointed out that prisons are not at all good at performing the function of disciplining the inmates. Riots, illegal behaviour and indiscipline seem to characterize contemporary prisons as much as the creation of docility. Does this resistance then refute Foucault's perspective on prisons as being the archetypal organization of the disciplinary society? Not so. For him, 'resistance is never in a position of exteriority in relation to power' (Foucault, 1979: 95). The very existence of power is seen as relying upon a multiplicity of points of resistance which play the role of adversary, target, support or handle within power relationships. Thus resistance is inconceivable without discipline. Prisons are there to demonstrate the futility of resistance and the importance of discipline. They may be hotbeds of resistance but they provide 'discipline' with an adversary and target against which to pit itself. The existence of resistance does not mean that discipline is threatened. It means that discipline can grow stronger knowing where its next efforts must be directed.

In summary then, Foucault maintains that the despotic character of the disciplinary mode of domination is built into the heart, the essence of contemporary society and affects the body of the individual, of whatever class, at the minutest level. This implies that as the reader peruses this page, the gestures, the posture, the attitude, 'the dressage' adopted in this literary task are part of the political anatomy of society. Even the mundane activity of reading is reflective of a discipline which is transmitted by and sustained within a homogeneous collective of organizational forms. According to Foucault, since all of us belong to organizations and all organizations are alike and take the prison as their model, we are all imprisoned within a field of bio-power, even as we sit alone. The relevance of this view to the critique of conventional approaches to organizational power (Hickson et al., 1971; Pettigrew, 1973; Mintzberg, 1983) should be obvious (Daudi, 1986).

In his last works, Foucault attempted to shift ground yet again from archaeology and genealogy onto the terrain of *ethics*. This area is conceptualized quite differently from the Anglo-American tradition in that he assumes a marked discontinuity between Greek–Roman ethics and those of Christian and modern times. In order to distinguish his study of ethics from the archaeological study of discourse and the genealogical study of power, Foucault's attention is drawn backwards two millennia. The later work is not what Foucault promised in *The History of Sexuality, Volume 1*, and its full relevance and meaning still remains an open issue (Davidson, 1986). Thus attention here will be redirected back to the major corpus of Foucault's writing.

The archaeological and genealogical methods compared

Table 2.1 attempts to highlight the difference between the two approaches found in Michel Foucault's work. What it does not reveal are the several continuities between the two methods, including those very features which identify Foucault as an anti-modernist. Common to the two periods are a commitment to a rejection of totalizing visions of history, to an image of discontinuous ruptures in social change, to a concern to decentre the subject and to a questioning of the idea of human progress and enlightenment. What Table 2.1 emphasizes is the profound shifts in methodological position undertaken by Foucault as his work developed (*pace* Daudi, 1986; Davidson, 1986).

Clearly, such changes in perspectives and conceptualizations are not unproblematic. In recent years, much justifiable criticism has been levelled against Foucault (Gane, 1986; Hoy, 1986). He has been attacked for his views on sexuality (Weeks, 1981; Brake, 1982), for his early concentration on the notion of 'discourse' (White, 1979), for his critique of Marxism, for his pessimism and for his conceptualization of power (Fine, 1979; Minson, 1980; Smart, 1983). Here, however, attention will focus on the positive aspects of Foucault's work and its relevance for organizational analysis. In this task, we may remember what Foucault has said of Nietzsche:

> The only valid tribute to thought such as Nietzsche's is precisely to use it, to deform it, to make it groan and protest. And if the commentators say that I am being unfaithful to Nietzsche that it is of absolutely no interest. (Quoted in Sheridan, 1980: 116–17)

As Foucault has done unto Nietzsche so are we able to do unto Foucault.

The relevance of Foucault for organizational analysis

A number of issues stand out for immediate concern at this juncture. Let us look first to some of the issues thrown up by the Foucauldian texts which deal directly with 'organizations' and their impact upon inmates.

Table 2.1 *Two analytical approaches found in Foucault's writings*

The Archaeological Method	The Genealogical Method
Uncover those rules which regulate and govern social practices, and which are unknown to the actors involved.	Record the singularity of surface events, looking at the meaning of small details, minor shifts and subtle contours.
It is possible to achieve some partial distancing from these institutional bonds by a bracketing of 'accepted truth'.	There are no fixed essences or underlying laws. There is discontinuity and arbitrariness. Since the world is as it appears, one seeks out the 'superficial secrets'.
Act as an 'excavator', revealing depth and interiority.	Act as a recorder of accidents, chance and lies. Oppose the search for depth and interiority.

To begin with, Foucault's work is worthy of consideration here for it illuminates, in particular, an area of increasing concern in organization theory connected with the heterogeneity or homogeneity of organizational forms. Are organizations all alike or are they all unalike? To what extent are organizations unique and contingent? How far can we generalize about them? Questions such as these raise important epistemological and methodological issues which have been aired in some recent literature. For example, McKelvey and Aldrich (1983) have drawn attention to the supposed utility of the population perspective in standing between two competing 'paradigms' which dominate organization theory. In their view, 'papers in the field generalize about organizations as if they were all alike or refrain from generalizing at all, as if they were all unique' (McKelvey and Aldrich, 1983: 101). The all-alike perspective assumes that administration processes are essentially the same in industrial, commercial, educational and other forms of organization (Litchfield, 1956). The 'unalike' perspective, on the other hand, stresses that organizations are so distinctive and particular that generalizable statements are not worth making. McKelvey and Aldrich (1983: 109) imply that the 'unalike paradigm' is in the ascendancy, for they claim that 'organizational scientists are beginning to believe that organizations come in so many varieties . . . that it no longer makes sense to search for a few essential attributes captured in an all encompassing definition of organization'.

Foucault is of relevance here because contained within his writings is a key to unlock the issues from prior conceptualizations. In this work, with its rich variety of empirical depictions, one finds a complex set of ideas which claim a homogeneity for organizational forms and suggest that all organizations are essentially alike. In Foucault's carefully chosen words, 'prisons resemble factories, schools, barracks, hospitals, which all resemble prisons' (1979: 83). Prior to this statement, Foucault had maintained that no two things are similar to one another in their particularity. All language, therefore, constitutes an abuse in so far as it gives a single name to things different in time, space and their external attributes (White, 1979: 94). 'Sameness' or analogy develops in a linguistic attempt to classify everything which is 'Different'. The perception of 'The Same in the Different' and of 'The Different in the Same' is the origin of all scientific classification schemes where Sameness comes to be formalized and submitted to rules as rationality becomes highly developed. The problem for Foucault is that such classificatory schemes are examples of the trope, 'catachresis', in which all analogies are abused. The reduction of a human's individuality to case notes, of the myriad variety of personalities to human 'types' are examples of scientific discourse in the field of classification which are fundamentally hierarchical (McKelvey, 1982).

Thus, the linguistic category 'organization' attempts to reduce 'Difference' to 'Sameness' by assuming that prisons and factories and hospitals are part of a wider scientifically acceptable category which we generically label as 'organizations'. The notion of 'organization' itself may well become, for

Foucault, a catachresis in that it falsely reduces differences and spuriously elevates similarities. In so doing, it contributes in some significant way to the scientific hierarchization of the disciplinary society.

Meanwhile, in a reaction against both 'paradigms', McKelvey and Aldrich seek to establish an intermediate position in which the view that 'some organizations are like some other organizations' is taken to represent the golden mean. We have already seen that a Foucauldian approach allows for both the search for generic principles and for detailed empirical investigations of strange local events in single organizations. What the approach is loath to permit is the segmentation and classification of organizational 'types'. In contrast, McKelvey and Aldrich's position can be seen as an attempt to enhance the globality of discipline. Their emphasis 'on research methods that improve the description and classification of organizational forms, define more homogeneous groupings and specify the limited conditions under which predictions may be expected to hold true' (McKelvey and Aldrich, 1983: 101) becomes highly suspect because once we follow the route of 'some organizations are like some other organizations' we begin the process of normalizing the field. Normalization, as Foucault shows, is a great instrument of power.

> In a sense, the power of normalization imposes homogeneity; but it individualizes by making it possible to measure gaps, to determine levels, to fix specialities and to render the differences useful by fitting them one to another. (Foucault, 1977c: 184)

Thus, whilst the option of 'some organizations are like some other organizations' seems at first sight to be reasonable, and as representing a professional compromise to the twin difficulties of universalism and particularism, we must remember that professionalism and discipline go hand in hand. By partitioning our multifarious subject matter into neat, manageable, hierarchically ordered categories, we actually contribute to the globality of discipline.

Moreover, McKelvey and Aldrich's (1983) discussion of the two 'paradigms' and the third intermediate option of the population perspective excludes a fourth option based upon a use of the two types of Foucauldian analysis. Such an analysis would focus on the multiplicity of factors involved in describing organizational life and events. It would emphasize the complexity, contingency and fragility of organizational forms as transitory manifestations of relationships of dominance–subordination *and* as mere embodiments of an underlying relationship of forces. Organizations come to be seen, therefore, as episodic and unpredictable manifestations of a play of dominations (Smart, 1983: 76). In Foucauldian analysis, the paradox arises when organizations are seen as totally contingent and particularly requiring patient, meticulous, documentary research of their individuality on the one hand, whilst on the other, they are viewed as manifestations of some underlying and generic Nietzschean 'will to knowledge'. Put simply, such a view implies that, at any one given moment in time, all organizations are unalike in terms of surface features, but are alike in so far as one can understand their underlying dynamics. *They are all-unalike and all-alike at one and the same time.* They need to be studied both archaeologically and genealogically – which is not at all the same thing as McKelvey and Aldrich are advocating.

Second, the issue of 'total institutions' (Goffman, 1961) and their relevance is thrown up by Foucault's work. In particular, Anthony Giddens (1984) has attacked Foucault's views of time and space, opening up issues of import to the present discussion. Foucault is accused of recognizing that the prison is an 'extreme' form of organization and that therefore it cannot be viewed as being typical of contemporary organizations. Certain organizations are 'complete and austere' institutions but, as Foucault admitted, other forms are not quite like this. Giddens remarks that Foucault's observations on this point are

> of some significance because complete and austere institutions are the exception rather than the rule within the main institutional sectors of modern societies. It does not follow that because prisons and asylums maximize disciplinary power, they express its nature more clearly than the other, less all-embracing organizations. (Giddens, 1984: 155)

As far as Giddens is concerned, 'carceral institutions' are akin to Goffman's 'total institutions' (Goffman, 1961) in that they fully control, in an unbroken way, the life of the inmate in both time and space. Thus 'total institutions stand outside others because of the daily life paths of those inside' (Giddens, 1984: 184). Conceptualized in this way, the character of other, less embracing non-carceral organizations is such that members move in and then out of them throughout the working week and that their experience of organizational life is intermittent. But Giddens's focus on time/space relations leads him to miss the point. He assumes that 'typical' individuals belong to only one organization and, on leaving it at the end of the day, cease to confront the organizational world by 'going home' and re-entering the non-organizational world of civil society. The geographical metaphor used by Giddens apparently involves an acceptance of the validity of the organization/non-organization spatial 'boundary' which people frequently cross. But such a metaphor is of limited utility since individuals confront, interact with and are encapsulated, not by one organizational form, but by many. Even as we sit in our studies, we confront a world organized for us by telephone companies, furniture manufacturers, publishers and clothes designers. The real point is not that most of us do not live in carceral institutions and can therefore escape from their discipline but that, as individuals, we are incarcerated within an organizational world. Whilst we may not live in total institutions, the institutional organization of our lives is total. It is in this sense that Foucault's comment 'prisons resemble factories, schools, barracks, hospitals which all resemble prisons' has to be understood. In this way, Foucault and Weber are not unconnected, for the 'bureaucratic' mode of domination (Weber, 1947) is also the 'disciplinary' mode of domination (Smart, 1983, 1985). Individuals may move in and out of given organizations but remain, for most purposes, within either a form of bureaucratic organization, or at least within a life space which is shaped and moulded by its confrontation with bureaucracy. For Weber, human life takes place within the 'iron cage' of bureaucracy. For Foucault, human life is existence within an institutional framework of incarceration. If we were to follow up these lines of inquiry then, control of space, particularly with regard to the 'life-paths' of organizational members, becomes crucial (Massey and Meegan, 1982). The ongoing movement of people and/or their fixed location within the boundary of the organization represents important evidence for the existence of a disciplinary mode of domination.

Third, the rise of information technology and knowledge engineering creates some theoretical space in which Foucauldian insights may be relevant (Poster, 1984). Investigation might be directed to microprocessor technologies and the ways in which the Panopticon has been updated by computer networking and 'computer architecture'. For example, to what extent has Bentham's geometrical mathematics for optical observation been replaced by the tachographic capabilities of electronic surveillance? Since electronics have largely replaced optics, it may well be that computer networks resemble in several ways the architectural design of the Panopticon – which in its day was 'the ultimate managerial tool'. Similarly, if we are attracted to the notion of the globality of discipline we must be aware that the control of human sexuality is an important research topic. This area, in particular, has the beginnings of a significant re-ordering of work in organizational analysis (Quinn, 1977; Hearn and Parkin, 1987). The control of time in religious houses, the control of space in modern factories and the gender-specific allocation of management tasks on the one hand and clerical activities on the other, are possibly linked to a generic process of organizational desexualization. The 'normalization' of sexuality carries with it everywhere the separation of gender in time and space. Organizations such as the prison, or the ship at sea or the commercial enterprise are all-alike in their attempts to suppress sexuality and are all-alike in their failure to do so (Ignatieff, 1978).

Finally, if one looks to the future development of organization theory in the light of the modernism–postmodernism debate, the message coming from Foucault is certainly not of a modernist kind. Enlightenment, progress, the history of ideas, truth, debate and knowledge for him are not part of some modernist march to a better tomorrow. His impact is of a decidedly anti-modernist kind. Moreover, his work presents organization theory with a contradiction. At its simplest it is this – it is important to know that the reality of organizations is that they reflect and reproduce a disciplinary society. But to talk about them, to develop discourses and classification schemes for their analysis actively contributes to the reproduction of this discipline. Reality, and our discourse about reality, are both ever more closely confining: we are imprisoned by our knowledge and made freer by our ignorance. Only to the extent that we stop talking about types of organizations do we succeed in not reproducing the disciplinary society. Only to the extent that we speak of 'the Same *and* the Different' rather than 'the Same *in* the Different' can we hope to develop a 'discursive ferment' in organization theory without developing discipline. Michel Foucault has provided us with a pessimistic vision of our role within organizational life, but it is a vision to be developed in fruitful and controversial ways by those interested in opening up our discipline and our organization. We must remember that 'Genealogical analysis stands in a relationship of opposition to the scientific hierarchization of knowledges and their effects, its status being that of an anti-science' (Smart, 1983: 77). In the light of all this, Foucault's work is certainly of an anti-modernist kind – and well worth reading at first hand.

Acknowledgement

This chapter originally appeared in *Organization Studies* (1988, 9 (2): 221–35).

References

Althusser, L. (1969) *For Marx*. Harmondsworth: Penguin.
Bourgeois, C.C. and Pinder, V.W. (1982) 'Controlling tropes in administrative science', *Administrative Science Quarterly*, 27: 641–52.
Brake, M. (1982) *Human Sexual Relations: A Reader*. Harmondsworth: Penguin.
Clegg, S. (1981) 'Organization and control', *Administrative Science Quarterly*, 26: 545–62.
Cooper, R. and Burrell, G. (1988) 'Modernism, postmodernism and organizational analysis', *Organization Studies*, 9 (1): 91–112.
Daudi, P. (1986) *Power in the Organization*. Oxford: Blackwell.
Davidson, A.I. (1986) 'Archaeology, genealogy, ethics', in D.C. Hoy (ed.) *Foucault: A Critical Reader*. Oxford: Blackwell, pp. 221–33.
Donzelot, J. (1980) *The Policing of Families*. London: Hutchinson.
Dreyfus, H.L. and Rabinow, P. (1982) *Michel Foucault: Beyond Structuralism and Hermeneutics*. Brighton: Harvester.
Fine, B. (1979) 'Struggles against discipline', *Capital and Class*, 9: 75–96.
Foucault, M. (1973) *The Order of Things*. New York: Vintage.
Foucault, M. (1975) *The Birth of the Clinic*. New York: Vintage.
Foucault, M. (1977a) *Madness and Civilisation*. London: Tavistock.
Foucault, M. (1977b) *The Archaeology of Knowledge*. London: Tavistock.
Foucault, M. (1977c) *Discipline and Punish*. Harmondsworth: Penguin.
Foucault, M. (1979) *The History of Sexuality, Volume 1*. Harmondsworth: Penguin.
Gane, M. (ed.) (1986) *Towards a Critique of Foucault*. London: Routledge and Kegan Paul.
Giddens, A. (1984) *The Constitution of Society*. Cambridge: Polity.
Goffman, E. (1961) *Asylums*. Garden City, NJ: Anchor Books.
Gordon, C. (ed.) (1980) *Power/knowledge: Selected Interviews and other Writings 1972–1977 by Michel Foucault*. Brighton: Harvester.
Habermas, J. (1981) 'Modernity versus postmodernity', *New German Critique*, 22 (winter): 3–18.
Hearn, J. and Parkin, W. (1987) *Sex at Work*. Brighton: Harvester.
Hickson, D.J., Hinings, C.R., Lee, C.A., Schenk, R.E. and Pennings, J.M. (1971) 'A strategic contingencies theory of intra-organizational power', *Administrative Science Quarterly*, 16: 216–29.
Hoy, D.C. (ed.) (1986) *Foucault: A Critical Reader*. Oxford: Blackwell.

Ignatieff, M. (1978) *A Just Measure of Pain: The Penitentiary in the Industrial Revolution*. London: Macmillan.

Lemert, G.C. (1979) *Sociology and the Twilight of Man*. Carbondale, IL: Southern Illinois University Press.

Litchfield, E.H. (1956) 'Notes on a general theory of administration', *Administrative Science Quarterly*, 1: 3–29.

McKelvey, B. (1982) *Organizational Systematics*. Berkeley, CA: University of California Press.

McKelvey, B. and Aldrich, H. (1983) 'Populations, natural selection and applied organizational science', *Administrative Science Quarterly*, 28: 101–28.

Massey, D.B. and Meegan, R.A. (1982) *The Anatomy of Job Loss*. London: Methuen.

Melossi, D. and Pavarini, M. (1981) *The Prison Factory*. London: Macmillan.

Minson, J. (1980) 'Strategies for socialists? Foucault's conception of power', in M. Gane (ed.) (1986) *Towards a critique of Foucault*. London: Routledge and Kegan Paul. pp. 106–48.

Mintzberg, H. (1983) *Power in and Around Organizations*. Englewood Cliffs, NJ: Prentice-Hall.

Morgan, G. (1980) 'Paradigms, metaphors and puzzle solving in organization theory', *Administrative Science Quarterly*, 25: 605–22.

Pettigrew, A. (1973) *The Politics of Organizational Decision Making*. London: Tavistock.

Poster, M. (1984) *Foucault, Marxism and History*. Cambridge: Polity.

Quinn, R. (1977) 'Coping with Cupid', *Administrative Science Quarterly*, 22: 30–45.

Rabinow, P. (ed.) (1984) *The Foucault Reader*. New York: Pantheon.

Sheridan, A. (1980) *Michel Foucault: The Will to Truth*. London: Tavistock.

Smart, B. (1983) *Foucault, Marxism, Critique*. London: Routledge and Kegan Paul.

Smart, B. (1985) *Michel Foucault*. London: Ellis Horwood and Tavistock.

Sunesson, S. (1985) 'Outside the goal paradigm: power and structural patterns of non-rationality', *Organization Studies* 6 (3): 229–46.

Weber, M. (1947) *The Theory of Social and Economic Organization*. New York: Oxford University Press.

Weeks, J. (1981) *Sex, Politics and Society*. Harlow: Longman.

Weeks, J. (1986) *Sexuality*. London: Ellis Horwood and Tavistock.

White, H. (1979) 'Michel Foucault', in J. Sturrock (ed.), *Structuralism and Since*. Oxford: Oxford University Press. pp. 81–115.

3

Foucault, Power and Organizations

Stewart Clegg

At the outset I will assume the following. In the broadest terms, language defines the possibilities of meaningful existence at the same time as it limits them. Through language we constitute our sense of ourselves as distinct subjectivities through a myriad of 'discursive practices', practices of talk, text, writing, cognition, argumentation, representation generally. The *meanings of* and *membership within* the categories of discursive practice will be a constant site of struggle over power, as identities become posited, resisted and fought-over in attachment to the subjectivity that constructs any particular individuality. Identity is never fixed in its expression nor given by nature. No rational, unified human being, or class or gendered subject is the locus or source of the expression of identity. Membership in a category as a particular type of subject is the effect of devices of categorization; thus identity is contingent, provisional, achieved not given. Identity is always in process, always subject to reproduction or transformation through discursive practices that secure or refuse particular posited identities. Identities are not absolute but are always relational: one can only be something in relation to some other thing. Identity implies difference, rather than something intrinsic to a particular person or category of experience. It implies possible signifiers of self, carrying complex, shifting, frequently ambiguous and contradictory meaning. All discursive practices have historical specificity, particularly as the work of Foucault (1977) interpreted them.

Meaning exists in the difference between relational terms to which current representations defer. However, there is no reason to expect that representations will remain contextually and historically stable and every reason to think that they will shift. Power implicates attempts to fix or uncouple and change particular representational relations of meaning, as is developed most explicitly in Foucault's (1977) historical ontology of subjectivities.

In constructing the knowledge/power relation as the object of analysis one dissolves the notion of any transcendent position constituted outside discursive practices. Within these, then, some representations achieve a power far greater than others, a power that is neither an effect of a human subject and its volition nor of a structure that works behind the backs of such subjects. Representations, the fundamental discursively formed ways of constituting relations, have a historically specific character constituted by strategies of discursive power, where strategicality becomes seen as an effect of distinctive practices of power/knowledge gaining an ascendant position in the representation of normal subjectivity: forms of surveillance or psychiatry, for instance, which constitute the normal in respect to a penology or a medical knowledge from whose 'gaze' and rulings no one can subsequently escape, whether prison or medical officer, or one imprisoned or medically confined.

Foucault writes concretely and descriptively on power, much as did Weber. The ontological foundations of modern institutions, the institutional sources of power, are his topic. Foucault (1977) sees the methods of surveillance and assessment of individuals that were first developed in state institutions such as prisons, as effective tools developed for the orderly regimentation of others as docile bodies, techniques that achieve strategic effects through their disciplinary character. This is so, he maintains, even when they provoke resistance. Resistance merely serves to demonstrate the necessity of that discipline that provokes it. It becomes a target against which discipline may justify its necessity because of its lack of omnipotence. These disciplinary practices become widely disseminated through schools, the army and the asylum, and eventually into the capitalist factory. They become strategic if they are effective constitutions of powers. As a form of knowledge they work through their own ontogenesis. Because they are knowledge constituted not just in texts but in definite institutional and organizational practices, they are 'discursive practices': knowledge reproduced through practices made possible by the framing assumptions of that knowledge. Moreover, it is a very practical knowledge: it disciplines the body, regulates the mind and orders the emotions in such a way that the ranking, hierarchy and stratification that ensues are not just the blind reproduction of a transcendent traditional order, as in feudalism. It produces a new basis for order in the productive worth of individuals defined by new disciplinary practices of power.

These new disciplinary practices of power are not, however, an intentional effect of any will, least of all of that traditional central condensation of power, the state.

> There is not, on the one side, a discourse of power, and opposite it another discourse that runs counter to it. Discourses are tactical elements or blocks operating in the field of force relations; there can run different and even contradictory discourses within the same strategy; they can, on the contrary, circulate without changing their form from one strategy to another, opposing strategy. (Foucault, 1984: 101–2)

If no given elective affinity exists between discourse, practice and interests, then images of power as a 'single, all-encompassing strategy' dissolve (Foucault, 1984: 103). Power will be a more or less stable or shifting network of alliances extended over a shifting terrain of practice and discursively constituted interests. Points of resistance will open up at many points in the network (Foucault, 1984: 95) whose effect will be to fracture alliances, constitute regroupings and re-posit strategies (Foucault, 1984: 96). Power appears in:

the multiplicity of force relations immanent in the sphere in which they operate and which constitute their own organization; as the process which, through ceaseless struggles and confrontations, transforms, strengthens or reverses them; as the support which these force relations find in one another, thus forming a chain or a system, or on the contrary, the disjunctions and contradictions which isolate them one from another; and lastly, as the strategies in which they take effect, whose general design or institutional crystallisation is embodied in the state apparatus, in the formulation of the law, in the various social hegemonies. (Foucault, 1984: 92)

Central to Foucault's conception of power is its shifting, inherently unstable expression in networks and alliances. Rather than the monolithic view of power as a 'third dimension' incorporating subjectivities, the focus is much closer to Machiavelli's strategic concerns or Gramsci's notion of hegemony as a 'war of manoeuvre', in which points of resistance and fissure are at the forefront.

Discourses are a means by which a certain power (of theorizing: a theorizing power) is itself constituted. For Foucault, the discursive field of formal academic theorizing about power primarily derives from notions of sovereignty. In this context sovereignty refers to an originating subject whose will is power. The allusion is obviously to Nietzsche. Daudi (1986: 152–6) explores the connections between Foucault and Nietzsche. Against this originary subject (which in Western history becomes transmuted from the monarch into 'the state'), Foucault argues for a reversal of Hobbes's terms. Instead of concentrating on the sovereignty of power, he argues that, on the contrary, we should 'study the myriad of bodies which are constituted as peripheral *subjects* as a result of the effects of power' (Foucault, 1980: 39; emphasis added). That theorists from Hobbes to Dahl might have imagined the subjects of power as 'individual(s) . . . a sort of elementary nucleus, a primitive atom, a multiple and inert material on which power comes to fashion or against which it happens to strike . . . is already one of the prime effects of power'. In other words, the episodic and agency view of power cannot be taken as any kind of analytic fundamental or primitive conception. Foucault's conception of power is one that attempts to break decisively with the 'mechanistic' and 'sovereign' view. He writes of the creation of new forms of social power that crystallize in the seventeenth and eighteenth centuries, outside the terms which by now have become quite conventional for addressing and constituting 'power'. What emerges during this period is a 'capillary form' of power, a power which 'reaches into the very grain of individuals', a 'synaptic regime of power, a regime of its exercise *within* the social body, rather than *from above* it' (Foucault, 1980: 39; original emphasis).

'Disciplinary power' is one of two distinctive conceptions of power which Foucault (1979) argues have characterized the 'modern' epoch, from the early nineteenth century onwards. The other term is 'bio-power' (Foucault, 1984: 140–4). Both contrast with the conception of 'sovereign power', a power tied irrevocably to the formal apparatus of the state in its complex organization. Whereas disciplinary power targets particular individuals or collections of individuals, bio-power orients to the subjugation of bodies and control of populations in general. Foucault concentrates on sexuality as an area of bio-power.

Sexuality stands as the point of intersection of not only the expressivity of human beings but also the reproduction of the species as such. From the nineteenth century onwards, contrary to the hypothesis of 'Victorian repression', Foucault sees an outpouring of talk, concern and writing focusing on sex. The effect of this discourse, he argues, is the development of a whole new realm of discourse attending to the definition of what is 'normal' and what is not, what is available for individuals to do, think, say and be and what is not. Indeed, Foucault focuses on the range of professional discourses that increasingly limit, define and normalize the 'vocabularies of motive' (Mills, 1940) available in specific sites ('situated contexts' in Mills's terms) for making sensible and accountable what it is that people should do, can do and thus do. Bio-power normalizes through discursive formations of psychiatry, medicine, social work and so on. The terms of these ways of constituting the normal become institutionalized and incorporated into everyday life. Our own reflexive gaze takes over the disciplining role as we take on the accounts and vocabularies of meaning and motive that are available to us as certain other forms of account are marginalized or simply eased out of currency.

Foucault's distinctiveness: the death knell of sovereignty

The distinctiveness of Foucault's conception is that it presents, in its historical inquiry into disciplinary power, an alternative view of power practices. Foucault suggests that a real world of new and distinct practices of power emerged far from the concern with sovereignty and the associated debates on power. The formal discourses available for the study of politics focused on conceptions of sovereign power, of an 'A getting a B to do something that B wouldn't otherwise do'. Power is negative. Why should this be so?

Foucault suggests that the interpenetration of the discourse of power at its modern inception was virtually synonymous with the institution of the monarchy, the sovereign power. Foucault argues that we are still very much in the thrall of a conception of sovereign power. There are two manifestations of this enthralment. First, that what one may term an 'episodic' notation for power has held sway for so long, such that, except when exercised, one should regard power as mostly absent. The exercise of power occurs only intermittently in discrete episodes. Ultimately this conception of episodic power derived from the feudal social relations that sustained it. These conditions were such that it was

> a power which intervened in the life of the producer only on occasion; its sole function was to assure the periodical transfer of the product of labour – not the administration of labour itself. (Bauman, 1982: 10)

The feudal monarch or lord did not personally subjugate these subject peoples:

> In such a society, surplus product was typically extracted from the producers, so to speak, in leaps and bounds; say, once or several times during the annual cycle of the essentially agricultural production, in the form of rent, or tax, or a levy, or a tribute or a tithe. The one function of power was to force the producer to part, of will or of fear, or of both, with a fraction of his product. Once he had done that, he could be (and should be, if the production was to continue) left to his own resources. It was largely irrelevant for the circulation of surplus how he went about his daily business, how he administered and deployed his bodily and spiritual powers . . . the customs and habits which ruled the daily life of the food suppliers were no concern of power. (Bauman, 1982: 40)

The absent, intermittent, episodic concept derived from sovereign power is all too evident in the incredulity and puzzlement of a contemporary power theorist, like Wolfinger (1971a, 1971b), when confronted with what very evidently strikes him as the bizarre idea that power is somehow present in its absence from the social terrain, in the normal routines of everyday organizational life generally. Sovereign conceptions of episodic power, constituted mechanically, mean that something has to be seen to have been done in order to say that power has been exercised. The very verb form of power's 'exercise' is redolent of the intermittent and episodic genesis of the applications of sovereign power.

Hobbes's *Leviathan* proposed a solution to what he saw as the anarchic, disorderly, 'state of nature': vast architectonic power in the body of the sovereign. Hobbes sought to rationalize and justify the re-ascendancy of the English monarchy to the throne after the bloody Civil War and Cromwellian commonwealth. The context of Hobbes's theorizing may not be unimportant. It provided the background for a distinctive foregrounding of power focused on power's majesty. Foucault's (1980: 121) acknowledgement of this is by means of both a question and a proposal. For one so sensitive to the corporeality of power the proposal takes the form of a bloody and spectacular metaphor that invites us to wield the executioner's axe or to unleash the terrible power of the guillotine:

> I wonder if this modern conception of power isn't bound up with the institution of monarchy. This developed during the Middle Ages against the backdrop of the previously endemic struggles between feudal power agencies. The monarchy presented itself as a referee, a power capable of putting an end to war, violence and pillage and saying no to these struggles and private feuds. It made itself acceptable by allocating itself a juridical and negative function, albeit one whose limits it naturally began at once to overstep. Sovereign, law and prohibition formed a system of representation of power which was extended during the subsequent era by the theories of right: political theory has never ceased to be obsessed with the person of the sovereign. Such theories still continue today to busy themselves with the problem of sovereignty. What we need, however, is a political philosophy that isn't erected around the problem of sovereignty, nor therefore around the problems of law and prohibition. We need to cut off the King's head: in political theory that has still to be done.

The radical nature of Foucault's enterprise thus becomes apparent: administer capital punishment to the theoretical corpus of power. Reverse the concentration of analysis on a mechanical and sovereign conception of power.

The project is thoroughgoingly 'constitutive'. Foucault shows how relations of 'agency' and 'structure' constitute discursively, how agency is denied to some, given to others, how structures could be said to have determined some things and not others. The focus is upon the constitution of certain forms of representation rather than a focus on the 'truth' or 'falsity' of the representations themselves, or the 'ideological' work that they do. Rather than focus on categories of 'ideology' as false consciousness or occlusion, Foucault returns our attention to Weber's (1978) stress on the importance of discipline. Disciplinary power works exactly through the construction of routine. Bauman (1982: 40–1) captures the processes of this new power perfectly:

> Power moved from the distant horizon into the very centre of daily life. Its object, previously the goods possessed or produced by the subject, was now the subject himself, his daily rhythm, his time, his bodily actions, his mode of life. The power reached now towards the body and the soul of its subjects. It wished to regulate, to legislate, to tell the right from the wrong, the norm from deviance, the ought from the is. It wanted to impose one ubiquitous pattern of normality and eliminate everything and everybody which the pattern could not fit. Unlike the sovereign power which required only a ceremonial reminder of the timeless limits to autonomy, the emergent power could be maintained only by a dense web of interlocking authorities in constant communication with the subject and in a physical proximity to the subject which permitted a perpetual surveillance of, possibly, the totality of his life process.

Foucault and the capitalist labour process

Writers like Marglin (1974) or Braverman (1974) limit consideration of new forms of disciplinary power solely to factory settings. In this context they regard them as an outcome of creative and intentional acts of power by capitalists. While there is no doubt that some of the new forms of disciplinary power proved 'functional' for capitalists, as Weber (1978) argued, it is, as Bauman (1982: 42) suggests, far more difficult to establish that they were 'necessary'. The causality is all wrong. New forms of disciplinary power preceded the establishment of the factory system by at least two centuries, he suggests. In fact, as Keiser (1987) demonstrates, one should, as Weber (1978) suggested, chart the early religious roots of modern disciplinary power as they emerged in monastic discipline. The availability of disciplinary power mechanisms facilitated the development of capitalism, suggests Bauman (1982).

The ideal type of the new disciplinary power for Foucault is Bentham's proposal for a 'Panopticon'. The Panopticon was an architectural device consisting of a central elevated watch-tower, a device that signals clearly the practical demise of the old sovereign concept. From this central point of inspection a circular disposition of cells radiated like spokes from the hub of a wheel to its rim. Each cell, illuminated with peripheral light that passed from the exterior rim of the building into the cell, made evident the person within. One observer, all-seeing but unseen in the tower, could in principle subject all in vision to surveillance. Surveillance was less in the actual superintendence, more in the sheer impossibility of avoiding the observer's gaze, and the realization that one was always, in principle, subject to it. It would thus become, in principle, 'internalized'. Power no longer based itself on the constancy of place and normative ties and occasional acts of expropriation. Power would now be regularized, routinized, cast not as an absent presence securing traditional norms, but as a constant surveillance constituting a new discipline of norms and behaviour. Subject to the Panopticon, inmates of whatever institution would be acutely aware that every action might be, with no way of knowing if indeed it was, subject to the supervisory gaze of surveillance. This knowledge in itself might be sufficient to produce disciplined obedience, as subjects learnt to survey themselves, to be reflexively self-regarding as if under the ever present and watchful eye of surveillance. Moreover, coupled with the therapeutic incitement to speak and to provide an account of themselves in the terms made available by the new disciplinary practices, power was now able to work not simply by silencing people but by giving them voice. Power, rather than occasionally imposing itself on the subjectivity of its subjects, now 'in its actual exercise must be ever constitutive of the subjectivity of the agents of power relations' (Minson, 1986: 113–14). Power subjects and now, in its disciplinary mode, subjectifies.

The planned apparatus was quite cunning in terms of its design. However, although examples of the Panopticon were built, it should be evident that a system of control that depends upon purpose-built and designed architecture is an expensive option and likely to be cast aside in favour of more cost-effective and flexible solutions. Very little flexibility attaches to a control system that can, because of its design, only hold a specific number of inmates. For expanding commercial enterprises this was an especial barrier. And an unnecessary one. It was not the Panopticon but what it could achieve that was important: subjectification. Subjectification identified with disciplinary power operates primarily though enhancing the 'calculability' of individuals (Foucault, 1977: 192–4). Minson (1986: 13) renders it clearly: 'The human individual constructed in such discourses is calculable to the extent of being subject to comparative, scalar measures and related forms of training and correction'. The objective of disciplinary techniques is normalization, representing the discursive 'fixing' of the conditions of subjectivity in particular places and times. Almost anything might become a resource in this process, from a religious vocation to the formation of discursive skills themselves (Clegg and Dunkerley, 1980: 59–63).

Disciplinary power, particularly in its 'time-discipline' (Thompson, 1967), clearly emerged from the monasteries, as Keiser (1987) argues. However, it is equally clear that it was rapidly adapted in the competitive learning environment of early capitalist industrialization. A general transition may be said to have taken place from a domestic economy premised on the 'putting out' system to one which was factory based (Clegg and Dunkerley, 1980: 49–56, 59–70), even though it is clear that, as O'Neill (1987: 47) observes, citing Laslett (1965) and Wall et al. (1983), it would be a myth to regard this family as a 'natural' economy. However, it is evident that the chronology of the world was transformed, often in a generation, from one of Holy days, local feasts and the unremitting but seasonally variable rhythms of agricultural production into one based on the rhythms of the industrial machine, overseer, and the clock of factory discipline applied to factory 'hands'. (Workers were interchangeable 'hands', recruited as such.) In the competitive ecology of nineteenth-century production regimes, the possibilities for theft, casualness and ill-discipline of the putting-out system of domestic production compared unfavourably with factory control (Landes, 1969; Marglin, 1974). The keynote of this factory control was what Weber (1978) referred to as 'military discipline'. Equally, this discipline had not only military but also monastic roots, particularly in the subjugation of one's own time to the externally imposed discipline of the master's time.

O'Neill (1987: 47–8) notes, after Smelser (1959), that certain technological changes such as steam power and mule spinning cemented the loss of workers' control and the ascendancy of the master's, in the spinning trades. These changes gradually spread in the weaving trades, with women and children replacing previously craft-based male labour, labour whose resistance was stubborn, violent, political and drawn-out. Indeed, some writers who focus on class struggle at the point of production (Burawoy, 1978, 1979, 1985; Edwards, 1979; Clawson, 1980; Littler, 1982) see this as a battleground in which a dialectic of capitalist control and worker resistance to it is played out, one that is structurally irresolvable as long as capitalist relations of production are reproduced. Hence, the dialectic of power and resistance has a precise structural location in Marx's (1976) general theory of capitalism as relations of production. From this basis develop quite general theories of capitalist organization and control of the labour process (Clegg and Dunkerley, 1980).

Foucault's (1977) conception of disciplinary power, although compatible with the Marxian focus on control and resistance in the capitalist workplace, differs from it in two important respects. First, control via discipline first develops not in the factory, but in various state institutions. Capitalist masters adopt it from prison masters, from beadles, and from superintendents of asylums. Second, it is not a control functionally oriented to capitalist exploitation but to the creation of obedient bodies. Foucault spends considerable detail on the 'embodiment' of power. This focus was not entirely novel, as Marx (1976) was only too well aware of the violence done to human bodies by the new capitalist discipline, as many of his more descriptive passages indicate. Gramsci (1971) was also aware of the impact of the 'Fordist' system on the bodies of workers. Weber (1948: 261–2) also wrote of the 'tuning' of the 'psycho-physical' apparatus produced by the 'ever-widening grasp of discipline', although his focus was more on the role that Protestantism could play in producing a morally tuned and willing apparatus (Weber 1976; see Poggi (1983) and Marshall (1982); also Thompson (1968), Hobsbawm (1969), Wearmouth (1939), Eldridge (1972), Anthony (1977) and Guttman (1977); all stress the role of religion in disciplining the workforce). Religion undoubtedly had a role to play, although as Eldridge (1972) notes, it is not always clear on the evidence of religious conviction that it was quite as dramatic as is sometimes assumed. Others see the Foucauldian stress on state institutions rather than testament as a more compelling locus of the new disciplinary power. Writing of the forced labour of the workhouses which followed the breakdown of the Elizabethan Poor Laws under the supply of increasingly surplus quantities of labour, driven off the land by enclosure, O'Neill notes that

> When labour became increasingly plentiful, unemployed and driven to crime and rebellion, the houses of correction became even more punitive, while labour in the houses of correction was limited to intimidating and useless tasks so that no one would ever enter them voluntarily. The overall effect was to teach free labour the discipline of the factory outside and inside the factory. . . . Thus, the employed and the unemployed learn their respective disciplines. Thereafter, we might say that in the bourgeois social order the prison, the factory and the school, like the army, are places where the system can project its conception of the disciplinary society in the reformed criminal, the good worker, student, loyal soldier, and committed citizen. In every case, it is a question of reproducing among the propertyless a sense of commitment to the property system in which they have nothing to sell but their labour and loyalty. (O'Neill, 1987: 51–2)

It is in this panoply of disciplinary organizations, in Foucault's account, that the new complex of bio-power emerges. It is this aspect of power, how it ties up with new discourses of medicine, administration and so on, which is additional to either Marx or Weber's accounts, and which provides a framework for the carrying capacity of new forms of disciplinary power to spread like a contagion from their initial institutional site. With DiMaggio and Powell (1983) one would see the carriers of institutional isomorphism in this respect as primarily the state and the professions. Moreover, as certain 'radical' organization theorists have argued, it is this knowledge and the practices which they license that produces what O'Neill (1987: 55) refers to as the *natural discipline* of the workplace and the wage system (see, for example: Clegg and Dunkerley, 1980). The Foucauldian twist is a useful corrective in making the process far less instrumental than these accounts presume.

Foucault's approach to discursive practices is not the relativism it might appear to be.

> It is not necessary to construe those differential advantages and disadvantages such as popular aspirations, morale, responsibilities, principles, rights or virtues as essential human or subjective factors belonging to a moral domain. Rather it is possible to treat these phenomena of the moral or personal life as always determined by the specific discourses and social relations in which they are formed and where they exercise definite, albeit limited effects. They are no less 'objective' or more conditional than a policeman's powers of arrest or the power of a gun to penetrate a body or of a manager to sack an employee. (Minson, 1986: 129–30)

Whatever phenomena of fixity exist result from those stabilized disciplinary powers and discursive practices that constitute them. This has considerable significance for studies of power in organizations. Power in organizations must concern the hierarchical structure of offices and their relation to each other, in the classical Weberian sense. Implicitly, this concerns 'legitimate power'. However, in addition to this perspective the organizations literature has also highlighted what Thompson (1956: 290) termed 'illegitimate power'. It was the dichotomy of the concepts of 'power' and 'authority' around the axis of legitimacy that became constitutive of the 'contingencies' and 'resource dependence' problematic of power in organizations. Subsequently, the concept of power applies to exercises of discretion by organization members that their position in the formal structure does not sanction. Such exercise, premised on an illegitimate or informal use of resource control, gains purchase from the member's place in the organizational division of labour.

Mechanisms of power: disciplinary practices of surveillance

'Obedience' is central to an analysis of the production of power in organizations, an insight shared by major precursors such as Weber (1978) and Etzioni (1961). Moreover, it is a focus that has received historical endorsement not only through the corpus of Weberian research (Matheson, 1987) but also through that recent and related work on the origins of disciplined obedience through 'disciplinary practices' in monastic organizations (see Assad (1987); Keiser (1987)). The concept of 'disciplinary practice' derives, as we have seen, from Foucault (1977) but is implicit in Weber (1978). It renders those micro-techniques of power that inscribe and normalize not only individuals but also collective, organized bodies. Surveillance, whether personal, technical, bureaucratic or legal, is the central issue.

Surveillance is not simply about direct control. It may range from cultural practices of moral endorsement, enablement and suasion, to more formalized technical knowledge. At one particular level of application these can include the use of new technologies such as computer monitoring of keyboard output and efficiency. At another more general level, one may be dealing with the development of disciplines of knowledge shaped almost wholly by the 'disciplinary gaze' of surveillance, as Foucault (1977) suggests was the case of much nineteenth-century social science, particularly branches of social welfare, statistics and administration. Organizationally, the twentieth-century development of the personnel function under the 'human relations' guidance of Mayo (1975) had a similar tutelary role with respect to organizationally dependent members (Rose, 1990). Through such mechanisms one discriminates individuals or bodies collectively, as well as abstract properties of goods and services, and categorizes them through diverse and localized tactics of ratiocination. At the more general level of discipline, this will form organizations into discursive locales of competing calculations.

Each disciplinary practice, in its applications, will calculate organizational rationality from distinct auspices of power and knowledge. From such potentially discursive babel any formally efficient organization will normally attempt to construct the architectonic of some overall strategic practices of discipline. A storehouse of disciplinary techniques is available for organizations to achieve this aim. Not only are there the services of those many agencies who specialize in selling specific disciplinary techniques on a consultancy, advisory or sub-contracting basis. There are also the enduring sediments of previous practice selectively structured into the rules of organization control. Not only are such practices capable of quite precise targeting within organizations; quite generalized but no less effective sanctions available as a result of the career structure and movement through it also buttress control. In addition, there are 'the files', the repository of all that is formally recorded and known concerning an agent or agency, of whose potency as a device Weber (1978) was only too well aware; there are the mechanisms of a 'span of control', of hierarchy, of divisional and departmental cleavage and so on (see Barnes, 1988: 117). Such practices will not be simply constraining: they do not only punish and forbid; more especially they endorse and enable obedient wills and constitute organizationally approved forms of creativity and productivity through a process both transitive (via authoritative externalities such as rules, superiors, etc.) and intransitive (via the acquisition of organizationally proper conduct by the member).

Any superordinate member of a complex organization will be just one relay in a complex flow of authority up, down and across organization hierarchies. Ideally, in any rationalistic view by organization elites, planners and seemingly many theorists, such relays should be without resistance, offering no impedance whatsoever, no 'problem of obedience'. Rarely, if ever, will this be the case. Resistance, to continue the metaphor, will tend to be pervasive. Authorities, to use the term as a plural noun, will rarely if ever be resistance-free and passive relays. An explanation for this is available through appreciation of the strategic relationship between organization and agency.

Strategic agency

Organizations are locales in which negotiation, contestation and struggle between organizationally divided and linked agencies are a routine occurrence, as Machiavelli saw so clearly. Divisions of labour are both an object and outcome of struggle. All divisions of labour within any employing organization necessarily constitute themselves within the context of various contracts of employment. Hence, the employment relationship, that of economic domination and subordination, is necessarily an organizational fundamental. It is the underlying sediment through which other organization practices stratify. Often these will overlap with it in quite complex ways.

The sociological consequences of this view of organizations are evident. Divisions of labour, along with their remuneration, as central aspects of the employment contract and effort bargain, will become foci of politics. In these politics, agencies interested in maximizing their strategicality must attempt to transform their point of connection with some other agency or agencies into a 'necessary nodal point': this would be a channel through which traffic between them occurs on terms that privilege the putative strategic agency. Otherwise, strategic inclinations will be unconsummated. From these observations follow the central points of strategic contingency theory (Hickson et al., 1971).

To achieve strategic agency requires disciplining the discretion of other agencies: at best, from the strategist's point of view, such other agencies will become merely authoritative relays, extensions of strategic agency (Law, 1986: 16). Whatever interests such relay-agencies would have would be entirely those represented by the strategically subordinating agency. A totally disciplined army squad in the field of battle, obediently subject to higher authority and its commands, would be the extreme example of this evacuation from agency of interests other than those authoritatively attributed to them. The actual agents, in this case the army squad, remain literally non-actors in this process: the only action formally allowed is for them to obey unquestioningly, sometimes on penalty of death for mutiny, desertion or insubordination in the field of battle. Ideally, they become agents without interests other than obedience to others' commands. In this respect the army, as Weber was well aware, represents only the most condensed and concentrated form of much 'normal' organizational power and discipline, at least along the transitive dimension as it applies to low trust, low discretion positions. It is expedient if moral authority buttresses one's military discipline also, such as, for instance, a religious vocation: soldiers of God, as Anthony (1977) suggests, historically have been the highest expression of obedient organization membership: commerce as a moral crusade would be, perhaps, the ultimate cultural evangelist's dream, as Weber (1976), of course, was not unaware.

High discretionary strategic agency is another matter, one for which power will be less prohibitive and more productive, more facultative of desired outcomes through the disciplined discretion of the agency of empowered authorities. Here the necessity is not so much to forbid or restrict or prohibit but to enable creativity that is imbued with positivity yet still constrained with discipline. The model, of course, is the classical conception of the professional discipline as a vocation whose testament Weber (1948) conveyed so exquisitely in his profession of faith in 'Science as a vocation'.

The articulation of interests by strategic agencies is thus the medium and outcome of unique positioning over the discretion of others in the organization field. It requires reproduction for existing structures of power to be reproduced. Indeed, its reproduction is a significant component of the phenomenon of power; its transformation effective resistance to it. It should be evident that such reproductions are never flat, one-dimensional topographies, always already structured. Topography in this instance will always be the result of previous and current contest. In organizational life such field structure requires reproduction by strategic agencies.

One consequence of the position taken here is that organizational locales will more likely be loci of multivalent powers than monadic sites of total control: contested terrains rather than total institutions. The theoretically most powerful delegation of authority depends upon the delegated agent acting as one who is 'obedient'. Other than this, there is no way that the delegated routines will occur as directed without discretion. 'Obedience' cannot be guaranteed, despite the search for a secular equivalent to divinely inspired obeisance, if only because of the complexity and contingency of agency, as a nexus of calculation. Discretion need not entail dissent: it may be organizationally creative, productive, reproductive. Nonetheless, to increase the power of a delegating agency does mean authorizing delegated others, and delegated authorities do not guarantee loci of wholly predictable and controlled agency, other than if they are dutiful servants. Thus the problematic of 'power in organizations' centres not on the legitimacy or otherwise of subordinates' capacities, as in the conventional view, but on the myriad practices that *incapacitate* authorities from becoming powers by restricting action to that which is 'obedient', not only prohibitively but also creatively, productively.

Power inscribes itself within contextual 'rules of the game' that both enable and constrain action (Clegg, 1975). These rules form the underlying rationale of those calculations that agencies routinely make in organizational contexts. Action designates itself as such-and-such an action by reference to rules that identify it as such. Such rules can never be free of surplus or ambiguous meaning: they are always indexical to the context of interpreters and interpretation. Where there are rules there must be indexicality, as has been demonstrated by texts as diverse as Wittgenstein (1968), Garfinkel (1967), Clegg (1975) and Barnes (1986). Rules can never provide for their own interpretation. Issues of interpretation always implicate the processes whereby agencies instantiate and signify rules. 'Ruling' is an activity. Some agency does it as a constitutive sense-making process that fixes meaning. Both rules and games necessarily tend to the subject of contested interpretation, with some players having not only play-moves but also the refereeing of these as power resources. Consequently, where we invoke rules there must be discretion. Thus, it is not only embodiment, labour power, which is the source of resistance. It is not only the gap between the capacity to labour and its realization that implicates power and the organization of control; it is also inherent in the regulation of meaning.

Here we confront the central paradox of power: the power of an agency increases in principle by that agency's delegating authority; the delegation of authority proceeds by rules; rules necessarily entail discretion and discretion potentially empowers delegates. From this arises the tacit and taken-for-granted basis of organizationally negotiated order, and on occasion, its fragility and instability. Events and others require rendering as routine and predictable if negotiation is to remain an unusual and out-of-the-ordinary state of affairs. Routines arise not so much by prohibition and intervention into states of affairs, but through the knowledgeable construction of these states of affairs so that subordinate agencies know what needs doing on their part if they are to minimize whatever sanctions may be directed at them by superordinates, or indeed by any others involved in their circuits of power. It is not only power that presumes knowledge, its exclusive control or privileged access. It is also subordination: as Barnes (1988: 103) puts it, such agencies 'must recognise that the output of appropriate action that they produce is what minimises the input of coercion and sanctioning which they receive'. It is for this reason that wherever questions of time–space extension become necessary for securing organization action, it becomes important to hold agents to some form of rules of practice. The freedom of discretion requires disciplining if it is to be a reliable relay. Whether this be achieved through what Foucault referred to as 'disciplinary' or some other modes of practice is unimportant. It may be direct surveillance, the interiorized, normalizing gaze of professional self-regulation, a standardized reporting scheme, common economic interest or client reports that serve as the rules of practice. In the absence of these, their evasion or malfunction, then organizations are ill-advised to put their trust in agencies, as Machiavelli knew only too well.

Authority implies power and rules constitute it; the interpretation of rules requires discipline, regulation, to avoid producing new powers or transforming existing powers. In fact, given the inherent indexicality of rule use, things will never be wholly stable; they will usually exhibit tolerances to stress, strain and strife in rule constitution whose limits become evident only through ill-disciplined breach of regulation. By definition, wholly effective discipline admits no breach, no 'disobedience', total rule-boundedness. None of this is far from Weber (1978) or for that matter Foucault (1977). Resistance to discipline will be irremediable. Not because of 'human nature', 'capitalism' or any other putatively essentialist category. It is irremediable because of the power/rule constitution as a nexus of meaning and interpretation that, because of indexicality, is always open to being re-fixed. This is what couples power/knowledge in Foucault's (1977) formulation, because, at its most pervasive, power positions the subject, through the organization of disciplinary practices that constitute the potentialities, incapacities and correlates of specific forms of agency.

Conclusion

Organization may seek to secure particular representations across specific spaces but can never arrest time: it always elapses. No insurance entails the continuity of any particular fixture. One implication of this is that the shackles of Weber's cultural pessimism do not have to bind us tight, either in his thought or that of his heirs presumptive (Donaldson, 1985). In concrete settings it is the play of people that undercut and remake fates for our times, not a logic of efficiency, a singular rationality or specific limited sets of contingencies and designs. Whatever 'image' of organization (Morgan, 1986) or 'vision' of its strategy (Hampden-Turner, 1991) is being implicated in the analysis, design or development of an organization it must work through the meanings that the members of the organization, and significant others in and around it, seek to fix discursively. Some important consequences flow from such a premise.

First, meanings are ineradicably indexical in nature. Consequently, the perspective offered here is not just another 'image' of organization or another 'paradigm'. It is far deeper. Any 'image' or any 'paradigm' of organizations may itself be subject to analysis in terms of its deployment of values, power, rules, discretion, organization and paradox. Such is the case both in its formal representation in theory and in the practical representation of whatever forms of organizationally or investigationally contrived data get constituted as its theoretical instantiation. Diverse theories, methods and objects of analysis are all cultural contrivances. For this reason the proper study of organization theory is its own forms of knowledge, whether lodged in formal theories or in the phenomena that such theories ostensibly are about.

Weber defined the contrivance that is culture as 'the endowment of a finite segment of the meaningless infinity of events in the world with meaning and significance from the standpoint of human beings' (translation adapted from Weber, 1949: 81). Hence, the analysis of organizations concerns the endowment of the material forms of institutional life, be it economic, religious, or whatever, with significance, both by the participants in and around these arenas and those who participate as members of the arena of organization theory. This means coming to terms with the culturally embedded modes of rationality that characterize various spheres of organized social life, including those of theorists and consultants as well as the actions of those whom they ordinarily address.

There is a further implication of the terms at work in this chapter. The very notion of 'address', as used in this context, entails communication. Communication without dialogue is impossible. Dialogue entails some limits to totalitarianism to the extent that its horizons are open and its participation not restricted, as Habermas (1984) works out in his late flowering of the Weberian, modernist project. Such dialogue, or conversation, invariably, will not be ideal where it is organizational. Organization means more or less domination and distorted communication. The flow of communication through, up, down, across, into and out of an organization structure, while it can qualify the extent of distortion, will rarely eliminate it. Complex organization entails that this should be so. Hence, any ideal of organization democracy, premised on an ideal speech situation, is chimerical.

Organization theory condemns us to a specific form of conversation, a further implication of the views developed here. Giddens (1976) writes about a particular form of the 'double-hermeneutic' that applies to organization theory. The discourse of organization theory represents and reflects back upon the practice of organization. This practice is irremediably part of the conversation that is culture, relatively enveloped and contained within the organizational form. It is a specific site of conversation for addressing which three broad methodological options present themselves. First, a monologically contrived conversation where theorists talk within their respective intellectual traditions but bound their rationality with respect to others, both in other traditions and in the context of mundane organization conversations (e.g. Williamson, 1985, in his production of an approach that makes an economic sense of hitherto organizational questions, yet does so largely divorced from some of the central traditions already established in this field); second, where they speak in a dialogue, across two or more intellectual traditions (e.g. Fligstein, 1985, with his strategy of hypothesis generation from rival theoretical camps capable of rudimentary address in terms of the same body of data) and third, where they speak dialectically, through intellectual traditions to those cultural practices that they study and through those practices to their intellectual traditions: here the best exemplar is probably Foucault, in his various revisions of our understanding of intellectual traditions, such as penology (Foucault, 1977), where the encounter arranged between the traditions and the archives transforms our understanding of knowledge (and, it should be added, power) in terms of practices understood as practical knowledge.

Organization theory involves less reflexivity where it proffers nostrums irrespective of their situational relevance and meaning. Yet, the more that it seeks to control others through its values, power, rules and discretion, the less is it likely to change meanings *in situ*, by virtue of being disinclined to hear them. Such is the paradoxical power of any organization theory that knows in advance what it prescribes. Given that what are prescribed so invariably are powerful and privileged sites of representation in the organization discourse, then it is not surprising that such power frequently wraps itself in what Fairtlough (1994) terms the security blanket of hierarchy.

What would it be like to develop power without being stifled by hierarchy? It would not mean the abolition of hierarchy: as is evident, differential power will always attend any moderate task, capital or knowledge complexity (see Clegg and Higgins, 1987). It would be a listening power, using office to be receptive and to encourage the voice of others, rather than to screen them out, ignore or marginalize them (Forester, 1989). It would entail the value of openness as the primary foundation for interaction.

Effective management is the extension of its agency across organization space and time. Such extension entails discretion, and discretion can potentially empower delegates in ways that are not necessarily organizationally authoritative. Consequently, organizational power, rules and domination never get irrevocably and automatically classified and framed in and by authority and authoritative relations. A certain indeterminacy, a certain openness, is always possible. Hence, the juxtaposition of organizational discretion and distributed powers always will entail heterodoxy and pluralism, many organizational viewpoints and conversations rather than a singular monologue capable of representation as such. One consequence of this viewpoint is that one must always ask what representational purposes are being served by any depiction, lay or academic, that privilege some over other organizational viewpoints? How is such closure effected? What does it marginalize, trivialize or exclude? What voices are silenced, muffled or distorted? What are the mechanisms, practices and routines of power that enable this monological representation to occur? How is openness avoided?

Some theorists of a critical nature have proposed that 'openness' be established as the norm for 'collectivist organizations'. Others suggest that open dissent is functional, anyhow. Dissent is not necessarily 'functional', however. It is not merely a matter of the 'functions' of social conflict. If dissent becomes too emotional in the person or too embedded in the organization, the paradoxical outcome may be that it undercuts further expression of that which it represents, as members shy away from hurt and pain.

One should not assume an analytical endorsement of 'openness' in favour of 'concealment'. Whereas concealment has been the basis for the practice of modernist organization in the past, and such practice has become increasingly subject to criticism (Clegg, 1990; Boje and Dennehy, 1992), one should not assume that technologies of openness will deliver a liberal ideal of an organization world of free and equal individuals. To practise openness, as much as concealment, also requires disciplinary practices of power – this much, at least, one should know from Foucault (1977). One can frame a normative order that encourages, rather than discourages, voice. Yet, where this is the case, strong organizational frames usually feature. Such framing devices, usually embedded in recruitment and containment constituted through a strong ideological commitment, as in most successful collectives, function as a form of surrogate control. Openness does not equate with non-distorted communication. Where recruitment in an ideological image premises openness, conversation in the organization becomes more monological, as values get cloned and reinforced in recruits. Cults exemplify this to the greatest extent, often tragically, as in the 1993 Waco tragedy. Any organization with a strong value base risks the ultimate paradox of becoming cultish and thus increasingly incapable of reflexivity regarding the environment in which it operates. Consequently, where a value of openness is paramount, successful organizations must build dissent into their practices, even as it may challenge the core values of the organization. Practising power in such a context thus becomes a case of listening acutely, to hear silences and ellipses, as well as what is evident; of seeking to draw others and oneself into discursive dissonance in order to find that which all agree as the basis for action so that none can deny consultation as to its wisdom; of building an organization environment of alliances, networks and overlapping conduits of interest. Such a *realpolitik* of power, one submits, will open the door to postmodern organization futures made more reflexive by less hierarchical distortion of power and more capable of learning from the potential voices for their conversation.

References

Anthony, P.D. (1977) *The Ideology of Work*. London: Tavistock.

Assad, T. (1987) 'On ritual and discipline in medieval Christian monasteries', *Economy and Society*, 14 (2): 159–203.

Barnes, B. (1986) 'On authority and its relationship to power', in J. Law (ed.), *Power, Action and Belief: A New Sociology of Knowledge?* Sociological Review Monograph 32. London: Routledge and Kegan Paul. pp. 190–5.

Barnes, B. (1988) *The Nature of Power*. Cambridge: Polity.

Bauman, Z. (1982) *Memories of Class*. London: Routledge and Kegan Paul.

Bauman, Z. (1990) 'Philosophical affinities of postmodern sociology', *The Sociological Review*, 38 (3): 411–44.

Boje, D.M. and Dennehy, R.F. (1992) *Managing in the Postmodern World: America's Revolution against Exploitation*. Dubuque, IA: Kendall/Hunt.

Bravermen, H. (1974) *Labour and Monopoly Capitalism: The Degradation of Work in the Twentieth Century*. New York: Monthly Review Press.

Burawoy, M. (1978) 'Towards a Marxist theory of the labour process: Braverman and beyond', *Politics and Society*, 8: 247–312.

Burawoy, M. (1979) *Manufacturing Consent: Changes in the Labor Process under Capitalism*. Chicago: University of Chicago Press.

Burawoy, M. (1985) *The Politics of Production: Factory Regimes under Capitalism and Socialism*. London: Verso.

Clawson, D. (1980) *Bureaucracy and the Labor Process: The Transformation of U.S. Industry 1860–1920*. New York: Monthly Review Press.

Clegg, S.R. (1975) *Power, Rule and Domination: A Critical and Empirical Understanding of Power in Sociological Theory and Organizational Life*. London: Routledge and Kegan Paul.

Clegg, S.R. (1987) 'The power of language, the language of power', *Organization Studies*, 8 (1): 60–70.

Clegg, S.R. (1989) *Frameworks of Power*. London: Sage.

Clegg, S.R. (1990) *Modern Organizations: Organization Studies in the Postmodern World*. London: Sage.

Clegg, S.R. and Dunkerley, D. (1980) *Organization, Class and Control*. London: Routledge and Kegan Paul.

Clegg, S.R. and Higgins, W. (1987) 'Against the current: sociology, socialism and organizations', *Organization Studies*, 8 (3): 201–21.

Clegg, S.R., Boreham, P. and Dow, G. (1986) *Class, Politics and the Economy*. London: Routledge and Kegan Paul.

Daudi, P. (1986) *Power in the Organization*. Oxford: Blackwell.

DiMaggio, P. and Powell, W. (1983) 'The iron cage revisited: institutional isomorphism and collective rationality in organizational fields', *American Sociological Review*, 48 (2): 147–60.

Donaldson, L. (1985) *In Defence of Organization Theory: A Response to Critics*. Cambridge: Cambridge University Press.

Edwards, R. (1979) *Contested Terrain: The Transformation of the Workplace in the Twentieth Century*. New York: Basic Books.

Eldridge, J.E.T. (1972) *Max Weber: The Interpretation of Social Reality*. London: Nelson.

Etzioni A. (1961) *The Comparative Analysis of Complex Organizations.* New York: Free Press.

Fairtlough, G. (1994) *Creative Compartments: A Design for Future Organizations.* London: Adamantine Press.

Fligstein N. (1985) 'The spread of the multidivisional form among large firms, 1919–1979', *American Sociological Review,* 50 (3): 377–91.

Forester, J. (1989) *Planning in the Face of Power.* Berkeley, CA: University of California Press.

Foucault, M. (1977) *Discipline and Punish: The Birth of the Prison.* Harmondsworth: Penguin.

Foucault, M. (1979) 'Governmentality', *Ideology and Consciousness,* 6: 5–21.

Foucault, M. (1980) *Power/Knowledge: Selected Interviews and Other Writings 1972–1977* (ed. C. Gordon). Brighton: Harvester Press.

Foucault, M. (1984) *The History of Sexuality: An Introduction.* Harmondsworth: Peregrine.

Garfinkel, H. (1967) *Studies in Ethnomethodology.* Englewood Cliffs, NJ: Prentice-Hall.

Giddens, A. (1976) *New Rules of Sociological Method.* London: Hutchinson.

Gramsci, A. (1971) *Selections from the Prison Notebooks.* London. Lawrence and Wishart.

Guttman, H.G. (1977) *Work, Culture and Society in Industrializing America.* Oxford: Blackwell.

Habermas, J. (1984) *Reason and the Rationalization of Society.* London: Heinemann.

Hampden-Turner, C. (1991) *Corporate Culture: From Vicious to Virtuous Circles.* London: Hutchinson Business Books / Economist Books.

Hickson, D.J., Hinings, C.R., Lee, C.A., Schneck, R.E. and Pennings, J.M. (1971) 'A strategic contingencies theory of intra-organizational power', *Administrative Science Quarterly,* 16: 216–29.

Hobsbawm, E.J. (1969) *Industry and Empire.* Harmondsworth: Penguin.

Keiser, A. (1987) 'From asceticism to administration of wealth: medieval monasteries and the pitfalls of rationalization', *Organization Studies,* 8 (2): 103–24.

Landes, S. (1969) *The Unbound Prometheus: Technological Change and Industrial Development in Western Europe from 1750 to the Present.* Cambridge: University of Cambridge Press.

Laslett, P. (1965) *The World We have Lost.* London. Methuen.

Law, J. (1986) 'Power/knowledge and the dissolution of the sociology of knowledge', in J. Law (ed.), *Power, Action and Belief: A New Sociology of Knowledge?* London: Routledge and Kegan Paul. pp. 1–19.

Littler, C.R. (1982) *The Development of the Labour Process in Capitalist Societies.* London. Heinemann.

Machiavelli, N. (1958) *The Prince.* London: Everyman.

Marglin, S. (1974) 'What do bosses do? The origins and functions of hierarchy in capitalist production', *Review of Radical Political Economics,* 6: 60–112.

Marshall, G. (1982) *In Search of the Spirit of Capitalism: An Essay on Max Weber's Protestant Ethic Thesis.* London: Hutchinson.

Marx, K. (1976) *Capital,* (vol. 1). Harmondsworth: Penguin.

Matheson, C. (1987) 'Weber and the classification of forms of legitimacy', *British Journal of Sociology,* 38 (2): 199–215.

Mayo, E. (1975) *The Social Problems of an Industrial Civilization.* London: Routledge and Kegan Paul.

Mills, C.W. (1940) 'Situated actions and vocabularies of motive', *American Sociological Review,* V: 904–13.

Minson, J. (1986) 'Strategies for socialists? Foucault's conception of power', in M. Gane (ed.), *Towards a Critique of Foucault.* London: Routledge and Kegan Paul. pp. 106–48.

Morgan G. (1986) *Images of Organizations.* London: Sage.

O'Neill, J. (1987) 'The disciplinary society: from Weber to Foucault', *British Journal of Sociology,* XXXVII (1): 42–60.

Poggi, G. (1978) *The Development of the Modern State.* London: Hutchinson.

Poggi, G. (1983) *Calvinism and the Capitalist Spirit: Max Weber's Protestant Ethic*. London: Macmillan.

Rose, N. (1990) *Governing the Soul: The Shaping of the Private Self*. London: Routledge.

Saussure, F. de (1974) *Course in General Linguistics*. London: Fontana.

Smelser, N. (1959) *Social Change in the Industrial Revolutions An Application of Theory to the Lancashire Cotton Industry*. London: Routledge and Kegan Paul.

Thompson, E.P. (1967) 'Time, work, discipline and industrial capitalism', *Past and Present*, 38: 56–97.

Thompson, E.P. (1968) *The Making of the English Working Class*. Harmondsworth: Penguin.

Thompson, J.D. (1956) 'Authority and power in identical organizations', *American Journal of Sociology*, 62: 290–301.

Wall, R., Robin, J. and Laslett, P. (eds) (1983) *Family Forms in Historic Europe*. Cambridge: Cambridge University Press.

Wearmouth, R.F (1939) *Methodism and the Working Class Movements of England 1800–1950*. London: Epworth.

Weber, M. (1947) *The Theory of Social and Economic Organization*. London: Routledge and Kegan Paul.

Weber, M. (1948) *From Max Weber: Essays in Sociology* (trans., ed. and with an introduction by H.H. Gerth and C.W. Mills). London: Routledge and Kegan Paul.

Weber, M. (1949) *The Methodology of the Social Sciences* (trans. and ed. E.A. Shills and H.A. Finch). New York: Free Press.

Weber, M. (1976) *The Protestant Ethic and the Spirit of Capitalism* (trans. T. Parsons and with a new introduction by A. Giddens). London: Allen and Unwin.

Weber, M. (1978) *Economy and Society: An Outline of Interpretive Sociology* (2 vols, ed. G. Roth and C. Wittich). Berkeley, CA: University of California Press.

Williamson, O.E. (1985) *The Economic Institutions of Capitalism*. New York: Free Press.

Wittgenstein, L. (1968) *Philosophical Investigations* (trans. G.E.M. Anscombe). Oxford: Blackwell.

Wolfinger, R.E. (1971a) 'Nondecisions and the study of local politics', *American Political Science Review*, 65: 1063–80.

Wolfinger, R.E. (1971b) 'Rejoinder to Frey's "comment"', *American Political Science Review*, 65: 1102–4.

4

Labour as Dressage

Norman Jackson and Pippa Carter

This chapter links two themes from the work of Foucault: *governmentality* and *labour as dressage*. Governmentality relates to the management of a population, at an aggregate level (the state) and also at a micro level. These levels are embedded in a matrix of apparatuses, logics, techniques, and so forth, of control – what Foucault calls the *dispositif*. The levels are linked through the overarching rationale of managing. Thus, management in its organizational sense, the management of labour and the organization of work, can be seen to constitute part of governmentality. Foucault identifies three functions of labour: the productive, the symbolic and dressage. We will argue that labour as dressage is a function of governmentality, that it is management not for economic or productive purposes, but for 'reasons of state', the reasons of the governors, which require in the governed docility, obedience, discipline and self-control.

Governmentality

Governmentality represents a shift from forms of rule which focus on the management of boundaries in order to protect the integrity of the state both as territory and as refuge, to forms of rule which focus on the disposition of the state's inhabitants. The shift reflects a change in concern from external threat to internal processes. Under sovereignty where the focus is external the behaviour of the population is a matter for local regulation, rather than a concern of the state. When the focus shifts, and the state does desire to concern itself with internal regulation, for that regulation to function it is necessary to have detailed knowledge of the population in order to label and organize it. In other words, it is not simply a shift of focus, but also involves the development of new – or, at least, different – knowledge which is also able to rationalize and legitimate the processes. Governmentality draws attention to

> 'the techniques and procedures designed to direct the conduct of men'. . . . The government of men demanded of men acts of obedience and submission, but also 'acts of truth'. . . . (Macey, 1993: 416)

All forms of government have a logic of truth which legitimates them. In a feudal or absolutist state, the logic of truth establishes the right of the ruler to own all that is in his/her domain, and so legitimates a locus of power. With the ongoing transition to a mercantilist state, and the significance of international trade and exchange, came the recognition of a 'floating population' operating, in effect, outside the state's 'laws' – not, strictly speaking, outlaws, but those who are somehow deviant in relation to the normal condition. The need to broaden out the law of the state to enable regulation of this floating population produced, Foucault argued (e.g. 1979a), a shift away from the locus of power towards the structure of the state – what might be termed a shift from the ruler to the rules. This could, perhaps, be seen in Weberian language as a move away from traditional authority – authority embodied in hereditament – to rational–legal authority, authority embodied expressly not in a person but in the rules. It is these rules which must be obeyed, and it is discursive formations which both make the rules possible and sustain and legitimate them: produce and represent the logic of truth.

The term 'governmentality' is usually understood by commentators as a Foucauldian neologism deriving from governmental rationality (e.g. Gordon, 1991), to denote what Foucault defines as 'a whole series of specific governmental apparatuses and . . . a whole complex of "savoir"' (1979a: 20). In this, governmentality refers to a way of thinking about, and a set of practices for, governance. It could also be understood as a neologism deriving from government mentality, and this would move the emphasis to what might be called the mind set of governance. This is a less neutral interpretation in that it draws attention to the colonization of the psyche which governmentality entails, where both the 'acts of obedience' and the 'acts of truth' seem normal and beyond contestation. Thus it is that governmentality is prosecuted, not only by the state and its formal structures, but also by other formal and informal structures which represent the internalization of the precepts of governmentality. Some of these other structures might be seen in terms of 'fellow travellers' – those which, while not directly part of government, have a vested interest in the maintenance of the status quo – for example, the Confederation of British Industry, the Institute of Directors, the General Synod of the Church of England; some are vicarious instruments of government, for example, quangos; some are social and/or economic formations, for example, the Church, the Boy Scouts, work organizations. Together such structures represent the imposition of compliance. What is referred to as the balance of compliance is supplied by the individuals who accept, in one way or another, wittingly or unwittingly, the legitimacy of government mentality.

The desired effect of these apparatuses and savoirs which make up governmentality is a population committed to obedience, that people should, voluntarily and willingly, delegate their moral autonomy and moral responsibility to obedience to the rules, to being governed in their conduct by a 'moral' force – the state – which is external to the 'self'. What is desired is a population of docile bodies: '[a] body is docile that may be subjected, used, transformed and improved' (Foucault, 1979b: 136). Nonetheless, failure to obey is not usually an option, and successful governance does not need to concern itself with why obedience is given, as long as it *is* given. Thus, for example, the penalties of non-compliance are made crystal clear by all and any of the structures which require obedience. The requirement for obedience can be based on autocracy – that is, on coercion – but more usually is rationalized and justified in terms of a greater, collective interest. Thus, in a democracy there is, at the level of the state, the notion of government *for* the people, and even at the corporate level there are claims to represent a collective utility through, for example, stakeholder models. But this altruistic framework is not impartial in respect of the values it represents. The general point is made by Foucault (1981: 77):

> . . . reason of state is not an art of government according to divine, natural or human laws. It doesn't have to respect the general order of the world. It's government in accordance with the state's strength. It's government whose aim is to increase this strength within an extensive and competitive framework.

In other words, governance is fundamentally conservative and rests on vested interest, and its object is, minimally, to maintain the status quo and, optimally, to increase the consolidation of these vested interests. Since even the non-state structures of governance represent these vested interests, it is quite normal for the population to be persuaded by their perceived duty to obey, to act on behalf of the vested interests even though it is contrary to their own perceived interests. Thus, for example, a recent study (reported in the *Guardian* (1995)) has demonstrated the extent of the impact of the newspaper media in the UK in influencing voting patterns, and that a press overwhelmingly (70 per cent) sympathetic to the Conservative Party has a significant impact on that party being re-elected. Hutton (1995: 35) provides a comment on Conservative government in the UK which elaborates Foucault's point:

> There is no constitutional protection of a public interest that transcends party concerns, because no conception of the public interest exists independently of what the Government defines it to be.

Control, carceration, checking

Governmentality seeks to control deviance. It enforces obedience to the rules, which are intended to control, in considerable detail, the 'conduct of men', and which are constituted and legitimated by a discursive logic of truth, informed by claims to represent public good. On this basis, behaviour which does not conform to the rules is, *de facto*, deviant. In reference to a French *cause célèbre*, the incarceration of Roger Knobelspiess, Foucault explains how 'deviant' becomes 'dangerous':

> . . . he was found guilty of a crime he strongly denies having committed. How could he accept prison without admitting that he was guilty? But you can see the mechanism: because he resists, he is put in a QHS [high security unit]. The reason why he is in a QHS is that he is dangerous. 'Dangerous' in prison, and therefore even more dangerous if he were at liberty. He is therefore guilty of having

committed the crime of which he was accused. That he denies it is irrelevant: he could have done it. The QHS supplies proof; . . . (cited in Macey, 1993: 421)

To resent the logic of control thereby justifies control, and its resentment justifies repressive enforcement. That Knobelspiess may indeed have been dangerous does not, in any way, legitimate the circularity of the argument for repressive action.

To prevent the deviant being a danger to the compliant they can be constrained within closed institutions, such as the prison and the madhouse. However, within the general logic of constraint the prison and the madhouse are only extreme cases of the more general condition of repression. Most people do not need to be so incarcerated to keep their deviant behaviour within tolerable limits. Institutions such as schools, churches, the family, and so forth, can perform the same sort of control functions without, generally, the need for physical restraint, although they may retain such restraint as a possibility. It is widely recognized that a primary function of such institutions is to train people in what is acceptable behaviour, and a 'reasonable' person is one who accepts this and behaves accordingly, who is self-policing. However, no institution which has responsibility for governance is simply assumed to do this successfully. An inevitable corollary of training in compliance is the process of checking that obedience is indeed the outcome.

The literal control by surveillance of the Panopticon has its principles perpetuated in a more general philosophy and practice of checking compliance, another aspect of governmentality which pervades contemporary life. Most forms of checking, however, are constrained to checking what can be checked, rather than being defined by what needs to be checked. In other words, what is checked is what is observable, and thus the emphasis focuses on visible compliance, rather than on, for example, the spirit of compliance (see, e.g., Power and Laughlin, 1992). Because a normative value is given to the checking of compliance, attempts are made to solve this recognized limitation by ever-increasing the levels and accessibility of detailed information held on individuals' behaviour. Nonetheless, the purpose of such checking is not prosecution of the public interest, or betterment in any context, but to reassure the powerful that order is being maintained. Checking always involves power relations (as implied by the word's etymology, which is, via Old French, from the Persian 'shah'), and it is a typical feature of it, as with the Panopticon, that it is unidirectional, always directed downwards in hierarchical terms (Jackson and Carter, 1995). While it is a current shibboleth that those with power should also be checked – if in terms of performance rather than of process, and so, in the UK, the generation of offices such as Ofwat, Ofgas, Ofsted, of school league tables, of Research Assessment Exercises, and so forth – this conviction does not generally extend to the upper levels of governance, whether in its formal or its informal sense, though lip-service may be paid (witness the brouhaha over acceptance of the principle that Members of Parliament should disclose remunerative affiliations which are a consequence of being an MP, but not part of the normal duties of representation of constituents). It is an oft-remarked irony that the recently created Ministry for Open Government is most noteworthy for its manifest desire to keep things secret 'in the public interest'. The unidirectionality of checking is also a cornerstone of Functionalist theories of management, from Taylorism to appraisal.

Labour and dressage

One arena of control of deviance to which Foucault did not devote much concentrated attention is that of work, but, in some ways, work can be recognized as a persistent sub-text, and he clearly had interests in developing this more directly. Macey (1993: 318) refers to a projected history of working class struggle, and there are many passing references throughout Foucault's work which suggest that he viewed 'factory' work as a form of incarceration, extensible from the more formally carceral institutions he studied. The significance Foucault gave to labour and its organization is manifested by the importance he accorded to it as an element in the change of episteme which he located in the eighteenth century (Foucault, 1970). In *Discipline and Punish* (1979b: 174–5), he comments on the organization of 'a new type of surveillance' associated with 'the great workshops and factories' which 'becomes a decisive economic operator both as an internal part of the production machinery and as a specific mechanism in the disciplinary power'. Later (1979b: 200), he comments on the Panopticon that

> [a]ll that is needed, then, is to place a supervisor in a central tower and to shut up in each cell a madman, a patient, a condemned man, a worker or a schoolboy.

A similar comment is made in Foucault (1977a: 147). In other words, a worker is just another observed subject/object. He further notes (ibid.: 161) that 'techniques of power are invented to meet the demands of production'. More significantly, Foucault follows this comment with the argument that labour has three functions: the productive, the symbolic and dressage. While the vast bulk of management and organization literature deals with the productive function and there has, latterly, been some interest in the symbolic function, there is very little – either in this literature or in Foucault's work – which focuses on the idea of labour as dressage. It is undoubtedly the case that all labour should have a productive function, whether direct or indirect – as, indeed, Foucault signals when, for example, he cites Ricardo's argument that all value is produced by labour (1970: 254). And, in a world construed as symbolic, labour could hardly avoid a symbolic function. But it needs to be asked, what could be the purpose or necessity of labour as dressage? What, indeed, does dressage signify?

Dressage means both discipline and taming. English uses the French word and, in both languages, 'dressage' has complex, and very similar, connotations. In English it is associated with the verb 'to dress' (also from the French), which itself has two closely connected senses: to make straight, bring into proper order, manage and to direct. A common context in the French use of 'dressage', and its most common usage in English, is the equestrian: the training of a horse in deportment and response to controls, its mastering. What this signifies is making horses perform unnatural movements and obey control which is for control's sake, for the gratification of the controller. In other words, equestrian dressage is non-utilitarian behaviour for the benefit of the master and, of course, as a spectator sport. It seems safe to assume that this was the context Foucault had in mind. Elsewhere, talking about prisons, he says of imprisonment:

> The profitability of work done in the prisons has always been negligible – it was work for the sake of work . . . [I]mprisonment . . . was after all a long elaboration of various techniques that made it possible to locate people, to fix them in precise places, to constrict them to a certain number of gestures and habits – in short, it was a form of 'dressage' . . . [I]n the eighteenth century, we see the appearance of the great workshops employing hundreds of workers. *What developed, then, was a whole technique of human dressage by location, confinement, surveillance, the perpetual supervision of behaviour and tasks, in short, a whole technique of 'management' of which the prison was merely one manifestation or its transposition into the penal domain.* (Foucault, 1984: 104–5; emphasis added)

Labour in its dressage sense, then, is non-productive, non-utilitarian and unnatural behaviour for the satisfaction of the controller and as a public display of compliance, obedience to discipline.

The carceration of labour

That organized work has a carceral function is implied on numerous occasions in Foucault's work, particularly in the connections he makes between work organizations and the prison, the madhouse, and so forth. Notwithstanding arguments about, and examples of, so-called new work practices, and unemployment, most workers still attend work organizations – and it is a cliché to point out that those who do not are still subject to, or object of, pervasive surveillance and control of behaviour. There are some obvious isomorphisms between work organizations and the more formally carceral organizations explored by Foucault. Workers are required to attend in a certain place at a certain time, to conform to procedure, to obey the rules. Their discretion is attenuated, they are required to accept control (Jackson and Carter, 1985). Another isomorphism is less frequently noted. At first glance it might be thought a significant difference that prisoners, and the like, are locked up, away from public view. Yet work organizations similarly exclude the public in various ways. For example, generally speaking, the public does not have unfettered access to work organizations and, even in cases where it is necessary to have public access, such as supermarkets, theatres or restaurants, areas available to such access are strictly defined and away from those areas where the work is done, with some 'special' workers having the specific task of policing the interface: for example, check-out operators, ushers, receptionists, waiters. In other cases, such as banks, there is a more precise caging of the workers, sometimes literally 'behind bars'.

This does not mean, however, that there is an absence of public display. Rather than unfettered access, the public is given controlled access. This is, also, exactly the case with formally carceral institutions. Chain gangs were a popular spectacle (and, apparently, are again since their reintroduction in some states of the USA), as were public executions (and may be again if demands in the USA to make executions public are satisfied). Bedlam was a tourist attraction. Even though inmates were/are formally incarcerated, there were/are facilities for structured public access. In analogous ways modern-day workers are put on display in controlled circumstances, ranging from open days, to public scrutiny of performance via the stockmarket, to the formal and informal mechanisms by which performance is spotlighted by, for example, government, such as the pillorying of public sector workers for inefficiency as a justification for privatization of the services they provide, and the publication of league tables for schools, hospitals, and so on.

Foucault notes (1979b: 300) that the carceral system also 'organizes what might be called "disciplinary careers" . . . [D]isciplinary "training" continuous and compelling . . . ha[s] something of the pedagogical curriculum and something of the professional network'. Precisely because the system is carceral, there is a need for people to serve the incarcerated, and people can secure comfortable existence thereby. This is clearly demonstrable in the realm of organization and management. The management function emerged from the preference for large-scale, factory-type production organizations. At first this was fulfilled by supervisors, foremen, charge hands, and so on, whose task was to exercise direct control over workers. But these people were drawn from the workers themselves, and the extent of their identity with owner interests could not be trusted. As owners' involvement became less direct they required agents to protect their interests and exercise control, and so a professional managerial class emerged. By the 1900s this class was, unsurprisingly, complemented by another group who could tell managers how to manage. With the establishment of a knowledge base the management function extended into what has been called the managerial society – but managerialism is less about production than it is about control. Management's successful development of techniques of dressage has all but eclipsed its productive function, so that all organizations are encouraged to accept managerial definition. A vast array of management experts fuels a vast array of techniques for managing. That their task is primarily disciplinary rather than productive is indicated by the general absence of advice and support directed at workers themselves. Thus, for example, there are many techniques for intensifying labour, but none for extensifying it.

These behavioural and procedural isomorphisms between carceral institutions and work organizations underline the significance of discipline in the latter. Foucault argues that all forms of discipline have a common rationality. All forms of carceral institution have ways of organizing and managing which right down to the way of conditioning individuals' behaviour, have a logic, obey a type of rationality, and are all based on one another to form a sort of specific stratum. (Foucault, 1984: 105)

This is part of the essence of government mentality.

Dressage: discipline

That organization requires disciplined behaviour is incontestable, as is precisely the force of such arguments as Freud's Reality Principle. In some organizations discipline is cherished and celebrated in its own right, such as in the military, where automatic obedience to orders is a primary objective of all training and acculturation. Indeed, the parade ground is a supreme locus of dressage in all senses of the word, both in its practice and in its language: for example, the 'dressing' of troops is a manoeuvre to arrange them with strict orderliness and pattern. The performance of those on parade is not just a visible display of functional obedience but also a demonstration of the skill of suppressing all difference for the sake of uniformity and compliance. At a secondary level there are organizations which, consciously or unconsciously, model themselves on a quasi-militaristic standard, such as the police, hospitals and schools. At a tertiary level are organizations such as bureaucracies which also exhibit strong attachment to discipline – and this is not surprising when it is recalled that many early organization theorists were themselves military men, and that much organization theory, past and present, is redolent with military terminology. (Another obvious relationship with military behaviour is to be found in 'parade ground' events, most notably the morning exercises, and the like, encouraged by Japanese managements, and the attempt to transpose these to their various multi-national settings.)

Discipline in such contexts refers to the ideal of order and, as such, is presented as rational, functional and productive. It represents attempts to regulate random or arbitrary aspects of organization by making responses to such aspects predictable. The goal is for everything to be done that should be done, and done at the right time and in the ways prescribed – a place for everything and everything in its place. However, this barely does justice to the significance of such discipline. It is a procedural device which does not, and is not intended to, question what is being done. That organizations require disciplinary procedures implies, minimally, that disorder is a constant, but repressed, presence. The depiction of discipline as functional presents it as benign, utilitarian, consensual, a good. The notion of labour as dressage offers a different view, that work is subject to control, not for functional reasons, but for the sake of control itself.

Dressage: taming

The second denotation of dressage is taming, the equivalent of breaking in a horse, which is 'to tame or habituate to obedience' (*Chambers English Dictionary*). We would suggest that this occurs in work organizations at a number of levels. At a primary level there is the straightforward issue of accepting the requirement of submission to discipline. For example, it is required to attend on certain days at certain times in certain places and to deliver a certain amount of finished work, however measured and in whatever time scale. In the early phases of the Industrial Revolution, when large-scale factories first appeared – which were and are more acceptably characterizable as carceral, reflecting the novelty of the transition to different ways of organizing and managing work – this primary taming was a more difficult achievement (see, e.g., Marglin, 1974). This is less the case now, when such requirements are generally accepted in their functional guise (except where the move to more decentralized work practices, such as home working, is desired).

A secondary process of taming concerns the modification and manipulation of behaviour in ways desired by those in control – a major focus of academic texts, both past and present, which address issues of 'organizational behaviour'. The focus of this process is on the selection and subsequent moulding of employees who fit some more or less explicit model of the ideal worker, who is a worker who is not only obedient but is willing to modify any behaviour which managers might define as deviant, and thereby to symbolize their submission to control. The ideal worker is one who 'doesn't rock the boat' (see Beynon, 1975: 90; in this case by being too intelligent). The modification of behaviour required extends far beyond questions of capacity and suitability to perform the tasks required. This is nicely illustrated by Doray's (1988: 30ff.) extensive lists of proscribed behaviours from the early industrial period, such as leaving the work station, wandering, loitering, acting disrespectfully, spending 'excessive' time in the toilets, whistling, singing, talking, combining – all activities punishable by fine or dismissal, and, in some cases, by being denounced to the courts. There are extant many similar examples of such restrictions on behaviour not obviously related to functional capacity, some much more recent. That such behaviours had to be banned suggests that they must have occurred, and that going to the toilet, talking, whistling, and so on, were natural acts on the part of workers. Doray points out (1988: 25; emphasis added) that most such regulations began 'by stating that the very fact that they have been posted inside the factory gives them the status of an *internal law*'. Although contemporary work organizations may be less obviously repressive, proscriptions of some of the above are still to be found: for example, excessive time spent in toilets (see Beynon, 1975: 135), leaving the work station, talking. Other activities, such as combining, are actively discouraged rather than literally proscribed. Furthermore, other similar controls, less common in the past, are more common today, such as dress codes, restrictions on smoking, and so forth, and some organizations specify in minute detail, including requirements such as eye contact and sincerity, how employees should interact with customers.

A third level of taming can also be identified, though much less clearly visible, which centres on the idea that work has intrinsic value. It is widely acknowledged that the 'governors' see work as a good in itself for the 'governed', who must therefore be encouraged, or if need be compelled, to do lots of it. Various explanations for this perception of value and for the encouragement/compulsion have been offered, ranging from its 'natural-ness', to acculturation, to preservation of the status quo – for example, the need to sustain society, constructive activity, the protestant work ethic, 'the devil finds work for idle hands', class relations, necessary control of the population, 'keeping people off the streets', and so forth. Equally, various mechanisms are used to promote such effort, such as stigmatization of unemployment, low wages, and punitive sanctions. However, more im-portant than what is done, is the faith in the moral injunction that it should be done.

That work is a good thing is such an entrenched conviction that its use as punishment for, and, more importantly, as corrective to, deviance is wide-spread. Prison sentences with hard labour were used to signify the difference between relatively major and relatively minor deviance. In all the more formally carceral institutions – prisons, workhouses, madhouses – and, notably, in the military, the deliberate use of futile work tasks has been a particular feature, classic examples being the crank and the treadmill. Such tasks have no useful purpose other than to impose the burden of labour on the body. More recently, and in the context of more 'ordinary' work organizations, it was a common requirement in an organization well-known to one of us that, should a worker be unable to perform his normal task because the day's work had been completed, he should take a broom and sweep, irrespective of whether there was anything to sweep. Task and finish systems, a rational scientific management incentive much lauded in the 1960s and 1970s, fell into disfavour with managers when they saw workers legitimately going home earlier than the notional finishing time, a 'perk' not available to managers. Work as punishment has also extended beyond such organizations, to be used, for example, as an educational aid: for example, writing lines, for deviant behaviour at school. Such examples of the use of work as discipline are only the most overt cases of the evidence that work does not have only a productive function. Work is not only a means to an end, but also an end in itself.

Dressage: performance

An important aspect of dressage in its equestrian context is that it is a spectator sport. We have already alluded to aspects of controlled display in the context of work organizations, which is part of the pervasive surveillance of work. But labour as dressage also contains significant connotations of performance. Surveillance observes what is done, for corrective purposes, but only requires that the body to be surveyed is visible. Dressage, however, requires the body to perform, requires knowing acts which, implicitly or explicitly, demonstrate compliance to whatever demands the controller seeks to have satisfied. Performance at work is the enactment of routines in specified ways, analogous to performance on stage. The point is that it is not sufficient that something should be done, it must be done in a particular way – and it is from being done in this prescribed way that the act derives its goodness. Thus, for Taylor, it was not enough to load pig iron, it had to be done in the ways he specified; more recently, it has been considered inadequate simply to work but required that when one worked one should self-actualize; even more recently, we are required to be empowered. However, what constitutes self-actualization or empowerment is not a felt condition but specified a priori and demonstrated by pre-defined indicators. Such responses reflect the desires of the governors (management, academics, etc.), rather than emanate from the desires of the skilled subject/object who works. They place an added burden on the worker, who must do and feel these things, and demonstrate that they are done and felt, as well as work. Yet there is no incontrovertible evidence that any such techniques contribute to the productive function of labour.

All performance needs an audience, and labour as dressage in this respect is no different. The audience is perhaps most simply defined in terms of the stakeholder model. For example, owners, managers and academics clearly have an interest in these routines; company practices are examined in academic and popular journals, and in the press; there is also the contemporary fashion of highlighting 'best practice' for bench-marking purposes; and there is the engagement of the wider public, such as in the case of one hotel chain which informs the public via its advertisements that it uses empowerment techniques, thereby enlisting their direct interest in matters of performance.

The issue of the performative character of work is well recognized. It might be suggested, perhaps, that Freud's Reality Principle is analogous to Foucault's productive function of labour, while Marcuse's reworking of this concept into what he calls the Performance Principle (Marcuse, 1987) – whereby we are defined as members of society in terms of our economic utility to it – may be analogous to labour as dressage. Lyotard's (1984) concept of performativity has many similar connotations, and he notes the role of performativity in business as a catechism defining what can be said and how it can be said (1984: 17). Lyotard (1988) also suggests that the performative is profoundly normative, which situates the 'author' in a position of sovereignty.

Dressage, deviance, dispositif

There is work that needs to be done, and work that does not need to be done, in terms of production. We would suggest that anything which falls into the latter category is an obvious form of labour as dressage. Dressage is those aspects of work which escape the imperatives of production. Dressage functions to suppress deviance and, successfully performed, dressage is taken as a visible indicator of the absence of deviance. Deviance may be seen as any act which expresses an identity beyond that of worker, and which therefore may escape the requirement to submit to control. Any resistance to control is itself deviant and, as Foucault argued concerning Knobelspiess, dangerous – deviance and danger are mutually defining. The automatic obedience which dressage requires also provides a powerful antidote to thinking. Dressage serves what Gordon (1980: 255) calls 'the fantasy of a disciplined society populated by docile, obedient, normalised subjects'. It serves the attempt to realize this fantasy in part because its features can be claimed, and indeed have been claimed, to be part of the productive function of labour. It is precisely this possibility of seeing dressage as functional which justifies and legitimates its techniques. This is because labour as dressage, and its potential justification as part of the productive function of labour, are elements of what Foucault calls the dispositif.

The dispositif is the 'apparatus' which, one might say, operationalizes governmentality. It is the apparatus of control which produces submission and compliance to the demands of governance. The dispositif is more than the discourse, more than the knowledge which is an essential prerequisite for the organization and management of populations, because it combines discourse with practices and effects and, most importantly, relates all of these to a strategic function. Examination of the dispositif reveals how these elements intersect and interact to realize governmentality. The force of the term 'dispositif' (apparatus) is the identification of the elements of govern-ance, how they are related to each other and how they function to respond to an 'urgent need' – in other words, 'the apparatus . . . has a dominant strategic function . . . for example, the assimilation of a floating population found to be burdensome for an essentially mercantilist economy' (Foucault, 1977b: 195). Some of the complexity of the operation of the dispositif can be illustrated by the

> definite strategies for fixing the workers in the first heavy industries at their work-place . . . : pressuring people to marry, providing housing, building cités ouvrières, practicing that sly system of credit-slavery . . . savings-bank systems, the truck system . . . the discourse of philanthropy and the moralisation of the working class . . . the problem of women's work, the schooling of children and the relations between the two issues . . . support mechanisms (unions of employers, chambers of commerce, etc.) which invent, modify and re-adjust . . . so that you get a coherent, rational strategy. . . . (Foucault, 1977b: 202–3)

These are all part of the processes which create the identity of worker as worker, rather than as person. Once this identity has been imposed, it itself justifies the formulation of particular modes of dealing with workers. The constitution of workers as workers is what makes the operation of the dispositif in the organization of work possible. The dissolution of such identity becomes a pre-requisite for dissolution of labour as dressage.

The condition of government in the contemporary world is that which concerns itself with the disposition of its internal population and, Foucault points out (1979a: 21), 'both refers itself to and makes use of the in-strumentation of the economic "savoir"'. Governmentality requires more than the management of a population at the level of 'the collective mass of phenomena . . . it also implies the management of the population *in its depths and its details*' (ibid.: 19; emphasis added). An apologist for what is characterizable as labour as dressage would argue that such aspects of labour are economically functional and, as such, should be seen as part of the economic savoir. The desirability of workers performing particular routines can only be legitimated by this economic reference. Within the concept of rational organization there can be no other justification for any form of working practice. We would argue, however, that they do not constitute part of the economic savoir, but are part of *the savoir of discipline*. In other words, labour as dressage does not form part of the economic imperatives of governance but is part of its need to control the population, to discourage deviance and to encourage obedience. Thus, both management knowledge and management practice can be seen as part of the dispositif of govern-mentality. The dispositif makes use of the economic savoir as part of its manifestation of truth, to legitimate its strategies, techniques and pro-grammes. But that the economic is their justification does not mean that it is, thereby, their function. This function is, rather, to produce obedience.

In the early days of industrialization the imposition of discipline may well have been necessary to break workers in for the unnatural ways of organizing work – necessary, that is, to the purposes of the governors. Part of this process was to divest the worker of the power to organize work, to establish submission to the organizational and managerial demands of those who owned the means of production (see, e.g., Marglin, 1974; Doray, 1988). This created the space in which the dressage function of labour was articulated. In contemporary organizations it is arguable that the 'factory mentality' is well internalized in the working population, and in the prospective working population, through the re-casting of education as preparation for work rather than, for example, for its own sake. Para-doxically, as the absolute demand for labour decreases, we are becoming increasingly defined in terms of work culture. Our capacity for work exceeds demand and at least 10 per cent of the UK workforce is permanently unemployed, yet this is seen as an aberration rather than as a new 'reality' (notwithstanding the use of 'structural unemployment' as a disciplinary technique). Evidence that those in employment work increasingly long hours is rife, yet the reduction of the working week, even as a means to decrease unemployment, is treated as anathema. Such contradictions cannot be explained within the context of a productive rationale but, on the other hand, dissolve when seen in terms of a disciplinary rationale: maintenance of the dressage function is more important than the resolution of its inconsistencies with the productive function. As Russell noted 60 years ago, it is seen as better to use unemployment as a punishment than as a potential for increased leisure and happiness (Russell, 1976).

The apparent reduction in demand for labour, and the creation of a sector of the population who desire employment but are, in effect, surplus to requirements, has increased demands on those in work to be obedient, to the extent that remaining in employed work becomes, itself, a reward for compliance and submission to control. This is manifested both in increasing interrogation of process (making it increasingly visible) and in increasing requirements for conformity to prescribed routines. Following Foucault's injunction that we should not speak for others (e.g. Macey, 1993: 269), universities can provide an example. These organizations might be thought somewhat less carceral than most, but are increasingly characterized by the institution of work measurements, such as Research Assessment Exercises (RAE) and Teaching Quality Assessments (TQA), practices instantly recognizable to any practitioner of Scientific Management.

'Dressaging the dons'

The government, through the dispositif, desires to exercise greater control over research, for example. Prima facie, there seem to be two possible objectives, the classification of departments as research or non-research, allowing the concentration of available research funds in the former, and/or to encourage more research by linking funds to the production of research. The chosen method is to measure research output and to rank departments accordingly. The RAE evaluates (valorizes) research in terms of a given output within a given time period. Thus the measure of research is not its contribution to knowledge, or to human happiness, but is simply quantitative. Articles are counted, rather than read. Sub-standard work – in the wrong journals or the wrong format – is dis-counted. But, since no university wishes to be seen as non-research oriented, pressure is applied to increase research output. As is well known in incentive theory, however, the incentive is to get the money, not to do the work, and this is widely recognized as increasing the volume of publications rather than the contributions to knowledge. This quantity is stimulated solely to satisfy the requirements of the RAE. The attempt to monitor quality as well as quantity amounts to a nominal, if not an ordinal, ranking of publications according to what are, in effect, arbitrarily imposed criteria, which do not, and cannot, reflect the effort involved in any particular piece of research. Neither the intention nor the effect of this technique can be rationalized in terms of the productive function of the labour of research. However laudable the principle of encouraging research, its operationalization has been to intensify the dressage function. TQAs, similarly, are redolent with the principles and practices of labour as dressage, including the obligation/duty to respond with remedy for deviation from the criteria prescribed, irrespective of any possible educational justification for such deviation. Both processes are methodologically flawed, to the extent that they claim to represent and produce knowledge on grounds that would not be acceptable within the rules of any discourse except the discourse of control. Yet, such is the success of the techniques of dressage which encourage self-policing, interrogation of these techniques is spasmodic, weak and fragmented – emphasizing its deviance – and the subjects/objects feel generally powerless to resist their rationale.

The RAE represents the importation of a managerialist function into a domain of activity which is, above all, celebrated for its embodiment of the principles of peer review – that is, the judgement of (anonymous) equals – and a system devised specifically to minimize the distortions on knowledge production of power relations. The RAE is, indeed, legitimated as an extension of this process. Nonetheless, the design and operationalization of the RAE clearly offends against the very principles of peer review. Those who act as judges are not selected by their peers but occupy a role which is the gift of the governors; they are not required to explain to their so-called peers how they reach their conclusions, or even to demonstrate how the criteria have been derived and operationalized; such criteria are not agreed by the population to be judged. Thus a small unrepresentative group with allegiance to those who appoint them are given extraordinary power to discipline and tame the production of knowledge through research, on the basis of pre-defined but arbitrary (and based on possible rather than relevant) criteria of performance.

None of this should be surprising. Derrida has recently commented that universities are part of the forces of 'techno-mediatic power' which 'communicate and cooperate at every moment toward producing the greatest force with which to assure the hegemony or the imperialism in question' (1994: 53). Universities are part of the discourse which produces knowledge for the dispositif, and they are work organizations which exercise the apparatus of control on their workers.

Conclusion

The concept of labour as dressage offers a fundamentally different perspective on the role of management and suggests a different perspective for its study. The continuing predominance of perspectives which view management primarily as a functional agency of production is unlikely to lead to an adequate understanding of the management process or to solutions to social problems that are identified with it – problems which might, indeed, be seen as emanating precisely from this misconception. Similarly, this blinkered approach avoids the possibilities for betterment of the human condition which might proceed from the organization of labour. But the dressage function of labour has, so far, received little direct attention.

Foucault has commented that what he calls 'local criticism', criticism which does not seek to present a global unity, stands against 'an entire thematic to the effect that it is not theory but life that matters, not knowledge but reality, not books but money, etc.' through 'an insurrection of subjugated knowledges' (1977c: 81). One characteristic of such knowledges is 'the historical contents that have been buried and disguised in a functionalist coherence or formal systematisation' (ibid.). Elsewhere he says that '[t]he role for theory today seems to me to be just this: not to formulate the global systematic theory which holds everything in place, but to analyse the specificity of mechanisms of power, to locate the connections and extensions, to build little by little a strategic knowledge' (1977d: 145). As Gordon notes (1980: 258), what Foucault offers is 'a set of possible tools, tools for the identification of conditions of possibility which operate through the obviousnesses and enigmas of our present, tools perhaps also for the eventual modification of those conditions'. We suggest, in this spirit, that labour as dressage and its location in the dispositif must be examined in terms of its consequences and its progeniture in order to understand how it arises, how it functions and whether it needs to be resisted.

References

Beynon, H. (1975) *Working for Ford*. Wakefield: EP Publishing.

Derrida, J. (1994) *Specters of Marx* (trans. P. Kamuf). London: Routledge.

Doray, B. (1988) *From Taylorism to Fordism: A Rational Madness* (trans. D. Macey). London: Free Association Books.

Foucault, M. (1970) *The Order of Things*. London: Tavistock.

Foucault, M. (1977a) 'The eye of power', in C. Gordon (ed.) (1980), *Michel Foucault: Power/ Knowledge*. London: Harvester. pp. 146–65.

Foucault, M. (1977b) 'The confession of the flesh', in Gordon, *Michel Foucault*. pp. 194–228.

Foucault, M. (1977c) 'Two lectures', in Gordon, *Michel Foucault*. pp. 78–108.

Foucault, M. (1977d) 'Power and strategies', in Gordon, *Michel Foucault*. pp. 134–45.

Foucault, M. (1979a) 'Governmentality' (trans. R. Braidoth), *Ideology and Consciousness*, 6: 5–21.

Foucault, M. (1979b) *Discipline and Punish* (trans. A. Sheridan). Harmondsworth: Penguin.

Foucault, M. (1981) 'Politics and reason', in L.D. Kritzman (ed.) (1990) *Michel Foucault: Politics, Philosophy, Culture*. London: Routledge. pp. 57–85.

Foucault, M. (1984) 'On power', in Kritzman, *Michel Foucault*. pp. 96–109.

Gordon, C. (1980) 'Afterword', in Gordon, *Michel Foucault*. pp. 229–59.

Gordon, C. (1991) 'Governmental rationality: an introduction', in G. Burchell, C. Gordon and P. Miller (eds), *The Foucault Effect*. London: Harvester Wheatsheaf. pp. 1–51.

Guardian (1995) 'Sun-powered politics', 30 October.

Hutton, W. (1995) *The State We're In*. London: Jonathan Cape.

Jackson, N. and Carter, P. (1985) 'The ergonomics of desire', *Personnel Review*, 14(3): 20–8.

Jackson, N. and Carter, P. (1995) 'Organisational chiaroscuro: throwing light on the concept of corporate governance', *Human Relations*, 48(8): 875–89.

Lyotard, J.-F. (1984) *The Postmodern Condition: A Report on Knowledge* (trans. G. Bennington and B. Massumi). Manchester: Manchester University Press.

Lyotard, J.-F. (1988) *The Differend: Phrases in Dispute* (trans. G. Van Den Abbeele). Manchester: Manchester University Press.

Macey, D. (1993) *The Lives of Michel Foucault*. London: Random House.

Marcuse, H. (1987) *Eros and Civilisation*. London: Ark.

Marglin, S. (1974) 'What do bosses do? The origins and functions of hierarchy in capitalist production', *Review of Radical Political Economics*, 6: 60–112.

Power, M. and Laughlin, R. (1992) 'Critical theory and accounting', in M. Alvesson and H. Willmott (eds), *Critical Management Studies*. London: Sage. pp. 113–35.

Russell, B. (1976) *In Praise of Idleness*. London: George Allen and Unwin.

II
CONSTRUCTING THE MODERN ORGANIZATION

5

Discipline, Surveillance and the 'Career': Employment on the Great Western Railway 1833–1914

Mike Savage

In 1908 a Director and future Chairman of the Great Western Railway Company (GWR), Viscount Churchill, informed his staff that:

> however subordinate your present position may be, if you will only take the trouble to make yourselves efficient you will, I am sure, rise to positions of trust in this great company. (GWRM, January 1908)

The same year his words were echoed by the staff journal of the GWR, which informed its readers that

> railway employees have never had such splendid opportunities to improve their position as they have at the present time, and if a man does not attain a reasonable measure of success he can only blame himself. (GWRM, August 1908)

This promise of career progress as a reward for merit, diligence and hard work has come to be regarded as – at least in principle – one of the most characteristic features of modern bureaucracies (see, most notably, Weber, 1978, and, more generally, Halford and Savage, 1995). Certainly, during the course of the twentieth century, increasing numbers of individuals have had the promise (if not the reality) of 'career' advancement held up to them. One survey indicates that in Britain during the later 1980s, nearly 80 per cent of those in professional, managerial or administrative jobs felt they were on a 'career ladder'. Over half of routine non-manual workers, foremen and technicians, and agricultural labourers defined themselves in these career terms, and even amongst other manual workers a substantial minority of between 22 per cent and 36 per cent concurred (Evans, 1992). Recent work has also begun to hint at the way that the career impinges on people's self-awareness. Grey (1994) draws attention to the way that young recruits in accountancy are encouraged to 'play the game', develop networks and so forth as a means of advancing their 'careers' and hence how young professionals come to internalize a distinct 'career ethos'. Yet despite the contemporary salience of the 'career' ethos, its historical construction is rarely examined.

This paper considers how Foucault's 'genealogical' approach might shed light on the career as a device tied up with the dynamics of modern disciplinary power. For, it is striking that although Foucault considers a remarkably wide array of disparate phenomena – from school examinations, military drills, medical quarantining, and punishment through imprisonment – as testimony to the development of modern forms of power relationships in the eighteenth and nineteenth centuries, he never so much as mentions how the varied practices associated with the development of the 'career' might be seen in these terms. This is despite the fact that the idea of the 'career' appears to be quintessentially 'modern' and closely associated with the emergence of large bureaucratic units. Thus Raymond Williams (1970) mentions that until the 1850s the term 'career' was used to mean unstable movement (as in the expression 'horses careering out of control'), and only took on its meaning as regularized and steady movement through a series of occupational stages in the second half of the nineteenth century.

But this is jumping ahead. This paper begins by considering what light a Foucauldian perspective might shed on the genesis of the 'career'. The body of the paper uses a case study of the construction of career ladders on the Great Western Railway in order to consider how the crystallization of the career was associated with new techniques of disciplinary power and surveillance. The second section provides an introduction to the GWR whilst the third points to the ramshackle, disorganized career ladders which existed in its early years. The fourth section examines the early use of discipline on the GWR, pointing to some problems with the military model. The fifth section then shows how the elaboration of more systematic career ladders between the 1860s and 1890s was dependent upon a reconsideration of management and discipline, and explores how this period saw serious attempts to use career progress as a device to secure consent from the workforce and to encourage the 'right' sort of employee. The sixth concludes by exploring some of the contradictions which this career culture then exposed. The conclusion elaborates on some of the general lessons to be drawn from the case study.

Weber, Foucault and the modern bureaucratic career

For Weber (1978), the career was a generic feature of a modern, rational society. For, in modern societies based on rational authority, it was essential to ensure that those individuals in positions of power would not be inclined to use such positions for self-aggrandizement. The 'career' was the rational solution to this problem. By emphasizing to individual employees that they could expect to be moved between jobs they would come not to treat any one job as a sinecure but would be more likely to develop a 'vocational' orientation to their work. The 'career' facilitated an impersonal, rationalized mode of administration by new legions of bureaucratic employees.

The implications of Weber's arguments are that the 'career' is essentially a by-product of a modern bureaucracy, and has therefore emerged in tandem with modernity itself. Thus, for writers such as Alfred Chandler (e.g. 1977), the career manager developed alongside the large business enterprise, so that the history of one can only be written with the history of the other. The career is fundamentally a device to secure efficiency and organizational cohesion, a way of knitting together large, complex organizations. It is therefore not primarily a means of exercising power over a workforce. Economists have explored the creation of career ladders (or internal labour markets) in similar sorts of ways, as rational economic methods of matching workers to jobs. For instance, human capital theory has explored how career ladders might be seen as ways of retaining skilled employees by securing their loyalty to specific firms.

It is these sorts of rather benign views of the 'career' which are problematized by Foucault's analysis of surveillance and his insistence on the power-laden character of bureaucratic development.[1] Foucault's emphasis is on the rise of 'governmentality' (see Miller and Rose, 1993), whereby authorities become concerned to supervise, administrate and organize various populations. This notion has some parallels with Weber's emphasis upon the rationality inherent in modern forms of power, but Foucault provides some distinct emphases. The originality of Foucault's analysis lies in his concentration on two rather different techniques by which modern 'capillary' power operates, firstly, through the elaboration of techniques of bodily control, and secondly, through the construction of new forms of 'self-monitoring' subjectivity. Surveillance operates on the 'body' and on the 'soul'. Admittedly, whilst Foucault does run these two themes together, notably in his celebrated analysis of Bentham's Panopticon as the crucible of modern power, he tends to hold these two issues apart in most of his work. In *Discipline and Punish* (1977) Foucault's emphasis is upon the construction of new disciplinary techniques designed to regiment and control bodies, focusing particularly on new forms of punishment. By the time Foucault came to write *A History of Sexuality* (1979), his emphasis had shifted more to the construction of subjectivities and in particular how modern power relationships depended on the need to construct one's self through processes of confession, and of ethics, defined as the study of the self's relationship to the self (see Davidson, 1986; Hacking, 1986).

Both books emphasize the distinctiveness of modern forms of power, but in rather different ways. *Discipline and Punish* focuses upon the emergence of new techniques of direct surveillance over bodily comportment and behaviour from the eighteenth century. Here, Foucault stressed how attention was directed to the precise coordination of bodily movements and the need for each individual to regulate their bodily actions. As a result, new disciplines 'made possible the meticulous control of the operations of the body, which assured the constant subjection of its forces and imposed on them a relation of docility–utility . . . the human body was entering a machinery of power that explores it, breaks it down and rearranges it' (Foucault, 1977: 137, 138). Crucial to all these techniques are various forms of inspection, as developed especially in the military (see also Dandeker, 1990).

But Foucault's most arresting point is his isolation of Jeremy Bentham's model prison, the Panopticon, as the culmination of this process. In many respects the Panopticon was simply another example of the new type of regulatory institution which allowed the detailed inspection and monitoring of individual bodily behaviour. But it differed in one vital respect. Because it allowed individuals to be inspected without their knowing whether they were in fact being observed, it marked a new stage in the elaboration of disciplinary power in which surveillance no longer depended on direct visual observation between people. This allowed surveillance to be extended much more deeply into social relationships. Power rested less on direct control of the body and more on techniques designed to elicit 'self-regulation' as people began to act as if they were being observed.

And yet it is important to recognize that this theme remains very underdeveloped in *Discipline and Punish*.[2] Foucault's main claim for the Panopticon, and for other forms of surveillance, concerns the emergence of new techniques of bodily inspection, and he plays relatively little attention to the subjective aspects of these new techniques. Thus he concludes his examination of the Panopticon by noting that 'the practice of placing people under observation is a natural extension of a justice imbued with disciplinary methods and examination procedures. Is it surprising that the cellular prison, with its regular chronologies, forced labour, its authorities of surveillance and regulations, its experts in normality . . . should have become the modern instrument of penality?' (Foucault, 1977: 227–8). There is little here about subjectivity or identity.

It is Foucault's later work which sees him play greater attention to the way that new forms of power call forth new types of subjectivity and permit the elaboration of a sense of 'self' as individuals 'confess'. Foucault's main interest here is how sexuality came to be defined as the key node for the construction of identity and subjectivity (see also Weeks, 1990). This emphasis marks a significant departure from his earlier work, since it places less recognition on inspection and direct surveillance, and more on how the crucial arena for modern surveillance takes place by individuals' disclosing themselves in confessional situations (an issue which was not discussed in *Discipline and Punish*). It is this which constitutes modern identity, which 'does not liberate man in his own being; it compels him to face the task of producing himself' (Foucault, 1986: 42).

It is striking that Foucault himself nowhere attempts to consider how the 'career' can be examined 'genealogically'. Yet there are a number of prima facie reasons for considering that it might be a highly pertinent case, particularly as a means of thinking about the interrelationship between new forms of bodily discipline and new subjectivities, and therefore as providing a bridge between the two aspects of modern power relationships elaborated by Foucault. The elaboration of the 'career' can be seen as depending both on the construction of forms of inspection, examination and control to regulate job movements and to decide who should be promoted, but also the construction of particular forms of 'selfhood', as individual employees themselves come to recognize the 'career' as something which they should pursue.

Subsequent work has begun to hint at the possible relevance of the 'career' to analyses of surveillance but only by undermining some of the central features of Foucault's account by appropriating them to more orthodox Weberian themes. Dandeker's (1990) generally insightful account of the development of modern forms of surveillance and bureaucracy is a good example. Dandeker does note that surveillance involved the elaboration of career ladders, initially in the military, and later in other spheres of employment. Dandeker's emphasis, however, is very much on the way that career structures were tied in to new forms of bodily control, rather than new subjectivities. Dandeker points to four main developments in the later eighteenth- and nineteenth-century military: central authorities controlled recruitment (rather than existing officers' nominating their favourites); training was formalized; promotion became based on formalized criteria; and compulsory retirement was introduced. The sum impact of these developments was to reduce the potential of military officers to 'buck the system'.

> [t]he creation of a modern war machine involved the crystallization of a career structure for the men. . . . Under traditional arrangements . . . [m]any of the men looked to their personal relationships with their superior officers rather than to the 'service' for career advancement or employment. (Dandeker, 1990: 96)

Dandeker clearly perceives the significance of the 'career'. However, he does so at some cost. For Dandeker dilutes the originality of Foucault's conception of surveillance and recasts it within an orthodox Weberian problematic. In fact, Dandeker's account of the military career is largely a restatement of Weber's own argument that the modern bureaucracy depends upon distinguishing individual members of staff from their specific jobs so that they do not use such jobs as devices for self-promotion. Furthermore, whereas Foucault sees surveillance as largely tied up with the regulation of 'populations', and places the control of individual bodies at its heart, Dandeker adopts a more technocratic line by arguing that many aspects of surveillance can be attributed to the need to coordinate large bureaucratic units. In this he adopts Giddens's (1985) distinction between 'authoritative' and 'allocative' aspects of control, which permits him to note that many aspects of surveillance are related to issues of allocation, and this also allows him to play down the role of social conflict in the development of the large business corporation (see, e.g., Dandeker, 1990: 190).

Dandeker's Weberian recasting of the concept of surveillance is made possible by his lack of interest in the link Foucault draws between new techniques of surveillance and the emergence of new forms of subjectivity and identity (or 'knowledge, power and self', as rehearsed by Kelley, 1994). This latter question is an area to which more thoroughbred Foucauldians such as Nikolas Rose (1985, 1990) have paid particular attention. Nonetheless, it is interesting that Rose's account of how technologies of the 'self' have been deployed in the modern workplace focuses on issues such as welfare provision, industrial psychology and training and is concentrated on twentieth-century developments. It will be one of the arguments of this chapter that we need to look further back, to the nineteenth century, and to focus on the development of career ladders as a crucible for new forms of surveillance.

This chapter therefore proposes to examine the murky origins of the 'career' by examining the changing nature of employment on the Great Western Railway. My aim is to argue against Weberian claims that the growth of the career was simply a by-product of bureaucratic expansion, and to show how the elaboration of notions of the career was critically tied up with issues of discipline and control. However, I also suggest that Foucault's own arguments about surveillance fail to register the degree to which the types of punitive discipline he discusses in *Discipline and Punish* were actually a failure. Before developing my argument, I briefly provide some background to my case study.

The Great Western Railway

The railways are a particularly interesting case to study the emergence of modern bureaucratic careers, since they are recognized as the pioneers both of the modern business corporation itself (Chandler, 1977; Dandeker, 1990) and of the development of internal labour markets and career ladders. Certainly, compared with the small-scale, fragmented units found in many parts of the British economy, railway companies were unusual in being centralized bureaucratic structures with a high degree of managerial control from a relatively early date. Railways were highly centralized, with the big four railway companies taking over 40 per cent of receipts from the mid-nineteenth century. They saw the early development of a sophisticated managerial hierarchy, based on the 'departmental system' in which officers in a number of discrete departments were allowed considerable autonomy in planning their activities. Such was the sophistication of the administrative apparatus that in 1919 the GWR had nearly 10,000, or 13 per cent, of its 75,344 staff working in supervisory or salaried grades – a proportion unimaginable in most sectors of the British economy (PRO Rail 786/2. Strike Book, 27 September 1919).[3]

The GWR was one of the 'big four' British railway companies, employing 40,000 by the 1880s and over 100,000 after the forced mergers of 1923. It was also the most glamorous of the railway companies. Founded in 1833 by a group of Bristol financiers intent on ensuring the prosperity of Bristol by creating good rail links with London and the new industrial areas, it soon came to monopolize railway transport in the West Country and developed links to the Midlands, south and mid-Wales, spreading its lines as far north as the Mersey. Its reputation owed something to its association with Isambard Kingdom Brunel, the best known of the Victorian engineers. It also rested on the fact that the GWR pioneered express travel, its early services being the fastest in the world, with its 'Flying Dutchman' being especially renowned. It also created a distinct livery and design, the browns and yellows, which marked out its carriage design. Perhaps above all, however, it owed its reputation to its championing of broad gauge, which it developed before 1850. It was generally reckoned that this was indeed technically superior to the narrow gauge, and its defeat, and ultimate removal by 1892, was due to the political strength of the other companies (Sekon, 1895; McDermott, 1927, 1929; Booker, 1977).

For the purposes of this paper it is also worth pointing out that the GWR was one of the first railway companies to repudiate traditional systems of recruitment and promotion based on patronage. As early as 1856 its Secretary and General Superintendent, C.A. Saunders, responded to a presentation by staff by stating that he had never employed friends or relatives, and that 'I have an earnest desire to see those rise who by their qualifications, their talent, their industry, and integrity are entitled to occupy better positions' (PRO Zlib 27/1).[4] This endorsement of the 'meritocratic' ideal, at a time when patronage remained common in public employment, the professions and on other railway companies, indicates the pioneering role played by the GWR in constructing notions of the modern career.

Although there are many books on the GWR (e.g. Sekon, 1895; McDermott, 1927, 1929; Nock, 1962; Booker, 1977), most of these concentrate on the promotion of lines and technical matters, though Russell (1983) describes the organizational structure of the GWR, and McDermott's history has some relevant material, though only for the period before 1863. Its policies on labour issues, and its industrial relations have never been studied. Indeed, research on railway employees at a more general level remains scanty. Kingsford's (1970) detailed and comprehensive account only covers the years between 1830 and 1870. McKenna's (1980) evocative study gives a superb general view of life on the railway but is not attentive to specific historical shifts in the nature of railway employment. Neither deals with the GWR in particular detail. Other studies, such as those by Hudson (1970), and Cohn (1985) examine particular aspects of labour relations on the GWR without systematically examining wider issues. The trade union histories of Raynes (1921), Allcock (1922) and Bagwell (1961) were concerned with national developments, and drew material indiscriminately from different railway companies to fit these purposes. It is indeed remarkable that despite major differences in the industrial relations of different companies, especially in the years before 1907 when each company was forced to introduce identical forms of collective bargaining with their employees, no serious explanations of such differences have ever been attempted.

The research reported in this chapter is a first step to rectify this. It is based on detailed examination of relevant parts of the GWR archives in the Public Record Office, together with a reading of the trade union journals, especially the *Railway Review*, and the considerable amount of published material written by contemporaries on the railways in the form of autobiographies, treatises and so forth. One of the most important elements of the archival research has been the construction of a data base of career records of different grades of workers employed by the GWR between 1840 and 1940.[5] These records vary in quality, but are extremely detailed for footplate workers, and for uniformed workers, where they include every job which an individual had, the stations at which they were based, as well as a full record of any offences committed or commendations they received.

Railway careers before 1860

It is well known that workers on the railways typically moved between jobs, and could expect to earn promotion to better-paying jobs, even from the earliest days. Existing accounts are not sensitive, however, to the important changes in the nature of career patterns and career ladders over time. McKenna (1980: 109), for instance, recites seven stages of career progress found on the footplate, where workers would begin as cleaners, become firemen, and finally engine drivers, through various intermediate stages. He does not point out, however, that these seven steps did not apply in all companies, or in the entire period covered in his book.

In fact, the types of career routes which workers had open to them, and the 'hoops' through which they had to pass to move into better-paid employment were subject to major change, especially in the period between 1860 and 1900. In the period before 1860 job mobility was not integrated into a disciplinary system. Career routes were not systematized, and a range of job movements was possible, there often being no clear ladders connecting jobs together.

This argument may appear to fly in the face of Kingsford's (1970) claim that there were 'well defined if limited channels of advancement' on the railways before 1870. Even Kingsford's own research indicates, however, that there was considerable variation in the nature of job mobility. Porters, for instance, could be promoted to up to 15 other jobs, including guard and clerk (Kingsford, 1970: 138, 135). He shows that there was considerable mobility between manual and clerical occupations. The railway police, porters, switchmen, signalmen, pointsmen, ticket collectors and guards could all become clerks. Porters had a particularly wide range of jobs open to them, ranging from signalmen to guards, and the police. Footplate workers were from the earliest days entirely separate from the other grades,[6] but within these grades the range of job mobility on the Great Western was chaotic. It was claimed that the first engine drivers were not recruited from within the industry, but from the ranks of the skilled fitters who had built the engines and who were lured into staying to work the engine by the offer of high wages. Only at a later date did firemen have the opportunity of earning promotion to become engine drivers (Vincit, 1847: 22). It also remained common for railway companies to poach drivers from other companies, so that many drivers continued to be recruited specifically as drivers. This was because the demand for skilled drivers was exceptionally high: as one contemporary put it, 'at first the demand so far exceeded supply that companies were glad to secure (drivers) on any terms, and a driver was no sooner dismissed from one line of employment than he found ready employment on another' (quoted in Bagwell, 1961: 19). It was only by the 1870s that the typical career route whereby boys were recruited as engine cleaners, who then became firemen and finally drivers was established (see Table 5.3).

In these early days many forms of job mobility and the development of particular wage systems reflected the fact that skilled workers, especially the engine drivers, held the whip hand in the labour market.[7] The GWR, like many other companies, responded by constructing an incremental wage system, which rewarded long-serving workers, so encouraging them to stay with the company. The GWR paid incremental wages to engine drivers, to guards and porters, paying staff extra for seven or eight years' experience (PRO Rail 267/51; PRO Rail 253/483). Premiums and gratuities were also used to induce loyalty, with up to £10 (with £5 being usual) being paid once a year for a good conduct – a sum which added up to 10 per cent to annual income (Kingsford, 1970: 104ff.). They also attempted to force loyalty by their insistence, from 1848, that workers had to join company-specific benefit societies. If workers left the company they lost their eligibility to get sickness pay, with the result that their contributions were effectively wasted (Bagwell, 1961: 22; Kingsford, 1970).

One of the most striking things about the early construction of career paths for engine drivers and incremental wages was the fact that it seems to have been divorced from the disciplinary regulations of the company. Increments were automatically paid and progress to higher-paying jobs did not seem dependent upon good behaviour or performance.[8] Table 5.1 examines whether those footplate workers who committed an offence early in their work life took longer to earn promotion than those who did not. The figures in Table 5.1 are striking. In the earliest cohort, those who entered before 1870, those who had committed an offence within the shortest time period – seven years – were also those who were promoted most rapidly, whilst those who took over 13 years to commit an offence were promoted considerably more slowly! For the middle cohort the same association can be found, but is less striking, whilst for those who entered after 1900 the association disappears altogether.

It is, however, necessary to point out that this association might be artefactual. It may be that many offences are only 'committable' once the worker is promoted to be an engine driver, so that workers are only in a position to be able to commit an offence once promoted. There may be some truth in this, but it is not enough to explain the entire picture revealed by

Table 5.1   *Speed of promotion to engine driver according to date of first offence (number of years)*

	Before 1871			1871–1900			1900 +		
	Mean	Median	N	Mean	Median	N	Mean	Median	N
Offended within 6 years	6.3	7	15	12.9	16	10	19.8	20.5	3
Offended 7–12 years	9.8	9	23	14.9	16	11	17.5	17.5	4
Offended 13–18 years	11.8	9.5	10	16.1	17.5	10	16	16	1
Offended after 18 years or never	10.5	10	8	14.7	16	21	18.2	18	124

Table only indicates the number of years it took workers to commit their first offence. Subsequent offences are not taken into account.

Source: Pathways and Prospects Database: footplate workers.

Table 5.1. Further analyses have examined the fortunes of those workers who committed offences *before* being promoted. Nearly half of those who were promoted quickly had committed offences before their promotion. Scrutiny of individual records of the earliest cohort of entrants suggests that the general impression given by Table 5.1 is correct. One man recruited as a fireman in 1845 became an engine turner in 1847. In this job he committed two major blunders (once letting the locomotive move off with no-one on board!) but was nonetheless promoted to be a full engine driver after only 11 months (PRO Rail 264/18: 4).

In general the idea of the career as a kind of disciplinary system in which the meritorious were rewarded by promotion did not appear to exist in the early GWR. Although there was a high rate of job mobility on the railways, it was not of a type which suggests fixed career ladders or which appeared to define job movement as a 'moral' project which workers should pursue. Job movement did not take place solely on fixed, established career routes, nor did it appear to be related to issues of discipline and authority. Rather than offences being seen as a factor which might affect a man's career progress, it may have been that fines effectively seemed to wipe the slate clean, so to speak. Punishment was geared to specific offences and not to long-term careers. I now turn to develop this point by considering the general issue of discipline on the railways.

Railways and labour discipline

The GWR, in common with all early railway companies, was faced with enormous problems in securing the legitimacy of rail transport. In part this was a matter of actually getting trains to run between stations roughly to time. This was no easy matter in a period when many of the technologies which made railways safe and reliable had not yet been invented. As G.P. Neele, one of the leading Victorian railway superintendents, looking back to the 1850s, put it:

> it is difficult for those, who in later years, have had the duty of conducting the outdoor working of railways with the modern equipment of telegraph and telephone, to place themselves in imagination in the position of those who struggled early in railway history with the task unaided by these appliances. (Neele, 1974: 31)

Neele conjured up a world in which if a train did not arrive at a station no one had the means to know why not, and if it was 20 minutes late another train had to be sent down the line to search for it.[9]

The railways also had to reassure the travelling public as to the safety of rail travel. This safety was partly physical – the poor safety record of Victorian trains being well known – but also social. The public needed to be made to trust the new type of proletarian railway worker who found employment on the railways. One station master summed up popular fears:

> In the coaching days the driver was the man whose society was most sought. Is it not again astonishing, that whereas the driver of a coach and four horses, value a few hundreds, and say twenty passengers, should have been a man, for the most part, from the middle classes, the driver of a railway engine and train with say one hundred passengers and so many thousands worth of property, should be from the lower orders? (Simmons, 1974: 61)

Using the railways was not simply a matter of travelling from one destination to another. Rather, it was one of the most visible arenas where many of the middle and upper classes came into personal contact with labourers, and hence where class relations had to be personally negotiated.[10] The early railway companies had not only to convince the – generally middle class – travelling public of the safety and reliability of rail travel but also to persuade them that the new class of railway workers could be trusted.

Yet at the same time that the railway companies faced these problems of ensuring the legitimacy of railway transport they also faced huge problems in securing it due to the spatial dispersal of their employees to a vast network of stations, signal boxes, yards and trains, with the result that direct supervision of all staff was never a feasible option. The sorts of 'paternalist' response possible in factory communities, such as Saltaire in Bradford, or New Lanark in Scotland, where employers could stamp their authority on an entire community were of little value in much railway work, given its spatial dispersal, though of course these strategies were drawn upon extensively in the railway workshop towns of Crewe, Swindon or Derby (see, e.g., Chaloner, 1950).

The early railway companies, faced with these problems, turned to the most obvious model which they hoped would ensure discipline and control – that based on the military. As Foucault and Dandeker observe it was in these military forces that procedures and technologies had been developed to control and subordinate large numbers of staff and which hence seemed an appropriate model for the railways to follow. The railway companies succeeded in securing special legislation to allow their employees to be treated in this way. The Report of the Select Committee on Communication by Railway reported in 1839 that,

It is essential to the safety of the Public and to the maintenance of regular intercourse by Railroads that the Companies should have a more perfect control over their servants. . . . where the lives of many persons depend on the good conduct and ready obedience of subordinate officers, and where the smallest irregularity may be attended with fatal consequences, a system of exact discipline should be encouraged. (quoted in Kingsford, 1970: 16)

The centrepiece of the disciplinary system was the Rule Book, issued to every recruit, and which laid down, with great detail and precision, the obligations on staff and the procedures which workers had to follow (Kingsford, 1970; McKenna, 1980). These rules specified working practices, laid down a list of punishments if these were infringed or if workers were negligent or careless, and forbade drinking, smoking, or leaving work without permission. They also typically included general clauses allowing the company to punish workers arbitrarily. The rules for the Swindon Works of the GWR stated that 'any workman guilty of disobedience to his superiors, or adjudged guilty of serious misconduct will be liable to instant dismissal' (Hudson, 1970: 42). The rules of the Lancashire and Yorkshire Railway, recited by William Smith at the Royal Commission of Labour in 1893, stated bluntly that 'every person employed by the company must devote himself exclusively to their service, he must reside at whatever place he may be appointed, attend at such hours as may be required, give prompt obedience to all persons placed in authority over him and conform to all the rules and regulations of the company' (PP 1893–4: Vol. xxxiii).

The sorts of punishments meted out for infringements to the Rule Book were either fines, or dismissal. The use of fining was well known in many other industrial sectors, such as textiles, but was particularly pronounced on the railways. The rules covering the GWR Swindon works in the later nineteenth century specified fines between 6d and 2/6d, but on the footplate fines of up to £1 were imposed for even minor offences (Hudson, 1970: 18; see also Kingsford, 1970).

McKenna (1980: 37) argues that these rules continued to be of major importance as disciplinary devices until the twentieth century. It is important to recognize, however, that they raised as many problems as they resolved. Whilst they laid down a set of formal procedures to be followed, they did not indicate how infringements were to be discovered. At the informal level a number of these controls were largely inoperable. It became commonly accepted that some rules simply could not be enforced. The law forbidding the 'tipping' of porters was widely recognized to be unenforceable, especially when railway companies came to realize that it allowed them to keep wages low. There were many other examples. William Smith, quizzed by the Royal Commission of Labour, stated that it was common for railway employees to travel free if they gave a password to ticket collectors, even though the rules stated that they needed a free pass (PP 1893–4: Vol. xxxiii).

G.P. Neele (1974: 31), though a stickler for legality, observed that an early rule instructing the guard to get off a late train in order to put warnings on the track for later trains was impractical since guards could often not get back on the train again!

In other cases, breaches of the rules could not easily be ascertained. This problem was revealed with the publication in 1879 of the notorious *Memoirs of a Station Master* by E. Simmons. Simmons gave such a frank account of life on the GWR that they banned the sale of his book on their stations.[11] The picture portrayed by Simmons was one where the GWR (or the 'Great Smash Railway', as he preferred to call it) lacked the disciplinary apparatus to effectively keep tabs on railway workers, dispersed as they were to far-flung stations and goods yards. He talked of booking clerks easily able to double their wages by defrauding passengers of their change, claiming that the GWR was content to let this practice continue since it allowed them to pay low wages.[12] He talked also of rural station masters who spent most of the day in the public house.

This same point – that, concealed behind the apparent disciplinary rigour, lay a rather more anarchic reality – was taken up in other contemporary writing. Reynolds, in a popular book, *Engine Driving Life* (1881), one of the first books to develop the myth of the 'heroic engine driver', pointed out that fiddling was common. Engine drivers received a premium if they were economical in the use of coal. The amount of coal they were expected to use was greater if they drove a longer train, and it was possible for engine drivers to bribe guards into recording that they had driven more carriages than was actually the case. The early railways had no technology of checking the facts other than relying on the word of the workers. Similarly, if an engine driver insisted that he had not passed 'down' signals, and a signalman insisted that he had, there was no way of checking who was telling the truth (Simmons, 1974).

The principal device by which railways attempted to monitor workers was though the classic form of surveillance, visual inspection. Railway companies were able to visually inspect operations within their workshops, where they were able to strictly enforce rules and impose a harsh disciplinary regime (e.g. Williams, 1969; Hudson, 1970). The GWR attempted to apply this principle elsewhere by the use of inspectors. In the early days the Railway Police force had a squad of Inspectors and Sub-Inspectors whose job it was to walk the line 'at uncertain intervals' to check up on any irregularities (McDermontt, 1927: 355f.). As the railway police lost their importance, these powers of inspection became concentrated in the hands of Superintendents who assumed a new prominence when the management structure of the GWR was reorganized in the 1860s. These reforms reduced the powers of the Board of Directors, and placed key decision making in the hands of the District Superintendents and the General Manager (a new appointment on the GWR from 1863). In 1867 the General Manager was given the right to fix rates and fares, negotiate with other companies, propose new lines, look after company houses and wharfs, as well as 'general superintendence and management of the line, stations, including refreshment rooms and staff connected with the Traffic Department' (PRO Rail 267/168). It was also agreed that the Superintendents were to have effective control over all matters of staffing and control, including appointments (except clerical ones), leaving the Board of Directors simply as a court of appeal. It is notable, however, that the Divisional Superintendents' jobs were largely defined in terms of their role as inspectors:

> It is an order of the Directors that Superintendents make it a constant practice to travel with all the trains running in their Divisions, so as to ensure a continuous personal supervision over their staff and to satisfy themselves that the trains are properly timed, that no unnecessary detention occur at the stations, and that every person engaged upon the trains does his work in the best manner. (PRO Rail 250/688)

A further clause emphasized that the Superintendents should have enough clerical support to allow them to spend as much as two thirds of their time travelling on trains. Far from carrying out strategic planning, or dealing with other managerial departments, or other divisions or companies, their job was hence defined in terms of a type of glorified inspection, in which they were to supervise staff personally through travelling on trains unannounced and observing their efficiency first hand.

These developments indicate how closely the restructuring of management was tied up with the need to find effective means of surveillance, and suggests that Dandeker (following Chandler) is wrong to argue that it was the need for technical coordination alone which drove the process of bureaucratization of the railways. But it is still interesting to note how much of the powers vested in these new Superintendents depended on the power of direct visual observation – the gaze – to supervise workers. The GWR did create a form of Panopticon here, by emphasizing that Superintendents were never to advertise which trains they were to travel in. Hence they hoped that railway workers would not know when a superintendent was about to turn up, with the result that they would routinely behave as if a Superintendent might actually appear to observe them. But in fact this Panopticon did not work in practice. Travelling superintendents rarely had the power of surprise. Simmons records how the visits of Inspectors were often forewarned by telegraph operators telling station clerks of impending visits, allowing the station master to be fetched from the pub and a hectic tidying up of the premises to ensue. Reynolds also refers to the way that engine drivers would give advance warning to station staff if they knew that a superintendent was travelling on their train. Despite the sophistication of superintendence, it seems unlikely that it was able to provide rigorous checks on workers.

By the 1870s a shift in management thinking was apparent, as it became clear that direct visual supervision was difficult to enforce, and as employers throughout the British economy began to consider more 'advanced' methods of management including the use of welfare provision (e.g. Melling, 1979). E.B. Ivatts, in *Railway Management*, one of the first general treatises on railway management, first published in 1861, criticized the use of punitive methods and pointed towards a more liberal regime in which the worker could be treated more 'humanely'. Central to his critique of old methods of management was that they did not subject the individual to punishment. 'It is the offence that is punished, rather than the individual' (Ivatts, 1885: 48). Ivatts pointed out that a worker who was fined would simply pass on the fine to his wife, presumably retaining the same amount of pocket money for himself. Parsloe, writing in 1878, noted that,

> there has, of late years, been a considerable increase in the number of officials, and perhaps an unnecessary increase. So much supervision by such a variety of overlookers naturally becomes irksome. As a rule men are most likely to perform their duties circumspectly when confidence is bestowed and they are left to work with a certain sense of personal responsibility. (Parsloe, 1878: 120)

Reynolds (1881) also noted that one problem, not easily tackled by fining, was of 'thoughtlessness', where offences were not committed through malice. He gave the example of an engine driver who was in the habit of stopping at stations he was not booked to stop at, simply because he felt sorry for the waiting passengers. He noted that fines were only ever retrospective punishments for committing a given offence, and that the only way to make workers not do such a thing was to make them aware of the consequences of their actions by encouraging them to develop 'fore-thought'.

It is indeed clear that the practice of fining was declining in the years after 1860. Table 5.2, based on the career records of GWR footplate workers, reveals a major shift in the way that offences committed by workers were dealt with. Until the 1860s, fines were the sole means of punishment, but after 1865 their frequency falls considerably, as more workers are cautioned. Nonetheless, until the 1890s they were the most common means of dealing with offences. They suddenly stop, however, in 1900, despite the fact that they remained in the rule books. After this date cautioning becomes the dominant mode of dealing with offenders. The other main means of dealing with offenders was the use of demotion, suspension, and reductions in pay (especially the engine driver's premium).

There is clear evidence that in the years after 1860 the heavy use of punitive discipline, though still sanctioned by the rule books, was becoming a less frequent response, and management was searching for other ways of disciplining their workforce. It was in this respect that the idea of the career as a project of the 'self' began to be attractive.

Reorganization and the genesis of the modern career

From the 1860s a major shift took place in the organization of labour on the railways, which heralded a new, more systematic construction of career routes. This was congruent with the new management thinking which recognized the deficiencies of the older punitive style and began to argue

Table 5.2 *Punishments given to footplate workers (as percentages of all punishments in each five-year period)*

	Fines	Cautions	Pay	Suspension	Dismissal	Demotion
1845–49	100					
1850–54	100					
1855–59	100					
1860–64	94	6				
1865–69	62	31	5			
1870–74	64	26		6	2	2
1875–79	59	25	2	10		
1880–84	54	34		14	2	3
1885–89	61	20		14	2	2
1890–94	65	23	1	5	3	4
1895–99	40	30		22	3	4
1900–04		43	10	32	2	15
1905–09		47	43		2	10
1910–14		48	26		4	13
1915–19		69	19		13	
1920–24		76	8	17		
1925–29		60		10		20
1930–34		33		17		17

'Pay', means pay reduced, for instance by deferring workers' premium.
Demotion includes promotion being deferred, or seniority altered.
Dismissal includes being made to retire early.
Numbers do not sum to 100 per cent since the balance have no punishment for their offence.
Source: 'Pathways and Prospects' database: footplate workers

that the best way to motivate workers lay in rewarding them for performing well. E.B. Ivatts argued that it was vital to develop methods for disciplining individuals according to their changing aptitudes.

> There are plenty of so called classifications on paper in respect to grade, salary, and length of service, but within our knowledge there is no *periodical* revising classification as to progressive experience and efficiency. (Ivatts, 1861: 7; original emphasis)

Ivatts emphasized the way in which allowing for career advance might serve to deal with the problem of discipline.

> The hope of reward particularly encourages the younger men who are in the cause of working up their attainable standard, and doubtless it inspires them during that time. . . . promotion incites esprit de corps, and encourages emulation among a staff. (Ivatts, 1861: 45, 489)

A similar emphasis can be found in Reynolds's work. He insisted that 'railway companies recognise the great principle of individual exertion: they make every man in the service stand alone on his merits, and strictly accountable for the rapidity of his own promotion' (1881: 34).

Admittedly, this shift in management thought may have been less important, initially, than the simple economic need to cut wage costs as the GWR attempted to stave off financial disaster in the 1860s. One obvious target was the use of incremental wage systems which massively inflated costs because they automatically meant that older workers were being paid more, even if they were not actually carrying out more skilled or arduous work than younger workers.

The first major changes took place in clerical work. In 1863, the GWR introduced 'lad clerks' in place of adult men. As Simmons recalled. 'The amount to be paid to these lads was £20 per annum, instead of £50 per annum, but they were promised a progressive rise of pay until they reached the magnificent sum of £50 per annum, after which time it was held out to them that even the post of general manager was open to them' (Simmons, 1974: 141). An analysis of salaries paid in 1870 showed that whilst in 1862 only five per cent of clerks earned less than £50 per annum, by 1870 this had risen to 28 per cent (PRO Rail 267/33). The GWR kept their wages low by imposing a rule that 'no youth should be appointed who cannot reside with his parents or other friend' (PRO Rail 267/144). Lad clerks were subject to a probationary period, and were not promised permanent employment, but had to sit examinations at the age of 18 or 19 in order to become a senior clerk. In 1870 only around a third of lad clerks were successful in becoming senior clerks (PRO Rail 267/33). The strategy of replacing men by youths continued to be deployed throughout the century, and a report issued in 1890 even quantified the money saved by using boys (PRO Rail 267/219).

Simmons was unimpressed by the new system:

> The only thing my experience allow me to liken this lad clerk system, is a number of people pushing on together in an enclosed triangular passage towards the narrow point, and for whom the only escape that I can see is to back out. (Simmons 1974: 141)

Nonetheless, the changes were far reaching. It became much more difficult for workers not initially employed as 'lad clerks' to become clerks, but, partly as a reward for their early sacrifices, all progress within management was claimed to be confined to the clerical grades. No manual workers were shifted into clerical work as had previously occurred.

For the adult, senior clerical grades, the GWR attempted to link pay increases to promotion, so that there were as few cases as possible of senior employees doing menial work on relatively high pay. In 1870 the Board noted that 45 per cent of clerks earning an increase in pay between 1867 and 1870 had done so without changing job, and they agreed that,

> as a rule . . . it is desirable for the purpose of keeping down the expenses that clerks should receive their promotion by removal to better positions as vacancies arise and this has been a subject that has been prominently brought before the Superintendents and Goods Manager. (PRO Rail 267/33)

The same procedures were applied to uniformed staff. Procedures were formalized whereby passenger guards were to be recruited from porters, police, and goods guards, whilst goods guards and brakesmen were to be recruited from porters. Just as with clerks, porters were to be employed initially as lads only, so that clear promotion channels would be open to boys joining the GWR. The same reforms also clearly stated that all promotions were to be dealt with on the basis of seniority (PRO Rail

250/688). By the 1870s the GWR was clearly aware of the value of offering wage increases to 'deserving' individuals. In 1871 they responded to an agitation for higher wages by 'recommending deserving men for advances and leaving the others to take what course they liked' (PRO Rail 267/51, General Manager's Report).

Such was the strategic power of the footplate workers that it was not until 1879 that the GWR attempted to challenge the incremental wage rates paid there. In that year they noted their awareness of spiralling wage costs in this area.

> a continual advance is taking place in the cost per train mile for the wages of Enginemen and Firemen, the yearly advances being out of all proportion to the numbers of promotions. (PRO Rail 253/483)

Under the existing system, wages for firemen began at 3/6d and rose to 4/- after three years. For enginemen, wages began at 5/- and rose to 7/6 after seven years' service. The GWR responded in 1879 by introducing the 'classification system' where footplate workers were divided into three classes, with main line passenger driving at the top, local passenger driving and main line goods driving in the middle, and branch line passenger and goods work at the bottom. Wages were related to the class of work, rather than seniority, with the result that drivers only got more money if they actually moved to more skilled driving – 'promotion will be made to a higher class when vacancies occur' (PRO Rail 253/483). Since there were more jobs in the lower classes rather than the higher ones, workers were frequently confined to lower-class work with their incumbent lower wages for many years. Figures released by the GWR in 1902 showed that there were 44 first-class drivers, compared with 523 second-class shunters, 951 on third-class and branch work, and 792 shunters (PRO Rail 253/484). A similar system was rapidly introduced for goods guards, who found themselves divided as first-class guards, second-class guards, first-class brakesmen, and second-class brakesmen (*Railway Review*, 11 March 1881).

Even though economic forces were significant in the restructuring of job ladders, there is no doubt that changing management thought played a key role, especially in considering ways of thinking about how and why workers should be promoted. From the later 1880s any assumption that promotion was automatic and based on seniority was hedged round by a series of regulations which allowed Superintendents to refuse to promote time-served workers. In 1883 it was stated that shunting firemen could only become registered firemen if the District Superintendent was satisfied of 'the number of vacancies and the suitability of the men', and the Superintendent also had the right to demote firemen back to cleaning jobs. From 1886 the GWR emphasized that there was no automatic progression from engine cleaner to fireman:

> it does not follow from the employment of young men as cleaners that they will subsequently be employed as firemen: on the contrary it should be understood that there are many more candidates for appointment as Fireman than there are openings and that only the most deserving cleaners will be recommended for promotion. (PRO Rail 253/483; 17 March 1886)

From the 1880s progress through the various classes of fireman's and engine driver's work became increasingly dependent upon formal tests. In 1889 all firemen who were liable to earn promotion were sent to Swindon to spend a week showing the Inspector that they were competent to drive and that they were familiar with the rules. From 1892, all second-class engine drivers had to go to Swindon for a further examination before they could be promoted to become a first-class engine driver, and in 1893 this was made retrospective, so that all first-class drivers had to be re-examined. By 1908 candidates for promotion were inspected at no less than four stages: as second-class firemen looking for promotion to first-class work; as first-class firemen looking for promotion to be engine turners; as engine turners looking for promotion to be third-class engine drivers; and when earning promotion to first-class engine driver. Anyone failing these tests was not promoted, and might even be offered alternative employment off the footplate. George Armstrong reported in 1885 that 'when a man is put back through misconduct he forfeits to a greater or lesser extent his position on the seniority list'. Significant numbers of workers failed the tests, and these examinations cannot be seen simply as rubber stamping. In 1903 280 candidates for shunting fireman passed first time, another 109 passed on a subsequent occasion, and 49 failed altogether (PRO Rail 253/483).

Table 5.3 shows that it was from the 1870s that a more regular career pattern took shape. Before 1870 many more workers were recruited as firemen than as cleaners. There is also evidence in the middle cohorts that some workers were demoted, with some who entered as firemen (and one driver 1875–9) ending as cleaners. All those who began as cleaners before the 1860s ended up as drivers (or supervisors), but this proportion declined slightly in the middle cohorts (1870s/80s). For the 1900 entrants rates of promotion return to 100 per cent, before falling off amongst those entering after 1910, possibly reflecting the existence of incomplete career records.

The signalmen were also incorporated into promotion ladders. In the early years they had been recruited from a variety of origins, frequently from the ranks of the police. Although commentators as late as the 1920s argued that they were 'recruited from no particular class or grade' (Chappell, 1924), it was clear that by the late nineteenth century they were nearly all promoted from the ranks of porters. Of the 37 signalmen appointed from our sample in the late nineteenth century, 22 (60 per cent) had begun as porters, and virtually all the others had been policemen. Once appointed as signalmen they were subject to their own classification system according to the complexity of the box they worked, and this determined their wages. By 1890 four classes of signalbox existed (*Railway Review*, 14 February 1890). Unlike other grades of workers, however, they had very little prospect of moving into supervisory positions outside the signalbox, and they could therefore expect to remain signalmen all their lives (see the *Railway Review*, 27 April 1883). The GWR increasingly policed entry to signalling work according to examination proficiency. It began a set of classes in signalling in 1903, which attracted over 500 students by 1905. Results in examinations

Table 5.3   *Mobility between first and last jobs (percent by job)*

First job	Cleaner	Fireman	Driver	Supervisor	N =
			Final job		
1845–49					
firemen			100		2
1850–54					
firemen			89	11	9
drivers			100		1
1855–59					
cleaners			100		4
firemen	50		50		4
1860–64					
cleaners		20	80		5
firemen			100		3
1865–69					
cleaners		9	73	18	11
firemen	15	8	54	23	13
1870–74					
cleaners	12	12	71	6	17
firemen		25	75		4
1875–79					
cleaners	17	17	67		12
firemen			100		1
drivers	20		80		5
1880–84					
cleaners	5	35	60		20
firemen		100			1
drivers		100	100		2
1900–04					
cleaners			97	3	34
firemen			83	17	6
drivers			100		1
1905–09					
cleaners			100		22
1910–14					
cleaners	7	14	68	7	28
1915–19					
cleaners	7	24	69		54

Sample misses those entering in later 1880s and 1890s.
Source: 'Pathways and Prospects' database

taken by students were increasingly used as a basis for promotion (GWRM January, August 1908).

The contradictions of career culture

The inculcation of the promise of career appears to solve a major problem facing employers, since it creates reasons for employees to monitor their own actions, relieving the organization of the burden of supervision, at least to some extent. Yet it exposes a major contradiction in turn. It creates enormous potential dissatisfaction since it unleashes a range of hopes which may be difficult to satisfy. If individuals are given the prospect of advance how can they be fulfilled if such advance is denied? On the other hand if they are not given much real prospect of advance then the career loses its moral function, and does not exercise significant control.

In 1880 an article in the Amalgamated Society of Railway Servants' paper, *The Railway Review*, was able to rejoice in the career opportunities open to footplate workers and porters, comparing them favourably with those of clerks:

> [a cleaner or porter] enters the service an illiterate lad and is put to clean engines or carry luggage; the [clerk] comes on the scene with unexceptional evidence of respectability and a fair education. In fifteen years time the cleaner is a driver earning 50 shillings weekly, or the porter is an Inspector in smart uniform earning 42 shillings weekly, while the respectable young gent, who disdains manual labour is still a clerk in receipt of £60 or £70 a year. (*Railway Review*, 10 September 1880)

Yet just as the career prospects for manual workers were being trumpeted in this fashion, the actual rate of promotion began to slow. This was partly a result of the fact that, as railway expansion slowed, and as most new lines were completed, vacancies at the top diminished (Bagwell, 1961: 67). The clearest evidence for this comes from the footplate workers.

Table 5.4 shows quite clearly that the length of time taken to become an engine driver increased steadily. In the heady days of the 1840s it took less than five years on average to become an engine driver. By the 1860s this had slowed to around 10 years, and by the 1870s it rose again to 15. It remained around this level until those entering after 1910, where rates of promotion reached an all time low. It should be emphasized that Table 5.4 only

Table 5.4   *Speed of entry to drivers' jobs (per cent by cohort)*

	< 5 yrs	5–9	10–14	15–19	> 20	Median yrs	Mean yrs	N =
1845–49	50	50				4.5	4.5	2
1845–54	60	40				3.5	3.6	10
1855–59	13	50	12	12	12	7.5	11	8
1860–64	–	38	62			11	10.8	8
1865–69	–	71	13	13	13	9	10.2	24
1870–74	6	–	11	84		17	15.9	18
1875–79	33	7	–	33	27	18	12.1	15
1880–84	–	–	–	100		16	16.3	13
1900–04	2	4	8	85		17	15.7	47
1905–09	–	–	37	63		15	14.8	35
1910–14	–	–	4	13	83	21	21.5	24
1915–19	–	–	3	–	97	21	20.9	38

Sample misses later 1880s and 1890s.
Cohort is cohort of entry.
Source: 'Pathways and Prospects' sample

indicates entry to the lowest class of engine driving work. It would take many extra years to reach the higher classed, and better paid, work. A memorial from footplate workers to the GWR Board in 1882 prayed

> that classification be abolished, the enforcing of which acts most disadvantageously on many of your memorialists, preventing them from rising to the position of first class man. (*Railway Review*, 28 April 1882)

It was to no avail.

The trends revealed in the small sample of Table 5.4 are easily confirmed by other sources. On the Vale of Neath Railway company, 27 drivers were recruited between 1853 and 1865, of which there are complete records for 19. The average number of years these 19 had spent as firemen before promotion was only four. The mean age at which they were appointed as engine drivers was only 24. Twenty years later, however, the average number of years it took the 56 footplate workers who began working for the Brecon and Merthyr Railway after 1880 to earn promotion was 14.[13]

It is also clear that promotion prospects were deteriorating in other areas. Promotion to the ranks of Station Masters and foremen also took longer in the years after 1890. In the years before 1870 it took only around five years for workers to become Station Masters (Kingsford, 1970). Table 5.5 shows that by the end of the century the length of time needed to earn promotion to supervisory jobs had lengthened considerably. Whereas for those promoted before the 1890s it took only about nine years, on average, to be promoted, this doubled to around 17 years for those promoted afterwards; 58 per cent of those in the early cohort earned promotion within 10 years, but only 19 per cent of those in the latter cohort did.

Promotion prospects in clerical work were also restricted. Although clerical staff entered as 'lad clerks', and in theory could move into senior levels of management, in practice very few did. It is true that the General Manager of the GWR from 1912, Frank Potter, had begun as a lad clerk in 1869, but his was a rare case, and only about 1 per cent of those recruited as clerks were appointed to an officer's position.[14] From the late 1890s, furthermore, the GWR began to consider the possible advantages of recruiting a special class of clerical entrants who would be given higher salaries and would have prospects of moving into higher ranked jobs more quickly. There was, however, a general hostility to this proposal from most senior

Table 5.5 *Years taken to become Supervisory Worker (per cent by year of promotion)*

	< 5 yrs	6–10	11–15	16–20	> 21	Median yrs	Mean yrs	N =
1870–1889	23	35	23	19	–	9.0	9.6	26
1890–1915	2	17	24	13	39	17.0	17.4	41

For technical reasons, the cohort refers not to the year when workers began work, but the year in which their (first) promotion was earned.

Supervisory workers are Foremen, Station Masters and Inspectors.

Source: 'Pathways and Prospects' database

managers who were consulted, all of whom felt that it would jeopardize the existing system whereby the career technically open to all served to motivate workers.

> The proposal, however, to attract to the Company's service as a special class those who have taken a University Degree, or who are otherwise qualified for the higher grades of the Civil Service would not in my judgement be wise. It is of the first importance that all youths entering the service should have before them the prospect of advancement to the higher positions. If the rank and file felt that such positions were reserved for a special class, it would cause discontent amongst them. It would remove the chief inducement to diligence and progress, and would lower the standard of the general staff by leading the best men to seek employment elsewhere. (Letter dated 21 February 1901 in PRO Rail 258/400)

These views were widely expressed by senior officers, and the only significant changes introduced were to make the senior clerks' examination more stringent, and to extend the period of probation. But the major contradiction with the reliance on regular promotion from clerical ranks was forcefully drawn to the attention of managers in 1910:

> while the circumstances of the Railway Service call for a number of men who will become competent to occupy the positions of importance and responsibility there must be a considerable proportion of the staff who cannot expect to reach beyond a small – or at any rate quite moderate – salary and who will be content with that outlook. Therefore it is not desirable to put the educational standard on too high a level but to regulate the examination test so as to enable lads from all quarters to be introduced – from Council Schools, Day Schools, and Public Schools. (PRO Rail 258/400)

This proposal clearly recognizes the chief contradiction of the career strategy. In any organizational hierarchy there have to be some people who do the menial jobs at the bottom, and the danger of opening up career routes for everyone is that it creates unsupportable demands. The response was to stream clerical entrants so that only a special class would be groomed for progress to the top.

In 1914 the GWR, copying the example of the North Eastern Railway Company, did indeed begin to construct a new 'special class' of clerks. In June 1914 Heads of Department were given powers to select six staff aged between 18 and 24 each year who would be given special training and salaries. The expectation was that these special clerks would reach Assistant District Superintendent grade by age 30. These staff were selected as being expected to place work above all else, in return for their special 'careers':

> we expect all our salaried staff to work hard but we expect the Traffic Apprentices to work harder. We expect the ordinary staff to work late when necessary, but we expect the Traffic Apprentices to work all night to accomplish a special task. . . . (PRO Rail 258/400)

The GWR was quite aware of the wider implications of this innovation:

> it was recognised that the scheme necessarily had the effect of cutting off from some of the older members of staff opportunities of advancement which would otherwise have been open to them. (PRO Rail 258/400)

The introduction of Traffic Apprentices marked a drawing back from a career culture for clerical workers. Real career progress was to be confined to a special type of worker, whilst most clerical workers were to be earmarked for steady and unspectacular progress.

Conclusions

Let me now return to some general issues. A number of points are evident from this case study which shed light on the relationship between the career and surveillance. First, we should be wary of any progressive or evolutionary account of the history of the 'career' which sees it as the by-product or reflex of wider, more general social changes. In this respect Foucault's genealogical approach, which searches out for discontinuity and unevenness in historical development, has much to commend it. I have argued that the elaboration of various procedures for regulating careers has a distinct history which does not simply reflect the growth of the GWR itself, but was critically dependent upon the isolation of specific managerial ideas which found ways of connecting careers to discipline. Hoy's observation about the genealogical method, that 'there is no essence or original unity to be discovered. When genealogy looks to beginnings, it looks for accidents, chance, passion, petty malice, surprises, feverish agitation, unsteady victories and power' (Hoy, 1986: 224) summarizes well the lessons from the empirical material presented in this paper.

Second, it would appear that the 'career' was indeed championed by the GWR from the later 1870s as a means of 'working on the soul', and in this respect it marked a major break in management thinking compared with earlier forms of punishment and discipline. The research presented in this paper suggests that the attempt to impose rigid work control through the construction of a punitive disciplinary regime based on direct visual observation (the 'gaze') was largely a failure. In this respect, the well-established historiography which sees industrial discipline as a product of industrialization (e.g. Thompson, 1967) rather misses the point (see also Whipp, 1987). Instead, it seems much more accurate to argue that truly modern ways of controlling workers were only pioneered in the later nineteenth century, and that they revolved around attempts to motivate and discipline workers by using career ladders to encourage workers to monitor and regulate their own actions. It is this attempt to 'work on the soul', rather than to inflict punitive punishments and fines on workers, which can be seen as the truly 'modern' solution to the problem of labour control.

However, if this point is granted, a number of interesting implications follow. It suggests, contra Dandeker, that the elaboration of career ladders on the railways did not involve simply copying the military example. Although early railway management was indebted to military example, it was the punitive elements of military discipline which they borrowed, and they did not take the idea of regularized career progress from them. It was not until management thought within the railways connected careers and discipline that the modern career developed. This also suggests, contra the Weberian view, that capitalist enterprises were significant in developing new forms of discipline and did not simply copy examplars pioneered by the state.

Furthermore, this example suggests that Foucault himself rather misunderstands the development of modern disciplinary power. For it was precisely the failure of attempts at bodily regulation and visual inspection (the sorts of topics he discusses in *Discipline and Punish*) which forced the emergence of a new approach to discipline and control. Whereas Foucault tends to run together bodily regulation and discipline of the soul, the case of the GWR suggests that the latter grew out of a recognition of the former's failure. Foucault's elision of these two processes depends on his adoption of the Panopticon as the key symbolic metaphor of modern power. But it does need to be emphasized here that, however powerful the imagery of the Panopticon may be, it was actually historically unusual.

The general point here is whether it might be more important to play down the relevance of the arguments of *Discipline and Punish*, and to explore Foucault's later work in more detail. It can be argued that *Discipline and Punish* is not actually one of Foucault's more important books. As Honneth (1985) has demonstrated, it has serious conceptual flaws by falling back on a latent functionalism in which techniques of surveillance are introduced to ensure the reproduction of power relations. As Honneth also notes, Foucault fails to address the subjective dimension, and it is precisely his attempt to incorporate this in his later work which suggests its greater interest. Foucault's later work, admittedly, is more concerned with antiquity than modernity, and tends to downplay the significance of power, but nonetheless it would be interesting to analyse the modern 'career' as a distinctly modern form of ethics. The sort of issues he raises in relation to ethics: how you internalize ethical concerns, how you comport yourself to an ethical project, how issues of ethical substance are decided upon, these are all questions posed by the modern career. What importance should individuals place on their 'career' as opposed to family, friends or other social activities; what sorts of activities are legitimate to advance one's 'career'; how important is to have a 'career' at all? These are all fundamentally ethical issues which are ingrained in the modern career culture, and which cannot be shrugged off or ignored by those who inhabit it. The career culture has indeed come a long way from its humble beginnings in the nascent bureaucracies of the nineteenth century.

Notes

1 It should also be noted here that a strand of Marxist work has also been attentive to the role of internal labour markets in generating worker control – see for instance Stone (1974), Edwards (1979), Gordon et al. (1982).

2 See Foucault's auto-critique of *Discipline and Punish* (1980): 'if one wants to analyze the genealogy of the subject in Western societies, one has to take account not only of the techniques of domination but also techniques of the self' (quoted in Habermas, 1994: 86).

3 Even in the 1860s the proportion of 'officers' to 'servants' was over 10 per cent on the railways as a whole. See Mills (1867).

4 Other railway companies allowed directors to nominate their favourites to certain posts in the company. See Ivatts (1861).

5 This data base was constructed as part of an ESRC project 'Pathways and prospects: the development of the modern bureaucratic career 1840–1940' (ref. No. R000 23 2803), co-directors Dr Hiranthi Jayaweera (University of Keele), Dr Andrew Miles (University of Birmingham) and Prof. David Vincent (University of Keele). Fuller details will be published in a co-authored book to be published by Cambridge University Press.

6 On the GWR all appointments except those of footplate workers were supervised by the Board of Directors, the footplate workers being appointed by the locomotive superintendent (McDermott, 1927, Ch XIV).

7 A good example of this was in 1867, when the GWR was on the verge of bankruptcy and was investigating all possible measures to reduce costs, but still was forced to concede wage demands to engine drivers who threatened to go on strike (Nock, 1962: 101).

8 Several amusing examples can be provided. One contemporary, whose work I consider below, also provides an interesting case. Having worked as a station clerk he threatened to beat up his immediate superior, called him to his face by his nickname, together with other sundry offences, yet still managed to obtain rapid promotion to Station Master's ranks within three years (see Simmons, 1974).

9 This practice continued on the GWR until the 1870s. See McDermott (1927: 365).

10 One amusing case is that of an indignant clergyman, told by a porter to go to a stand with the letter L to pick up his luggage, who complained bitterly about the porter's conduct. He thought that the porter had told him to 'Go to Hell'. See Simmons (1974: 7–8).

11 Indeed, this book is not referred to in any of the company histories, even though McDermott (1927: 370) quotes an incident from it.

12 This practice was also reported in the trade union journal *The Railway Review*. See its article on clerks, 10 September 1880.

13 Figures from Vale of Neath Railway come from PRO Rail 264/310. Brecon and Merthyr records are in PRO Rail 264/309. The 56 records are for those starting work between 1880 and 1910.

14 This figure is derived from our sample of 504 male clerks recruited between 1860 and 1890. The details on Potter come from McDermott (1929: 236). Most senior officers appear to have been recruited directly from the professions.

References

Note: all references to PRO material are to the Great Western Railway archives at the Public Record Office, Kew.

Allcock, G. (1922) *Fifty Years of Railway Trade Unionism*. London: Unwin.
Bagwell, P. (1961) *The Railwaymen: the History of the National Union of Railwaymen*. London: Allen and Unwin.
Booker, J. (1977) *The Great Western Railway: A New History*. Newton Abbott: Tavistock.
Chaloner, W.H. (1950) *The Social and Economic Development of Crewe 1780–1923*. Manchester: Manchester University Press.
Chandler, A.D. (1977) *The Visible Hand*. Cambridge, MA: Harvard University Press.
Chandler, A.D. (1990) *Scale and Scope: Dynamics of Industrial Capitalism*. Cambridge, MA: MIT Press.
Chappell, H. (1924) *Life on the Iron Road*. London: John Lane.
Cohn, S. (1985) *The Process of Occupational Sex Typing: the Feminisation of Clerical Labour in Great Britain*. Philadelphia: University of Philadelphia Press.
Coleman, D.C. (1973) 'Gentleman and Players', *Economic History Review*, xxvi: 92–116.
Dandeker C. (1990) *Surveillance, Power, Modernity*. Oxford: Polity.
Davidson, A.L. (1986) 'Archaeology, genealogy, ethics', in Hoy, *Foucault*. pp. 221–34.
Edwards, R.C. (1979) *The Contested Terrain*. New York: Basic Books.

Evans, G. (1992) 'Testing the validity of the Goldthorpe Class Schema', *European Sociological Review*, 8: 211–32.

Foucault, M. (1977) *Discipline and Punish*. Harmondsworth: Penguin.

Foucault, M. (1979) *A History of Sexuality, Volume 1*. Harmondsworth: Penguin.

Foucault, M. (1986) 'What is Enlightenment?' in P. Rabinow (ed.), *The Foucault Reader*. Harmondsworth: Penguin. pp. 32–50.

Giddens, A. (1985) *The Nation State and Violence*. Oxford: Polity.

Gordon, D., Edwards, R. and Reich, M. (1982) *Segmented Work, Divided Workers*. Cambridge: Cambridge University Press.

Grey, C. (1994) 'Career as a project of the self and labour process discipline', *Sociology*, 28: 479–98.

GWRM (various dates) *Great Western Railway Magazine*, Swindon.

Habermas, J. (1994) 'Some questions concerning the theory of power: Foucault again', in Kelley, *Critique and Power*. pp. 79–107.

Hacking, I. (1986) 'Self-improvement', in Hoy, *Foucault*. pp. 235–40.

Halford, S. and Savage, M. (1995) 'The Bureaucratic career: demise or adaptation?', in T. Butler and M. Savage (eds), *Social Change and the Middle Classes*. London: UCL Press. pp. 117–32.

Honneth, A. (1985) *Critique of Power*. Boston: MIT Press.

Hoy, D.C. (ed.) (1986) *Foucault: A Critical Reader*. Oxford: Blackwell.

Hudson, K. (1970) *Working to Rule*. Bath: Adams and Dart.

Ivatts, I.B. (1861) *Railway Management at Stations*. London: McCorquodale. (2nd edn 1885: 3rd edn 1910.)

Kelley, M. (ed.) (1994) *Critique and Power: Recasting the Foucault/Habermas Debate*. Boston, MA: MIT Press.

Kingsford, P.W. (1970) *Victorian Railwaymen: The Emergence and Growth of Railway Labour*. London: Cass.

McDermott, E.T. (1927, 1929) *A History of the Great Western Railway* (2 Vols). London: Ian Allen.

McKenna, F. (1980) *The Railway Workers 1840–1970*. London: Faber.

Melling, J. (1979) 'Industrial strife and business welfare philosophy: the case of the South Metropolitan Gas Company from 1880s to the war', *Business History*, XXI, 2: 163–98.

Miller, P. and Rose, N. (1993) 'Governing economic life', in M. Gane and T. Johnson (eds)., *Foucault's New Domains*. London: Routledge. pp. 75–105.

Mills, W.F. (1867) *The Railway Service: Its Exigencies, Provisions and Requirements*. London: W.J. Adams.

Neele, G.P. (1974) *Railway Reminiscences*. London: EP Publishing. (Originally published 1904.)

Nock, O.S. (1962) *The Great Western Railway in the Nineteenth Century*. London: Ian Allen.

Parsloe, J. (1878) *Our Railways*. London: Kegan Paul.

Pollard, S. (1965) *The Genesis of Modern Management*. London: Edward Arnold.

Raynes, J.R. (1921) *Engines and Men*. Leeds: Goodall and Sudcock.

Reynolds, M. (1881) *Engine Driving Life*. London: Crosby, Lockwood.

Rose, N. (1985) *The Psychological Complex: Psychology, Politics and Society in England, 1869–1939*. London: Routledge.

Rose, N. (1990) *Governing the Soul*. London: Routledge.

Russell, J.K. (1983) *Great Western Railway Company Servants*. Upper Buckleberry: Wild Swan.

Savage, M. (1993) 'Career mobility and class formation: British banking workers and the lower middle classes', in A. Miles and D. Vincent (eds), *Building European Society: Occupational and Social Mobility in Europe, 1840–1940*. Manchester: Manchester University Press. pp. 196–216.

Sekon, G.A. (1895) *A History of the Great Western Railway*. London: Digby, Long.

Simmons, E.J. (1974) *Memoirs of a Station Master*. Bath: Adams and Dart. (Originally published 1879.)

Stone, K. (1974) 'The origins of job structures in the steel industry', *Review of Radical Political Economics*, 6: 113–74.

Thompson, E.P. (1967) 'Time, work and industrial discipline', *Past and Present*. 38: 56–97.

Vincit, V. (1847) *Railway Locomotive Management*. London: Simplex.

Weber, M. (1978) *Economy and Society*. Berkeley, CA: University of California Press.

Weeks, J. (1990) *Sex, Politics and Society*. London: Longman.

Whipp, R. (1987) 'Time to work, time to play: a critique of EP Thompson', in P. Joyce (ed.), *The Historical Meanings of Work*. Cambridge: Cambridge University Press. pp. 210–36.

Williams, A. (1969) *Life in a Railway Factory*. London: Fontana. (Originally published 1915.)

Williams, R. (1970) *Keywords*. London: Fontana.

6

Examining Accounts and Accounting for Management: Inverting Understandings of 'the Economic'

Keith Hoskin

Signs of change

> Management is possible only when the strength of a firm is known . . .
> The firm's capacity and the means to enlarge it must be known. The
> strength and capacity of other firms, rivals of my own firm, must also be
> known. . . . A certain specific knowledge is necessary: concrete, precise
> and measured knowledge as to the firm's strength. The art of managing
> . . . is intimately bound up with the development of what is, from this
> moment, nameable as accounting.

This is a monstrous hybrid, a deliberate misquotation from Foucault: yet it is
one which may go some way to explaining why, within the field of
management, accounting has proved such a fertile area for applying Foucault's way of seeing. Foucault's original quotation was remarking on the
phenomenon which he called 'governmentalization', which he saw as the
distinctive mode of modern political power, the basis for the developed
nation state (regardless, paradoxically, of its particular political complexion): in which case, for 'management' in the above, read 'government', for
'the firm' read 'the state', and for 'accounting' read 'political arithmetic'.[1]
So why not choose to begin just with Foucault? Because, one might say, the
pastiche is more apt than the original. It would be only half-joking to say
that virtually nothing gets changed, and yet, as Borges (1981: 101) puts it, in
his story of Pierre Menard (who sets out, in the twentieth century, to recreate
the *Don Quixote* word for word), the second time around the passage is
'almost infinitely richer'. For here we have, as if in parallel, the most
exemplary summary of what enables management's invention and continued
success – that is, knowing one's own strength and how to build on it, while
knowing the strength of one's competition – and here we have the most
concise designation of what enables such strengths to be known, the
powerful kind of knowledge which embodies the certainty which comes
from specificity and measurement: but then, in an even more shocking
paradox than Foucault's original, we discover, behind and before management, accounting . . .

However, there are, I suggest, other reasons for not simply beginning with Foucault. For one, we ought, perhaps, in principle to mark our distance from him. For the strange fact is that Foucault wrote virtually nothing on management or accounting, yet has, even so, become a theorist of major influence within these fields.[2] By thus tracing but displacing his words, we may be reminded of how, while we all try to say something new, certain thinkers, even when not ostensibly talking of particular fields and problems, appear in retrospect to have been talking of them all along. But perhaps the most necessary and pressing reason for choosing this subversive inversion of his text is precisely because subversive inversion is Foucault's special trick, his *modus operandi*, his *pièce de résistance*.

In the case of 'the political', inversion is his way of counteracting what he sees as 'the excessive value attributed to the problem of the state', whether viewed as a monolithic totality, a '*monstre froid*', or else as object of a fractioning analysis 'that consists in reducing the state to a number of functions such as the development of productive forces and the production of relations of production' (Foucault, 1991: 103). The problem, in either case, is that the state, as metaphysical construct, remains an untouched and unquestioned presence, 'absolutely essential as a target needing to be attacked and a privileged position needing to be occupied': in which case, analysis never begins to think the strangeness of how we have reached a position where the state, as object and as sign, should seem so obviously, massively there. There is no distinct and separate starting-point from which to diagnose effectively the unreason in its forms of reason. Accordingly, he recommends beginning from such micro-practices of 'governmentality' as political arithmetic, precisely to get inside the workings of 'the state', in its mundane forms of effectiveness. For 'what is really important for our modernity – for our present – is not so much the *étatisation* of society, as the "governmentalisation" of the state' (ibid.).

So, similarly here, we arguably now require an inversion in our ways of thinking about 'the economic' – one which also adopts Foucault's tactic of inversion, as the means to destabilize the sign 'economics'. So we should be more ready to think in terms of saying: let us address great and momentous themes, but, to do so, let us talk of a grey and unprepossessing 'precise and measured knowledge' – and *revel* in the fact that we therefore talk of accounting. Yes, we know that it is the very archetype of 'backroom knowledge', something conventionally seen (except perhaps among accountants) as purely secondary: secondary in practical terms to more dynamic and significant practices, such as strategic management and marketing, and in theoretical terms to the bellwether field of economics (and as such, best avoided).[3] But what if this secondary knowledge is, in some way, central? Rather as political arithmetic may now be seen to be?

Suddenly comfortable assumptions about the economic world may become a little less comfortable, and unquestionable premises begin to be thrown into question, as the Foucauldian gadfly gets to work, goading us towards a re-thinking of 'the economic' from the bottom up, starting from simple little practices, and then tracing their effects. In Foucault's wake, we may begin to subvert that well-trodden and noble path of thought, which so effortlessly works from the top down, beginning from the empyrean height of those abstractions which – as with 'the state' – we assume we understand: 'the market', and that great denizen of the modern market, 'the multi-national'. For in the era of supposed globalization, these constructs have become their own form of frozen monster, as governments and businesses across the world bend the knee before 'the disciplines of the market', and the 'oligopoly power' of the multinationals. Each has also proved equally susceptible to being reduced to its productive functions, a whole supposedly captured and dissected In these functional parts, not least by all the disciplinary and sub-disciplinary forms of economics and the management 'sciences'. Indeed, those functional parts arguably then become little monsters of their own.

But we now have a new intellectual purchase on these monsters, large and small. We may, after Foucault, think of managing, and its relation to accounting, in an unprecedented way, as accounting may be brought to play a similar role to political arithmetic in re-orienting our thinking. What, in particular, needs dwelling upon is how these practices produce new possible relations between forms of knowledge and the exercise of power. This is not to suggest that they are therefore vehicles of a prior 'power–knowledge' (which would then be just another form of prior metaphysical construct). It is rather to focus on them in their simplicity, in the way that the very generation of their written, numerical evaluations makes 'the strength of the state' or of 'the firm' known – and so, *ipso facto*, makes the state/firm appear as having a 'strength' which is most purely and properly expressible in concrete, precise and measured terms. By extension, of course, what is then rendered true of one state/firm becomes a truth applicable to many, or all: there emerges a whole domain of states/firms, which can be totalled up, or analysed down, in their specificity, and evaluated in terms of their pasts and futures, generating a whole archipelago of new expert knowledges and truths. That, at least, is the possibility which I wish to consider here, by examining accounting, and accounting's relation to certain other little practices, such as those of writing, and indeed of examining. But I recognize that, in doing so, I am putting a great deal of theoretical weight on accounting and its significance, which accounting is not accustomed to bear. It is an issue which perhaps requires some reflection, before going further.

Examining accounting: the theoretical inversion

So why attempt an inversive critique of economics and managerialism from accounting, rather than, say, political arithmetic, or even pure arithmetic (since economics so often seems to present itself as purely numbers)?[4] One might respond that, empirically, accounting can be seen as the 'master metaphor' of economics (cf. Klamer and McCloskey, 1992), being the raw data (often, sadly, seen as unproblematically raw) which forms the warp and weft of economic theorizing, even including econometrics. Or one may observe (not least by drawing on Foucauldian categories) how often accounting and its related form, accountability, turn out to be at the heart of economic and managerial activity in the modern world.[5] But in addition I suggest that there is a still more important theoretical reason, which has everything to do with developing and extending Foucault's inversive way of seeing. While there remains no last word in the game of interpreting Foucault's own theoretical project (see, for instance, the range of contributions in Gutting, 1994 and Kelly, 1995), it is clear that one major theme in his last series of works was the analysis of practices. Here the work on governmentalization is just one example of a more general approach, which was concerned, in various ways, with the question of how practices make possible both social and individual regularities. So, alongside the work on governmentality and 'the State', we find the work on the 'care of the self', engendering a parallel new understanding of that other central metaphysical category, 'the self'.[6] In both cases, one starts from the bottom up, without presuming a theoretical priority to the traditional categories, a move which prevents the categories from intervening in their usual massively unquestionable way, before debate and analysis even begin.

For myself, I would suggest that this is a theoretical breakthrough of massive significance (cf. McNay, 1994). Foucault's principle of beginning from practices was perhaps first evident in works like *Discipline and Punish*, where he discusses how power and knowledge effects are produced from practices of hierarchical surveillance and normalizing judgement, including of course the examination, the practice in which 'the superimposition of the power relations and the knowledge relations assumes . . . all its visible brilliance' (1975: 185). By these last works, one may see this less as just a principle, and more a general 'theory of practices', which is offering a new kind of reasoned analysis of both social and individual worlds (one which gets beyond the twin culs-de-sac of sociologism and psychologism).[7] For practices – or practices in the way that Foucault makes it possible to conceive them – are neither locatable purely at the social level, nor within the self, insofar as they are secondary or background 'technologies which socially we cannot avoid yet which individually we internalise in varying ways, with effects that are both socially regular and personally differentiated' (Hoskin, 1994: 78). The possibility now extended is that, by beginning analysis from such practices, we may develop a new kind of reasoning, beyond the traditionally deficient forms of reason which fall prey to such 'isms' (including also 'logicism', the idea that there is a sovereign rational subject surveying a world of timeless ideas and truths – that Platonic vision which launched the moves into sociologism, etc., in the first place). As such, this bottom-up approach may even open a new regime of truth, beyond disciplinary knowledge and its peculiar forms of power. Such at least is the possibility which Foucault himself, at least some of the time, seems to have entertained.

In saying 'seems to have', I have in mind, particularly, the enigmatic case of the entry by the otherwise-unknown 'Maurice Florence' on 'Michel Foucault' in a French Dictionary of Philosophers (Gutting, 1994: 314–19). Here 'MF' suggests that in all 'MF's' work there have been 'certain methodological choices': 'a systematic scepticism with respect to all anthropological universals . . . so as to interrogate them in their historical constitution'; a move away from studying 'the constitutive subject' in favour of a 'return toward the study of the concrete practices by which the subject is constituted in the immanence of a domain of knowledge'; from this 'a third methodological principle follows: that of appealing to "practices" as a domain of analysis, of approaching one's study from the side of what "was done"'. Such 'practices' comprise those which are 'more or less regulated, more or less conscious, more or less goal-oriented . . . practices understood simultaneously as modes of acting and thinking'. Of course, the question remains: is 'MF' the authentic voice of Michel Foucault? But then, the question also remains: 'What is an author?'[8]

The theoretical question which remains, however, is what practices constitute the 'domain of analysis' here? In other words, what sort of practices, situated at what level, may constitute the basis for a general theory of practices on these lines? This is not just a historical issue – although it will always require historical investigation, since such practices, being 'more or less regulated and conscious', will vary with time and place, with changes at the social level and within the self (if only because such changes will themselves be products of changes in the practices through which we act and think). However, it is also, seriously, theoretical. Through the historical investigation, we are zeroing in, narrowing down, to certain types of practice, which have general significance for us in enabling us to act and think (and speak, write, sign, sing, draw, dream, articulate, calculate, etc.). In considering what practices qualify for this role, I suggest that the first factor is that they will indeed be secondary practices, behind or beneath the explicit word said, thought written, sign visualized, picture drawn, and soon. The second is that they will have a generality, a coherence, beyond the specific form they take, at any given time, as what we may call 'processes'.

Such general 'processes' may perhaps include communicating, and possibly learning – that is, processes which are conventionally invoked as 'essentially' human, even if they so often seem elusive of precise definition and knowledge (which is perhaps because we never encounter them as such, but only through historically specific practices: which, in turn, is why they then remain, as processes, subject to such confusion and misunderstanding). But in addition, there may, as a third such process, be 'valuing'. Again resistant to logical analysis, this is another supposed 'essential' aspect of humanity. But leaving aside such essentialist debate, we now know that as a *practice*, valuing was already a feature of the social and the self, from before the invention of writing. For, before writing, there was a first system of accounting, utilizing three-dimensional clay tokens (Schmandt-Besserat, 1992). Using these tokens – which both named and counted the objects accounted for, in what was therefore a sign-system before writing – humans engaged, from around 8000 BC, in a practice of valuing for stewardship, though not exchange, purposes (Schmandt-Besserat, 1992: 168). This evidence suggests that accounting-based stewardship of goods and produce stored is what made possible the first known agricultural societies: and, further, that the extension of the accounting sign-system, from around 4500 BC, was crucial to the success of the first city-based (or *polis*-based) cultures. Indeed, in Schmandt-Besserat's thesis, this token-accounting was then the system out of which the first separate counting and writing systems were derived, in Mesopotamia, *c.* 3200 BC. Out of accounting, writing: a sign of change indeed, as the central sign-systems of civilization, and indeed of those talismanic cultural signs, the political and the economic, appear to be secondary to accounting.[9]

Following Schmandt-Besserat's pioneering work, it is now possible, in a new way, to see accounting as having a very special significance, as the first-known visible system of valuing, and as a practice preceding and making possible, writing, counting, the political and the economic. Beginning one's inversive critique of the economic from accounting is therefore a move not justified purely because accounting is the master metaphor of economics, nor even because forms of accounting are so embedded within modern systems of economic analysis and management. It is a move which goes to the heart of the issue of developing a more rigorous 'theory of practices', if we are to do so in a way which focuses on the practices through which we communicate, learn and value. Still assuming that such practices are background and purposive, we may now more rigorously, after Foucault, suggest what they may be. Such a suggestion will, of course, never then be purely theoretical in its detail. On the contrary, it will need to be informed by re-examining Foucault's own analyses of practices, and extending them further. What follows is just the product of one such re-examination.

For myself, on reading and re-reading Foucault (e.g. Hoskin, 1990, 1994), it has always been striking how central, from *Discipline and Punish* on, practices of writing, examining and grading are to his analyses. Indeed, I have suggested that he might be taken as a 'crypto-educationist' (Hoskin, 1990), for the way that practices which are pedagogic and pedagogic-related keep appearing at the heart of his texts, to the point where occasionally the analyses themselves lose historical precision. 'In certain passages, he can be seen to claim that particular practices were at work in eras when they were not, as such, available; or alternatively, he perceives practices as purely modern, when they have an older and significant history.'[10] However, if he sometimes erred in detail, this does not necessarily invalidate the approach as such; it is, rather, a matter of specifying historical developments, and their theoretical basis, more closely.

So, for instance, I may have argued that examining in itself cannot be accepted as the new practice which, around 1800, captured the 'superimposition of the power relations and the knowledge relations' of modern disciplinarity; but closer historical investigation only suggests a revision and respecification of the theory of practices, identifying what is new as a combination of writing, examining and grading: a new configuration, in other words, of the processes of communicating, learning and valuing, in which students, from this modern moment on, learn to learn that significant communications are written not oral, that proper learning and new knowledge are the product of constant examination, and that evaluation of the true is embodied in the numerical. Given that, then other historical moments can also come more sharply into focus, as moments when similar discontinuities in how we act and think took place: that moment, for instance, before the invention of writing, when token-accounting – not in itself, but in conjunction with new oral forms of communicating and some integrally necessary mode of pedagogy (for how else was a knowledge of what the tokens signified ever disseminated?) – made possible the first agricultural economies; or that moment, around AD 1200, when the first form of oral examining – in conjunction with a new practice of silent reading, plus the development of an 'alphanumeric' writing-system, plus the spatial gridding of texts, plus the expert evaluation of individual acts and their intentions by constant re-examining – produced those new commitments to method and system which are frequently attributed to the later invention of perspective and print (e.g. Ong, 1982; Hoskin and Macve, 1994).

In such ways, I have suggested, one version of a more general 'theory of practices' can be articulated. But it is, necessarily, a version in which accounting now has a surprisingly significant role, before writing and also possibly after (e.g. with the invention of management), as the practice through which significant modes of valuing become made possible. It is that possibility which I now propose to examine in relation to that distinctive feature of our modern disciplinary/economic world, managerialism.

Which brings me back to my initial misquotation, and a necessary qualification which must now be conceded. For although, dramatically, there is a certain inversive *frisson* in claiming that accounting, so to speak, 'made management possible', the claim as such clearly will not do, historically or theoretically. Historically, 'accounting' manifestly cannot have emerged as something unprecedented, to constitute management, in the way that political arithmetic can be argued to have done *vis-à-vis* government: for while the latter is an invention of the seventeenth century, the former, by my own admission, predates the invention of writing. Theoretically, it cannot have emerged as something monocausal (nor indeed, I suggest, did political arithmetic). For what this bottom-up approach entails, in every case, is beginning from a certain range of secondary practices, and then seeing how, in their interplay, they exert a certain kind of power, by generating particular kinds of knowledge, and enabling certain things to be said and thought. It is here that I find myself not simply examining accounting for its effects, but examining accounting, writing, grading, *and* examining, altogether, as practices which socially, over the past two centuries, we have been increasingly powerless to avoid, but which individually we have internalized in dizzyingly multiple ways: not least, in the economic world of modernity, as the means to rendering management so central.

The space for Foucauldian inversion: beyond misunderstandings of 'the economic'

What, then, can be added that is new concerning management and its genesis, by going through this long theoretical digression? I suggest that the ultimate outcome (which as yet is only vaguely discernible) is the super-seding of economics, its vocabulary and ways of theorizing: something which will happen, however (if it does), for the only necessary and sufficient reason, because of the internal collapse of economics as a reasoned way of making sense of 'the economic'. What we shall then find, in its place, is a more reasoned discourse, which will be concerned, in its vocabulary and ways of theorizing, with accounting, writing, grading, and all the other supplementary disciplinary practices which have now made management so central, in practice, to 'the economic'.

Now arguably such a possibility is not so far-fetched as it might have seemed a generation ago. Not only are the nostrums of economists, and their claims to theoretical coherence, more fiercely critiqued from within the field than ever (e.g. Ormerod, 1994; Hutton, 1995), but there is also, particularly in books such as this, an increasing critique of economics, which puts it under a new and unaccustomed type of theoretical pressure from outside. But perhaps most significantly, there is already lurking within economics, a theoretically and historically devastating critique of market-based 'invisible hand' theorizing, which has in a sense already done the hard theoretical work, and which only requires now to be framed within a theory of practices for this to become properly apparent. That it has not, as yet, is the result of a classic discursive irony. The work I refer to is that of Alfred Chandler.

Chandler's monumental work on the emergence of the world of the modern business enterprise, with its corporations, strategies, capital move-ments, globalization, and so on – massive metaphysical categories, all – has as its central thesis one simple point: that market-based economics, of the kind so researched and fetishized by economists (*pace* Keynes, both those defunct and most of those still alive and kicking) is dead, and has been dead since the genesis of management, approximately 150 years ago. For the invention of management, as his work details in great care, is what made possible the triumph of that quite unprecedented organization, the multi-divisional, multinational corporation: since when, as the title of perhaps his most significant book declares (Chandler, 1977), the reign of the market, and its 'invisible hand', has been displaced by the power of the 'visible hand' of management, which has enabled the creation of the oligopoly power of the multidivisional multinationals, which now dominate the world economy.

One can, after Foucault, suggest that Chandler already had the necessary weaponry, the point of theoretical purchase, to undermine economics definitively. For he very precisely defines management in terms of practices, explaining that it is not charismatic leadership, nor entrepreneurial zeal, but simply 'administrative coordination': and that proves to be nothing more than techniques of book-keeping, for recording and evaluating cost, time and productivity, supported by a system of organization charts and systems, leading to coordination via plans, budgets and reports derived from these techniques – in other words the familiar mundanities of modern business life.[11] As *The Visible Hand* then documents, it was the application of the technologies of administrative coordination which then made it possible to construct organizations on a new hierarchically integrated model, based, in the USA, on the line-and-staff structure, and so to construct them as organizations where, for the first time in history, managers managed other managers. 'Markets', with decreasingly few exceptions, began from that moment on to be restructured in favour of oligopoly: slowly at first, but then as the early line-and-staff organizations were supplemented by larger divisionalized corporations, with increasing rapidity.

Now it is only fair to say that accounting has a significant role in Chandler's story here, for the bottom line is that the day-to-day running and control even of early unitary (U-form) companies was unfeasible without the implantation of techniques for managing 'by the numbers'. Furthermore, it gained in significance from around 1900, as more elaborate forms of number management led to the development of systematic budgeting and techniques for measuring Return on Investment (first in the du Pont Company, where it was used only by top management). It then came into its own – or, in the contrarian thesis of Johnson and Kaplan's 1987 book, lost its relevance – as it was applied at General Motors, by Alfred P. Sloan, to enable the construction of the multidivisional (M-form) corporation, where divisional heads, with devolved powers of investment, could in effect manage companies within the company.[12] It was, for Chandler, from this point on that the full effects of the 'visible hand' became apparent, as these corporations gained the potential, first for internal elaboration into various structures, depending on the strategy evolved by analysis of the data provided via administrative coordination, and second for external market control, by forming oligopolies, with attendant barriers to entry, and so on.

Now one possible conclusion to this would be that the use of the term 'markets' (as if there were some unchanging identity of the market, running through the various transformations engineered by administrative co-ordination) would be the most frozen and monstrous misrepresentation of 'the economic'. Assuming that markets had ever been free (a dubious assumption, from Sahlins's stone-age world on) what they now became was an arena where an increasingly disparate power was exercised by larger businesses over smaller, via the practices of coordination. Chandler does not mince words, concluding that there is no residual possibility that perfect competition 'remains the most efficient way to co-ordinate economic activities or allocate economic resources' (1977: 4); for the 'modern business enterprise' has come to control such large sectors of the world economy that it has 'altered the basic structure of these sectors and of the economy as a whole' (1977: 4).

Yet, ironically, the conclusion to Chandler's work, in the sense both of his own elaboration of it, and its appropriation by others, such as Williamson, has proved to be a continuation of economics by another means. The initial insight is compromised by a return to the metaphysical vocabulary of old, to construct an alternative version of economic rationalism. 'Strategy precedes structure' because strategy is what the rational re-examining and evaluating of the new writing produces; and the new practices are themselves a rational response to economic-technical demands, such as the invention of interchangeable-part manufacture, the telegraph and the railroad, over the period 1830 to 1860. That response was in turn forthcoming thanks to a group of businessmen, the 'pioneers of modern management' (Chandler, 1977: 95), who recognized what was demanded, by seeing the economic truth clear.

Chandler provides three propositions 'to help explain the initial appearance of the modern business enterprise' (1977: 7–8). It happened, firstly, when 'administrative co-ordination permitted greater productivity, lower costs and higher profits than co-ordination by market mechanisms'; second, this did not occur 'until a managerial hierarchy had been created', something which needed managers 'to invent new practices and procedures which in time became standard operating methods in managing'; and third, success only followed 'when the volume of economic activities reached a level that made administrative co-ordination more efficient and profitable than market co-ordination' (1977: 7–8). But this is all *ex post* rationalization, and confused at that: propositions one and three declare that managerialism was only invented when the time was metaphysically right – that is, at the moment when economic reality, functioning as a form of bottom line, justified it; meanwhile proposition two has pioneering individuals, who cannot know the truth of this economic reality, providentially coming up with the solution that will make it come true, and so evolving, in social Darwinist terms, into that new 'subspecies of economic man – the salaried manager' (1977: 4). Given this ironic turn to an invisible-hand framework of explanation, it is perhaps not so surprising that Chandler should have been claimed as a source by Williamson's transaction-cost economics, even though that inverts Chandler's thesis in an almost-parodic way. For Williamson (1980: 190–1), in noting that administrative coordination produced a new '*differential* effect' on costs in favour of factory-based divisionalized organizations, for instance by 'the joining of differential inventory economies (made possible by the development of infrastructure) with greater specialisation', ignores the fact that this power is exerted by the visible hand of management; instead (exploiting Chandler's metaphysical turn) he re-defines it as a power exerted by the invisible hand of the market, since the change to coordination always happens, even initially, when it is *economically* rational in terms of lower transaction costs. Yet this is precisely what is never knowable except *ex post*.[13]

The only possible reasoned justification for such theorizing would be if it were indeed the case, in Williamson's immortal phrase, that: 'In the beginning there were markets' (1985: 87). But even that, after Schmandt-Besserat, looks untrue. And worse, the historical evidence now points systematically in another direction, largely thanks to Chandler himself, to a supra-economic level of explanation for managerialism's genesis. If we do not presume a providential invisible hand, there are awkward questions to be answered. In particular, what made managerialism's pioneers so specially insightful? Especially since they had no special economic motive to capture greater productivity, lower costs and higher profits, being, as Chandler acknowledges (1977: 95), 'salaried employees with little or no financial interest in the companies they served'? And why, if economic demand was the spur, did this breakthrough happen in the economic backwater which, in the 1840s, was the USA, rather than, say, in Britain, which had been experiencing the Industrial Revolution for some 60 years?

Examining, accounting and the genesis of managerialism

These questions can now be given a reasoned answer, by taking up Chandler's insight, but eschewing the move back to the metaphysical vocabulary of economics: in other words, by using a Foucauldian theory of practices. The answer that can then be given may seem surprising, but is so only if one still presumes that 'the economic' is the boundary within which explanation must be contained. For, as my research with Richard Macve has detailed, the practices of administrative coordination are precisely those of writing, examining and grading, translated into the economic arena from other sites where 'disciplinarity', in a double sense, was already being exercised, socially and within selves. Such sites, as indicated above, were primarily educational, since it was in the world of elite education that the now-familiar practices of written, graded examination were first imposed upon us, and internalized by us, to produce both new disciplinary knowledges and new disciplinary power.

Historically, what we have now pointed out is that the new managerial practices have a precise genealogy, which stretches from the elite educational world of Europe into these US businesses, via the apparently unlikely conduit of the US Military Academy at West Point. For Chandler's 'pioneers' of modern business prove not to be businessmen at all, but West Point graduates. The detail is as follows. Founded in 1801, West Point was in 1817 handed over to a reformist Superintendent, Sylvanus Thayer, who introduced, from the French *École Polytechnique*, its then-unparalleled scientific/engineering curriculum, along with its rigorous pedagogic regime based on constant writing, grading and examining, and then added certain refinements. These doubly disciplinary practices were then internalized by the cadets at the Academy, who then, a generation later, being the most knowledgeable engineers of their day, found themselves in economic situations, where they then deployed the practices of writing, examining and grading, thus translating disciplinary modes of knowledge and power into the economic arena, and so initiating modern managerialism.

In other words, the transformation identified by Chandler was real enough, but the reasons for it (and the detail of its development) require reassessment. Chandler had discerned at the earliest stage of managerialism two separate if parallel developments. Single-unit management, in his words, 'had its genesis in the United States at the Springfield Armory' (1977: 75). Supposedly as a result of innovations such as detailed quality control and inventory accounting systems, Springfield, a government armoury, played a major role in the development of a low-cost high-productivity manufacturing system, the 'American System of Manufacture', the first system to succeed in achieving integrated mass production using interchangeable parts (1977: 72–5). Meanwhile multi-unit management was being pioneered on the US railroads. Here, first on the grandiosely named Western Railroad (which ran all the way west from Boston, Massachusetts to Albany, New York), a line-and-staff system of organization was introduced, following an accident in 1841. It was 'the first modern, carefully defined, internal organizational structure used by an American business enterprise' (1977: 97).

But we may now see Chandler's two developments as linked aspects of one transformation. First at Springfield Armory, our reappraisal of the evidence (Hoskin and Macve, 1994) indicates that the breakthrough to managerialism is due neither to the technological achievement of mass interchangeable-part manufacturing nor to the control of inventory; instead it was the result of the application of the practices of writing, grading and examining to institute a new form of human accounting. Just as grades had rendered West Point cadets 'educationally calculable selves', so they could be combined with cost data to render workers 'economically calculable selves'. This is what happened in 1832 (some 50 years before Taylor's time-and-motion studies), as a young army lieutenant named Daniel Tyler spent six months 'watch in hand' examining every aspect of production not just to establish averages of what was done, but to calculate norms of what could be done in every production activity (with standard times calculated down to tenths of a second, even though the stop-watch was not yet invented). Now, cost data, on objects and processes, had existed before (there was indeed a profusion of it at the Springfield Armory). But it had not been systematically combined, even at Springfield, with data on worker performance to produce standards, based on a cost/time calculus. This mathematization of time and action is what writing, grading and examining produced, thereby conferring on accounting a historically new significance (which it has retained to this day). Now, the workforce, seeing what was at stake, at first resisted Tyler's proposed new work-regime successfully; but when it was finally introduced in 1842, a new quality of economic gain was produced (for instance, in the barrel-welding department, within three years, productivity doubled while unit costs halved). This all took place, be it noted, in the absence of technological change, since interchangeable part manufacture was not adopted till the mid-1840s.

Similarly, on the railroads, we can now see that the new line-and-staff organizational structure on the Western Railroad pre-dates the 1841 accident, for it was introduced as soon as the Western began operations in 1839. Interestingly, though, the man credited with developing this new organizational system is another young Army officer: George W. Whistler, who had been seconded, because of his engineering skills, to survey the Railroad's path, and was then asked to stay on as its Chief Engineer. Whistler's structure was fully developed, right from the outset. He headed up a system with a central staff office plus three operating divisions; he personally had direct line responsibility for the Roads division, but also ran the Central Staff Office through which information flowed to and from the heads of the other two lines: Transportation and Machinery. Each of them in turn had three regional managers under them, who in turn had local managers below them. Where though did this come from?

If one looks more closely at the biographies of both Tyler and Whistler, it turns out that neither of them ever ran a business in their lives. However, both graduated from West Point in the Class of 1819, and so lived through the first phase of the disciplinary revolution engineered by Thayer. The details of his intensified disciplinary system are amazing, if only because they are so modern. For he added his own 'managerial' dimension, creating files for all aspects of behaviour and running the academy almost like a modern CEO, issuing his orders in writing and hardly ever being seen in person (and this in an institution of just 200 cadets). He also constructed a line-and-staff system, by dividing the Academy into two 'divisions', and creating in each a line management system (involving both teacher-officers and cadets), wherein daily, weekly and monthly written reports were required, all in writing. All material passed up and down relays of command, before being consolidated and passed to the central 'Staff Office', which consisted of Thayer, a personal clerk and two hand-picked cadets. As it happens, one of Thayer's first two cadet staff officers was George Whistler.

Hence the lines in the genealogy may be filled in. The time-and-motion study and the line-and-staff system lead back equally to Thayer's West Point system. Hence Chandler's two parallel forms of management should be read as two aspects of one disciplinary transformation, with administrative coordination embodying a new power of writing, examination and grading.

Conclusion: examining accounting and management

Theoretically, it is doubtless significant just to recognize that administrative coordination is more than economic, and more, even, than just a normalizing of performance and an imposition of constant panoptic surveillance, being a doubly disciplinary transformation, bringing powerful expert knowledge into the heart of 'the economic'. The knowledges now available are potentially infinite (i.e. we never reach a definitive list): to the mathematical, statistical, engineering, we now add the sociological, psychological, rhetorical, and so on. But the significant factor, in terms of a theory of practices, is that this is always a knowledge which writes, examines and grades, to extract from performance (human and machine) objective measures which can then become standards and targets for future performance: and which similarly tracks and accounts for past performance and transactions (financial and non-financial), in order to extrapolate trends and forecasts of profitability and market share. It is here that accounting proves so central. As the knowledge which not only renders the financial 'concrete, precise and measured', but also, in the guise of human accounting, coalesces the human into the financial, it has a special and central role. Hence the continued justification for the misquotation of Foucault.

At the same time, this is not a ringing endorsement for accounting, as technical key to managerial success. It is rather an acknowledgement that accounting exemplifies, in an extreme form, the paradox that infects all these disciplinary managerial knowledges – that of reading the future from the past. In other words, it is most accurate when most redundant, and most useless when most needed. But still it remains at the heart of managing, as the (to date) central set of numbers. There is, I suggest, a reasoned explanation even for this (though it is not, sadly, an economically rational one). All these knowledges have a certain degree of success, since individually and together they have contributed to re-writing the future so as to become more like the past. Accounting is here no exception. At the same time, its particular competitive advantage is that, in a world whose central truths are all expressed as a mix of financial and non-financial measures, it continues to have a certain centrality. That renders it centrally significant: at the same time, it has only a negative justification for its significance: it is, to date, the least bad alternative.

Perhaps one final theoretical observation should be added. I suggested at the outset that the misquotation of Foucault was more apt than the original. Though a light aside, it had a serious intent. For there must be a serious question (see note 4) as to whether the 'economic' does emerge out of governmentality, and behind that out of political arithmetic. The relation between the governmental and the managerial remains less clear-cut, not least as managerialism begins to displace the high-modernist governmental form, bureaucracy, across so much of the public sector in so many countries. The prior question, I suggest, is whether political arithmetic as such underpins modern governmentality, in the way that accounting underpins managing by the numbers. For, as we may now see, when accounting began to grade performance, to impose a principle of calculability, it did so both socially and within the self. Like the mark, it puts not just a number on what you do, but a value on who you are. So, endemically, managers, like students, now live by their results, grubbing for success points, as the affirmation of identity. But political arithmetic, as invented by William Petty in the 1600s, is, I suggest, less than this: it writes and counts, but only outwardly, to make evaluations of the *polis*. It is therefore not, in itself, a means of producing governmentality, both without and within. That is what happens, governmentally as economically, with the shift in pedagogic practice, and the doubly disciplinary transformation into modernity. It is arguably, therefore, the disciplinary descendants of Political Arithmetic, like Political Science, which signal the success of governmentality (Sylvan, 1991). Such disciplines now compete with accounting, because they are like accounting: forms of expert knowledge which examine the statistical regularities of our subjectivity as much as those of whole population sectors. They fight their own battles, with their warriors those of us who have successfully passed through the practices of writing, examining and grading, so to become the producers of a truth manufactured via those self-same practices.

Notes

I would like to thank Mahmoud Ezzamel and Richard Macve, both for the discussions that lie behind this chapter, and for the pleasure of the joint writing which lies behind much of what is said here.

1 In his own words, Foucault writes: 'Government is possible only when the strength of the state is known. . . . The state's capacity and the means to enlarge it must be known. The strength and capacity of other states, rivals of my own state, must also be known. . . . A certain specific knowledge is necessary: concrete, precise and measured knowledge as to the state's strength. The art of governing . . . is intimately bound up with the development of what was called, from this moment, political arithmetic' (Martin et al., 1988: 151).

2 Figures may lie, but he has certainly been one of the most-cited authors in journals such as *Accounting, Organizations and Society*, *Accounting, Auditing and Accountability Journal* and *Critical Perspectives on Accounting* in the past few years. In addition, as a measure of 'quality', he is the inspiration for perhaps 10 per cent of the articles included in a recent survey of 'classic' and 'near classic' accounting articles, based on citation count over the past three decades (Brown, 1996).

3 Indeed, accountants, or accounting academics at least, are themselves often the first to concede this intellectual priority. For instance, one best-selling accounting textbook tells us: 'Accounting is an applied subject. . . . Financial accounting and part of management accounting are related to *economics* . . . part of management accounting is related to *social psychology*' (Anthony and Reece, 1989: 523). Such a view has of course always been the unquestioning stock-in-trade of *economists* (see, most recently, Napier, 1996).

4 If arithmetic is understandable as a starting-point, why though political arithmetic? This is Foucault's suggestion, in another essay: i.e. that 'it was through the development of the science of government that the notion of economy came to be recentred on to that different plane of reality which we characterise today as the "economic"' (Foucault 1991: 101). Here we may applaud the general theoretical point, that practices made possible the new disciplinary discourses, such as economics and politics, without necessarily accepting that it was government (and so political arithmetic) which were the knowledges which constituted the modern economic plane. There are, we shall see, both historical and theoretical reasons for thinking otherwise.

5 Leading work which has begun to sensitize us to accounting's economic significance in this way would include (without being limited to) that of Hopwood, Roberts, and Miller and O'Leary, which has now shed new light on such issues as the archaeology of modern accounting systems, the constitution and dissemination of modern forms of accountability, and the production both of 'governable selves' and of the world-class manufacturing organizations which live and die by the application and variation of accounting technologies (e.g. Hopwood, 1987; Miller and O'Leary, 1987, 1993; Roberts, 1991; see also Hopwood and Miller, 1994; Munro and Mouritsen, 1996).

6 It is instructive to revisit the last full volume Foucault completed, *Le Souci de Soi* (1984b), and see just how far practices prove to be central to his concerns (not least because the focus on practices neatly avoids the reflexive problem of how a self may ever speak of 'the self' without being trapped before starting to speak). Chapter 2, 'The Culture of the Self', discusses how practices produce a self which then acts on its self, like a teacher on a recalcitrant pupil: adults have to turn themselves into 'over-age schoolboys', following formulas of good practice, undertaking exercise for 'care of the body, regimes of health, physical exercises but not to excess', and engaging in care of the soul through 'meditations, lectures, notes taken on books or extended conversations, which one will re-read subsequently, the recalling to mind of truths already known but which must be internalised still better' (1984b: 64–5). Out of such practices emerges a discourse, wherein a pedagogic voice speaks, as superior double, to that 'self' which will be presumed to lurk as coherent entity behind the incompetent, putatively prior voice thus addressed.

7 See Hoskin (1994), especially pp. 70–9, for a discussion of Foucault's reasoned rejection of the self-defeating beliefs that either the social or the psychological is prior, approaches which always leave the idea of the 'sovereign rational subject' in place, since they apply to everyone except, of course, the author articulating them. The recognition of Foucault as a 'theorist of practices', particularly in his last works on the 'care of the self', is now being put to use in various ways, e.g. in relation to feminism (McNay, 1994).

8 (© M. Foucault) For those who insist on their author-functions being unitary, there are, thankfully, similar passages at other strategic points. So, in the introduction to *L'Usage des Plaisirs* (1984a: 19), Foucault refers to his new project as a cross-breeding of 'an archaeology of the problematics of, and a genealogy of the practices of, the self'. Similarly, in the essay 'What is englightenment?' he proposes – having advanced the thesis that 'Modern man . . . is the man who tries to invent himself' (1987: 42) – that the way to understand this self-invention is through 'the at once archaeological and genealogical study of practices' (1987: 50).

9 For if there is no *polis* before token-accounting, it is also etymologically the case that the 'eco-nomic' is absent. Agriculture displaces the hunter-gathering world of what Sahlins (1974) called 'stone-age economics', but which is literally the 'aneconomic' world. For agriculture displaces the principle of mobility with that of dwelling in one place, in the *oikos* or home, which is successfully achieved only through the careful stewardship and allocation (*nomos*) of goods and produce. Hence the 'economic' is nameable only after and through the practice of token-accounting.

10 His analysis of 'the examination' was particularly prone to this, from *Discipline and Punish* to the last works on the care of the self. In the latter (Foucault, 1984b: 77–9), he names examination of conscience as the climactic caring technology in ancient Rome, as described by Seneca; Foucault uses variations on the French term *examen* some 10 times in three pages, but Seneca never uses such a term once (although he does refer to 'accounting' for what one has done). In the former, as noted above, he identifies formal examining as the new technology which combines hierarchical surveillance and normalizing judgement, and so produces humans as subjects within a new field of disciplinary knowledge and disciplinary power. However, in the invention of double-entry book-keeping, formal examination as such is an earlier invention, being the practice (as *oral* examination) which, from before AD 1200, enabled expert teachers to begin evaluating students for their 'degrees' of excellence, and in the process to invent both formal qualification and the university (Hoskin and Macve, 1994).

11 It is the micro-techniques of administrative coordination, he argues, which enable the key superior economic outcomes, for example by routinizing transactions between units, so lowering costs: linking the administration of production, upstream and downstream, to buying and distribution; and coordinating the flow of goods through internalized enterprise units (Chandler, 1977, Introduction). The economic payoffs came largely through increased productivity and reduced costs, plus more predictable cash flows and control over systems of payment collection.

12 The Johnson and Kaplan argument was a *cause célèbre*, both because it broke with the ahistorical and technicist view of accounting so widely held in the USA, and then suggested

relevance could be regained by wresting the numbers away from the tyranny of short-term financial reporting and by more enlightened teaching of accounting as more than disembodied technique. The issue, however, is whether there ever was, in the presumed technicist sense, a 'relevance' to be lost (Ezzamel et al. 1990). Their history, of course, fails to recognize the possibility that the numbers were always 'disciplinary', in their genesis and effects; but it also passes over the technical limitation of all accounting data, its logical inability, being historical data, to deliver information relevant to future decision-making (see note 13).

13 There are certain non-trivial accounting points here: profit calculation, even more so then, frequently failed to track economic gains and losses effectively; and even today, since overhead costs have to be allocated on an arbitrary basis, the most *meticulously* calculated cost data remain a notoriously hazardous guide to economic decision-making. Williamson has been critiqued (e.g. Kay, 1992), for conceptual confusion between physical transactions and economic contractual ones, and seeing all the former, many of which will take place by fiat, not contract, as the latter. Williamson's response is breathtaking, claiming that 'any problem that arises as, *or can be reformulated as*, a contracting problem, can usefully be examined in Transaction Cost Economising terms'. Consequently, 'the fact that fiat is now used to avoid or settle disputes does not eliminate a contractual relation but *merely transforms* it.' (1992: 336; my emphases)

References

Anthony, R. and Reece, J. (1989) *Accounting: Text and Cases* (8th edn). Homewood, IL: Irwin.

Borges, J. (1981) 'Pierre Menard: author of the Quixote' in E. Monegal and A. Reid (eds), *Borges: A Reader*. New York: Dutton. pp. 96–103.

Brown, L. (1996) 'Influential accounting articles, individuals, PhD granting institutions and faculties: a citational analysis', *Accounting, Organizations and Society*, 21 (7/8): 723–54.

Chandler, A. (1977) *The Visible Hand: The Managerial Revolution in American Business*. Cambridge, MA: Harvard University Press.

Ezzamel, M., Hoskin, K. and Macve, R. (1990) 'Managing it all by numbers: a review of Johnson and Kaplan's *Relevance Lost*', *Accounting and Business Research*, 20 (78): 153–66.

Foucault, M. (1975) *Discipline and Punish*. Allen Lane: London.

Foucault, M. (1984a) *Histoire de la sexualité, Volume 2: L'Usage des plaisirs*. Paris: Gallimard.

Foucault, M. (1984b) *Histoire de la sexualité, Volume 3: Le souci de soi*. Paris: Gallimard.

Foucault, M. (1987) 'What is enlightenment?', in P. Rabinow (ed.), *The Foucault Reader*. London: Penguin Books. pp. 32–50.

Foucault, M. (1991) 'Governmentality', in G. Burchell, C. Gordon and P. Miller (eds), *The Foucault Effect: Studies in Governmentality*. London: Harvester. pp. 87–104.

Gutting, G. (1994) *The Cambridge Companion to Foucault*. Cambridge: Cambridge University Press.

Hopwood, A. (1987) 'The archaeology of accounting systems', *Accounting, Organizations and Society*, 12 (3): 207–34.

Hopwood, A. and Miller, P. (1994) *Accounting as Social and Institutional Practice*. Cambridge: Cambridge University Press.

Hoskin, K. (1990) 'Foucault under examination: the crypto-educationalist unmasked', in S. Ball (ed.), *Foucault and Education*. London: Routledge. pp. 29–53.

Hoskin, K. (1993) 'Education and the genesis of disciplinarity: the unexpected reversal', in E. Messer-Davidow, D. Shumway and D. Sylvan (eds), *Knowledges: Historical and Critical Studies in Disciplinarity*. Charlottesville, VA: University of Virginia Press. pp. 271–304.

Hoskin, K. (1994) 'Boxing clever: for, against and beyond Foucault in the battle for accounting theory', *Critical Perspectives on Accounting*, 5: 57–85.

Hoskin, K.W. and Macve, R.H. (1988) 'The genesis of accountability: the West Point connections', *Accounting, Organizations and Society*, 13 (1): 37–73.

Hoskin, K. and Macve, R. (1994) 'Writing, examining, disciplining: the genesis of accounting's modern power', in A. Hopwood and P. Miller (eds), *Accounting as Social and Institutional Practice*. Cambridge: Cambridge University Press. pp. 67–97.

Hutton, W. (1995) *The State We're In*. London: Jonathan Cape.

Kay, N. (1992) 'Markets, false hierarchies, and the end of the modern corporation', *Journal of Economic Behaviour and Organization*, 17: 315–32.

Kelly, M. (1995) *Critique and Power: Recasting the Foucault/Habermas Debate*. Cambridge, MA: MIT Press.

Klamer, A. and McCloskey, D. (1992) 'Accounting as the master metaphor of economics', *European Accounting Review*, 1 (1): 145–60.

Martin, L., Gutman, H. and Hutton, P. (eds) (1988) *Technologies of the Self: A Seminar with Michel Foucault*. London: Tavistock.

McNay, L. (1994) *Foucault: A Critical Introduction*. London: Polity.

Miller, P. and O'Leary, T. (1987) 'Accounting and the construction of the governable person', *Accounting, Organizations and Society*, 12 (3): 235–65.

Miller, P. and O'Leary, T. (1993) 'Accounting expertise and the politics of the product: economic citizenship and modes of corporate governance', *Accounting, Organizations and Society*, 18 (2/3): 187–206.

Munro, R. and Mouritsen, J. (1996) *Accountability: Power, Ethos and the Technologies of Managing*. London: International Thomson Business Press.

Napier, C. (1996) 'Academic disdain? Economists and accounting in Britain, 1850–1950', *Accounting, Business and Financial History*, 6 (3): 427–50.

Ong, W. (1982) *Orality and Literacy*. London: Methuen.

Ormerod, P. (1994) *The Death of Economics*. London: Faber and Faber.

Roberts, J. (1991) 'The possibilities of accountability', *Accounting, Organizations and Society*, 16 (4): 355–68.

Sahlins, M. (1974) *Stone Age Economics*. Chicago: University of Chicago Press.

Schmandt-Besserat, D. (1992) *Before Writing, Volume I: From Counting to Cuneiform*. Austin TX: University of Texas Press.

Sylvan, D. (1991) 'The qualitative–quantitative distinction in political science', *Poetics Today*, 12 (2): 267–86.

Williamson, O. (1980) 'Emergence of the visible hand: implications for industrial organization', in A. Chandler and H. Daems (eds), *Managerial Hierarchies: Comparative Perspectives on the Rise of the Modern Business Enterprise*. Cambridge, MA: Harvard University Press. pp. 180–202.

Williamson, O. (1985) *The Economic Institutions of Capitalism: Firms, Markets, Relational Contracting*. London: Free Press.

Williamson, O. (1992) 'Markets, hierarchies and the modern corporation: an unfolding perspective', *Journal of Economic Behaviour and Organization*, 17: 335–52.

7

The 'Velvety Grip': Managing Managers in the Modern Corporation

Alan McKinlay and Ken Starkey

This paper applies the work of Michel Foucault to organizational analysis and accounting theory. Foucault's work provides an important alternative to modernist conceptions of organizations as expressions of planned, rational thought and technically calculative action. In this sense, 'modernist' includes the influential labour process perspective which, despite its opposition to Taylorism, shares certain key assumptions with orthodox 'management science'. Both perspectives assume that managers gradually monopolize all relevant knowledge within the organization; that a sharp divide between 'thinking' and 'doing' is an essential prerequisite of competitiveness and profitability; and, finally, that organizational structure unproblematically follows corporate strategy. Instead Foucault construes organizations and the 'knowledge' they utilize as grounded in power relations. In particular, he offers an image of organizations as disciplinary modes of domination. We explore the Foucauldian perspective in an analysis of the Ford Motor Company since the Second World War. We emphasize that the 'carceral gaze' of the modern corporation encompassed not just the assembly line but also all areas of managerial work. We then turn our attention to Ford's attempt to break with the tight financial control system which was the key disciplinary device inside the post-1945 corporation. The company's obsession with control threatened to destroy its competitiveness and led to experimentation with new ways of organizing and controlling managerial work. Profit, not control, remains, after all, the overriding purpose of the capitalist enterprise.

Constructing manageable organizations

Foucault's work has received increasing attention in attempts to theorize accounting and, in particular, to open its study to theoretical and historical debates in the social sciences (Miller and O'Leary, 1987). His work has influenced critical accounting theory and history with its aim of subverting 'the belief that accounting develops functionally as a passive tool of economic efficiency'. According to critical theory the history of accounting needs to be interpreted as a complex web of economic and political occurrences rather than a progressive technical rationality (Arrington and Francis, 1989: 2).

The Panopticon provides a powerful image of management control in general and of accounting controls – fundamental to the development of large corporations (Chandler and Daems, 1979) – in particular. A central problem from the Foucauldian perspective is 'an unravelling of the relations of power within which accounting is embedded, and which in turn it has helped to fabricate' (Miller et al., 1991: 401). Morgan (1988) analyses the manner in which accountants construct reality, using a variety of metaphors and images (Boland, 1989). Some of the most important metaphors and images have a distinctly Foucauldian ring – accounting as information control, as politics, as mythology, as disciplined control. Some would add domination and exploitation to this list (Armstrong, 1985). Foucault consistently distanced himself from any social theory which claimed universality. Respectful of Marx, he was, however, dismissive of attempts to understand every institution – clinic, prison, asylum, factory – as expressions of a singular class project (Poster, 1984: 78). Crucially, whereas, in Marxist analysis, power and control are negative and exploitative, for Foucault the refinement of technologies of power is a positive and creative process. There is no universal fault-line running through society which defines power and powerlessness. Indeed, it is the variety of forms of power which provides established social formations with such resilience.

Hopwood (1987) offers an account of accounting which draws together many of these themes. He critiques the notion of accounting change as a process of the application of objectively defined technical expertise towards ever more predictable outcomes. He argues for an alternative view of accounting in action, an 'archaeology' of accounting, that reveals the role served by accounting discourse in the construction of organizational and social order.

> Accounting, when seen in such terms, is not a passive instrument of technical administration, a neutral means for merely revealing the pregiven aspects of organisational functioning. Instead its origins are seen to reside in the exercising of social power both within and between organisations. (Hopwood, 1987: 213)

Such an approach demonstrates accounting's pivotal role in the creation and maintenance of manageable organizational domains, the 'genesis of accountability' (Hoskin and Macve, 1988) in those organizations in which the rules of the bureaucratic game (Crozier, 1964) are defined and from which they are diffused. This is a theme further developed by Miller and O'Leary (1987: 235) who analyse accounting practices' contribution (for example, standard costing and budgeting) to 'the construction of the individual person as a more manageable and efficient entity'.

Accounting is construed in our analysis in a generic sense as 'that broader range of subjects which include its [accounting's] technologies as core elements' (Armstrong, 1985: 134). The historical moment starts in the period immediately after the Second World War. This was a pivotal moment in one company's history but also in the history of corporate control, the rise to power of finance and accounting and the rise to dominance of a financial concept of control (Fligstein, 1990). We emphasize the use of finance and accounting 'discourse' and techniques as 'weapons' and symbols in a political arena, a struggle for legitimacy and power which led to the definition of a particular form of organizational reality. This reminds us of the Foucauldian view that 'truth' and 'knowledge' are socially constructed products of interests and power relations (Hines, 1988) rather than 'the passive mirror of a technical reality' (Covaleski and Dirsmith, 1988: 1).

The corporate Panopticon

> Sloan's administrative ideology and 'scientific' methodology . . . were applicable at the top level, and it is in no way disparaging to Taylor to say that Sloan, rather than Taylor, was a pioneer of scientific management. (Dale, 1956: 52)

Foucault's work suggests that we question received practice and the thinking upon which it is based. We do this by examining its historical emergence. Such an examination leads us to question dominant paradigms of thought and practice. Foucault's driving hypothesis is that such an examination will locate the roots of 'knowledge' in evolving relations of power. It is to the strategies of power and their association with the finance function in one of the world's largest and historically most successful companies that we now turn in the empirical part of this chapter. Here we examine the role of the accounting and finance function (hereafter Finance) in the Ford Motor Company at a particular historical moment and the way in which Finance's definition of management control created a kind of discipline that came to define Ford's key management tasks in terms of mechanisms of financial control, 'instruments that render visible, record, differentiate and compare' (Foucault, 1977: 208).

The Ford Motor Company was once synonymous with the creation of a particular management style, Fordism, based on bureaucratic organization, hierarchical decision-making with strict functional specialization and tightly defined job design (scientific management) and specialized machinery to mass produce a standard product for mass markets. Historically, Alfred Sloan's work at General Motors provided the 'necessary complement' to Henry Ford's development of the assembly line (Womack et al., 1991: 39–41). Managerial professionalism, however, came to Ford late and only after the death of its founder. Henry Ford distrusted everyone but himself so he was unwilling to share the reins of power. Ironically, in the company which pioneered the moving assembly line and the rationalization of product design and work organization, Henry Ford's personal control amounted to a system of monarchic power.

Alfred Sloan's General Motors became the archetypal form of American big business. Refined over 20 years, Sloan first developed the multi-divisional corporate structure which clearly separated strategic and operational management in 1920. Innocuously entitled 'The Organization Study', Sloan's 1920 28-page memorandum was intended to stave off the imminent financial collapse of General Motors' independent and uncontrolled businesses (Chandler, 1962: 133–42). In the longer term, Sloan's administrative design decisively shaped the structure and management processes of the American corporation for over 50 years. Drawing on internal accounting procedures pioneered by Du Pont to relieve executives from information overload, Sloan had the dual purpose of integrating General Motors and establishing centralized administrative surveillance (Yates, 1989: 266). Between 1900 and 1920 Du Pont refined its executives' oversight function to exclude all operational information and judgements; only divisional financial data was monitored. To allow comparability between divisions and over time, Du Pont divisions reported their financial performance using a standard formula: Return on Investment (ROI). ROI was the statistical vehicle for Sloan's progressive centralization of vital information and control of managerial decision making. By combining ROI as the single commensurable measure of divisional effectiveness with the multidivisional structure, Sloan pioneered the archetypal form of power/knowledge within the modern corporation. The simplified budgetary process was central to the corporate Panopticon, allowing a penetrating one-way gaze while eroding any vestige of divisional privacy:

> the simple 'threat of review' kept the divisional decision makers adhering to corporate directives. GM's designers further enhanced the headquarters' observational power by having divisional financial staffs report to the corporate officers rather than to the division managers. The divisional financial officers thus acted as 'reliable local data sources' for the central office. Sloan also used his powerful Advisory Staff to break down 'institutions of privacy' protecting divisional autonomy, and he declared that nonfinancial functions should be *audited* just as financial results. To conserve his own audit capacity, Sloan concentrated on the auto divisions, which in turn monitored the parts divisions' price and quality performances. (Kuhn, 1986: 25–6; original emphasis)

Continuous and intensive administrative scrutiny of managerial decision making was Sloan's prime concern. Sloan explained the panoptic logic behind his new organizational design: 'Essentially it was a matter of making things visible' (Sloan, 1963: 142).

Built on an elaborate hierarchy of dedicated expert committees continuously directing and monitoring strategy formation and operational efficiency, GM defined, in Peter Drucker's classic account, the very 'concept of the corporation' (Drucker, 1946: 267). Sloan's vision of the disciplined corporation was the very antithesis of Henry Ford's autocratic management and his disdain for expertise. As one of Ford's most trusted lieutenants, Charles Sorensen, put it, 'Ford was not an expert, and he didn't rely upon experts whether they were scientists, engineers, railroad men, economists, educationalists, business executives, or bankers' (Sorensen, 1957: 39). Sloan, by contrast, was convinced of

> the necessity of the scientific approach, the elimination of operation by hunches; this affects men, tools and methods. . . . Scientific management means a constant search for the facts, the true actualities, and their intelligent, unprejudiced analysis. Thus, and in no other way, policies and their administration are

determined. I keep saying to General Motors organization that we are prepared to spend any proper amount of money to get the facts. (Sloan 1970: 140)

It was Henry Ford II who was left to bring order to the chaos his grandfather left in 1945, the worst-run large company in America, rife with waste. To this end he recruited to Ford the 'Whiz Kids' – the brightest graduates of the best business schools, whose skills had been honed in the US Air Force during the Second World War – chief among whom was Robert McNamara. Originally known as the 'Quiz Kids' then Whiz Kids, the group constituted corporate Jesuits. The ascetic McNamara was much feared but little understood by Ford managers outside his immediate group. Even the epithets attached to this group resonate with the transition in Ford from one mode of power to another – from a sovereign to an architectonic regime, from their initial interventions as quizzical powerless newcomers, a period in which they were aliens within the host organization, to their ultimate role as the overseers of the corporate Panopticon. Contemporary definitions of corporate America in the first decade of peace consistently draw upon conflicting images of the organization as technocracy *and* management as a secular priesthood. This imagery depicts the corporation as an '"organisation cathedral", complete with an organisation bible, commandments, rites, liturgy, inquisitions, crusades, holy wars, martyrs, and saints' (Dale, 1956: 33). This language of rival faiths reflects the penetration of planning and control into ever-lower levels of management:

> To some line chiefs, change based on staff ideas will be disastrous for they represent instability, impracticality, and unpredictability. They are 'snoopervisors' who may uncover workable but forbidden practices and label them 'inefficient' and 'unscientific' in terms of their holy procedures. (Dalton, 1959: 100)

In Foucauldian terms, Henry Ford exercised an essentially pre-modern form of power, a visible sovereign power imposed from above rather than invisibly suffused throughout the routine of the organization (Clegg, 1989: 155). Such sovereign power is invested in the body of the owner and is only apparent during moments when it is exercised. The distant, arbitrary and episodic nature of sovereign power is the antithesis of the constant, routinized, anonymous power inscribed in the very architecture of the modern organization. Power/powerlessness is the unspoken meaning of every task. Extraordinary displays of power, whether they be acts of magnificent beneficence or cruel punishment, are unnecessary in the corporate Panopticon. Henry Ford, observed Drucker (1955: 111–12), attempted 'to run the billion dollar business without managers'. The task of Henry Ford II, who became Chairman in 1945, was not so much to modernize Ford's management structure as to transform the nature of power in the organization, to dismantle the sovereign power regime maintained by the company's founder.

> The concept of the executive as a personal delegate of the owner has been replaced by the concept of the manager whose authority is grounded in the objective responsibility of the job. Arbitrary orders have been replaced by

performance standards based on objectives and measurement. (Drucker, 1955: 114–15)

McNamara joined Ford in 1946. He became Director of the Financial Analysis Department then President, leaving in 1961 to become Secretary of State for Defense. Ford's official historians of this period describe conditions in the company at the time of his arrival:

> They [the Whiz Kids] were appalled by the conditions they found. The company had no proper records, no certified balance sheet, and 'a fantastic cost system.' The old merchandising type of accounting was used: 'You took the purchases, took the sales, and the difference between the two was the profit.' [One] found a large fund in the bank drawing no interest whatever. 'The bankers must have loved us,' he remarked. [Another declared]: 'The whole system was incredible. I thought I'd never tell anyone but the Lord himself, because nobody would believe it.' In milder phraseology, former and present finance officials . . . agreed that a complete renovation was essential. 'I wouldn't attempt to defend our old system . . . It was really ridiculously crude.' The job in this area was a modern version of the labors of Hercules. (Nevins and Hill, 1962: 327)

Such was the mesmeric hold of Sloan's creation on Henry Ford II's imagination that he kept a GM organizational chart on his office wall for over forty years (Hayes, 1990). As Drucker put it, GM had perfected 'not a mere technique of management' but nothing less than 'a universally valid concept of social order' (Drucker, 1946: 46–7).

McNamara was to be the Jeremy Bentham of the Ford Motor Company, the architect of the corporate Panopticon. 'My real contribution to Ford', McNamara reflected, 'was to turn a family company into an omniscient operating system . . . a modern American corporation'. If the Taylorized assembly line pursued the domination of workers' bodies, then McNamara shifted the 'carceral gaze' of the corporation to the minds of its managers. Drucker (1955: 109) summed up the agenda of the time: 'The fundamental problems of order, structure, motivation and leadership in the business enterprise have to be solved in the managing of managers. Managers are the basic resource of its enterprise and its scarcest.'

McNamara's contribution to Ford was to bring discipline to the accounting system. What he and his group of Whiz Kids introduced into Ford was a management discipline based upon the power of numbers, a discipline the lack of which, under its founder, had brought the company close to disaster. Under McNamara, for the first time for more than twenty-five years, the company always knew how much it was spending and how much it was making, and it could project both costs and earnings in a consistent manner (Halberstam, 1987: 210). Profit was no longer a fortuitous residue but the outcome of a rational, predictable and, above all, disciplined process. The beancounters brought the promise of 'rational' decision making based on notions of efficiency and bureaucracy, the power of facts and numbers to set against the intuition of the product men who were arguing taste and instinct, uncertainty and risk, against the Finance people's certitude.

Just as the organizing principle of Bentham's Panopticon was continuous, impersonal and ubiquitous surveillance, so McNamara disseminated the quantitative logic of management accounting throughout Ford. Ford progressively extended the scope and ambition of financial control. Under the original Sloan regime, divisional managers were accountable on a monthly basis, a regime in which corporate executives exercised negative, reactive sanctions (Miller, 1992: 86). From a time horizon of just four months in 1946, by the mid-1950s Ford aspired to forecast financial performance for up to 10 years ahead (Secrest, 1966: 4). For the mid-century corporate manager, the intensification of the administrative gaze engendered a psychology of conformity. The 'velvety grip' on the *Organization Man*, wrote William Whyte in 1957, was such that 'he must not only accept control, he must accept it as if he liked it' (Whyte, 1957: 151). The higher the office, the greater the individual's visibility and the greater the pressure for conformity, an expectation evident even in the executive's posture and bearing:

> for now they must conform *downward*, just as much as upward. Less than before can they afford the luxury of the inadvertent frown, for their position now means that it will be transmitted all down the line, and eventually come back and smite them. . . . More and more, the executive must act according to the role that he is cast for – the calm eye that never strays from the other's gaze, the easy, controlled laughter, the whole demeanour that tells onlookers that here certainly is a man without neurosis and inner rumblings. (Whyte, 1957: 155–6; emphasis added)

The coming of McNamara to Ford, according to his protégé Lee Iacocca, was one of the best things that ever happened to the company. Iacocca added that McNamara's departure was also one of the best things that ever happened. The beancounters knew first and foremost how to minimize costs and maximize profits. The one thing that McNamara did not understand was cars. Ironically, it was the emphasis on numbers, the 'bottom line', and maintaining the rigid management control system that brought the company to the brink of disaster in the late 1970s.

The beancounters' legacy was a company dominated by Finance. Its power is captured in the following quotation.

> One of the many stringent tests which all Ford cars have to pass is to sustain a crash at 30 mph into a concrete barrier with less than five inches of steering column penetration. This means that the steering column must not move more than five inches towards a driver. In management terms in Ford, the nearest thing to that concrete barrier is probably the finance staff – and many projects are fated to crumple entirely on impact. (Hackett, 1976: 9.1)

Before 1945 Manufacturing had been all-powerful. Gradually under the beancounters power moved from the factories to Detroit headquarters. The product engineers were also brought to heel. Traditional product development in Ford is described by Don Frey (1991), who was vice president of product development at Ford in the 1960s. Frey is highly critical of what was, in his time at Ford, the 'normal' approach to product development. The process was controlled by a centralized industrial research organization, typically far-removed from both operations and markets. 'Bean counter designs' dominated. Quality and innovation suffered in the trade-off with cost. Frey (1991: 48) illustrates this point in a description of a new car development:

The quality problems were overwhelming. Someone had to 'dry the car up' – which meant stop it from leaking oil all over the place. I was that someone.

We attacked the power steering pump, which one of the old hands said was 'a piece of junk.' When I asked how it got that way, he said the 'bean counters' had taken a dime of cost out of assembly each year. I said 'fix it' – and we did. I wondered (in my naiveté) how financial planners could have anything to say about the matter in the first place. A bean counter's idea of cost control, I surmised, was to take an inch off the tail pipe every year. (Frey, 1991: 48)

The overriding product planning philosophy of the traditional approach is encapsulated in a quote attributed to a new product planning chief: 'we're the champions in popular cars. . . . Value for money. The maximum of amenities at the keenest possible price. That's our credo' (Seidler, 1976: 19). The key strategic focus was cost control. This required 'total discipline'.

Post-1945 product development was structured in the typical Ford top-down manner. Development was a sequential activity composed of distinct stages allocated to different functional groups. Supervising each of the stages were the architects of the overall discipline of the process, the cost analysis experts, whose task was to judge both the quality of a component, the most efficient way of producing it and what it would cost. They negotiated the cost–quality trade-off, usually, critics of the system argued, in favour of cost. One of their key roles was competitive benchmarking. They did this by stripping down the cars produced by Ford's competitors and estimating to the last quarter of a cent the cost of component parts. They then used these figures as the benchmark for setting the targets for Ford's own components. These were the 'high priests' of the disciplined approach:

[They] knew all the rules by heart and all the parameters in the tablets of the law: the quality standards, the rigorous criteria for durability, the targets for weight and cost. They were the ones to choose between the various components brought in for their appraisal; condemning this one because it weighed too much, awarding that one the prize for durability, arriving finally at an order of merit for all the comparable components under two headings, weight and cost. These, after all, were the great enemies, the two culprits on which they had to pass judgment: excessive weight and abnormal cost. (Seidler, 1976: 64–6)

Quantification ruled. Out of such analysis came the Red Books, volumes specifying objectives for each component of the car in terms of cost and weight and the investment needed to achieve them. The Red Books provided the base-line for forecasting variable costs and programme investment. In this process financial imperatives dominated – reducing the total cost of the investment while increasing the return on capital employed. The Finance function had one clear mission – to support management decision making with the objective of maximizing profit at least cost. Its influence was omnipresent and a constant source of tension between functional areas. New ideas were treated with 'a scepticism elevated into a system, a Cartesian philosophy anglo-saxon style' (Seidler, 1976: 23) and seldom survived the piercing analysis of the financial equivalent of the test crash at 30 mph. The 'normal' outcome was that innovation crumpled on impact.

A crucial emphasis in the system was a concern with discipline and punishment. The system developed a design and release manual which included every engineer involved in the process: individuals were allocated to specific components rather than integral sub-assemblies or complete designs.

> You knew you would only survive if you made your numbers, if you were the best: you were always looking over your shoulder.
>
> Ignorance, uncertainty and error were all taboo for the Ford manager: 'the three toughest words in Ford were – "I don't know"'.
>
> That's why you had such stiff quality control, because it was the policeman catching the thieves. Production was known as the thieves, and they'd try to push through the numbers at any cost, to beat the quality control. It was pretty funny the strokes people used to pull to get the numbers. (Starkey and McKinlay, 1993: 87)

Quality control was synonymous with search and punish in a 'rational' system where the outcome of behaviour was made increasingly visible and which increasingly and inevitably was losing touch with the people it thought it was serving.

After Japan

Analytical rigour was the great strength of the system established by McNamara after 1945. In the words of one vice-president:

> I grew up in Finance: joined it in 1962 and I helped develop it, to perfect it, to defend it. And I agree that Finance have strong power and influence within Ford Motor Company, but financial control is important. . . . The 'System' has forced me to think rigidly about alternatives, it's forced me to answer all kinds of stupid questions, and it's taken far longer to get things done. That's the negative; the positives are that people don't do things off the cuff. There's no back of the envelope calculations in Ford Motor Company. It does force you to think through alternatives; it does force you to be logical. In meetings I'd say, 'is that a fact or an opinion?' Ford Motor Company is an arena in which there are very few times that you express an opinion as a fact without the system itself correcting you. And that's a good self-discipline. (Starkey and McKinlay, 1993: 98–9)

The negative aspect of the system was that too many decisions were taken on the grounds of price alone. Financial controllers made financial projections but had no feel for the product and no idea about how to make the company grow through building market share by introducing exciting new product. Frey describes what he had to learn in pursuit of good products:

> First was to 'feel' my way through products, or rely on the intuitions that came from working from the ground up, not from the market data down. I had to learn the difference between the uncertain costs of experimentation and the certain disaster of standing pat. I had to learn to break down barriers in our corporate environment so that R&D people would explore customer needs, designers would learn to count on manufacturing, financial people would not kill projects just when they were about to pay off. (Frey, 1991: 46–52)

It was the advent of Japanese competition that finally revealed the 'irrationality' of the old system and its damaging effects, particularly on product development. The average Japanese firm has almost double the product development productivity of the average Western firm and can develop similar products on average a year faster. In an increasingly dynamic global market, speed of model-change has emerged as a significant competitive advantage. Japanese firms introduce far more new products, maintain a much shorter model life and expand their product lines more rapidly than Western firms, averaging less than five years between model changes, compared with American firms which average eight and European firms more than a decade (Womack et al., 1991; Clark and Fujimoto, 1991).

These products are also generally of high quality, and the Japanese firms use resources 'saved' in product development to invest in new technologies. Western companies, with their inefficient product-development processes, have found that they do not have the money or spare engineering capacity to expand their product range and renew their products as frequently.

The growing awareness of Japan's competitive advantage initiated a major rethinking of Ford's management system and culture. No group of Ford managers returned from a series of study trips to Japan in the early 1980s more chastened than those from Finance. Ford's financial controllers concluded that, in comparison with their own organization, the Japanese control process is simple; that control is shared throughout functional areas rather than monopolized by Finance; and that the entire Japanese enterprise is organized for cost reduction (Strebel, 1987: 120–8). It was not simply the organization of the Finance function that differed between Japanese and Western companies. Rather, the dispersed nature of financial control in Japanese companies represented a qualitatively different balance between trust and control – supported by a different organizational culture – than in the concentrated functional specialisms in Ford.

The target set for Ford of Europe in a series of changes introduced in 1980 that became known as the 'After Japan' (AJ) initiative was to reduce its Finance headcount by 30 per cent within three years. As Bud Marx, then Ford of Europe's Finance Vice-President, acknowledged, not only did this target mean stripping out layer upon layer of procedural controls it also entailed a radical change in the nature of Finance's role within the organization. This involved a relaxing of the scope of financial control but an intensification of internal audits (Strebel, 1987: 120). Cost control mechanisms were dramatically reduced. For instance, checking frequencies were reduced by up to 60 per cent, monthly reports by 25 per cent, and in major investment and product programmes only indicative rather than comprehensive costs were considered necessary at the initial strategy and concept stages.

> AJ was a significant event. AJ meant a major upheaval, a complete reconstruction of the Finance community. Prior to AJ we had armies of people checking what other people had done. . . . It was a nonsense system, a nonsense process. We now believe our management are responsible, why employ armies of people at all levels simply to check and recheck what responsible people have done? AJ finally

recognized that. Large chunks of the finance community disappeared overnight. . . . Along with that was hacked away a lot of administrative overheads we had accumulated in the numbers of forms which detailed every step for even the smallest decision or transaction. (Starkey and McKinlay, 1993: 91–2)

Within Finance the headcount reductions were uneven, varying between the 30 to 40 per cent achieved in Purchasing Cost Analysis and Financial Analysis and the nine per cent reported by Systems Group. The most significant reductions, in other words, were among 'checkers checking checkers'.

One of the clearest examples of the low trust between Finance and the rest of the organization and of the time-consuming bureaucratic controls eliminated by AJ was the monthly reports compiled by section managers which costed every member of staff's activity to the nearest half hour against an individual task. In turn, these reports were cross-checked and managers asked to account for any discrepancies between projections and actual time budgets. Now the cost of control was seen as an extravagance the company could no longer afford and as incompatible with good management practice.

Before AJ the manager had to be a good administrator of pseudo information flows. There were so many rules and regulations that you spent half your time administering routines rather than managing. Ford managers are now much less system administrators than businessmen of some kind. Managers in all functions and at all levels are expected to have a much wider appreciation of the business and its inter-dependent nature. The ideal Ford manager is more dynamic, reacting to change, to problem-solving, rather than grinding the Ford system, facilitating other people to do their job better rather than operating the routine of the system. (Starkey and McKinlay, 1993: 94)

Post-AJ the nature of quantitative information has been qualitatively changed. Before AJ all plant-level statistics were transformed from useful information about, for example, headcount and absenteeism to the dollar values necessary for Finance's centralizing and highly esoteric purposes. Since the early 1980s this logic has been reversed. Operational utility is the prime objective of plant-level statistics. Using physical values to identify scrap levels at different locations in the plant is part of the wider philosophy of empowering operational managers 'rather than channelling all contentious decisions upwards'. As a result of the process of change set in motion by AJ, financial analysts retained control over budgets and yields but devolved authority for approving investment up to $100,000.

This delegation of investment decisions was accompanied by a shift away from Ford's inherited faith in the absolutes of rational planning and an acceptance that responding quickly to increasingly uncertain markets necessarily involves intuition and risk. 'As a consequence of PM', a manufacturing plant manager suggested, 'decision-making in Ford has become more relative whereas before it was black and white. As managers we now accept that there are grey areas, that there are differing interpretations . . . and no single "correct" answer'.

Conclusion

After Japan was a watershed in Ford's conception of work organization and its approach to routine management and financial control. It signalled the need to radically alter the company's culture. AJ's cost comparisons challenged not just Ford's manufacturing efficiency. It also served notice that the bureaucratic control mechanisms of mass production were a dead-weight in terms of cost and time. The use of 'hot paper', the omnipresent evidence of the visible hand of management, and the layer upon layer of 'checkers checking checkers' were finally identified as a brake upon progress. The role of the powerful Finance function within Ford was called into serious question for the first time since 1945. Reductions in Finance personnel and the decentralization of decision making were the structural results of AJ.

> Ford has always been criticized for having too many administrative layers. We now realize that they were not, as they seemed to the outsider, layers of effective control. They were layer upon layer of reporting and review institutionalized by managers forced to justify regularly their existence which actually pushed up costs. The system, ironically, was both self-perpetuating and self-defeating. The company got into the habit of reporting the costs rather than controlling them. (See Starkey and McKinlay, 1993: 93)

The real problem was that planning and apparently rational processes had been developed too far, beyond their rational limits. They had taken on a life of their own. The formal process squeezed out dissenting voices, challenges to the received wisdom. Innovators 'just got worn down'. In the words of one Finance veteran, 'We'd bludgeon every investment proposal until it stopped moving.' Ingenuity, accountability and personal responsibility were stifled by fear. Individual initiative suffered 'because they know the bureau-cracy will review the hell out of it'. To be competitive the company realizes it cannot afford its previous 'enormous' bureaucracy based on the fetish that it has to 'police everything'. Managers lamented 'the amount of paperwork that circulates with no one actually being accountable for it because I know if someone else has to sign it I'm not going to review it'.

The 1980s After Japan programme saw a new concern in the company with human resource management and initiatives to replace control with a sense of commitment (Walton, 1985; Pascale, 1990; Starkey and McKinlay, 1993).

> We used to rule by fear, and fear breeds cynicism. It was that vicious circle which After Japan and all that followed tried to break. The 'bedrock' of the company was specialized technical expertise, primarily in finance. Ford are now saying that softer skills, interpersonal skills are increasingly important to the survival of the company because 'you've got to have a motivated organisation in which all the brainpower in the company is used to its maximum'. (See Starkey and McKinlay, 1993: 83–5)

AJ was the first step in 'a much wider organizational audit. But it went further than just the numbers. We . . . did a lot of soul-searching about our own conduct, the way we did our business, so it was as much a cultural audit as anything else',

> The nature of the dialogue in the company changed. Some of the questions we asked were very basic. Is our prime objective cost control or increased quality? And hours of debate went on around that single issue. The point is that as a manager you can't expect a clear answer: the terms of the question are ambiguous and can conflict. The business answer is you balance cost and quality – it's a trade-off. You can't enforce the full Ford cost control disciplines while you pursue enhanced quality. The point is that these issues are the subject of free debate whereas [before After Japan and the ensuing initiatives] they were not. Not only would they not have been debated, the issue would not have arisen: cost reduction took overriding priority. (Starkey and McKinlay, 1993: 120)

In the words of a former Ford of Europe chairman,

> what's changing now and hopefully it's going to change even more is that the manager begins to understand that his success is more interdependent with some of his colleagues, his peers, rather than his own. [The] whole psychology [that] drove the cost system we had, the fact that individual performance and the need to excel were very complementary to this cost system, the cost focus we had, was a deadly combination. One of the biggest contrasts would be a core understanding that teamwork and team involvement is going to get you better solutions. (See Starkey and McKinlay, 1993: 148–9)

Here we would qualify Foucault's view of the Panopticon. The experience of control and discipline, the burden of work in 'the field of visibility', was not light. Indeed, it was felt as increasingly heavy. The question from a Foucauldian perspective is: does the move away from the old forms of discipline represent a transcendence of the old need for discipline or merely its transmutation into a new form? After Japan we find a new rhetoric of human resource management in many companies not previously noted for their human resource focus. This new discourse, despite its emphasis on individual empowerment and the devolution of responsibility, has been criticized by some as nothing but the old control imperative in new clothing (Ray, 1986). Some managers at Ford share this view. And, indeed, one Finance specialist – 'I'm one of the guys in grey suits with sharp pencils' – suggested that new initiatives such as employee involvement and participative management were designed to compensate for the loss of traditional procedural controls.

> After Japan didn't just take out costs. It also took out a certain amount of our structural controls and a certain amount of our Finance capabilities. All our 'people' initiatives have been surrogates for our old controls. (Starkey and McKinlay, 1993: 100)

This was a view echoed by another manager in Manufacturing.

> Participative management is really making a virtue out of necessity. With fewer people in the organization we had to relax our little box mentality. Lateral communication [as opposed to top-down] might be the long-term strategic goal but it also had the short-term benefit of helping us paper over the cracks in the

organization as we shed manpower, *managerial* manpower. (Starkey and McKinlay, 1993: 100; original emphasis)

References

Armstrong, P. (1985) 'Changing management control strategies: the role of competition between accountancy and other organisational professions', *Accounting, Organizations and Society*, 10: 129–48.

Arrington, C.E. and Francis, J.R. (1989) 'Letting the chat out of the bag: deconstruction, privilege and accounting research', *Accounting, Organizations and Society*, 14: 1–28.

Boland, R.J. Jr (1989) 'Beyond the objectivist and the subjectivist: learning to read accounting as text', *Accounting, Organizations and Society*, 14: 591–604.

Chandler, A.D. (1962) *Strategy and Structure: Chapters in the History of the Industrial Enterprise*. Cambridge MA: MIT Press.

Chandler, A.D. Jr and Daems, H. (1979) 'Administrative coordination, allocation and monitoring: a comparative analysis of the emergence of accounting and organization in the USA and Europe', *Accounting, Organizations and Society*, 4: 3–20.

Clark, K. and Fujimoto, T. (1991) *Product Development Performance: Strategy, Organization and Management in the World Auto Industry*. Cambridge MA: Harvard Business School Press.

Clegg, S. (1989) *Frameworks of Power*. London: Sage.

Covaleski, M.A. and Dirsmith, M.W. (1988) 'The use of budgetary symbols in the political arena: an historically informed study', *Accounting, Organizations and Society*, 13: 1–24.

Crozier, M. (1964) *The Bureaucratic Phenomenon*. London: Tavistock and University of Chicago Press.

Dale, E. (1956) 'Contributions to Administration by Alfred P. Sloan, Jr, and GM', *Administrative Science Quarterly*, 1 (1): 30–62.

Dalton, M. (1959) *Men who Manage: Fusions of Feeling and Theory in Administration*. New York: Wiley.

Drucker, P. (1946) *Concept of the Corporation*. Boston: Beacon Hill Press.

Drucker, P. (1955) *The Practice of Management*. London: Heinemann.

Fligstein, N. (1990) *The Transformation of Corporate Control*. Cambridge, MA: Harvard University Press.

Foucault, M. (1977) *Discipline and Punish: The Birth of the Prison*. Harmondsworth: Penguin.

Frey, D. (1991) 'Learning the ropes: my life as a product champion', *Harvard Business Review*, September–October: 46–56.

Hackett, D. (1976) 'The big idea – the story of Ford of Europe'. Brentwood: Ford of Europe.

Halberstam, D. (1987) *The Reckoning*. London: Bloomsbury.

Hayes, W. (1990) *Henry: A Life of Henry Ford II*. London: Weidenfeld and Nicolson.

Hines, R.D. (1988) 'Financial accounting: in communicating reality, we construct reality', *Accounting, Organizations and Society*, 13: 251–61.

Hopwood, A. (1987) 'The archaeology of accounting systems', *Accounting, Organizations and Society*, 12: 207–34.

Hoskin, K.W. and Macve, R.H. (1988) 'The genesis of accountability: the West Point connections', *Accounting, Organizations and Society*, 13 (1): 37–73.

Kuhn, A. (1986) *GM Passes Ford, 1918–1938: Designing the General Motors Performance–Control System*. University Park, PA: Pennsylvania State University Press.

Lyotard, J.F. (1984) *The Postmodern Condition*. Manchester: Manchester University Press.

Miller, G.J. (1992) *Managerial Dilemmas: The Political Economy of Hierarchy*. Cambridge: Cambridge University Press.

Miller, P., Hopper, T. and Laughlin, R. (1991) 'The new accounting history: an introduction', *Accounting, Organizations and Society*, 16: 395–403.

Miller, P. and O'Leary, T. (1987) 'Accounting and the construction of the governable person', *Accounting, Organizations and Society*, 12: 235–66.

Morgan, G. (1988) 'Accounting as reality construction: towards a new epistemology for accounting practice', *Accounting, Organizations and Society*, 13: 477–85.

Nevins, A. and Hill, F.E. (1962) *Ford: Decline and Rebirth*. New York: Charles Scribner's Sons.

Pascale, R. (1990) *Managing on the Edge*. London: Viking.

Poster, M. (1984) *Foucault, Marxism and History: Mode of Production versus Mode of Information*. Cambridge: Polity.

Ray, C.A. (1986) 'Corporate culture: the last frontier of control', *Journal of Management Studies*, 23: 287–97.

Secrest, F.G. (1966) 'From Bookkeeping to Decision Theory', *Management Accounting*, December: 3–9.

Seidler, P. (1976) *Let's Call It Fiesta: The Autobiography of Ford's Project Bobcat*. Lausanne: Edita.

Sloan, A. (1963) *My Years with General Motors*. London: Sidgwick and Jackson.

Sloan, A. (1970) *Adventures of a White-Collar Man*. Freeport, NY: Books for Libraries Press.

Sorensen, C. (1957) *Forty Years with Ford*. London: Jonathan Cape.

Starkey, K. and McKinlay, A. (1993) *Strategy and the Human Resource: Ford and the Search for Competitive Advantage*. Oxford: Blackwell.

Strebel, P. (1987) 'Ford of Europe', *Journal of Management Case Studies*, 3 (3): 138–57.

Walton, R.E. (1985) 'From control to commitment: transforming work force management in the United States', in K.B. Clark, R.H. Hayes and C. Lorenz (eds), *The Uneasy Alliance: Managing the Productivity–Technology Dilemma*. Boston, MA: Harvard Business School Press. pp. 237–65.

Whyte, W.H. (1957) *The Organization Man*. London: Jonathan Cape.

Womack, J.P., Jones, D.T. and Roos, D. (1991) *The Machine that Changed the World*. London/New York: Rawson Associates/Macmillan.

Yates, J. (1989) *Control through Communication: The Rise of System in American Management*. Baltimore: Johns Hopkins University Press.

8

Management Accounting Numbers: Freedom or Prison – Geneen versus Foucault

Trevor Hopper and Norman Macintosh

> We are much less Greeks than we believe. We are neither in the amphitheatre, nor on the stage, but in the panoptic machine . . . is it surprising [then] that prisons resemble factories, schools, barracks, hospitals, which all resemble prisons? (Foucault, 1979: 217, 228)

Harold Geneen's (1984b) memoirs regarding his tenure as Chief Executive Officer (CEO) of International Telephone and Telegraph (ITT) can be read as a striking and illuminating example of the way large, complex, multinational firms make use of management accounting and control systems as a major apparatus for the surveillance, discipline and control of their managers and employees. These systems proceed according to the general disciplinary drive that appeared during the Modern epoch of Western civilization as outlined by Michel Foucault (1975, 1979) in his historical account of the sundry disciplinary techniques that came into being during Modernity, particularly within, but by no means limited to, penal institutions. Foucault's identification of specific devices, techniques and apparatuses that objectify individuals, including managers, as subjects and produce them as docile, obedient bodies are seen to be exemplified in the conventional management accounting and control literature as well as in practice. Even more disturbing, if ITT is typical, they are ubiquitous in today's large public and private sector organizations.

This chapter has four main intentions. It extracts a model of the main principles of discipline and control from *Discipline and Punish: The Birth of the Prison*, Foucault's most celebrated piece of writing.[1] It then illustrates, using ITT as a case history, the relevance of this model for providing a broader understanding than that of the traditional view of management accounting and control systems. We begin by providing detailed bibliographical background data on Harold Geneen – the 'super-accountant' who acted as CEO at ITT for nearly 20 years. Next, it sketches out the principles of Foucault's model of discipline and control and illustrates them with specific examples from Geneen's and others' accounts of the financial-based control systems at ITT. Finally, it outlines the insights and implications that emerge from the analysis.

Harold Geneen: a disciplined disciplinarian

Harold Geneen seems almost an archetype of Foucault's disciplined subject. His father, always optimistic in spite of a series of ups and downs as a small-time entrepreneur, married Geneen's mother, a light opera singer, when she was 17. They divorced when Geneen was five and sent him to a convent boarding school:

> where the discipline was strict and the nuns loving. I can still picture in my mind Sister Joseph, who more than once whacked my outstretched hand in punishment, not for any infraction of discipline, but because I had misspelled a word. It instilled in me, I think, a serious appreciation of my responsibilities as a student; certainly I learned to do my homework. (Geneen, 1984b: 56)

Each summer, Geneen went to a boys' camp where he encountered the discipline of the camp counsellors. By the age of six, however, he was content during holidays such as Thanksgiving and Christmas to sit by himself reading books. He recalls one day when Mother Superior seemed concerned about his lonely holidays:

> She smiled at me sympathetically, perhaps I noticed pity in her expression. What remains with me is the feeling that she was wrong, that I never felt uncomfortable about being alone. I thought that I could always find something to do, even at that tender age. Perhaps the isolation back then taught me to be independent, to be able to think through my small daily problems, and to achieve a sense of self-confidence. (Geneen, 1984b: 56)

Although no more than a small child, Geneen was well on his way to becoming a model of the disciplinary individual.

During his adolescence, Geneen was enrolled at Suffield Academy, a military-style college preparatory school based on the West Point model.[2] The academy had a balanced mixture of boarding and day students as well as a good proportion of scholarship students who set high standards for the others. During his stay there, Geneen waited on tables and worked in a local bakery. Although the general atmosphere was democratic and egalitarian, 'within that academic freedom there was a discipline and a value system and a reverence for life that I absorbed, which would stand me in good stead all the days of my life' (Geneen, 1984b: 56).

Geneen continued in summer camps until the age of 15 when he took a job as an errand boy for a lithograph company on New York's west side. His duties entailed carrying heavy packages all over the city, often travelling by subway and frequently working until 9 pm:

> The sharpest memory of that summer was a crisis and furor over a lost piece of copy that I had delivered to the printing room. A major client was furious. I was called into the manager's office to explain what I had done with the papers involved. I explained and he agreed that I had left the documents in the proper place. He thanked me and sent me back to work. For many years, that man's polite and fair treatment of me remained in my mind as a lesson. (Geneen, 1984b: 57)

Discipline, Geneen learned, gets recognized and rewarded. When he graduated from Suffield he got yet another lesson in discipline. His diploma was unsigned. However, the headmaster assured him that the moment his outstanding boarding and tuition bills were paid the diploma would happily be completed – 'It was a number of years before I was able to retire the debt' (Geneen, 1984b: 58).

Instead of university, Geneen had to go to work. He took a job as a floor page at the New York Stock Exchange, but also attended evening classes, where he studied accounting. Six years later, he witnessed the great crash of October 1929 and watched in wonder as great fortunes disappeared in a few hours. He was more impressed by the way fortunes were being made by cunning short-sellers. After the crash, things took a turn for the worse. His salary was cut, he lost his 200 dollars of life savings in a bank failure, and he had to live on day-old bread and taffy candy. A series of jobs followed – a book salesman, newspaper advertisement salesman, bookkeeper for a small investment firm, and para-professional for a large public accounting firm where

> My job was temporary and seasonal and I was promptly assigned to help in the audit of Floyd Odlum's Atlas Corporation of Journal Square in Jersey City, which had become notorious and highly profitable in buying up bankrupt and near-defunct mutual funds and companies. Atlas Corporation owned a grab bag of securities representing hotels, barge lines, frozen foods, utilities, as well as a wide variety of other assets. The job was conspicuous, most of all, for its overtime. We worked on that audit until ten o'clock at night, five and sometimes six days a week, and in the final three weeks until three or four o'clock in the morning. Considering that I had to take the tube back to New York, sleep at home, and return to work at 9 a.m., I think I slept about two hours a night those last three weeks. When the audit certificate was signed I requested an audience with Mr Lenhart. 'What's on your mind?' he asked. 'Well, I haven't had but nine hours sleep all week and I can't help worrying about this job,' I said, 'I just want to know whether I am permanently on the staff or not, so I can go home and get a good night's sleep.' I got the job and a good night's sleep. (Geneen, 1984b: 64)

As before, discipline saw him through and got its just rewards.

Geneen revelled in the work of a public accountant. He got to see inside many companies. He liked his colleagues and co-workers. But best of all, he liked the training: 'Public accounting taught me analytical approaches to business problems, objective reasoning, and the highest order of discipline in making factual presentations' (Geneen, 1984b: 65). He stayed six years and successfully took the CPA examinations.

Yet professional life, as with stock brokering, somehow seemed empty. He missed the active side of being on the firing line of commercial and industrial life. As a consequence, he took a series of jobs in industry serving with American Can, Bell and Howell, Jones and Laughlin Steel, and Raytheon Electronics. While these were mostly in finance and controller positions, he was involved also in getting new plants and ventures up and running, and, in some cases, divesting existing ones. Geneen, an extra-ordinarily disciplined individual, accepted the CEO job at ITT and transformed it into a disciplinary organization. He did this by following, almost to the letter, Foucault's principles of discipline and control.

Foucault's principles of discipline and control

In his classic book *Surveiller et punir: La naissance de la prison* Foucault detailed the emergence from the Classical era of an all-encompassing disciplinary drive that became ubiquitous during the Modern era. Foucault identified three general principles underlying the way the disciplinary society functions: the principle of enclosure; the principle of the efficient body; and the principle of disciplinary power. The enclosure principle includes concepts like the cell, useful sites and rankings. The efficient body principle stems from ideas of timetabling, manoeuvres and dressage, and the exhaustive use of time. The principle of disciplinary power includes concepts such as: hierarchization, panopticons, normalizing sanctions and examinations.

Disciplining space: the enclosure principle

Discipline proceeds initially, according to Foucault, by the careful distribution of heterogeneous individuals over space–time locations. In the first instance there is general confinement. This involves specifying special purpose, self-enclosed locations (*clôtures*) inside which individuals can be contained and sheltered in a monotonous disciplinary state. Monasteries, poor houses, schools, military barracks, factories, prisons, hospitals and even universities are examples.

Partitioning Enclosure, however, is insufficient in itself to achieve disciplinary spaces. It is also necessary to partition enclosures to make them amenable to discipline. Partitioning involves dividing up the general enclosure into as many self-contained locations or 'cells' as there are elements (bodies) to be distributed. This makes it possible to know, master and make useful each and every individual.

The principle of enclosure can be traced back to the monastery of the classical era where each monk had his own cell. With each individual in his or her own space and, importantly, each space with its own individual, the troublesome aspects of large transient groups and their confused collective dispositions could be avoided. Enclosure, confinement and partitioning were the necessary first steps for turning a heterogeneous mass of humans into a homogeneous social order.

Functional, useful, serialized spaces Enclosure and partitioning make it possible to effect the 'rule of functional sites'. In the first instance each site is defined in terms of the specific function performed there. Then it is necessary to spread out the individual partitions in a perfectly legible way so they can be linked in a serial fashion thus forming a permanent grid of functional, useful, serialized spaces:

> It was a question of distributing individuals in a space in which one might isolate and map them; but also of articulating this distribution on a production machinery that had its own requirements. The distribution of bodies, the spatial arrangements

of production machinery and the different forms of activity in the distribution of 'posts' had to be linked together. (Foucault, 1979: 145)

So each site is converted into a functionally useful place where tight control can be exercised over each and every individual. 'Particular places were designed to correspond not only to the need to supervise, to break dangerous communications, but also to create *a useful space*' (Foucault, 1979: 143–4).

This distribution and partitioning of disciplinary space, Foucault observed, worked not only to achieve specialization within the production process but also to assure the fragmentation and deskilling of labour power. Here, then, Foucault is in concordance with Marx's notion of the deskilling and the commodification of labour. Within a disciplinary grid, each space and every individual could be analysed, measured and assessed according to criteria for the strength, skill, promptness and constancy of the individual occupying that space, criteria which arose from the requirements of the production machinery. Thus the body could be matched perfectly with the machine.

Ranking   Another important aspect of the principle of enclosure involved the art of ranking each disciplinary space. Everyone is defined by the rank he or she occupies in the hierarchy and by the space that separates each rank from the one immediately below and above it. Individuals are not only distributed across a network of relations, but also circulated – moved up or down or across – in the network. Ranks remain permanent but the individuals change according to their most recent assigned rank. What is important is the place the individual occupies in the ranking.

Spaces so constituted are real in a material sense, in that they dictate the distribution of physical objects like buildings, rooms, machines and furniture. But they are also *idealized* spaces. They are constituted in terms of their function, their relationship to other spaces, and their rank within the power hierarchy. The effect is to create a *tableau vivant*[3] that transforms 'the confused, useless or dangerous multitudes into ordered multiplicities . . . and so is the basis of . . . a microphysics of what might be called a "cellular" power' (Foucault, 1979: 148–9). The individual's obedience is pretty much guaranteed.

The principle of enclosure at ITT

The principle of enclosure and its counterpart, the principle of responsibility centre accounting, is illustrated vividly in Geneen's story. Once installed as CEO, Geneen moved quickly to reorganize the company. He replaced the old functional/geographic organization structure with one featuring decentralized profit centres. Managers became fully responsible and accountable for financial performance. By 1977, ITT's line operations consisted of nearly 400,000 employees enclosed in 250 profit centres. Following the principle of enclosure, each space had its own manager and each manager had his or her own space.

Having neatly partitioned the company into profit centres, Geneen made each responsibility centre analysable through what he called 'the discipline of the numbers'. For most people, he postulated, numbers are much more easy to read than words. They use unambiguous symbols which measure the tasks and operations of the organization and, most importantly, they inform upper management about what is going on:

> The difference between well-managed companies and not-so-well managed companies is the degree of attention they pay to numbers, the temperature chart of their business. How often are the numbers reported up the chain of command? How accurate are those numbers? How much variation is tolerated between budget forecasts and actual results? How deep does management dig for its answers? (Geneen, 1984a: 80)

His financial control system provided Geneen with continuous, functional surveillance of each enclosed responsibility centre. For Geneen, this was absolutely essential if ITT was to become a disciplined and productive company. It seems clear that Geneen, deeply influenced by his own educational experiences, his knowledge of control systems at General Motors, his attendance at courses at Harvard Business School, and his own accounting background, relied heavily on the principle of enclosure inherent in the management accounting axiom that organizations should be divided up into responsibility centres headed up by an accountable manager.

Disciplining time: the efficient body principle

With individuals enclosed in identifiable, ranked, serialized and functional spaces, the principle of the efficient body can be brought to bear on them. This principle is realized through three additional disciplinary practices: the timetable; the articulation of body and machine; and the exhaustive use of time. It is important to recognize that just as the principle of enclosure disciplines space, the principle of the efficient body disciplines the individual's time in each enclosure.

The timetable   The timetable is the first stage in disciplining time. It articulates each functional partition in terms of when specific activities and routines are to be performed. It establishes a rhythm and a regularity to actions. It can be formulated in terms of days, hours, minutes and even seconds. It defines a time 'without impurities or defects; a time of good quality, throughout which the body is constantly applied to its exercise' (Foucault, 1979: 151). The timetable effects a clockwork-like world of daily repetition and regular cycles of 'useful' activities. It programmes each individual in a constraining chain of detailed, minute actions for the entire time the individual occupies that space. Foucault traces the timetable to the strict regimen adhered to in monasteries in pre-modernity where routine and regimen produced a 'disciplined disciple'.

While the timetable specifies at what moment the activity is to be performed and defines the general framework for an activity, the 'temporal elaboration of the act' goes even further by specifying the precise way to perform the activity. (Foucault cites the transmutation of the correct way of marching for French soldiers as an example.) Efficient body movements and the timetable, however, are necessary but not sufficient conditions for fully achieving the principle of the efficient body. It is also necessary to achieve a systematic and meticulous meshing of the body to the specific object – pen, rifle, wagon, machine or whatever.

The correct technique for handwriting, for example, resembled gymnastics. The position and movement of the feet, the arms, the index finger, the elbow and even the chin were rigorously prescribed. Each movement was assigned a direction, a range and a duration within a prescribed sequence. Each part of the body was disciplined. The disciplinary power thus achieved is not so much a forceful extortion of the product as it is a coercive chain binding the body to the apparatus of production. The detailed prescriptions (the knowledge) carried in the regulation (the discourse) and imposed on each individual (power) converted him or her into a manoeuvre: that is to say a 'man (body)-machine'. Both the individual and the machine, objects of discipline, were chained together.

The exhaustive use of time   These techniques, however, still were not enough to effect the principle of the efficient body. In addition, time had to be used exhaustively. As Foucault explains, in the Classical era, the principle of non-idleness prevailed. Since God counted time and men paid for it, to waste it was a mortal sin in the eyes of God. Moreover, it was economic dishonesty in the eyes of fellow men. During Modernity, however, this negative conception took on a positive economy of wasted time in the form of a demand for the continual increase in the utilization of time. 'Time was money.'

Detailed concern with the efficient use of time proved a definite competitive edge. For example, it was a strategic advantage in the mid-1700s for the Prussian army under Frederick II whose brilliant victories caught the attention of all Europe. Armies in other countries soon followed suit – as did schools, hospitals, workshops and universities. The principle spread throughout society and the 'educated, useful body' became commonplace.

The exhaustive use of time also calls for the incorporation of highly trained individuals in a body–machine system. As a consequence, *bon dressement* ('dressage' or 'correct training') emerged as an important disciplinary technique. Dressage today is taken to mean the habitual training of an animal, particularly a horse, in obedience and deportment. In the case of humans it can be applied in the same sense. The disciplined soldier, for example 'begins to obey whatever he is ordered to do; his obedience is prompt and blind; an appearance of indocility, the least delay would be a crime' (Boussaneile, 1970, quoted in Foucault, 1979: 166). More importantly, dressage automatically triggers a reflexive response from the disciplined body. It places the individual in a world of signals, each with its unique response and its moral imperative.

Dressage not only restrains the subject, but also links individuals together and so multiplies their usefulness.

It is important to realize that for Foucault the efficient body principle is not a celebrated, triumphant power. Instead, it works in a modest, calculating and constant fashion. It must be exercised gingerly in order not to weigh too heavily on the individual. Nevertheless, its effects are remarkable. It forms an otherwise mobile, confused and useless mass of individuals into obedient objects whose deportment can be counted on to conform to the prescribed actions.

For Foucault, these new techniques of subjection – the timetable, the temporal elaboration of the body, the articulation of body and machine, and the exhaustive use of time – led to a metamorphosis of the treatment of the body. It became a target to be manipulated, to be exercised in correct movements, and to be available for the imposition of ever more knowledge. Thus subjugated, the individual functions as obedient, docile and willing flesh (Foucault, 1979).

The efficient body principle at ITT

Geneen's financial control system at ITT bears more than a little correspondence with the principle of the efficient body. In terms of timetabling, each profit centre manager and staff divisional head submitted their annual budget and business plans in February for review and revision at both the local level and at headquarters. Then in November and December Geneen and other key headquarters officials met face-to-face with each manager and his or her own staff to discuss, review and finalize the plans and budgets. The finalized budget, now 'carved in stone', became the benchmark for performance in the ensuing year:

> Each division manager and his own management staff had negotiated an agreement with headquarters on his budget and business plan for the following year. He had made a firm commitment to ITT. His subordinates down the line had made their commitments to him for the integral parts of his budget. He would hold them to their word as we would hold him to his commitment – or know the reason why. (Geneen, 1984b: 92)

Geneen also required each manager to sketch out two-, three- and five-year profit plans of the profit-centre as well as anticipated capital expenditures. He did not, however, put a great deal of stock in long-range, qualitative strategic plans but instead focused on the current year: 'The budgets and business plans for all our divisions, bound in loose-leaf books, occupied more than thirty feet of bookcase shelves. But those books were the bible we lived by' (Geneen, 1984b: 93).

The cornerstone of the financial control system, however, was the monthly operating report. Each profit centre manager submitted to headquarters, by the fifth working day of each month, reports which included pertinent and detailed information on: sales, earnings, inventory, receivables, employment, marketing, competition and R&D along with any current or anticipated problems. The manager also reported on the current economic and political situation in his or her territory. Divisional comptrollers also made a monthly financial report to the headquarters comptroller. Moreover, all headquarters staff division heads (engineering, accounting, marketing, R&D, etc.) sent Geneen a monthly report about the situation in their specialized area, as did the product line managers. Geneen and his head-quarters staff personally scrutinized each and every report. He summed up his surveillance network this way: 'Information flows up the chain and orders flow down. Everyone knows his or her own place and responsibilities in the hierarchy. Logic and order are supposed to reign supreme' (Geneen, 1984b: 85).

The profit-centre philosophy also served to train managers to act like 'individual entrepreneurs'. Geneen selected each manager carefully to en-sure that only those persons who fitted his predetermined mould got the job. He did not want geniuses who could not communicate with ordinary, hard working people. Nor did he want people who got by on their good looks, smooth talk or family connections. Instead, he looked for people who shared his enthusiasm for hard work: 'what we sought were capable, experienced men who were motivated, who wanted to achieve and to make something of their lives, and who were not afraid to work hard for what they wanted' (Geneen, 1984b: 138). Intelligence, knowledgeability and experience were necessary, but not sufficient, characteristics. Each manager also had to display 'an enthusiasm for labouring'. Geneen's normalizing mould was clear for all to fit into.

More specifically, the information in the financial controls became the basis for the dressage-like training of ITT's managers. The on-site, monthly meeting with 150 European General Managers and 40 headquarters staff managers quickly became Geneen's 'training-grounds'. As Geneen de-scribes it:

> Soon after I came to ITT I saw the advantages of meeting face to face with our European directors, rather than trying to solve problems over the transatlantic telephone or telex systems. The look on a man's face, his tone of voice, his body language made a difference in the decisions I was making. We started out in Europe in small, smoke-filled hotel rooms, but as the company expanded and built its own European headquarters in Brussels, the monthly General Managers meeting usually consisted of 120 to 150 managing directors. Every month I flew to Europe with about forty headquarters staff, and we sat down together and went over the monthly operating reports. The pertinent figures from the comptrollers' reports and the managing directors' reports were flashed on giant projection screens in three corners of the room. Everyone on the headquarters staff had read every monthly report to be reviewed. We were informed. In going through the two large brown leather-bound loose-leaf books of reports, I made it a practice to jot down my queries in red ink and turn down the corner of the page to mark any item I wished to query at the meeting. We sat around a large U-shaped table, covered in green felt, facing one another, and I asked questions based upon the notes I had made on their monthly operating reports. Why were the sales down? Was he sure of the reasons? Had he checked it out? How? What was he doing about it? What did he expect in the month or two ahead? Did he need help? How did he plan to meet or outdistance the competition? (1984b: 96–7)

Geneen came armed with a series of 'red-ink queries'. He exhorted the others to do likewise:

> Not only I but anyone else at the meeting could say anything, question anything, suggest anything that was pertinent. Each man had a microphone in front of him. With the figures on the screen, we could all see how each profit centre measured up to its budget commitments, its last year's performance and whatever, in sales, earnings, receivables, inventory, etc. (Geneen, 1984b: 96)

Differences and queries were handled on the spot as everyone learned from each other: 'It was at times almost group therapy' (Geneen, 1984b: 97). The financial control system and the monthly meetings provided the means for training ITT managers in the correct manoeuvres. The signals from Geneen and the financial control system automatically triggered the required proper behaviour. ITT managers performed as docile, efficient bodies.

Sampson captures the dressage image in describing ITT's takeover of Avis Rent-A-Car. Many people at Avis complained that they now spent more time dealing with ITT than they did renting cars. The new president (who replaced Townsend – the consummate artistic, anti-bureaucratic manager) 'had the task of fitting the company into the hard shafts of the ITT harness' (Sampson, 1974: 79). The metaphor of shafts and harnesses captures well the spirit of dressage – a key ingredient in Geneen's control system.

The principle of disciplined bodies: the means of correct training

The third principle in Foucault's model is the principle of disciplined bodies or the means of correct training. This final link in Foucault's chain of disciplinary power involves the use of hierarchical surveillance, normalizing sanctions, examinations and the Panopticon. These 'instruments of organization' were, he believed, the means that led to the successful imposition of the principles of enclosure and efficient bodies.

Hierarchical surveillance   Hierarchical surveillance emerged in the eighteenth century as a special kind of 'looking on' or 'gaze' that constrained the individual without the watchers being seen or, even without them looking. This discreet art of close watching consisted of 'the minor techniques of multiple and intersecting observations, of eyes that must be seen without being seen, using techniques of subjection and methods of exploitation, an obscure art of light and the visible was secretly preparing new knowledge of man' (Foucault, 1979: 171). The gaze constrained as it watched.

The disciplinary gaze was not complete, however, without a system to relay information. This called for a pyramid-like administrative network, discreet enough that it did not appear to weigh too heavily on the individuals in the hierarchy, yet sufficient to act as either a brake or an obstacle to each individual's activities. The pyramid was decomposed into small but precise units of surveillance, and the levels and numbers of administrators were increased. The disciplinary gaze could have no missing links.

Surveillance was best accomplished, however, in the confines of 'human observatories'. This was exemplified in the military camp. The geometry of alley ways, the number and distribution of tents, the facing direction of tent entrances, and the rules governing the disposition of officers' and the soldiers' encampments were precisely drawn out so that power could be exercised by a network of single, exact glances. The encampment idea soon penetrated the design of many other institutions: schools, prisons, hospitals and asylums. Even workers' housing developments were constructed to facilitate constant observation. Architects no longer designed buildings to be seen nor did they design them so that occupants could look on a spectacular view; but rather buildings were patterned to permit a constant 'gaze', one which looked in on and articulated control over the inhabitants (Foucault, 1979).

Normalizing sanctions   Hierarchical surveillance, however, required a system of rewards and penalties. As a consequence, the new layer of supervision developed a system of 'normalizing sanctions' which moved into spaces of indifference not covered by the general statutes of the state. It put into place its own laws, its own ranges of proper behaviour, its own rules for solicitous judgements, its own designated infractions, and its own appropriate sanctions for deviance. It operated, in effect, like a miniature legal and prison system. Surveillance and sanctions spread throughout society. In the workshops, the schools, the military, the bureaucracy, and so on, deviant behaviour was ferreted out and appropriately sanctioned. Everyone was enmeshed in an *ex legalis*, punishable–punishing world.

These disciplinary sanctions, Foucault emphasized, were basically corrective. Alongside the regular punishments of the legal system (fines, whippings and solitary confinement) were erected a different series of punishments – drills, long and arduous apprenticeships, repetitious exercises and so on – to sanction and reduce nonconformity. In school, for example, a student whose behaviour was deemed 'uncooperative' was made to memorize long passages by heart or to write repeatedly one or two lines of verse. Punishment was not so much for avenging an outraged law. Nor was it for expiation or repentance. It was inflicted to correct behaviour and minimize non-conformism – it was outside of the legal, juridical systems.

Most of these normalizing sanctions, importantly, were not punitive. The use of penalties was avoided if at all possible. Instead, the master, teacher, boss or reformer tried to mete out positive recompenses more frequently than painful ones. Superordinates held to the prevailing belief that lazy individuals are more incited by a desire to receive the same rewards as diligent ones than they are motivated by the fear of penalties. A judicious mixture of gratifying and negative sanctions – along with drilling, repetition and correction – made improper behaviour all but impossible.

These new techniques of sanctioning, however, were not mere carbon copies of the legal and official tribunal system. They moved into spaces previously unobservable, unfettered by any rules, or untouched by formal and legal regulation. One of Foucault's great insights is that disciplinary punishment colonized those areas not already ruled by society's judicial system, spaces which were until then the only 'natural' places left for the individual. The soldier, for example, who did not raise his rifle to the required height during drill, or the worker who did not hold his tool correctly, found himself or herself victimized as the object of a series of penalties. Under the normalizing gaze, even these domains, previously indefinite and non-conforming, became penalizable.

Moreover, these gratification–penalty structures were readily quantified. Behaviour was calibrated along a continuum with positive and negative ends. Individuals received points for their behaviour according to where it fell on the continuum, making it possible to maintain an on-going, real-time accounting table (*grand tableau*) for each individual. The military, the workshops, and the schools soon employed these 'personal accounting' systems. Punishing, ranking, sanctioning, promoting and demoting, were integrated into a cycle of complete knowledge about the individual. Each teacher, officer, master, overseer or reformer was required to perform the essential surveillance, ranking and punishment functions, and to keep a written record of subordinates' progress and comportment. The record served as a rationale for the distribution of sanctions, promotions and demotions. Each person was not only completely known, but also completely 'written'. This constant 'accounting' for the individual completed the 'cycle of knowing'.

The art of punishment within the realm of the disciplinary power gaze, Foucault observed, was neither retributive nor restitutive. Rather, it put into play five other processes: it set up an entire field of comparisons for individual actions; it differentiated each individual in terms of his or her minimal, average, or optimal rule-following behaviour; it measured, quantified, ranked and valued each person according to his or her capacity, level of ability and 'general nature'; it introduced the constraint of conformity through the valorization of specific activities and behaviour; and it defined both extreme limits or frontiers of the abnormal. Differentiation, hierarchization, homogenization and exclusion combined to effect a ubiquitous, penalizing gaze on each subject. Appearing through the disciplinary gaze came the power of the norm.

The examination   The next element of the principle of disciplinary power is the 'examination'. As with the other techniques of discipline and control, it developed into a major vehicle of power in the late seventeenth century. The examination incorporated aspects of surveillance, hierarchization, measurement and normalization. Through its ceremony of power, it established 'the truth' about each individual, and became one of the most effective instruments of discipline and control in Western society (Foucault, 1979).

The hospital, previously little more than a poorhouse, was an archetypal example of an examining apparatus. Doctors conducted daily ritualistic examinations of patients. Clergy made regular visits to patients to make sure they were 'spiritually well'. And hospital administrators carried out daily rounds to 'check up' on patients. The disciplined hospital with its 'power-seeing' (*pouvoir*) combined with the medical practitioners' 'knowledge-seeing' (*savoir*), to produce an 'examinatory of objects'. Patients became the object of perpetual surveillance, examination and normalization. Schools, military institutions, universities, insane asylums, professions, trades, and so on, all followed suit to become vehicles for continuous examination.

The examination also left behind a perpetual, detailed, archival documentation of each individual and so provided material for databases available to calculate national averages and to construct norms for the entire population. This made it possible to compare and classify individuals, along with particular segments of the population, according to predetermined 'desirable' features. The seemingly trivial techniques of data collection, notation, registration, files and compilation of tables and columns proved to be the raw material for the developing of new 'sciences of man' which, according to Foucault, placed everyone in a state of perpetual subjugation. Constantly in the light, each individual could be seen, examined, categorized, rated, ranked, sanctioned and normalized.

The examination inverted the old system of punishment and control. In the Classical era, power was exercised on the individual's body in public displays where the subject was vilified, tortured or executed. Importantly, however, the sinner's soul was saved and went to heaven. In the Modern era, in contrast, punishment came to be exercised behind closed doors. It constituted a sort of ceremony whereby it arranged subjects in classifications and exercised a constant punishing gaze over them. This new form of power, Foucault believed, was far more insidious than public torture and execution. It inflicted its mark, not on the body, but on the mind. The new clinical experts measured, described and normalized the individual. They saved the body, but crushed the soul.

The Panopticon   These 'techniques of correct training' – hierarchical surveillance, normalizing sanctions and the examination – worked best within the Panopticon. Originally designed for prisons, the Panopticon featured a unique architecture. A central tower looked out in all directions into layers of solitary cells arranged in the periphery ring. The cells, or cages, acted as tiny theatres, putting each prisoner on the stage, alone and individualized, but with uninterrupted visibility from the central tower. The inmate, although constantly aware of the outline of the central tower, could never be sure at any given moment whether or not he or she was being watched. The central tower was designed with venetian blinds, specially angled partitions, and zig-zag internal openings that could scan in different directions. As a result, the presence or absence of a guard or director in the central tower was unverifiable from the cells. Spectacular manifestations of power in the old dungeons gave way to anonymous but constant surveillance.

The principle of disciplined bodies at ITT

Geneen's account of his financial control system at ITT typifies many aspects of the principle of disciplinary power. One of his first, but perhaps most critical, moves in reorganizing ITT was to restructure the comptroller's organization. Under the old system, field comptrollers reported directly to the field managers and only indirectly to headquarters. Geneen changed this to direct and primary reporting to headquarters, with secondary direct reporting to the field general managers. Initially, this move met with stiff resistance. Line managers, fearful that their comptrollers would turn into 'home-office spies', submitted formal protests. Yet as Geneen (1984b: 90) explains:

> They wanted complete control over their domains and the absolute loyalty of their financial men. But I wanted an independent check on their activities by comptrollers who would be personally responsible for the figures they submitted to headquarters. It is all too easy to fudge or cover up the facts with numbers as well as with words. The temptation is always there. Even without conscious lying, different men honestly interpret events and situations differently. Company or division managers can exaggerate anticipated sales or underestimate costs or whatever and the men under them will go along because their jobs depend on it. I wanted the comptrollers to feel free of that pressure and be able to give the home office their honest opinion. . . . If the division manager and his comptroller could not agree, we would settle it at a higher level after a full and open hearing.

Geneen completed his system of hierarchical surveillance by setting up a cadre of technical staff and product managers in his central headquarters 'panoptic tower'. Technical personnel, experienced and proficient in all aspects of ITT's activities (such as telecommunications, electronics, consumer goods, engineering, accounting, marketing and personnel) were organized into specialized headquarters staff offices. These managers also reviewed and analysed the monthly reports. Then they were free to go to an ITT location without an invitation to investigate anything within their area of expertise. On the site, they asked questions, got answers, and reported their findings back to Geneen. Before reporting to Geneen, however, the staff people had to tell the local manager involved, as well as their own boss, exactly what they were doing and what findings they came up with. This way the manager had a chance to correct (normalize) the situation. Geneen (1984b: 88–9) describes it thus:

> These staff men out of headquarters cut through the structured rigidity of the formal organization, monitoring each of the subsidiaries. The accounting staff man monitored the profits, the engineering staff monitored the engineering department, and so on with marketing, personnel, legal, etc. The staff people worked very closely with the men out in the field, and they made their reports and recommendations, and they were held equally responsible for whatever went well or poorly in the unit they were monitoring. . . . Eventually, the operating men came to look upon the headquarters staff as 'outside consultants' who could be relied upon to help when needed.

This part of the hierarchy played out its normalizing, disciplinary gaze over the surface, lines and fibres of the entire line organization.

As well, any manager or employee who had a suggestion for an improvement anywhere in any aspect of the company's operations, regardless of geographic location, was encouraged to write a signed report, have her or his superior initial it, and send it directly to Geneen. If Geneen had a question he talked directly to the person who wrote the report: 'I really wanted to know what was going on in the company. I thought it was essential' (Geneen, 1984b: 88). He also appointed a dozen or so senior, product-line staff managers who:

> roamed over complete product lines, representing competition. He was monitoring the competitive ability of an ITT subsidiary in the marketplace. The product line manager was paid to look cold turkey at an ITT company and its competition and raise questions as he saw fit. . . . They had in effect a license to speculate on what could be done differently and better. (Geneen, 1984b: 89–90)

Product line managers did not, however, have any authority to give orders to line managers. Instead, they had to sell them their ideas. But they also had to report any disagreements directly to Geneen who 'quickly settled them'.

Geneen held strong opinions about organizational hierarchies. Although he believed in the conventional, textbook version of organization – a pyramid, layers of supervision, a labour force at the bottom supporting the pyramid, and a regular chain of command – he was convinced that such a structure had serious flaws, the most important of which involved information flows and their limitations for surveillance of the entire organization. The way he saw it, critical information was often a distorted gaze. It frequently got delayed, twisted and even suppressed as it wound its way up and then back down the hierarchy: 'Managers often become paper pushers, reports stack up, recommendations are made wearily, decisions are delayed, actions are not taken. The company stagnates' (Geneen, 1984b: 86). As a consequence, he demanded that all important information came directly to him and his staff. 'At ITT, we cut through two or three levels of upper management, so that my management team and I could talk and deal directly with the men on the firing line' (Geneen, 1984b: 96). ITT utilized accounting as its disciplinary gaze; but it was a highly personalized and penalizable one.

Geneen also initiated a system of ranking for each and every responsibility centre in ITT. A typical example is the rating system he set up for the field comptrollership units. In the late 1970s, ITT employed nearly 23,000 persons in the comptrollership activities, including 325 corporate headquarters staff. Each field comptroller was examined and rated by an effectiveness score based on 30 identified areas of comptrollership, including, for example, intercompany accounting, budgets, cost accounting, capital expenditures, payables, debt management and foreign exchange, the comptroller's monthly operating and financial review, and the comptroller's interface with both the unit general manager and the director of financial controls.[4]

These ratings were displayed on a massive colour-coded 'Comptrollership Grid'. The grid listed each of the 250 comptroller field units on the vertical axis and each of the 30 areas of comptrollership on the horizontal one. As a result, Geneen and other top level executives could see at a single glance how well any particular field comptroller was performing as well as get the picture for any specific function. Newly acquired units and units featuring a 'high situation complexity' (unfavourable business environment, inadequate staff, degree of multiple operations, troublesome governments or tricky foreign exchange transactions) frequently received poor ratings. Here the measure of the unit comptroller's effectiveness was the time he or she took to remedy the situation. Thus each comptroller's exact actions were detailed in minute fashion. The Comptrollership Grid provided an exhaustive, automatic examining, ranking, sanctioning and promoting or demoting of the comptrollers. The result was obedient, disciplined and willing comptrollers.

Such disciplinary practices prevailed throughout the company. Each of the line and staff managers received a similar dose of surveillance, discipline and sanctions. Each operating and staff manager included in their monthly report a brief description of any significant problems they were facing, a clear statement of the action recommended, the reasoning and numbers used to analyse the problem, and a brief opinion statement regarding the resolution of the problem. These problems remained 'red-flagged' until they were solved. They also became part of the agenda at the monthly face-to-face meetings:

> If the man knew [of a problem] and was reluctant to put the facts in the open, my questions would force him to admit what he was trying to hide. If the man did not know or understand his own lines, which was often true because he had not written them, then my questions, doubly embarrassing, would force him to do his homework. (Geneen, 1984b: 100)

While Geneen's disciplinary grid provided hierarchical surveillance, the numbers were the most critical part of it. In fact, 'the numbers make you free' became his famous credo. Managers were required in formulating their budgets to put down on paper the 'whole gamut of costs of the product, supplies, production, labour, plants, marketing, sales, distribution – and also anticipated income from sales based upon market share, back orders, and what have you' (Geneen, 1984b: 191). These numbers, however, were not merely pulled out of the air. Nor were they to be based on 'hopes' or 'whims'. Rather, they were to be carefully gathered by the line managers and based on the best possible available figures and facts.

As the budget year unfolded, a similar set of numbers flowed into headquarters each month, or weekly in the case of red-flagged units. Geneen scrutinized every piece of information, searching for anything that might be off plan. He believed fervently that 'unshakable' facts, along with hard-headed, hard-hitting cross-examinations, were essential in order to instil the requisite degree of discipline into the organization.

> It is discipline that is built into the credo *management must manage*. Part of that discipline is recognizing that the first answer you receive is not necessarily the

best one. That is why I put so much emphasis upon probing for unshakable facts, (Geneen, 1984b: 123; original emphasis)

Geneen insisted on receiving timely, detailed and accurate information from every nook and cranny of the organization. He was convinced that if executives looked closely at the numbers, any company could slowly but surely emerge as a well-managed enterprise. If, however, they did not keep at the numbers constantly, they would soon slide downhill. Consider Geneen's own account of the obsessive self-discipline this demanded:

> There is a price to pay for all this analysis, of course: paying attention to the numbers is a dull, tiresome routine – it's drudgery. The more you want to know about your business, the more numbers there will be. They cannot be skimmed. They must be read, understood and compared to other sets of numbers that you have read that day, that week, or earlier that year. And you have to do it alone, all by yourself, even when you know that it would be far more stimulating to be doing almost anything else.
>
> If you are running a well-managed company, most of the numbers will be those you expect. That makes them even more mundane and dull. But you cannot skip over them; you dare not allow your concentration to flag. Those numbers are your controls, and you read them until your mind reels or until you come upon one number of a set of numbers that stand out from all the rest, demanding your attention, and getting it.
>
> What you are seeking is *comprehension* of the numbers: what they mean. That will come only with constant exposure, constant repetition, retention of what you read in the past, and a familiarity with the actual activities that the numbers represent. You cannot speed up the process. Comprehension seeps into your brain by a process of osmosis and gradually you find yourself at ease with numbers and what they really represent.
>
> The truth is that the drudgery of the numbers will make you free. The confidence that you are in control, that you are aware of the significant variations from the expected, gives you the freedom to do things that you would have been unable to do otherwise. You can build a new plant, or finance risk laden research, or go out and buy a company, and you can do it with assurance because you are able to sit down and figure out what that new venture will do to the balance sheet. You will be able, in short, to manage. (Geneen, 1984b: 81; emphasis added)

Rather than using committees Geneen preferred to 'examine' the managers of the operating units himself. The notorious monthly meeting in Brussels of 150 of ITT's top executives served as Geneen's examinatory:

> The invited 150 officers hear introductory remarks by Geneen, an operations report from Dunlevy, and reports on such matters as inventory levels and receivables. Then the action begins. The heads of the bigger companies and the line group vice-presidents responsible for the others track the performance of their operations against their budgets. Anybody attending can ask questions and make suggestions.
>
> Some former employees complain that the big meetings reek of Kafkaesque courts, of volleys of verbal invective fired at underachievers. 'Many of us have frankly, left the organization for having been spat upon publicly', says a former European unit manager. Geneen, by contrast, views the meetings as open, business-like forums at which participants try to help one another. (*Business Week*, 3 November 1973)

This examinatory practice, featuring an alphanumeric-inquisitional process of reading, examining and re-writing each manager as a text, was seen by the managers not so much as a 'help' session, but a 'hell' session.

Geneen also believed ardently in the exhaustive use of time and the perpetual struggle for improvement. He writes extensively about his own working habits when he constantly travelled back and forth to Europe, took home huge cases of office work each weekend, and normally worked 12 to 16 hour days for seven days a week. He did so, he recalls, not simply to get his own work done competently, but more importantly to establish standards of hard work and commitment for the entire organization – to set the 'norm':

> I worked as long and hard as any man at ITT and they knew it. . . . I did set an example, an honest example, which travelled down the ranks of management and, to an extent, established a standard of performance for the whole company. . . . If I could do it, so could the next man. (Geneen, 1984b: 136)

Along with gruelling standards for working hours, Geneen constantly harangued the organization for more productivity. He set what he thought were challenging and competitive goals of steady, stable increases in earnings of 10 per cent to 15 per cent each year. Any chance he got he talked about growth. His expectations were for everyone to stretch beyond the ordinary. He never let up and he did not hesitate to reward those who followed his dictums:

> I wanted to create that kind of invigorating, challenging, creative atmosphere at ITT. I wanted to get the people there to reach for goals that they might think were beyond them. I wanted them to accomplish more than they thought possible. And I wanted them to do it not only for the company and their careers but also for the fun of it. I wanted them to enjoy the process of tackling a difficult piece of business, solving it, and going on to bigger, better and tougher challenges. I wanted them to do this, not for self-aggrandizement, but as part of a greater team effort, in which each player realized his own contribution to the team, knew that he was needed and appreciated, and took pride and self-satisfaction from playing a winning game. (Geneen, 1984b: 135)

This process of self-normalization was Geneen's ultimate aim.

Geneen also believed that raising standards beyond what most managers thought was possible was one of his major personal contributions to ITT. He was convinced that the levels of achievement he insisted upon penetrated the entire company: 'We stretched and stretched, we reached and reached, we managed, and we achieved our goals. And we felt good about it' (Geneen, 1984b: 129). Standards for long working hours and constantly increasing goals put into effect a system that exemplified the principle of the exhaustive use of time.

Geneen was also a master of 'dressage'. Each manager had to at least posture as a user, and more importantly a believer, in 'managing by the numbers'. They were trained to meet face-to-face, to look into each other's eyes, to listen carefully to the tone of others' voices, and to pay attention to their 'body language'. Telephone or telex would not do. You had to see the other person's reactions.

Geneen's management accounting and control system also mirrored the ideals of the Panopticon. From the central headquarters office, the accounting system cast its constant normalizing gaze into every responsibility centre throughout the organization. At a glance, it could monitor any part of ITT. It effected a continual flow of both formal and informal information into Geneen's office. Individual managers, however, never knew at any particular moment whether or not Geneen was 'gazing' directly at them through the windows of the numbers, or if not he personally, then some other member of the anonymous headquarter's staff. Within this accounting and control Panopticon, the line organization anxiously conformed to the 'prescribed normalization of the numbers'.

Geneen's position – 'the numbers will make you free' – it is important to realize, is the antithesis of Foucault's. For Foucault, they would be a critical part of the 'accounting prison' which incarcerates managers in their responsibility centres. 'For the disciplined, as for the believer, no detail is unimportant, but not so much for the meaning it conceals within it as for the hold it provides for the power that wishes to seize it' (Foucault, 1979: 140).

Management accounting, Foucault and ITT

ITT's control systems resembled the components of disciplinary power as described by Foucault. Accounting made managers governable by creating abstract calculable spaces. The ITT case indicates that accounting controls, reinforced by direct, personalized celebrations of accountability, are akin to a panoptical gaze. Their effects upon managers were marked and, in some instances, disturbing. The combined effects of output controls and accountability produced a feeling of perpetual observation not dissimilar to that of the victim of a Panopticon. As an ITT manager recounts, 'You'd realize that being an ITT manager is like living in a room with closed circuit television and a bug up your ass' (Sampson, 1974). There is little doubt that Geneen's methods intensified managerial work: whilst the financial rewards for executives who complied could be high, they carried heavy personal costs, as was reflected in high rates of managerial turnover (Menzies, 1980). As Sampson (1974: 126) graphically observed:

> For a newly joined manager . . . the ordeal can be terrifying: there are stories of one man fainting as he walked in, and another rushing out to get blind drunk for two days. For the hardened ITT man it is no more than a routine test of sang froid; 'You have to be prepared' said one of them, 'to have your balls screwed off in public and then joke afterwards as if nothing had happened.'

Geneen advanced and refined the principles of disciplinary power through the aggregative abstractions of management accounting controls. Supplemented by interrogation, control could be extended over time and space, and, most importantly, it came to be self-policed by creating within the minds of managers a conception of what being an effective manager entailed.

Management accounting's origins and relationship to knowledge are hazy to say the least, yet it has increasingly permeated broad sectors of society. This phenomenon – how accounting came to create an aura of truth for itself – is of essential import. Through Foucauldian analyses, Hoskin and Macve (1986, 1988) have traced it back to the military academy and the examination system, and Miller and O'Leary (1987) to the Efficiency Movements in the USA at the turn of the century. These searches for origins receive some credence in the empirics of ITT. Geneen acknowledges the import of examinations during the nineteenth century upon his systems of management:

> Upon reflection, I can see that it probably goes back to my days as a student at Suffield Academy. I worked conscientiously because I liked to get good marks and it bothered me if I got bad ones: . . . So at ITT I instinctively sought to install something of the same in the company. (Geneen, 1984b: 134)

These early educational influences were reinforced by his accounting experiences and training. Courses at the Harvard Business School and New York Unversity impressed upon him the role that management accounting methods pioneered at General Motors played in making large and diverse corporations governable (Sobel, 1982).

Although Geneen himself was not militarily trained, many of ITT's senior managers from its inception were. An ex-major-general, Harrison, effectively succeeded ITT's founder, Colonel Behn (a military reservist), and instituted tighter financial controls in ITT. Upon Harrison's death, Leavey, a former general and West Point colleague of Eisenhower, assumed the Presidency of ITT. Leavey demanded frequent and detailed reports and tightened financial controls, thereby imposing a new form of discipline on managing directors (Sobel, 1982). Geneen was recruited to extend these financial policies. Geneen's short-lived successor, Hamilton, saw military service as a mere midshipman followed by an extensive governmental career. He was followed by Askarog, a West Point graduate (class rank 126th of 512). Askarog retained the ITT tradition of financial engineering and control through accounting, albeit in a more constricted delegated form. Prima facie, the history of ITT provides evidence of Foucauldian-inspired accounts of management accounting's origins in the examinatory system and American military academies, especially the West Point connection.

Not all the empirics fitted neatly into Foucault's model of analysis. Foucauldian analysis, if it is to provide a basis for full theorization, may need extension and refinement. This was apparent in three respects. First, whilst accounting controls in ITT effected a disciplinary gaze upon management, their features did not exactly mirror the principles of discipline and control detailed by Foucault. Moreover, accounting controls evolved and changed in ITT over time: accounting was not always the principal mode of control and it did not take a single form. If accounting is an expression of modernity then Foucault's bi-polar turning point for change of pre- and post-modernity cannot explicate subtle shifts in the means of control within ITT. Second, whilst Foucauldian analysis picked up the significance of discourse and disciplinary power, it failed to encompass other important factors affecting modes of control within ITT, especially financial markets, corporate relations with states and technologies. Third, panoptical control is not absolute; resistance within and without ITT helped shape its transformation.

Management accounting in ITT post-Behn was abstract, indirect, written and controlled through aggregated outputs, whereas the panoptical gaze is physical, direct and seeks to control immediate behaviour. Management accounting and associated controls in ITT under Geneen were a technologically more sophisticated adaptation rather than an isomorphism of the principles of surveillance outlined by Foucault, though it must be pointed out that the accounting controls needed supplementing by direct and visual interrogatory processes of accountability meetings. Such accounting may be an expression of power–knowledge in modernity, but ITT's initial growth under Colonel Behn, who eschewed detailed internal controls and instead relied on diplomacy with client Governments (Sobel, 1982), is a reminder that non-panoptical controls also exist in this period. These shifts in types of control in ITT were not restricted to the time of Geneen's accession: post-Geneen, ITT recognized major deficiencies in its systems and modified them, including shorter accountability meetings, reduced headquarters staff, an emphasis on high-tech research and development, and divestment (e.g. Thackray, 1981; Colvin, 1982; *Business Week*, 1984; Brody, 1985; Stevens, 1985).

Yet significantly the dual reporting system for comptrollers remained intact (Alleman, 1985). The central point is that controls in ITT never exactly corresponded to a panoptical gaze, nor were they constant over time. The explanation of changes in organizational controls requires a richer extended framework than that utilized in *Discipline and Punish*. As Foucault explicitly stated that his text concentrated on but one of several mechanisms of power in modernity and he never claimed his models exactly correspond to actuality, our observations may not be unexpected. Nevertheless, they do call for further development of Foucault's work. As Foucauldian accounting research has rarely ventured beyond the 1920s, opportunities to extend and refine Foucault's ideas according to the empirics of today's large and powerful corporations have been neglected.

Geneen's methods may have been awesome and encompassing, but points of resistance within and without ITT did occur. For example, European managers, many of whom were unsympathetic to Geneen's strategies and methods, utilized Geneen's visiting acolytes' devotion to timetables to their advantage by deferring discussion of key topics until shortly before their visitors' return flight times. More importantly, the series of Federal investigations into ITT's involvement with the overthrow of the Allende government in Chile, anti-trust investigations, and the 'San Diego Affair' concerning ITT's financial involvement with a Republican Party convention, were all fuelled partly by a series of internal leaks from ITT (Sampson, 1974; Sobel, 1982). The resultant political pressures contributed significantly to Geneen's demise. The essential point is that ITT was unable to totally control its subjects and their resistance played a crucial role in delimiting ITT's actions. Moreover, nation states and consumer groups were not passive and compliant. The role of these events is crucial to any understanding of transformation within ITT.

Conclusion

We shall conclude by returning to Geneen in person and his story. When Geneen took on the CEO post at ITT in 1959 he inherited a loosely managed but profitable company which was little more than a New-York-based holding company investing in plants and operations around the world and hoping for the best. Most of its earnings came from outside the USA in countries deemed by Geneen to be politically unstable (Sobel, 1982). In a decade, with Geneen at the helm, ITT had been transformed into a profitable and growing conglomerate operating globally with a wide variety of unrelated products. ITT's profits grew from \$30m in 1961 to over \$406m in 1971, coming equally from internal operations and outside acquisitions. By 1971, ITT ranked twelfth in the Fortune 500 list of industrial enterprises.

Geneen did not see himself first and foremost as a capitalist (or as an unwilling dupe of the capitalist system) but as a manager. He believed fervently in the virtues of managing. In his own words, 'MANAGEMENT must manage! Management MUST manage! Management must MANAGE! It is a very simple credo, probably the closest thing to the secret of success in business. The strange thing is that everybody knows it, but somehow managers forget it all the time' (Geneen, 1984b: 78). For Geneen this meant the arduous, lonely and tedious process of management by the numbers. Thus his famous slogan, 'The truth is that the numbers will make you free.'

For Geneen this means that *real* managers study and pore over the accounting numbers until their minds spin. Then suddenly one number or set of numbers suddenly stands out, gets the attention it demands, comprehension slowly seeps in, at last the manager is 'at ease with numbers and what they really mean.' With this comes the feeling of confidence that one is in control, aware of why variations from expectations come into being, and *free* to do things – build a plant, invest in risky research, buy a company – that he or she would otherwise not do and 'do it with assurance because you are able to sit down and figure out what the new venture will do to the balance sheet' (Geneen, 1984b: 81). When this happens, the manager is free at last.

The message from Foucault is quite different. He would see how Geneen's panoptic accounting regime of truth acts as an extra-juridical network of surveillance and discipline meting out its examinatory-justice throughout ITT. The carceral accounting pyramid (to paraphrase Foucault) 'naturalizes' Geneen's disciplinary power to inflict legal punishment on his sundry managers. Organizations like ITT are societies of 'accounting-judges' on whom: 'the universal reign of normative is based; and each individual, wherever he may find himself, subjects to it his body, his gestures, his behaviour, his achievements', and so the accounting carceral is 'a certain way of rendering the group of men docile and useful' (Foucault, 1979: 304–5).

Management accounting, re-constructed in Foucault's terms, is a major apparatus of discipline and punishment in large organizations. Following the principal enclosure, management accounting calls for the detailed partitioning of the organization into 'responsibility centres' which are partitioned further into homogeneous types of employees, identified in terms of use, and ranked within an explicit hierarchy of authority and accountability. Financial controls, mirroring the principle of the efficient body, call for a rigorous timetabling and reporting process which situates the manager in a world of signals and which serves as a means of correct training in planning, coordinating, measuring and controlling activities within the manager's responsibility centre. They also stress that managers must make exhaustive use of their time in order to assure efficient and effective task performance but that financial control discipline should be exercised gingerly, not in a heavy-handed manner.

Finally, conforming to the principle of disciplinary power, financial controls act as an apparatus for the totalizing, normalizing surveillance of each responsibility centre and the constant examining, ranking and sanctioning of the employees. This all-seeing, all-knowing disciplinary power produces docile obedient managers who willingly carry out the work of the organization. These ideas are illustrated vividly in Geneen's account of his tenure as CEO of ITT.

In closing, Foucault's revelation of the disciplinary, punitive, carceral nature of Modernity's life world was neither inaccurate nor inappropriate. Yet on its own it was inadequate for fully capturing the rich dynamics of management and management accounting control systems. This gestures towards a more eclectic and pluralistic attitude by management accounting researchers to theory and the need for scepticism towards those seeking to give any theory or concept a privileged position. And who knows, perhaps such a stance might pave the way – to return to our opening epigraph – for a new social order where institutions such as hospitals, barracks, schools, factories and industrial enterprises no longer resemble prisons.

Acknowledgements

We gratefully acknowledge the financial support of the Queen's University, School of Business, Summer Visiting Research Scholar Program which enabled us to work together on this paper. N.B. Macintosh is also grateful to the Social Sciences and Humanities Research Council of Canada, the School of Accounting, University of New South Wales, Australia and the Naval

Postgraduate School, Monterey, California for providing research stipends and support services for the research.

Notes

1 While some might object to the idea of consolidating these ideas into a specific model or set of ideas, it is clear enough that in *Discipline and Punish: The Birth of the Prison*, Foucault (1979) comes across in a very systematic, structuralist fashion. In fact, in the book he uses phrases (italics added) such as: 'a new political *anatomy*' (p. 138); 'the *rule* of functional sites' (p. 143); 'the *principle* of enclosure' (p. 143); 'the *universal* jurisdicism of modern society' (p. 223); 'the carceral *system*' (p. 293); 'superimposition of different *models*' (p. 294); 'the carceral *archipelago*' (p. 298); 'mechanisms of *normalization*' (p. 301); 'the *universality* of the carceral' (p. 303); 'the carceral *texture*' (p. 304); and 'the *modality* of disciplinary power' (p. 221). These descriptors (anatomy, system, universal, models, archipelago, universality, texture and modality) signal that Foucault was not averse to systematic thinking regarding the disciplined, disciplinary texture of society and its major social institutions. In speculating on 'the date of completion of the carceral systems' Foucault fixes on 20 January 1840, when the penitentiary at Mettray, France, officially opened. 'Why Mettray? Because it is the disciplinary form at its most extreme, the model in which are concentrated all the coercive technologies of behaviour' (p. 293). Clearly, Foucault had no qualms about models or systems of thought.

2 See Hoskin and Macve (1986, 1988) for a detailed history of the disciplinary practices at West Point in the nineteenth century.

3 An assembly of live subjects arranged to depict a scene with a subject or a purpose.

4 A 'yes–no' type questionnaire was developed for each comptrollership area with some 30 to 60 'yes–no' type questions, depending on the area. Each unit comptroller answered nearly 1,600 self-evaluation questions in completing the examination while the divisional financial comptroller (DFC) answered over 150 questions. The self-evaluation items, based on a 0 to 5 point scale, were weighted one and the divisional comptroller's items carried a weight of five. Thus, the final score was weighted about 70 per cent on self-evaluation and 30 per cent on DFC's ratings. The two ratings were then combined to get an overall score where a perfect evaluation equalled 100. The ratings for each of the 250 field units became the basis for a colour-coded ratings timetable (blue, green, yellow and red) where blue (the highest rating) indicated satisfactory performance and another rating in two years, while red (the lowest rating) meant unacceptable performance and another rating in three months.

References

Alleman, R.H. (1985) 'Comptrollership at ITT', *Management Accounting (USA)*, May: 24–30.

Brody, M. (1985) 'Caught in the cash crunch at ITT', *Fortune*, April: 62–4.

Business Week (1984) 'ITT's Big Gamble', 2865: 114–21.

Colvin, G. (1982) 'The de-Geneening of ITT', *Fortune*, January: 34–9.

Foucault, M. (1975) *Surveiller et Punir: Naissance de la Prison*. Paris: Gallimard.

Foucault, M. (1979) *Discipline and Punish: The Birth of the Prison*. New York: Vintage Books.

Geneen, H. (1984a) 'The case for managing by the numbers', *Fortune*, October: 78–83.

Geneen, H. (1984b) *Managing*. New York: Avon.

Hoskin, K.W. and Macve, R.H. (1986) 'Accounting and the examination: a genealogy of disciplinary power', *Accounting, Organizations and Society*, 11 (2): 105–36.

Hoskin, K.W. and Macve, R.H. (1988) 'The genesis of accountability: the West Point connection', *Accounting, Organizations and Society*, 13 (1): 37–74.

Menzies, H.D. (1980) 'The ten toughest bosses', *Fortune*: 62–72.

Miller, P. and O'Leary, T. (1987) 'Accounting and the construction of the governable person', *Accounting, Organizations and Society*, 12 (3): 235–65.

Sampson, A. (1974) *The Sovereign State of ITT*. London: Hodder and Stoughton.

Stevens, C. (1985) 'Off the critical list', *Financial World*, 154 (20): 103–4.

Sobel, R. (1982) *The Management of Opportunity*. New York: Truman Tulley/Time Books.

Thackray, J. (1981) 'Nemesis at ITT', *Management Today*, July: 46–51.

III

(RE)CONSTRUCTING THE MODERN ORGANIZATION

9

Discursive Formations, Strategized Subordination and Self-surveillance

Stanley Deetz

> It is one of my targets to show people that a lot of things that are part of
> their landscape – that people think are universal – are the results of some
> very precise historical changes. All my analyses are against the idea of
> universal necessities in human existence. They show the arbitrariness of
> institutions and show which space of freedom we can still enjoy and how
> many changes can still be made. (Foucault, 1988: 11)

Workplaces throughout the world are rapidly changing owing to new
technologies, new market conditions, and new conceptions of employer–
employee relations. With this has come new concerns with workplace
control – concern from dominant groups with how to acquire and exercise it,
and concern from others with new forms of domination, representational
failure, and less satisfactory company performance. My concern here aligns
with these latter groups.

Older forms of domination clearly still exist. Research concern with
oppressive work conditions, authority relations, processes of coercion,
dominant ideologies, work rules, and various other forms of manipulation
and oppression must be continued, and we have many excellent conceptions
for doing so. But with new 'high-end' industries, participation and empowerment plans, and shifting work forces, new and more subtle forms of
domination are emerging (see Barker, 1993; Alvesson, 1993a). While it may
be more difficult to have great concern with these 'middle-class' problems,
the limitations they put on organizational learning and positive use of
resources as well as the way they politically reconstruct a large active class
of people leave them of great importance (see Heckscher, 1995). These new
forms of control are most present in so-called 'knowledge-intensive' industries and in the 'knowledge-intensive' portions of other companies.
Understanding such organizations and these units is also important as they

make up a growing portion of the work force, at least in the economically advanced nations (Quinn, 1992; Drucker, 1993).

Foucault's conceptions of 'disciplinary power' and 'social technologies of control' have been very important in understanding new forms of domination arising in a variety of social institutions. Here I wish to use Foucauldian concepts to analyse a knowledge-intensive unit of a large multinational telecommunication corporation. Foucault's own analyses focused on major historical transformations, especially as they pertained to knowledge, health, order, and sexuality and the institutions specializing in them. And despite the constant expressed concern with micro-empirical events, more often his empirical discussions were illustrative rather than demonstrative. Organizational researchers inspired by Foucault have tended to work in a similar fashion. Highly successful analyses like those of Townley (1993), Knights (1992), and Knights and Morgan (1991) have looked at large discursive formations like the development of expertise in human resource management or the discourse of strategic planning, but rarely show how these are enacted in specific organizational contexts. The focus has been more on the university's role in producing knowledge about organization, and how that is utilized, than on the knowledge produced within corporations. I have done much the same in earlier works considering the conditions leading to the prevalence of disciplinary over sovereign power (Deetz, 1992a, Ch. 10) and generally how disciplinary power produces particular types of human subjectivity, especially the managed subject (Deetz, 1992b). Detailed case studies, however, have been less common. A case study can show how corporate processes become treated as natural and non-arbitrary and can display the unrealized freedoms remaining in these sites. That is the point of this analysis.

I wish to situate only briefly this analysis in Foucault's work before turning to the case example. In summarizing his own work, Foucault defined four major types of technologies of self-understanding that enter into the power games of truth. Each is a matrix of practical reason and each is associated with a certain type of domination. They are:

> (1) technologies of production, which permit us to produce, transform or manipulate things; (2) technologies of sign systems, which permit us to use signs, meanings symbols, or signification; (3) technologies of power, which determine the conduct of individuals and submit them to certain ends or domination, an objectivizing of the subject; and (4) technologies of the self, which permit individuals to effect by their own means or with the help of others a certain number of operations on their own bodies and souls, thoughts, conduct, and way of being, so as to transform themselves in order to attain a certain state of happiness, purity, wisdom, perfection, or immortality. (1988: 18)

These four 'technologies' interplay in particular sites, enabling productivity and defining satisfying personal identities and social relations. But they also lead to unnecessary conformity, restrictions of personal and organizational learning, and one-sided identities and relations. The processes of enablement and constraint arise together; one cannot exist without the other. So the point of looking at these technologies is not to argue for some form of autonomy or freedom through the critique of these constraints. Rather, the attempt is to resist the freezing and generalization of constraints and to ultimately reclaim social actor efficacy in working within these arbitrary bounds to make more satisfying choices. The problem is not the presence of constraint *per se*, but domination – the naturalization of arbitrary productions and closure of responsive options. The analysis is not directed towards determination by reason without power relations, but towards constant reconfiguration of power relations. This is a perpetual actor and researcher task initiated by insight into the logic and form of domination. As Foucault suggested:

> a society without power relations can only be an abstraction. . . . [However] to say that there cannot be a society without power relations is not to say either that those which are established are necessary, or, in any case, that power constitutes a fatality at the heart of societies, such that it cannot be undermined. Instead I would say that the analysis, elaboration, and bringing into question of power relations and the 'agonism' between power relations and the intransitivity of freedom is a permanent political task inherent in all social existence. (1982: 208)

While each of the four 'technologies' is of concern in the site studied, this essay primarily focuses on 'technologies of the self' which are central to domination in highly professionalized workplaces. Primary concern will be with how employees in the site studied consented within a discursive formation through strategizing their own subordination and engaged in active self-surveillance and self-control. I will begin with a brief consideration of the work organization, consider how workplace control is shaped by the nature of the business, and then consider how these 'technologies' work in this site.

The case study

The case study was an open-ended exploratory analysis of the relations among corporate cultural features, communication processes, and methods of coordination and control.[1] The data for this analysis were collected during a four-month period in the autumn of 1993. The group studied, Applied Integrated Management Systems (AIMS), is a professional service component of a large, multinational telecommunication corporation (LTC).[2] AIMS normally employs around 90 people; about 35 of these are considered temporary since they are hired on fixed-term contracts for specific projects and receive no standard employee benefits. About two thirds of all AIMS permanent employees work from the district's principal site in eastern USA. At the end of their most recent reorganization, AIMS was composed of six work groups ranging in size from six to 15. Two of these are branch offices: one in a neighbouring state and the other on the west coast.

AIMS was founded within LTC in 1991 with a very strong mission and vision to form a 'consultancy style' group providing 'integrated' solutions to various business problems, mostly involving computer and network systems.

Prior to the formation of AIMS most of the service functions were diffused throughout LTC in service centres or were performed as required by outside consultants. These services ranged from developing software for new billing and product control systems for other units of LTC to various types of personnel training. Many of these service centres prior to AIMS's formation were 'fully funded' through a budgeting system that treated them as a company-wide overhead cost. They responded to the needs of other units as requested on a loose priority system.

The reorganization that formed AIMS brought together a variety of different groups from LTC to form a division within AIMS. The reorganization was championed by the person who would become the Divisional Director as well as by others already in consulting-style services within LTC, including the present District Manager of AIMS. The conception of internal profit centres and the ideology of consultancy were considered able to break down the bureaucracy of fully funded centres, increase employee motivation, and improve accountability. From a company standpoint, internal profit centres changed political battles for resources among service units to economic competition. Rather than managers cutting services, the market would make the determination. As described by one manager:

> I was always in a funded, ya know some kind of funded organization where you were on retainer to a business you knew or a project and beginning of the year you would figure out how many people you needed for a project, it'd be 8, and you made damn sure you spent 8 people because otherwise if you only spent 7 next year your budget was cut. So there was a lot of resources ah, the other thing that happens if the project gets cut and that is out of your control now you have to lose people. Whereas consultancy whatever you can sell whatever services you have your group goal'll shrink your business goal'll shrink by what you can sell not by someone else's budget problem. That's why I like consultancy.[3]

The consultancy concept has clear ideological value and highlights important aspects of modern corporate life, and has considerable rhetorical power through easy coordination with extended discourses throughout the organization.

The employees of AIMS are highly educated (most with master's degrees in technical fields), well paid (upper seven per cent nation-wide), and have high degrees of job security and potential for career mobility. Their specialities range from computer software and information system design and implementation to human resources and job design. Nearly all AIMS members interviewed have worked for LTC for their entire professional career (averaging 12 years) and for AIMS since it was pulled together out of different parts of LTC 18 months prior to my interviews. AIMS members invest a high degree of their personal identity in their work and employment situation. Many seem more connected to their work than to their families or any outside group. Most hope to continue doing what they are doing and would be willing to take pay cuts to work on the projects they liked. Still, many of the employees and project managers work at client locations for extended periods of time and often feel cut off from AIMS.[4] Mixed loyalty is common since client evaluations of services is a significant portion of the employee's annual review. And, predictably, it is not uncommon for employees to take jobs with client organizations (nearly all are other parts of LTC).

During the study period AIMS is experiencing an economic crisis owing to bidding and billing mistakes and the loss of a significant contract. Even during this crisis, however, morale is high. Most employees have been through several reorganizations at LTC and are reasonably confident that even if AIMS were to be disbanded, they would be employed in a similar capacity somewhere in LTC. As will be shown, management members, however, appear to have more to lose if AIMS is reabsorbed into LTC. They have tried to increase employee loyalty to AIMS and have tried to evoke some fear of AIMS's demise.

Knowledge-intensive work and control processes

The work at AIMS can be defined as knowledge intensive. As such it shares characteristics with a growing list of professional service organizations and industries which rely primarily on individual and collective forms of intellectual capital. Numerous studies have shown that the management of employees in such companies is different from that in manufacturing and manual service companies (e.g. Greenwood et al., 1990; Hinings et al., 1991; Normann, 1991; Alvesson, 1992, 1994; Starbuck, 1992). These differences clearly impact on the forms of control and domination. In general the following can be said about knowledge-intensive work.

First, work groups in most knowledge-intensive organizations are explicitly characterized by high levels of autonomy and self-management. The viability of direct control processes is reduced by employee conceptions of autonomy entitlement, the specialized nature of the expertise, the lack of clear normative standards for the product, the presence of powerful professional codes, the presence of work activity outside the employment site, and the presence of alternative employment opportunities. Generally these characteristics reduce the legitimacy of managerial control and reduce what Foucault called 'sovereign' power.

The capacity for direct control is further reduced owing to the difficulty of observing the work process and the difficulty of measuring and attaching financial rewards to specific product characteristics. This is not to suggest that more traditional forms of control are absent at AIMS or similar companies. Orders are given, people are watched, products are measured. Simply these occur relatively infrequently, are comparatively subtle, are reserved for the most extreme cases, and are subject to justification demands when they are present. At AIMS, for example, in the tight economic situation the District Manager has assigned people to jobs where they previously had choices in job selection. While compliance is present, it has led to unhappiness and is treated by all, including the manager, as a necessary but undesirable short-term practice.

Additionally, the relative weight of the various forms of capital are different in knowlege-intensive companies from more traditional ones, and this has consequences for control processes. More traditional companies rely primarily on financial capital which is used to produce a relatively fixed work site. Ownership rights, and managerial prerogatives extending from them, rely on the assumption of capital investment and risk and employee dependency on someone else having made an investment. The three primary forms of 'capital' for knowledge-intensive companies, however, are 'intellectual' (skills and knowledge unique to specific employees), 'relational' (networks and trust relations with clients), and 'artefactual' (data bases and files containing technical data and client data). All three forms of capital are highly symbolic, thus need constant reproduction and secondary systems of justification, and are highly mobile. Further, each is more a property of the employee than anyone else.

As a result of these differences, in the place of authority relations and direct supervision, most control is 'normative' (Kunda, 1992; Barker, 1993). The control processes are unobtrusive and use group processes and standards to normalize behaviour. The presence of a 'strong' culture and shared internalized values provide control and coordination (Ouchi and Maguire, 1975; Alvesson, 1993a). At LTC and AIMS this has often included developing vision statements, shared value principles, company images, and active socialization programmes as well as managing cultural characteristics of the work environment. In Foucauldian terms, these control processes use *technologies of power*, in this case disciplinary power (Foucault, 1980; Clegg, 1989; Deetz, 1992b). But employees are often subject to competing cultural influences arising from internal and external relations with professional groups and client organizations. This complex of professional and exchange relationships leave all control processes fragmented and tenuous. For example, being a good engineer may be more prized than being a good manager of engineers, yet managerial demands may supersede professional standards (see also Kunda, 1992). Still these may be articulated together in ways that suppress or distort the conflicts and reduce contestation and full representation of each in choices.

The reduction of direct control leaves employees with a sense of liberation and capacity for negotiated self-identity and reality, as well as potential for different operations of power and forms of domination. Cultural and other forms of disciplinary control in these contexts become operant only to the extent that they are either internalized or reproduced in daily discourse and activities as a form of self-control (Knights and Willmott, 1985, 1989; Knights and Collinson, 1987). At AIMS, as will be developed, Foucault's conceptions of discipline and self-surveillance are especially useful in both showing how control works and the difficulties it creates.

Secondly, tasks are often uncertain and ambiguous in knowledge-intensive work, and agreement on problem definitions and solutions requires active communication and negotiation. Even the products of most work processes at AIMS are hard to measure based on intrinsic characteristics. In these environments messages serve a number of fairly explicit social purposes in addition to providing information. For example, since the nature of an individual's work and the quality of products produced often remains uncertain and open to social determination, both work-related roles and identities and professional competency are actively established in interaction (see Alvesson, 1993b). While organizational positions, certifications, and seniority exert constraints, employees frequently engage in role creation and negotiation to determine what needs to be done, how to do it, and their personal responsibilities. Since the need for products is often vendor driven and vendors and products are not easily compared, personal and organizational images are especially important. The largely fluid nature of anything external to interactional accomplishments, provides for very active symbolic labour. This leaves what Foucault called *technologies of sign systems* somewhat more visible and explicit than is the case in more stable environments with relatively constant, reproduced object distinctions. Differentiation, de-differentiation, re-differentiation through measurement and classification devices, naming and euphemisms, are on-going political acts (see also Bourdieu, 1991). At AIMS, such processes are clearest in the 'consultancy' business concept but spread through classification of people, activities, and products (see also Deetz, 1997).

Thirdly, the client–service-provider relationship assumes special significance. Most often the client participates in task activities by defining needs, soliciting attention, and being the primary evaluator of service quality. The personal relationship between the employee and client takes on special importance for several structural reasons: '(1) the problems facing the professional are not highly structured, (2) crucial information needed for task completion can be secured only by the individuals, (3) solutions must be accepted by the client to ensure implementation' (Manz and Sims, 1980). To the extent that each of these conditions is present in a high degree, power shifts from the providing firm's management to employees. Role definitions are quite fluid, and many traditional managerial responsibilities, such as interfacing with the client or determining work methods, are shifted to the employee (Mills et al., 1983). The result is usually a very loose work arrangement with managerial control concentrated at the outcome rather than the work process (Slocum and Sims, 1980).

In this regard, the *technologies of production*, as conceptualized by Foucault, have significant meaning. The often hidden and mysterious work, plus the absence of a clear physical product with measurable characteristics, leaves identity to be acquired from the projection of the subject rather than drawn from the product or work activity. While some of AIMS's products were more material and measurable than others, e.g. a software programme either ran or it did not, some are fast and others slow, most products were sufficiently ambiguous to leave an indeterminant reflection on the provider. Often the provider's symbolically produced identity was more secure and lasting (and accounted more for a client's product assessment) than the work product. But a lingering sense of falseness and insecurity comes with the symbolic identity.

Each of these 'technologies' present in knowledge-intensive work have their own forms of domination which played together at AIMS. In many ways they over-determined the specific *technologies of self* which became the most prominent way that domination was played out.

Consent or voice

Given these work conditions, AIMS employees have the potential for comparatively high degrees of personal autonomy. The unit members are minimally supervised, often working at home or in remote sites. They are valued by the company, and the company loses much if they leave. For many reasons, the company has to be more committed to keeping the employees than vice versa: (1) the retention of employees is critical from the company's standpoint since an employee can carry substantial capital with them if they leave; (2) client retention efforts make specific employees more valuable and increase the risk of their exit; (3) perceptions of stability have high value in themselves; and (4) the price of down time, recruiting and retaining clients and other 'overhead costs' is relatively high.

On first glance, AIMS appears to have a beneficial arrangement where employees make decisions presumably fulfilling their personal desires in this open choice context, which also potentially pays off well for the company. Even problems at AIMS demonstrate a clear sense of commitment and alignment of employee and unit goals (even though sometimes poorly thought out). For example, managers identify the tendency for employees to under-report their hours on their time forms as a problem. This problem has been a recurring theme at managerial meetings and subsequent extensive discussion with employees. For AIMS this is a problem since most employee hours are billable to outside units. In my interviews, however, employees describe under-reporting as a way to show their commitment to both AIMS and clients, to compensate for their mistakes or time in learning, and to disallow their social-chat time and various meetings at their home site. Certainly, this problem differs much from the more expected management–employee difference which might lead to over-reporting hours to demonstrate more work effort and to earn more money.

The apparently positive relation between the company and employees might well be considered to be unproblematic and even enviable, but a more careful analysis poses questions to this general consensus. One might reasonably ask how open the agreements are or to what extent arbitrary and harmful social configurations are reproduced without exploration or contestation. Further, one can ask what the costs and benefits of these arrangements are to the employee, company, and outside groups if different, but unthought, assessments are used.

In looking carefully at AIMS, despite these workplace characteristics and reported values of self-management, lattice structure, and autonomy, a dominant logic was reproduced through various material and symbolic formations to the long-term detriment of both the employee and company. For Foucault, this type of a 'logic' constitutes a discursive formation: a complex system for giving meaning to the world, organizing social institutions and processes, and naturalizing such structures and meanings. The formation was enabled through organizing the unit as an 'internal consultant group' and enacted through active employee 'consent'. The difference between autonomy used to accomplish self and company goals and subdued autonomy which provides consent to dominant configurations deserves some attention before looking at how the consultancy conception was used to facilitate consent.

Following along the general line of Hirschman (1970), employees who choose to stay in a company choose to varying degrees 'loyalty' or 'voice'. From Foucault's conceptions, loyalty can be thought of as a kind of 'consent' to arbitrary institutional arrangements as if they were natural and incontestable. 'Consent' processes designate the variety of situations and activities where someone actively, though often unknowingly, accomplishes the interests of others in the faulty attempt to fulfil his or her own. The person does not have a false sense of self nor a lack of connection to subjective experiences. Rather the social arrangements create a well-knowing subject fully imbued with experiences, but one which is partial and preferential. As a result, rather than having open discussions, discussions are foreclosed or appear unnecessary. The interaction processes reproduce fixed identities, relations, and knowledge, and the variety of possible differences are lost. Consent often appears in direct forms as members actively subordinate themselves to obtain money, security, meaning, or identity – things which should result from the work process itself without the necessity of subordination. In fact the presence of subordination hampers the accomplishment of self and company goals.

'Voice' can be considered as an attempt to open discussion about issues that apparently need no discussion and to act *on*, rather than simply *in*, present institutional arrangements. Voice, thus, is the presence of active resistance to consent processes. 'Voicing' opens both the corporation and individuals to learning through reclaiming differences and conflicts overlooked or suppressed by dominant conceptions and arrangements. All discursive formations centralize particular concerns and interests and marginalize others. Dominant arrangements normalize people and events along the lines of certain interests. Voice reclaims that which was marginalized, putting it back into a competitive relation with the dominant interests.

At AIMS, to reduce the risk of exit, the management group was enticed to increase either employee loyalty or voice. Through the contrived discursive arrangement, the potential autonomy provided only a type of loyalty. Thus, AIMS employees primarily engaged in consent rather than voice. Where voice existed at all it tended to be highly privatized, leading to empty complaints and ineffective local acts of resistance. Consent occurred in the active production of a particular type of self-understanding produced and reproduced by discursive and institutional arrangements. Employees further reproduced this consent through strategically utilizing these produced selves to define systems and acquire rewards. They exercised what autonomy they had to acquire financial and identity securities that left them progressively more dependent on AIMS and less capable of voice. As developed below, with the consultancy arrangement, the subjectivities of the employees were metaphorically produced as autonomous, self-employed, owners and experts, and contradictions within these subjectivities and alternatives to them were suppressed. This was willed by, rather than forced on, employees, yet created a condition of domination which distorted goal accomplishment by the employees, AIMS, and LTC and created potential harms to clients and employee families.

The discourse of consulting and the production of the AIMS employee

Prior to the formation of AIMS, most employees were performing professional services on a 'fully funded' basis. They were hired by LTC and provided services to other groups as needed. Budgeting processes within the organization were explicitly value-laden and political. The value of the services and financial support for them had to be defended in each budgeting cycle. This provided some inefficiencies and gave managers certain powers while it also provided the employee with considerable autonomy. Management in rather traditional ways worked to get the most for the salary assigned to employees. Management control of employees was largely direct through monitoring the work effort. The employee had both the freedoms and constraints given to a 'professional worker' in the linguistic distinctions and structural arrangements in LTC.

Conceptualizing the unit as an 'internal consulting group' made AIMS into a 'profit centre' where it was paid for the services provided and had to pay for its own costs, including personnel. This led to significant changes in the identity of employees and in control processes. Employee commitment and loyalty increased as it was now 'their company' (though they owned it no more now than before). Employees' perceived autonomy and responsibility increased since the success of the company was now more in their own hands. And the employee-acquired identity of 'consultant' had higher status (it suggests expertise and independence) than the service provider/worker designation. The employees are not just workers offering services in a bureaucracy, they are consultants. To the extent they took on this identity as their own, the personal/identity costs of 'their company' failing became higher. And loyalty was further increased, even though that meant losing autonomies granted to workers and only having the symbolic appearance of autonomies given to owner/consultant. Conceptions of self-value changed from pleasing a client and doing a good job as goods in themselves or as a fair exchange of labour for pay to the instrumentalization of these in the service of making money for the 'firm'. Most worked harder for the same pay. Employees' self-worth changed from being based on product quality or social standing to being based on feeling more important if someone was paying the company for their services.

Many interviewees discussed the good feeling that came from knowing that a client rather than employer was willing to pay for what they did. The institutional arrangement and client gave them identity rewards rather than just pay for their labour. And interestingly, the less their services seemed understood or appreciated by AIMS management, the more pressing being defined by client satisfaction ('by being wanted') became. Considerable identity is invested in being defined as good by others, a conception from which AIMS as a consulting type company gains financially. In this discursive set-up, AIMS's financial gain is greatest the closer they can keep employees to the very brink of exit.

Consulting, as the discursive self-conception, produces consent to worth's being determined by money. A couple of quick examples:

> As a consultant everyone you deal with you know that they want you there, because they are willing to pay.

> I feel like they're paying me to do something I better be doing it to the best of my ability.

There seemed to be little discussion of the other side of measuring self worth by money, the transforming of self into a commodity. They seemed happy to do that if it had identity pay-off (see Knights and Willmott, 1989). Rather than the self being an end, with labour and money as means, the self becomes a means to money. The company in no direct way violates Kant's moral imperative to treat people as ends, the person does it on the company's behalf.

A constant refrain was attention to the customer. The line most often repeated was, 'in consulting if you don't please your customer, you're out of business'. The seriousness of this construction is shown in an annual review system which emphasizes customer rating forms. But the conception is tautological and self-sealing. No evidence is given that clients are being treated better, rather the clients' self-reports are uncritically accepted. The possibility of vendor-driven 'needs', the influence of personal relations, or increased overhead cost and short cuts to improve profits are not considered. But even at the personal level of the employee, one does not have to follow the discourse very far to find gaps and contradictions. In their work discourse 'consulting makes money the game', but their private talk is far different.

Rarely is there evidence that money is the primary motivator for the individual 'consultant' at AIMS. Ironically, the person is defined by money, but does not especially work for money. Nearly all reported satisfaction in doing a good job, in solving a problem, and in simply pleasing a customer. Even the focus on integrated services is advocated so that the project can be seen through to the end, so that the work is more innovative and at a higher skill level, never because it is more profitable. Certainly there is no inherent contradiction between these intrinsic values and consultancy or making money, but they would seem just as likely in a funded agency. And most do not seem terribly concerned that the unit is currently unprofitable.

While the monetary conception does not seem to enter into motivation, it does into conceptual relations. Little attention is paid to the way the consultancy conception instrumentalizes each of these desires that do seem to motivate and how it transforms social relations into economic ones. Additionally, several of their current complaints of having to take jobs that they did not want and having to engage in marketing activities certainly come with a consultancy mentality. So while the instrumentalization of the self is felt, it does not appear to be able to be discussed, thus conceptualized, clearly. When money is not a primary motivator, management seeks other means of increasing work effort. They can satisfy other employee desires like those listed above. Or as in AIMS they can contrive an arrangement where economic determination re-enters. To the extent that a consultancy identity is accepted, the financial arrangement leads employees to control themselves, rather than management's having to do it.

The instrumentalization of the consultant–client relationship created its own forms of unpaid labour and control. In placing the client as central in evaluations of work activities and in definitions of identity, the employee is called upon to engage in activities that no employer could require or monitor and ones that few employees would be willing to give to their employer. An example of this, though unique in being somewhat to AIMS's disadvantage, was shown in the under-reporting of work time at client sites. Few employers could require that workers under-report work hours, but here it is done voluntarily often in subtle and disguised form. More significant was the amount of 'emotional labour' required (Hochschild, 1983). Several clients bordered on being abusive as well as making unrealistic work demands. Such clients did not appear to relate to their own employees in this way. The sense of these was, 'I have paid for this, I have a right to have it delivered no matter what you have to do'. In this surrogate management situation, not only did AIMS employees lack normal worker rights, since they complied voluntarily to meet the client needs, they were 'expected' to placate clients and maintain friendly, supportive relations. AIMS employees were generally 'required' to work extraordinary hours to meet client 'needs', including occasionally sleeping on cots in client work sites and working weekends to meet unrealistic deadlines which they themselves co-created in the bidding process. And additionally they were 'expected' to be happy, engaging, and attentive. Terms like 'expected' and 'required' are meant here in a 'consent' sense, since AIMS's management could not require such behaviours. Extra work and personal relations were being sold on behalf of AIMS. If anything, AIMS's management deplored such clients (thus helping to reduce exit) and openly acknowledged such pressures and even offered support. Yet, the command to please the client as a part of the consultancy 'self-employment' and a reward system all enhanced consent to management control only accomplished through clients rather than directly by AIMS managers.

Further, the discursive formation reproduced a conservative political ideology spread across other areas of life: economic calculations are to be preferred over social or political discussions as a means of decision making; people work harder and better if their effort is measured by money; a large corporation composed of entrepreneurial groups through self-interest, self-management and economic initiative can contribute to the greater good as if guided by an invisible hand. In interview descriptions most of these values of economic rationality as connected to good decision making and employee motivation were assumed as an intrinsic quality of a consultant mind-set. As in most cases of ideology, no one sought or offered data to support the value of this relation.

> I think not being funded, having to have the customer commit the dollars to the project has a lot of benefits. It validates that your organization is doing something worthwhile. Like I don't know, I guess it's like the free market economy theory of, you know, 'cause I guess having been in IMS a number of years and seeing some of the other organizations in IMS and, yeah, I think it sort of transforms the focus of the organization somewhat.

> If you're doing good work and you're getting paid for the work you do, then as long as you continue to you can do this kind of thing. If you're a funded organization you're at the mercy of someone up top who knows nothing about what you're doing, just to say, well, this morning I think I'm gonna cut by fifty percent so okay everyone down there, you know. With no rhyme nor reason, you know, the organization, you might be doing well and. . . .

> I tend to think that people in funded organizations, in that type of work, tend to get lazy, ah that may be a broad statement but it is easier to not to have something to get done in that type of organization. . . .

Contrary possibilities that internal marketing costs are collectively high for the parent company, that vendor-driven creation of needs are a costly inefficiency, that economic instabilities drive good people away or keep them from doing good work, or that the pursuit of self-interests do not magically add up to company gain were not discussed, let alone assessed. And all this at a time when AIMS was not even making money. Consultancy may have been questioned by some as a good way to do their work, but neither the hidden economic dysfunctions nor the dominant market economy discourse from which it drew its power could. Criticisms were easily dismissed as backward looking ('not able to give up old ways') or simply 'self-interested' 'scared' and 'weak willed'. As one of the supporters of the consultancy idea before AIMS reflected on the transitions at AIMS:

> Uh, as we became merged into AIMS and there was a different culture, ya know. It was the old [LTC] culture that's still persists as you're regulated, you're funded, we do whatever we want. And bringing those people along kind of diluted the culture that we had and it wasn't a matter of diversity getting new ideas in it was a matter of getting some old ideas that we got away from back in.

Proclaiming the consultancy model could thus be used to justify and legitimate any decision that could be coded in economic language (see Deetz, 1995, Ch. 4). This brief analysis is not to suggest a preference for 'funded' over 'consulting' arrangements for internal service groups. In a fuller account, they can both be shown to have opportunities for multiple stakeholder representation or consent and other control processes. But, the presumed autonomy and invisibility of this control process led to choices that reduced representation and suppressed important conflicts.

Strategizing one's own subordination

In direct systems of control, management watches the work effort, rewards and punishes according to personal preferences or standards for desired work characteristics. In more subtle versions, management instrumentalizes the employee – turns him or her into a production means – and hires experts to construct systems to get the most from the employee (see Hollway, 1991; Townley, 1993). In any number of control systems, individuals assume the particular subjectivities posited in systems as their own. These are un-critically accepted since they are considered natural and unproblematic. But this is largely passive. A false sense of autonomy, however, is also a basis for more active consent processes. The most widely discussed was devel-oped by Michael Burawoy as 'strategizing one's own subordination'. Reflecting on his earlier work experience, he argued: 'We participated in and strategized our own subordination. We were accomplices in our exploitation. That, and not the destruction of our subjectivity, was what was so remark-able' (1985: 10). In the advanced control system discussed here, employees (and managers as employees) instrumentalize and strategize themselves. Through self-surveillance and control of their bodies, feelings, dress, and behaviour, they use themselves for their own strategized employment and careers movement (Foucault, 1977, 1980, 1988; Deetz, 1992a, Ch. 11, 1995). This self-management frequently benefited managerial interests more than company or employee ones. Self-management is management of the inner world along normative lines through the use of self and professional knowledge.

Strategized subordination happens as members actively subordinate them-selves to obtain money, security, meaning, or identity. Not only should each of these result from the work process rather than requiring subordination, but the outcome of the subordination is different than expected. The employee strategizes the self toward increases in power and money, but since these are themselves simply more instrumental means and not ends, the quest is never complete. The future is deferred and the quest endless. While there is an expectation and even some appearance of gain, significant hidden costs accrue to both the corporation and employees. When employees strategize their own subordination for the sake of private gains, they surrender whatever power they have to change their conditions and have the corporate experience better fulfil their needs. Consent to domination occurs since the processes of the production of the self remain unproblematic, conflicts which could produce contestation and display construction processes are sup-pressed, and a false sense of autonomy exists which leads to the mistaken presumption of an open construction process.

Suppressed conflict

In many workplaces like AIMS, individuals have mixed and often con-
flictual identities, many of which arise from cross-group membership. For
example, personal identity is often as much invested in their profession as in
their particular workplace roles. This leads to conflicts around authority and
order, since authority is vested in a managerial role that conflicts with the
authority vested in professional expertise (see Kunda, 1992). Further, the
sales and marketing orientation of the unit often conflict with both the
professional scientific ethic of knowing for its own sake, and the intrinsic
interest in the production activity itself. Other potential conflicts arise from
commitment to particular clients (especially after having spent time at their
work site), from membership in other groups in the corporation (for
example, one woman was on the corporate diversity committee), or from
family and other non-work commitments.

Suppressed conflict occurs when a pre-resolution of such conflicts exists
which appears to reduce the tension but does so by making unthinkable,
undiscussible, or marginal one pair in the conflict. The tension remains in a
now hidden form: for example, the formation of routine practices leaves
alternative practices overlooked; the concept of 'private' removes concerns
with child rearing from the workplace; or 'cold medications' suppress the
intrusion of the body's self-defences into work effort. If not suppressed, each
of these tensions could lead to significant change, learning, and creative
solutions.

Further, work conceptions may organize conflicts, making some 'approved' and suppressing others. In so doing, pressures from suppressed
conflicts become displaced into approved forms. For example, the consultancy discourse at AIMS constructs a non-traditional relation among
expressed and suppressed conflicts. This is perhaps clearest in the conception of the 'enemy'. In 'traditional' 'funded' work discourse, the principal
conflicts are expressed as employee versus management interests. Management expresses a desire for more control of the work process and greater
production with lower labour cost. And employees express the desire for
shorter working hours at greater pay and more autonomy in work processes.
Everyday conflicts arising from such desires are channelled into periodic
negotiation of work rules and the employment contract. In this traditional
discourse both management and production employees have a sense of
solidarity within their groups organized around labour and management
contract negotiation and work direction. Most organizational theory came to
extend this discourse and form of interest constitution and expression
through conceptualizing their theory and research in terms of control
processes and productivity needs, organized around the question of how to
get workers to work harder and better.

Consent rearranges these relations. As Michael Burawoy (1979) suggested, if we wish to understand these new relations we should begin by
asking why workers work as hard as they do. This question is partly

answered in looking at the shifts in conflicts. AIMS employees do not express a concern that the employer wants more work; their primary expressed concerns are that their body, their social needs, their incapacities, or families do not let them do more work better. The enemy is no longer the managers' expectations. The company is integrated into the self, leaving one's body and non-work relations as oppositional (see also Martin, 1990; Deetz, 1994a, 1994b). In this logic, work is not supposed to be for body sustenance and support of external relations. Rather the reverse: the body and social relations are positive only in so far as they support work. Certainly this relation is softened in the expressions of hope that the financial pay-offs from such demanding work can enrich one's outside life, but this is consigned to an ever-receding future. Even this future hope turns to support ever-more commitment to the work arrangement in the present.

Competing identities and needs are suppressed and are considered, to the extent that they are considered at all, as intrusive and leading to in-efficiencies. The body is medicated (with caffeine, cold and stomach medications) to mask the symptoms of stress and fatigue, and the heart and home are replaced with consumption and hope of what 'we' will have. All other social institutions and their demands are conceptualized as constraints on employees' work success and their personal motives for identity, order, and money. Moral standards, government regulations, and children, are each expressed as limiting the employee in different ways. The employee colonizes the home, community, educational institutions, state, and church. The managers in the name of the corporation need not do so. The discourse structures the conflict as between the unity of self/employee (elaborated in this site with a discourse of consulting and self-employment) and a body and outside, thus these must be contained. The discourse also suppresses the conflicts within the matrix of self–corporate relations.

The discourse is not as complete as expressed here in this character-ization. At moments, other discourses can be heard, and without a doubt most employees know that if they did not work this way, direct forms of control would quickly reappear. The dictator may be primarily inside, but also resides just over the horizon. What is interesting is not the completeness of this discourse but the growth of this insidious means of control. Productive diversity is lost and members reproduce a conception of a homogeneous community within a heterogeneous context. The differences are lost that allow members to interrogate common-sense experiences to regain choices. In place of differences there appear to be already answers, answers embodying a narrow range of interests and often the arbitrary though naturalized interests of dominant groups, in this case making a profit arising from the consultancy model.

Fear, commitment and self-subordination

Obedience, rather than voice and self-determination, is produced from fear and commitment, (see Flan, 1993; Deetz, 1995). Direct control processes largely use forms of fear. Consent uses commitment. Both fear and commitment are highly contrived and mystified. The management at AIMS created contrived fears and demands for commitment. For example, to the extent that the corporation can entice the employee to invest his or her identity in the corporation, the fear of loss of position is greatly enhanced and acts of obedience become more likely. Or, the more an expensive life-style is encouraged, given, or required for the job, the greater the control that can be exacted from pay systems.

The consultancy conception added instability and fear to the AIMS system, ironically increasing loyalty and consent. In light of AIMS's current economic difficulties, the economic arrangement meant that any project had to be accepted if it would improve the company's position, while other employee values were disregarded. The concerns were (re)directed, however, most often to management choices and the temporary economic problem, rather than instabilities inherent in the market-driven consultancy conception. In many ways, the combination of the consultancy conception and economic crisis strengthened management's hand even as individual managers were criticized. Their power resided in the co-occurrence of people fearing AIMS's demise and an economic crisis which might lead to it. The removal of either would weaken management's control. The construction of fear of an unspecified, but implied, negative consequence was a clear part of silencing alternative voices thus reducing uncertainties and the choices offered in them. Not sharing in the dream of AIMS was heresy punishable by ostracizing.[5]

Commitment and loyalty, properly by-products of interesting or meaningful work or fair pay, are displayed to the corporation and required as a condition *for* interesting work or adequate pay. Paradoxically, perpetual economic crises did not generate wider questions of equity and economic organization. To the extent that the company owns their soul, employees respond to crises with fear *and* loyalty. In a vicious cycle, as the employee increasingly strategizes feelings, life style, home situations, the having of children, work effort, and relation to management for what the company offers, the consent grows and the consequences of not consenting (identity loss, exit costs) are perceived as greater. The behaviour of AIMS employees can be characterized as 'anxiety-driven enthusiastic play acting' (Flan, 1993: 69). Nor is this optimal for the company, which loses insights and the capacity to provide the meaningful work that would justify such loyalty. The concept of personal autonomy directly contributes to this. This becomes one of several active consent processes operating in AIMS.

Misrecognition of agency

LTC and AIMS are self-consciously active in managing workplace culture, integrating work efforts through teaching values, and using other forms of unobtrusive controls. Despite this, AIMS employees have little concern with the intrusion into the employees' inner world or the reduction of employee

voice. While jokes are often made about the company's cultural management programmes, and especially about their 'hokeyness', most individuals
quickly define themselves and their work activities within the values and
slogans they provide. Indeed, most employees are more concerned that
everyone knows that they are aware of the instrumental nature of these
programmes than about the presence of manipulative intent or effects. Thus
they assert their sense of autonomy in opposition to these programmes as a
way of denying that others are controlling them, and then enact the
programmes as if they were affected by them. Most seem more than willing
to learn new means of strategic self-manipulation offered in such programmes if a pay-off can be gained and if it is clear that they are
manipulating themselves rather than others doing it. But the effect is that
they control themselves on behalf of others. The consultancy formation's
implied self-management and control of one's own economic fate continually reproduced a concept of freedom, though one actualized in the
accomplishment of corporate control through self-control.

At AIMS, individuals are produced (or strategically deployed for the sake
of the larger system) who inadvertently reproduce power configurations,
who are precluded from participation in the production of the future in
which they exercise their apparent freedoms, and who are constantly anxious
(though imaged as confidently certain) about their identities. Employee
pronouncements of autonomy sound vaguely like some adolescent males'
treatment of sexual identity: the certainty speaks insecurity. The positive and
negative forces apparent in this are similar to those identified by Knights and
Willmott:

> Positively, the modern subject is constituted as 'independent' and 'responsible,'
> partly as a result of the institutionalization of 'natural' rights and obligations of
> democratic self-autonomy. Negatively, individuals have been 'split' off from each
> other, and this is experienced as a vulnerability to the judgments of 'significant
> others,' and as a recurrent anxiety about whether external social evaluations will
> continue in a favourable direction. The pressure is upon individualised subjects to
> secure an identity for themselves . . . [and there is] difficulty of so doing in
> institutional circumstances . . . where recognition is a scarce and competitively
> achieved commodity. . . . (1989: 549)

Despite the sense of autonomy in the employees, there is a constant sense
that they are being evaluated and that, if they complain or object, something
negative will happen. They work to sustain an image that will allow them
power and security. But ultimately the image more controls them than they
control the image.

Unfortunately, the person becomes like other products in this system. The
individual is the most important and lasting product since the material
products and their qualities float. More to the point, there were *models* of
talk and persons which superseded any lasting 'actuality' (see Jackell, 1988:
101ff.). AIMS employees demonstrate a strong version of consent. In this
site the rules are not set by management. These are self-devised for one's
own success. And these rules are not seen as a false shadowy display of a
complicated self. Rather the self is seen as a confused, imperfect rendition of

the model. Effort is not put into maintaining a front, but into self-surveillance and social technologies of control in order to get the self to behave (see Foucault, 1980, 1988). The ability to strategize subordination counts as autonomy, but the strategized image is given more agency than the now lost person. Management could never accomplish such clear silencing. But conceptions of the organization and managerial activities are essential to keep it in play.

But if I were to raise questions of voice, to suggest that their experience or identity might be socially constructed and working against their own reported interests, my questions would be seen as political rather than the reproductive processes in the workplace. This is of little surprise. While such a discussion might be practical for them in light of a broad range of interests, it could only hamper 'success' at work. Opening a reconsideration of basic fixed identities and experiences has a potentially costly ripple effect across the web of relations that reproduce them, with few quick rewards. Still if people and corporations are to be responsive to a rapidly changing environment and diversifying work force, such reconsiderations are crucial. Even personal gains need not necessarily stop an open dialogue about experience and identity.

Conclusion

Is this the best or worst workplace? Generally most employees are very happy in their positions, but they also report many sacrifices made owing to the work expectations, unit instabilities, and long hours. They seem to have struck an implicit Faustian bargain with the company to accept conditions of subordination for the sake of pay-offs in term of identity, financial standing, and job security. If AIMS were doing well financially, all would appear to be worth it. It could be described as a model workplace. But the economic issues give an opening for a discussion which otherwise would seem impossible, a place for voice. Unfortunately, the arrangement also limits voice in this context and advances consent and loyalty instead. Learning is stopped.

A careful look at the discourse of AIMS suggests an intricate set of relations between structural, economic, and personal discursive processes passing through the consultancy conception as a central node in the circuit of power (Clegg, 1989). The concept is part of the formation and internal politics of the organizations, favouring groups, and suppressing conflicts and alternative thoughts and actions. The power of the concept rests in the capacity to close off certain discursive options rather than in simply its rhetorical appeal. The conception deployed allows the discussion to seem complete and neutral, thus hiding the tensions and incompletion. With such a closed set of discursive options the employee is basically left to choose loyalty or exit, but not voice. In choosing loyalty they gain membership, clarity, status, and specific identities, but they also re-enact a dominant set of power relations with costs. The reported workplace characteristics and values of self-management, lattice structure, and autonomy help hide the various material and symbolic formations, to the long-term detriment of both the employee and company. The loss of contact with an outside environment and various tensions provides a certain ease and comfort, but these are themselves deceptive. The personal strategies to get the best deal in this fundamentally uneasy situation provide an appearance of agency but still no voice. Recovery of suppressed conflicts becomes a first step toward the possibility of voice. These are best unpacked by starting with the particular illusions built into the consultancy model itself.

Notes

1 This study is a part of a larger multinational study of knowledge-intensive workplaces. Questions on the interviews and many of the observations concern issues different from the ones addressed in this paper. More details of the company and study are found in Deetz (1997).

2 The names used in this paper are fictitious. The company asked as a condition of access that its identity be protected.

3 The statements reproduced here are not 'cleaned-up'. While extra-linguistic notations are not given, linguistic uncertainties and self-corrections as well as moments of great fluency provide important texture to the reports.

4 Nearly all off-site project locations were at other LTC offices; most were less than 30 miles from AIMS main office, though some were elsewhere in the USA and a few in Europe.

5 This became clearer after the time period of the interviews reported here. AIMS was reorganized in January of 1994 and moved to another company within LTC. 'The vision [consultancy and integrated services] saved them' were the words of one manager. But the 'them' has an interesting ambiguity. Is 'them' the unit or the individual employees? Both? Clearly the unit is still in existence, but what were the employees saved from, what was the price, and 'saved' to do what? Deeper questions are very difficult to raise even as an outsider.

References

Alvesson, M. (1992) 'Leadership as social integrative action: a study of a computer consulting company', *Organization Studies* 13: 185–209.

Alvesson, M. (1993a) 'Cultural-ideological modes of management control', in S. Deetz (ed.), *Communication Yearbook* 16, Newbury Park, CA: Sage. pp. 3–42.

Alvesson, M. (1993b) 'Organizations as rhetoric: knowledge-intensive firms and the struggle with ambiguity', *Journal of Management Studies*, 30: 997–1016.

Alvesson, M. (1994) *Management of Knowledge-intensive Companies*. Berlin/New York: de Gruyter.

Barker, J. (1993) 'Tightening the iron cage: concertive control in self-managing teams', *Administrative Science Quarterly*, 38: 408–37.

Bourdieu, P. (1991) *Language and Symbolic Power*. Cambridge, MA: Harvard University Press.

Burawoy, M. (1979) *Manufacturing Consent: Changes in the Labor Process under Capitalism*. Chicago: University of Chicago Press.

Burawoy, M. (1985) *The Politics of Production: Factory Regimes under Capitalism and Socialism*. London: Verso.

Clegg, S. (1989) *Frameworks of Power*. Newbury Park, CA: Sage.

Deetz, S. (1992a) *Democracy in the Age of Corporate Colonization: Developments in Communication and the Politics of Everyday Life*. Albany, NY: State University of New York Press.

Deetz, S. (1992b) 'Disciplinary power in the modern corporation', in M. Alvesson and H. Willmott (eds), *Critical Management Studies*. London: Sage. pp. 21–45.

Deetz, S. (1994a) 'The micro-politics of identity formation in the workplace: the case of a knowledge intensive firm', *Human Studies*, 17: 1–22.

Deetz, S. (1994b) 'Representative practices and the political analysis of corporation', in B. Kovacic (ed.), *Organizational Communication: New Perspectives*. Albany, NY: State University of New York Press. pp. 209–42.

Deetz, S. (1995) *Transforming Communication, Transforming Business: Building Responsive and Responsible Workplaces*. Cresskill, NJ: Hampton Press.

Deetz, S. (1997), 'The business concept, discursive power, and managerial control in a knowledge-intensive company: a case study', in B. Sypher (ed.), *Case Studies in Organizational Communication* (2nd edn). New York: Guilford Press. pp. 183–212.

Drucker, P. (1993) *Post Capitalist Society*. New York: Harper Business.

Flan, H. (1993) 'Fear, loyalty, and greedy organizations', in S. Fireman (ed.), *Emotion in Organizations*. London: Sage. pp. 58–75.

Foucault, M. (1977) *Discipline and Punish: The Birth of the Prison* (trans. A. Sheridan Smith). New York: Random House.

Foucault, M. (1980) *The History of Sexuality* (trans. R. Hurley). New York: Vintage.

Foucault, M. (1982) 'The subject and power', in H. Dreyfus and P. Rabinow (eds), *Foucault: Beyond Structuralism*. Chicago: University of Chicago Press. pp. 208–26.

Foucault, M. (1988) 'Technologies of the self', in L. Martin, H. Gutman and P. Hutton (eds), *Technologies of the Self*, Amherst, MA: University of Massachusetts Press. pp. 16–49.

Greenwood, R., Hinings, C.R., and Brown, J. (1990) '"P²-form" strategic management: corporate practices in professional partnerships', *Academy of Management Journal*, 33: 725–55.

Heckscher, C. (1995) *White-collar Blues: Management Loyalties in an Age of Corporate Restructuring*. New York: Basic Books.

Hinings, C.R., Brown, J. and Greenwood, R. (1991) 'Change in an autonomous professional organization', *Journal of Management Studies*, 28: 375–93.

Hirschman, P. (1970) *Loyalty, Exit and Voice*. Cambridge, MA: Harvard University Press.

Hochschild, A. (1983) *The Managed Heart*. Berkeley, CA: University of California Press.

Hollway, W. (1991) *Work Psychology and Organizational Behaviour*. London: Sage.

Jackell, R. (1988) *Moral Mazes: The World of Corporate Managers*. Oxford: Oxford University Press.

Knights, D. (1992) 'Changing spaces: the disruptive impact of a new epistemological location for the study of management', *Academy of Management Review*, 17: 514–36.

Knights, D. and Collinson, D. (1987) 'Disciplining the shop floor: a comparison of the disciplinary effects of managerial psychology and financial accounting', *Accounting, Organizations and Society*, 12: 457–77.

Knights, D. and Morgan, G. (1991) 'Corporate strategy, organizations, and subjectivity: a critique', *Organization Studies*, 12: 251–73.

Knights, D. and Willmott, H. (1985) 'Power and identity in theory and practice', *The Sociological Review*, 33: 22–46.

Knights, D. and Willmott, H. (1989) 'Power and subjectivity at work: from degradation to subjugation in social relations', *Sociology*, 23: 535–58.

Kunda, G. (1992) *Engineering Culture: Control and Commitment in a High-tech Corporation*. Philadelphia: Temple University Press.

Manz, C. and Sims, H. (1980) 'Self-management as a substitute for leadership: a social learning perspective', *Academy of Management Review*, 5: 361–67.

Martin, J. (1990) 'Deconstructing organizational taboos: the suppression of gender conflict in organizations', *Organization Science*, 1: 339–59.

Martin, J. (1997) 'The organization of exclusion: the institutionalization of sex inequality, gendered faculty jobs, and gendered knowledge in organizational theory and research', *Organization*, 1: 401–31

Mills, P., Hall, J., Leidecker, J. and Margulies, N. (1983) 'Flexiform: a model for professional service organizations', *Academy of Management Review*, 8: 118–31.

Normann, R. (1991) *Service Management: Strategic Leadership in Service Business* (2nd edn). New York: Wiley.

Ouchi, W. and Maguire, M. (1975) 'Organization control: two functions', *Administrative Science Quarterly*, 20: 559–69.

Quinn, J. (1992) *Intelligent Enterprise: A Knowledge and Service Based Paradigm for Industry*. New York: Free Press.

Slocum, J., Jr, and Sims, H., Jr (1980) 'A typology for integrating technology, organization and job design', *Human Relations*, 33: 193–212.

Starbuck, W. (1992) 'Learning by knowledge-intensive firms', *Journal of Management Studies*, 29: 713–40.

Townley, B. (1993) 'Foucault, power/knowledge, and its relevance for human resource management', *Academy of Management Review*, 18: 518–45.

10

Through the Looking Glass: Foucault and the Politics of Production

Alan McKinlay and Phil Taylor

Critical assessments of contemporary human resource management (HRM) have been dominated by categorization – 'hard' versus 'soft', programmatic and coherent or pragmatic and *ad hoc* (McKinlay and Starkey, 1988; Storey, 1992). Macro-level surveys have registered the emergence of a new dis-course of work: employment becomes membership, control is redefined as commitment, management transmutes into leadership. The new language of employment denies the very possibility of class conflict at work. Challenges to specific managerial judgements are encouraged, but collective opposition to corporate authority is deemed illegitimate. So powerful is this new corporate unitarism that workers even lose their capacity to express opposi-tion to management except in ephemeral parodies of the official language of the workplace. We agree that HRM, in all of its many guises, represents a departure for Western management, a decisive, if often incomplete break with Fordist assumptions and practices. The emergence of a new language of work has been paralleled by the rise of teamworking, a form of work organization in which groups of employees assume responsibility for com-plete production processes, including administrative and organizational functions. Together, the ideology and the reality of teamworking constitute a significant new politics of production. For our purposes, this new politics of production is a labour strategy which goes beyond the admixture of direct control and corporate welfarism of Fordism: the most sophisticated HR strategies are those which envisage workers as active participants in the construction and refinement of hegemonic factory regimes, complicit in their own subjugation. The contribution of Foucault – and its limits – is the subject of the opening section of this chapter. Unlike previous flurries of interest in job enrichment, however, current moves towards teamworking have little to do with enhancing the quality of working life in response to union bargaining strength or rapid labour turnover. Rather, establishing teamworking on the shopfloor has become a key route to the flexibility, efficiency and rapid product innovation essential to competitiveness in global markets.

SiliCon is an American multinational which operates in the consumer electronics, communications and semiconductor industries. SiliCon experi-enced major reversals through the 1970s in its core markets, all inflicted by

Japanese competitors. This chastening experience triggered a radical switch in corporate strategy and structure. From the early 1980s SiliCon rejected mass production and managerial bureaucracy in favour of flexibility, quality and organizational innovation. In the chapter's second section we consider the architecture and organizational design of Pyramid, a greenfield site with a dual purpose: to manufacture mobile telephones for the global market and to act as a testing ground for the most radical form of teamworking yet attempted by SiliCon. SiliCon designated Pyramid as nothing less than 'the factory of the future'. The cornerstone of Pyramid's teamworking regime was peer review, a continuous process of mutual supervision which made each workgroup responsible for its own internal discipline. The design and operation of peer review is the subject of the chapter's fourth section.

Our purpose in this chapter, however, is not simply to explore the dynamics of labour regulation in the 'factory of the future' but to offer a commentary on Foucault's concept of surveillance and his comparative neglect of resistance. There is a real danger that Bentham's image of the Panopticon used by Foucault in *Discipline and Punish* becomes not just a metaphor for the institutionalized pursuit of social control but an authoritarian dystopia latent in every social setting. We shall suggest that this gloomy determinism *is* present in Foucault's work, and one which he made only belated and limited attempts to correct. On one level, the Panopticon was simply an efficient administrative machine, that the many can be governed by the few. This was certainly a concern for SiliCon in its determination to avoid the fixed costs of a managerial bureaucracy: teamworking held the promise of maximum surveillance at minimum cost. The place of resistance in Foucault's work and how it developed in the 'factory of the future' is the subject of the chapter's final section.

Foucault and the politics of production

The leitmotif of twentieth-century management theory has been the pursuit of knowledge of the psychology of work and organization. That is, the construction of a language and technology which seeks to lay bare the physical, cognitive, and interpersonal dimensions of work, and so to render them calculable and susceptible to managerial manipulation (Rose, 1990: 95). This process has reached new heights with current attempts to construct high-commitment workplaces. Employee involvement and teamworking regimes are 'successful' to the extent that they impose increasing psychological pressures on workers to seek personal satisfactions through their assimilation – and realization – of corporate goals of quality and flexibility. Bereft of the job controls inherent in craft skills or developed in response to the refinement of Fordist labour processes, the individual's very soul is exposed to interrogative pressure (Townley, 1994).

Consider the sheer range of managerial technologies which assail the employee of the ideal-typical high-commitment work regime. Recruited only after the most searching examinations of their psyches and social life;

ensnared in just-in-time and total quality management regimes designed to ratchet up efficiency and isolate idle human resources; monitored daily by peers and periodically assessed through attitude surveys. Relentless examination, comparison, and individuation underpin regimes in which pervasive control becomes subliminal, all the more powerful for being intangible. Such is the tyranny of teamworking as an ideological construct that it camouflages 'coercion and conflict with the appearance of consultation and cohesion' (Sinclair, 1992: 611). So profound is the normative control exercised within high-technology corporations that their employees can comprehend their working lives only as theatres in which they enact a role even more alienating than those of their forebears (Kunda, 1992). This is particularly true of service corporations, in which management strategy in the workplace and the market-place hinges on reducing the psychic distance between feigned emotional labour – the role – and the individual (Hochschild, 1983: 185):

> although the individual personality remains a 'medium of competition', the competition is no longer confined to individuals. Institutional purposes are now tied to workers' psychological arts. It is not simply individuals who manage their feelings in order to do a job; whole organisations have entered the game.

Beguiled by Foucault's Panopticon metaphor a number of labour process writers have inverted the euphoric rhetoric of HRM to produce gloomy analyses of emerging factory regimes in which workers lose even the awareness of their own self-exploitation (for an extended critique, see McKinlay and Taylor, 1996a). Lavishly supported by quotations depicting carceral regimes and omniscient surveillance, such studies squeeze out the contested dynamics of power, knowledge and authority in the workplace. But the factory and the office are neither prison nor asylum, their social architectures *never* those of the total institution (Lyon, 1993; Thompson and Ackroyd, 1995). Nor was Foucault under any illusions about this. In an interview entitled 'Questions of method', Foucault distanced himself from any literal reading of Bentham's authoritarian vision as a description of the reality of nineteenth-century prison regimes. 'It is absolutely true that criminals stubbornly resisted the new disciplinary mechanisms in the prison; it is absolutely correct that the actual functioning of the prisons, in the inherited buildings where they were established and with the governors and guards who administered them, was a witches' brew compared to the beautiful Benthamite machine' (Foucault, 1991: 81).

More than this, however, there is a contradiction at the core of teamworking which necessarily leaves a social space for worker autonomy and unregulated collectivity, a space which *can* become a domain of resistance, not domination. Maintaining an unmanaged space for worker activity is a necessary precondition if teamworking regimes are to deliver their promised flexibility and innovation. For this unmanaged space is where workers' intimate understanding of production can be articulated and refined in a continuous process of incremental innovation without fear of managerial appropriation. To violate this space is to jeopardize the foundations of mutual control, to shatter the illusion that team decision-making has completely superseded managerial control.

But to rely on the reports of managers and the public responses of employees is virtually certain to produce hegemonic accounts of power relations. We should not be surprised that what Scott (1990) terms the 'public transcript' – the surface language of domination – of subordinate groups is saturated with the discourse of accommodation rather than resistance. 'Any analysis based exclusively on the public transcript', argues Scott (1990: 4), 'is likely to conclude that subordinate groups endorse the terms of their subordination, and are willing, even enthusiastic, partners in that subordination'.

As Frederic Jameson (1991: 5–6) points out, the obliteration of resistance from the theoretical lexicon of crude Foucauldian analyses is not entirely due to a misreading of Foucault. Rather, the omission of resistance is a manifestation of the danger in a 'totalizing dynamic' which disables critique and disarms the very possibility of meaningful opposition. Each act of opposition is, at best, futile, and, at worst, serves only to aid and abet the established system of power/knowledge (see Burrell and Deetz in this volume). Resistance, whether individual or collective, purposeful or aimless, although inevitably doomed to failure, alerts the powerful to chinks in their armoury of power/knowledge and so results in the ever-more-profound subordination of the powerless. Foucault was dismissive of such a melancholy interpretation of his work. It is not that Foucault was ignorant of how far Bentham's Panopticon was from the reality of prison life nor, indeed, of his neglect of resistance. But to acknowledge this empirical *and* theoretical lacuna does little to rectify it. We shall return to this issue in the final section of this chapter.

Through the looking glass

> It will be a lantern; it will be a bee-hive; it will be a glass bee-hive, and a bee-hive without a drone. (Bentham cited in Semple, 1993: 116)

SiliCon's 'factory of the future' – Pyramid – is surrounded by an extensive tract of land which acts as a *cordon sanitaire* isolating it from the neighbouring town. The plant's physical separation is also a symbolic space distancing it from the mining and manufacturing traditions of local labour. Part of the induction programme for new hires was to assemble inside the plant's west wall and to be asked the rhetorical question of what they could see: a desolate, weed-strewn car park. They were reminded that this vacant lot used to be a truck plant, an implicit warning of what happens when a workforce – and management – believes itself exempt from the dictates of the global market-place. The single road to the plant is private, all but eliminating the possibility of any embarassing union recruitment campaign on the corporate doorstep. The plant's isolation and proximity to the nearby town echoes SiliCon's hiring policy. SiliCon was determined not to create a company town and deliberately avoided hiring from the locality, preferring instead to draw its new labour from a hundred mile radius. Union membership was prohibited as an unwelcome intermediary, intervening in the corporation's pursuit of the most intimate, unmediated of psychological contracts with individual employees. Equally, the only recruitment path was through an elaborate series of psychometric and dexterity tests: personal recommendations were totally discounted. Only one member of a family was permitted to work in the plant, and the well-established practice of hiring through family and friendship networks was rejected (see Grieco, 1987). If the prohibition of a union presence foreclosed one important route to alternative collectivities then excluding locality, family and friendship ties also limited the potential for informal social networks inside the factory as alternative foci of worker loyalties. The rationale was simple: management wanted a geographically dispersed, socially individuated workforce whose only shared allegiances were to their team and the 'factory of the future'.

At first sight, Pyramid is the antithesis of Bentham's Panopticon. Where the Panopticon orchestrates physical separation and mental isolation before an unseen gaze, the organizing principles of the 'factory of the future' are inclusion and cooperation rather than confinement and control. Not only is there no physical equivalent of the central inspection tower, there are no hidden spaces occupied solely and in private by managers or technicians. There is minimal spatial separation between production and support activities. Computer workstations are routinely used by line workers without seeking any prior permission. The absence of covert spaces or forbidden areas is intended to symbolize the absence of any covert managerial agenda, to speak rather of openness, equality and meritocracy. But it is equally appropriate to regard the plant's architecture as symbolic of a hidden discourse of control and surveillance. The factory is no less 'a machine of observation' than the archetypal panoptic clinics and prisons of the nineteenth century (Hirst, 1994: 57). The plant's most striking physical feature is its glass exterior and interior walls. The external glass walls are not reflective: the plant's exterior announces the building's presence, not merely reflections of its surroundings. Perhaps the contrast with Bentham's Panopticon is more apparent than real for, contrary to his often callous rationality, he envisaged the Panopticon not as an intimidating gothic structure but as an elegant, uplifting public building made of the most advanced materials, iron and glass. In an unpublished passage which resonates across the centuries with Weber's famous description of the modern bureaucracy, Bentham envisaged his ideal prison as 'A Iron cage glazed' (Bentham cited by Semple, 1993: 116). Glass, as Gane (1991: 39) reminds us, is a material which 'can be lived as a new liberation, indeed as a new intensified interpenetration of interior and exterior, a new transparency and visibility, a new purity, yet . . . it does not facilitate a genuine opening on to the world while it abolishes its mysteries'. Glass was selected as the dominant building material to symbolize the organization's transparency. In practice, however, we shall argue that the glass walls lay open the factory's structure of domination for inspection by all and understanding by none.

The relationship between the factory's architecture and social engineering is evident even in the detail of the canteen lay-out. The canteen's wedge shape means that there is no focal point for any assembly. Tables are arranged in a fixed mosaic which precludes their rearrangement. Each table has four fixed seats which makes it physically impossible to hold a conversation with the occupants of a neighbouring table. There are no fixed times for breaks, which are allocated within the workgroup to avoid disrupting production. By making break times relatively fluid, self-managed breaks naturally reinforce the tendency to socialize within work teams. One final detail confirmed the importance management ascribes to maximizing unseen corporate control even over informal socializing. Newspapers are forbidden in the plant – even in the canteen. Nor is the ban to avoid contamination from newsprint. The real purpose, one manager explained, is to minimize discussion of external events, even trivial ones, inside the factory – to reinforce the workgroup, tasks and production as the dominant themes of informal socializing.

The 'factory of the future' operates in a global marketplace characterized by rapid technical change, dramatic reduction in selling prices, and intensifying volume competition. SiliCon operates in a high-tech consumer goods market, dominated by short product life cycles and explosive volume growth. Rapid product innovation *and* the ability of manufacturing to cope with abrupt switches to mass-produce new products are essential to survival. If first-mover advantage in each product generation is rewarded by increased market share and windfall profits then delays threaten market presence and risk a failure to amortize huge upfront investments in product development.

This market context was vital in shaping factory organization. Only a radical decentralization of management's coordinative and control functions could yield both the responsiveness and low fixed cost base essential in such a hostile marketplace. The consignment of 'managerial' functions to the workgroups fundamentally altered the nature of authority on the shopfloor. Each member of a team had a 'secondary' job such as recording yields and qualities, maintaining team records, improving logistics, and so on. Each secondary job was rotated every month, and no team member was permitted to break the sequence. The objective was not simply to construct teams with complementary skills but also to make each individual and every team a composite 'manager'. Managers, or Staff Associates, performed few administrative or control tasks. Staff Associates provided technical expertise, the link between corporate headquarters, and broad nebulous 'leadership' roles. In team-based organizations managerial authority is derived from interpersonal skills and technical competence rather than office or hierarchy. But if the authority of the individual manager is opened up to inspection from below through employee involvement, then managerial power *per se* becomes more opaque. By dispersing the functions of management, efficiency, flexibility and quality became the rationality of the organization as a whole rather than the prerogative of specific functionaries (Cressey et al., 1985: 53–4). The authority of the individual manager became more personalized and contingent as the factory's power structure became more anonymous and unquestioned.

This, then, is a physical and social architecture which speaks of an aspiration to create a total space, a closed environment whose very fabric spoke of intensive, self-reinforcing surveillance. In the factory of the future, then, the ubiquity of surveillance was reflected in the transparency of its physical and social architecture. The same principles also informed the architecture of the factory's management information system. Above all, as one of the plant's process engineers explained, the objective was to absorb line workers '*inside* the factory control system (FCS), to allow the operatives to ask more of the system itself ', to replicate, reinforce and monitor the process of mutual control on the shopfloor.

> We think of the FCS as a sponge in the manufacturing area which soaks up data. . . . The trick is giving people appropriate information. Do you want to give people on the line only the information for their own specific task? No: you want to increase the visibility of the whole system from any vantage point. Every Associate can assess their performance compared to a similar task on another line. FCS allows continuous, dispersed monitoring of individual performance, checking the number of Associate interventions, changes in machine and material characteristics. (Process engineer, June 1993)

Sweeping his arm over the shopfloor, the process designer insisted 'my job is to capture all the brains, all the ingenuity out there'. But if the objective echoed classical Taylorism, then implementation was qualitatively different. The plant's information system centralized all technical data but was not scrutinized by managerial technicians but rather as a check on the embeddedness of self-discipline and mutual control (see Poster, 1990). Process designers concentrated on the functioning of the network as a whole rather than comparing individual worker efficiencies: 'we leave the comparisons of micro data to the teams'.

The architecture of Pyramid's surveillance system is all the more thoroughgoing because of its invisibility. The plant's design, recruitment processes and information systems were saturated with a desire for control: glass walls symbolized that surveillance was constant and ubiquitous; recruitment reflected detailed corporate social engineering rather than the espoused meritocracy; and information systems open to line worker interventions masked the potential for a more penetrating managerial gaze.

Peer review and normative control

> It is often difficult to say who holds power in a precise sense, but it is easy to see who lacks power. (Foucault, 1989: 79)

> Basically they are trying to change your personality. (Line worker, 1993)

Foucault opens *Discipline and Punish* with a famous extended description of the slow, spectacular public execution of the regicide, Damiens. Each incision, each tear of Damiens's sinews was an exquisite metric of punishment, a just measure of corporal pain and psychic agony. For Foucault, Damiens's extended torture epitomized a system of domination which characterized the pre-modern era. Displays of power in the pre-modern era were public spectacles, dramatic affirmations of sovereign power. But sovereign power was power uncoupled from knowledge, a power which did not necessarily depend upon the construction of knowledge. Pre-modern power was a discontinuous, forgetful form of power. This, argues Foucault, is precisely the novelty of power in the modern era: power is quite literally unthinkable without the construction of *local* knowledges of specific populations, of 'workers', of 'the sick', of 'deviants'. Modern power, in other words, is the construction of calculable subjects; the exercise of power is both constitutive of and dependent upon that knowledge. But this is more than tautology. Rather, Foucault's concept of power/knowledge is a methodological injunction that power and knowledge are mutually constitutive. Power and knowledge are not conceived of in terms of cause and effect but as necessary complements, a method which rejects totalizing philosophies in favour of tracing the historicity of specific disciplinary practices and their institutional forms.

The original Benthamite Panopticon principle sought to modify the behaviour and moral codes of prisoners, workers or state bureaucrats through the illusion – or reality – of constant surveillance of their *bodies*. This was the alchemy of Bentham's Panopticon: 'a mill for grinding rogues honest and idle men industrious' (Bowring, 1838–43, x: 226). Similarly, F.W. Taylor pursued managerial control through physical dressage, a corporeal regime which aspired to the complete elimination of worker control. For both Bentham and Taylor, controlling recalcitrant bodies was the key to reshaping obdurate minds. Taylor's 'scientific management' resembles Bentham's administrative principles 'in objectives, devices, principles and above all . . . spirit' (Hume, 1981: 6). Both share 'the objective of exploiting resources scientifically through the careful analysis and study of activities and actions to find the "one best way", a systematic division of labour, the design and construction of systems of rewards and penalties to operate as precise incentives, . . . the limitation of initiative and discretion on the part of the individual worker and the centralisation of information and authority at the top'. Contemporary team-based work organizations share at least one key objective with Taylorism: both aim to generate a form of social control which does not involve a direct confrontation between management and labour. Whereas Taylorism focused on discovering and imposing a fixed pattern of physical movement from above, team-based organizations focus on monitoring and remaking employee attitudes. The high-involvement workplace aims not at the managerial choreography of bodies but constant improvisation in work organization and the unobtrusive orchestration of employee values. Contemporary organizations' pursuit of competitive advantage through innovation and efficiency demands not the compliant bodies of Fordism but active minds on the shopfloor. Worker discretion and creativity is no longer necessarily conceived as an obstacle to competitiveness but as 'a central economic resource' to be mobilized if ever-higher standards of efficiency, quality and product innovation are to be achieved (Miller and Rose, 1990: 26).

In Japanese transplant factories in the West, peer review is the institutional cornerstone of a dense web of governance practices which identity worker opposition, squeeze out inefficiency, and reward congruence with the corporate agenda (Kenney and Florida, 1993: 27–8; Graham, 1995). Outside of Japanese transplants, however, peer review has been introduced by very few companies and in only the most limited way (Hodson and Hagan, 1988). In SiliCon's 'factory of the future', peer review took a qualitatively different form. Not only was SiliCon's peer review process formalized and applied to the entire workforce, it was administered not by supervisors but by line workers. Peer review was not Taylorist control from *above* but intended to embed mutual- and self-discipline from *below*, with no visible role for management. Peer review is a systematic form of mutual control in which team members – *not* supervisors – rate each other on a variety of technical, task and behavioural scales. In theory, the disciplinary matrix of peer review explicitly focused on the constant, microscopic policing of the team member's subjectivity (May, 1992; Cutrofello, 1994: 67–9). The novelty of peer review is that colleagues have to exercise a normalizing gaze – have to assess and rank – each other and themselves. All aspects of worker behaviour and attitudes were incorporated into a ten-category grid which each team member used to rate themselves and their immediate colleagues. The categories ranged from relatively unambiguous matters such as individual efficiency, through grey areas such as perceptions of skill acquisition, into uncertain territory such as quality consciousness. No category was privileged: adherence to the team culture was given equal weight to task performance. But even apparently mundane 'objective' matters such as time-keeping were to be read by their team-mates as indicative of a person's reliability and collegiality, their assimilation of the 'team' culture. To 'show a willingness to change' was defined as being:

> flexible, open to new ideas, willing to learn, quick to take on new responsibilities, encourages others to change. (SiliCon, internal briefing, May 1993)

Through peer review the intuitive judgements made by the teams of fellow workers, which normally remain hidden from managerial view, are formalized and transformed through the imposition of a corporate schema: subjectivity is opened to intimate scrutiny and managerial intervention. Surveillance registers not simply the worker's physical presence and adherence to Taylorized motions but also the depth of psychological commitment.

Peer review was an integral part of the teamworking regime of the 'factory of the future', a collective, transparent and continuous process radically different from episodic, individual appraisal systems. And, as an event and collective process, peer review was insulated from the demands of production: discussion of targets, performance and quality were barred. Monthly meetings would convene for the sole purpose of reviewing graphs illustrating the relative scores of all permanent team members. The team would then focus on three individuals' performance and each team member would make their judgement. Alternatively, the team had the option of focusing on a lone individual if a more intensive examination was considered necessary. This was a form of summary justice predicated on a permanent anticipation of treachery. As the team members each gave their judgement in turn, the three contrite subjects were to remain silent and contemplative, to let the cumulative weight of judicial opinion build before they were permitted to reply. The monthly peer review was, then, a spectacle of discipline, an event which reminded the individual of the supposedly constant, inescapable, and silent scrutiny of her/ his workmates. In the metaphor of the Panopticon, the monthly meeting was the equivalent of the prisoner's quizzical glance at the Judas hole, uncertain of the watchfulness of his gaoler. Bentham was aware that the power and efficiency of the Panopticon effect depended upon maintaining the illusion of constant surveillance, and that the illusion had to be reaffirmed periodically. 'I will single out the most untoward of the prisoners', wrote Bentham, and 'keep an uninterrupted watch upon him.'

> I will watch until I observed a transgression. I will minute it down. I will watch for another: I will note that down too. I will lie by for a whole day: he shall do as he pleases that day. . . . The next day I produce the list to him. You thought yourself undiscovered: you abused my indulgence: see how you were mistaken. Another time, you may have rope for two days, ten days: the longer it is, the heavier it will fall upon you. Learn from this, all of you, that in this house transgression never can be safe. (Bowring, 1838–43, iv: 81–2)

Peer review did not simply expose the individual to power/knowledge but contributed to its formation. Inside Pyramid, peer review was essential to the mobilization of the discourse of empowerment, a discourse which decentres managerial power and which makes the individual an object of knowledge. Each individual's team's scores were reported to a central database which normalized and compared the average and range of scores across the factory. Any team whose scores diverged from the factory norm could then be subjected to further training in the peer review process or remedial team-building interventions. The calibration of employees' minds also occurred during the peer review meetings themselves. The very act of interrogating the performance of three individuals relative to the rest of the team and factory norms was in itself a form of discipline, a public reminder of laudable and unacceptable behaviours. But peer review went further than behavioural issues such as attendance and time-keeping. Rather, the real novelty of peer review was that it required participants to delve beneath behaviour and question the attitudes of their fellows: the depth of their commitment to a system of mutual surveillance and control. The disciplinary potential of mutual surveillance was not lost on Bentham. A cell occupied by two or three prisoners could intensify the Panopticon effect: 'so many comrades, so many inspectors; the very persons to be guarded against are added to the number of the guards' (Bowring, 1838–43, iv: 164). Or, as Foucault would have it, after Rousseau, 'each comrade becomes an overseer, each overseer should become a comrade' (Foucault, 1980: 152). As one of the main architects of peer review explained, the intimacy of mutual inspection was central to the organizational imperative of constant, incremental innovations in work organization.

> I start with a model that has two basic processes: disclosure and feedback. Knowledge of self and others increases. I believe that knowledge is the central mechanism in relationships. A team is a relationship and it has to have that knowledge *inside* it. . . . I believe in peer review 100 per cent as a knowledge device, as vital to a learning – a *self*-learning – organization. (HR manager, 1992)

This, then, was a therapeutic model of developing individual self-awareness bound to a corporate agenda of organizational innovation: remaking the individual employee's consciousness was essential to securing competitive advantage. Peer review was understood by management as a vehicle for team building, supervision and sustaining continuous incremental innovation in work organization. Indeed, for the plant's management, given the absence of traditional supervisors, the team *necessarily* became a critical disciplinary device. 'Discipline', explained one of the plant's HR advisors, 'is a group-based process'. Self-inspection and constant comparison with immediate colleagues was an interrogative process designed to generate visible mutual- and *self*-control among line workers. Peer review was a collective process to increase the individual's regulation of the *self*. Peer review incorporated testimony, testing, observation and confession – the elements Foucault analyses as constituting the modern Western 'techniques for producing truth' (Foucault, 1979: 59).

It is difficult to overstate SiliCon's ambition in its attempt to go beyond the rhetorics of flexibility, commitment and quality: to achieve nothing less than a total colonization of the consciousness of the Pyramid workforce. For those who came to SiliCon from outside the microelectronics sector particularly, teamworking was an extraordinarily liberating experience. 'I find working at SiliCon a refreshing change', said one 34 year-old female line worker, 'it's different from any other company I have worked for before . . . I like working in a team and you are treated like a person and not just another number.' Without doubt, the boundary of the 'private' and 'work' self is blurred by the emotional intensity of the high-commitment workplace. To paraphrase Hacking (1986: 236), the mutual surveillance regime goes far beyond the exercise of external constraints on worker behaviour. The ambition underpinning Pyramid is nothing less than to reshape 'the permanent heartland of subjectivity', to supplement the classic form of organizational discipline with self-discipline. Over time, the SiliCon workforce gradually confronted teamworking itself as a disciplinary device rather than solely as novel and positive. Gradually, even generally supportive comments included qualifications, shading into outright hostility. 'Although you do feel more responsible I do think that this is a clever ploy to make you feel more independent. After all, we're basically "puppets on a string" ' (Line worker, 1994).

Thinking resistance, doing resistance

On the question of power and resistance Foucault is at his most ambiguous, his most wilfully elusive (Dews, 1984). Debate over Foucault's notion of power/knowledge has centred on the extent to which freedom and resistance are possible. But as McCarthy (1994: 257) points out, even in the atypical disciplinary settings studied by Foucault human agency is not snuffed out: 'Since rules do not define their own application, rule following is always to some degree discretionary, elaborative, *ad hoc*' (see also Visker, 1995: 103). Foucault consistently denied that his was a search for the archetypal form of power/knowledge which defined Western societies and their institutions from the Enlightenment. Rather, his objective was more modest: not a theory of power as such but a series of histories of specific power/knowledge configurations. Whatever allusions Foucault made to resemblances between prison, asylum, school and factory, these should be regarded as no more than grandiose asides made before returning to the particular. Equally troubling is the determination to read Foucault as a theorist of power when he could more profitably be considered to be offering a *method*. Who can doubt, for example, that power and resistance are mutually constitutive, that one is the precondition of the other? Certainly not Foucault, for whom power relations are not external to other relationships but immanent within them.

> Resistance is integral to power. The existence of power relationships depends on a multiplicity of points of resistance which are present everywhere in the power network. Resistances are the odd terms in relations of power; they are inscribed in the latter as irreducible opposite. (Foucault, 1979: 95–6)

There are several points to note here. First, Foucault acknowledges and tries to avoid the 'winner loses' logic of *Discipline and Punish*. Resistance need not necessarily be in vain nor must it inevitably augment the 'stock' – if we may be forgiven such a tainted modernist term – of power/knowledge held by dominant groups. Indeed, to think of 'power' and 'resistance' as separable resources or strategies is to succumb to the very dualism Foucault sets out to avoid. The danger in this solution is that 'resistance' becomes a metaphysical category (Fine, 1979: 91). The verb 'to work', for instance, carries with it two hidden imperatives: 'to control' and 'to resist'. Second, Foucault insists that power relations and scientific discourses are mutually constitutive: one is literally unthinkable without the other. And just as power and truth are completely entangled so, equally, power and reistance form 'a knot that is not meant to be unravelled' (Simons, 1995: 27). If we regard this as a *theory* of power then it is, at best, a tautology. Alternatively, if we consider this as a *methodological* injunction, then the dynamic of power/ knowledge and resistance becomes an empirical issue *not* an abstract question. This is certainly Foucault's own view of his work as providing a toolkit for empirical investigation and political intervention. Theoretical labour is not abstract system building but is always through reflection on empirical and historical processes (Foucault, 1980: 145). If we accept this re-interpretation of Foucault's project it places him on the same ground as Marx. Listen to the echoes contained in Derek Sayer's (1983) classic statement of Marx's historical method. At the core of Marx's thought lies an understanding of social and structural conditions based on internal relations of entailment rather than external ones of cause. Marx's much-abused metaphor of base and superstructure is thus transformed from an analytical straitjacket to a metaphorical reminder of the need for empirical analysis to tease out the necessary connections and contingent strategies pursued by manager and managed.

For all that, however, Foucault's historical analyses of power/knowledge regimes are eloquent in their silence when it comes to the capacities and experiences of subordinated groups' resistance. Implicit in Foucault's scattered remarks about resistance is that the nature of power/knowledge is always contested, always strategic, and never complete (Simons, 1995: 83–6). And this, of course, is especially true of non-carceral institutions such as the factory. To understand the dynamics of teamworking regimes we must begin from an appreciation of the differences in power/knowledge inherent in the employment relationship. Employers enjoy organizational advantages in any factory setting: capital is *necessarily* organized and strategic. For labour, organization is contingent and partial, strategies sectional and localized (Offe, 1985). The imbalance in the organizational capacities of managers and managed was particularly extreme in Pyramid: a greenfield site specifically designed to construct a self-reinforcing mutual control regime using labour which was selected for its tractability and systematically deprived of trade unionism as a vehicle for building oppositional forms of power/knowledge.

Pyramid offered a singularly unpromising site for worker resistance to mutual surveillance and control. From the first, however, there was a widespread awareness that teamworking and peer review were alternative forms of management control rather than its antithesis. More than two thirds of the Pyramid workforce surveyed confirmed that they understood the disciplinary principles and purposes of peer review. But although peer review was understood as a management control device it was evaluated by the workforce in terms of its impact on the *ideal* of the team. Assessing and being assessed by one's immediate colleagues was rejected by a majority of seven to one. Just 11.1 per cent of respondents felt that peer review helped to develop their own self-confidence, and only 6.7 per cent regarded it as beneficial to the team as a whole. For the workforce, peer review was not supportive and developmental but intimidating; it sharpened rather than reduced internal tension in the team; and it personalized and discredited rather than legitimized the team as the main site of discipline. Although four out of five employees distrusted peer review, the intensity of opposition was greatest amongst those with an employment history outside microelectronics, particularly those with previous trade union membership.

This widespread antipathy towards the principles of peer review was confirmed by the teams' experience. Growing production pressures provided teams with a ready excuse for neglecting to hold monthly meetings. Where teams persevered with peer review the meetings became increasingly divisive, often embittering personal relationships. 'People come back from peer review meetings with red eyes from crying' (Line worker, June 1993). As one young male worker subjected to an hour-long dissection of his performance put it: 'they are a bit like those executions . . . in the French Revolution. They sit around knitting while the blood flows' (Line worker, January 1993). The paradox was that the silent witnesses were – unlike the Parisian *tricoteuses* – repelled by the spectacle of confrontational peer reviews. Such was the revulsion of a young female assembly worker compelled to witness the ritual humiliation of her silent colleague that it eroded the credibility of team control over discipline.

> Team involvement can result in a situation where a small minority of the team through manipulation can gain a very firm hold of power over other team members. This is OK as long as it is controlled by an observant 'supervisor'. This does not happen at SiliCon and therefore the possibilities of 'mob rule' are increased. (Line worker, 1994)

More than 25 per cent of those surveyed felt 'intimidated' by peer review. Even more strikingly, for 68.9 per cent of the respondents peer review did little to dissipate tensions within the teams. This criticism found no collective voice beyond the individual team. But a variety of strategies were developed to defuse the system of mutual surveillance. The key to the workforce's resistance was, ironically, the public nature of peer review. Public scoring rendered those who continued to exercise the normalizing gaze visible. The disciplinary intent of peer review was inverted: public scoring identified not the deviants from the factory culture but its strongest adherents. And group pressure was applied to 'the space cadets', who became the focus of the workforce's resentment at the rapid deterioration of the team concept and the reduced scope of collective decision making. 'When I make reviews I am very honest', reflected one line worker ruefully, 'and that sometimes does not go down too well – it puts you on the spot rather than the person you have reviewed' (Line worker, February 1994). Opposition to peer review was not simply individual and unfocused. Rather, the teams – particularly those which included workers from a non-microelectronics manufacturing background – quickly developed strategies to neutralize peer review. Retaliatory scoring – marking down any individual who had scored you low in the previous month was not uncommon: 'you do get revenge. You get a low score off somebody, and you say, "Right, I'll get that bastard back next month" ' (Line worker, 1993). Retaliatory scoring was not simply an expression of personal vendettas. Indeed, both by prior arrangement and by demonstration, this strategy developed as a collective strategy rather than a solely individual response. As one 'space cadet' exposed to this tactic put it, he had been 'tamed' of his readiness to engage in rigorous scoring when he was transferred to a new team:

> If you come in and start giving people 2s, which is saying that there's room for improvement, people will stop talking to you. So you change and start giving people higher scores. The minimum you give is a 3. (Line worker, April 1993)

Additional risks for anyone complying with the disciplinary purpose of the system included the partial withdrawal of sociability or complete shunning. But by far the most common strategy for disarming peer review as a reflexive process was an extensive campaign of passive resistance. The workforce simply utilized their knowledge of the normalizing gaze to rob of it any real impact. Team members tacitly traded scores about the mean, compressing the spread of scores and robbing the system of any way of identifying deviant individuals. The team withdrew from their judicial role in the peer review process. Monthly meetings were reduced to anodyne unanimity rather than ever-more-open spirals of criticism directed at silent penitents. There were attempts by management facilitators to inject a critical edge to the sessions but these proved counter-productive, further confirmation that the original ideals of teamworking were being debased (See McKinlay and Taylor, 1996b: 479). Quietly and systematically, peer review was dismantled by a combination of workforce resistance and tactical choices by a plant management under intense pressure for output.

There is no doubt that the experience of peer review and the shift away from the early liberatory exuberance of teamworking was a seminal moment in the development of the Pyramid plant. However, the resistance to peer review did not create a permanent site for future opposition, nor did it decisively shift workforce opinion against the *ideal* of teamworking; workforce opinion only became more sceptical of the reality of teamworking in the 'factory of the future'. Here again we return to Foucault's insistence that resistance is contingent in both form and content and does not necessarily flow from societal fault lines of, say, class or gender. 'Radical ruptures, massive binary divisions' remain possible but exceptional, argues Foucault. More commonly 'one is dealing with mobile and transitory points of resistance, producing cleavages in a society that shifts about, fracturing unities and effecting regroupings, furrowing across individuals themselves, cutting them up and remoulding them, marking off irreducible regions in them, in their bodies and minds' (Foucault, 1979: 96).

The irony is that employee resistance to peer review and the increasingly debased reality of teamworking produced a system of supervision which actually stripped away some of the decision-making power valued most by the workforce (Knights and Verdubakis, 1994: 189–90). Successive ramp-ups in production volumes rapidly reduced team meetings in duration, scope and levels of participation. Shift meetings became dominated by top-down directions regarding targets and left little or no space for collective discussion of work organization. Corporate pressure for volume also lessened management's attachment to 'the purity of the original team idea. . . . We were idealists but those phones have got to keep bumping off the end of the line: that's what really matters. We now realize teams were an important route to efficiency but not an end in themselves' (production manager, October 1995). But there is more to the SiliCon experience than a familiar tale of an ambitious managerial project being eroded by economic pressure. The integrity of the original teamworking vision was fatally compromised by its internal contradictions rather than by external factors. Indeed, our surveys revealed that so disenchanted was the workforce with the unevenness and uncertainties of team-based discipline that there was growing support for the installation of traditional supervision and bureaucratic rules. Here again, Scott (1990: 94) captures the dynamic of the process using an image of prisoners as agents – not as victims – shaping the nature of their own domination.

> What the prisoners resent most about daily prison life is their powerlessness before the seemingly capricious and unpredictable distribution of privileges and punishments by administrative personnel. In their dogged attempts to domesticate the power arranged against them and to render it predictable and manipulable they pursue a strategy . . . stressing the established norms of the rulers of their small kingdoms and claiming that these rulers have violated the norms by which they justify their own authority. Prisoners press constantly for the specification of procedures, criteria, and guidelines that will govern the granting of privileges. . . . They are partisans of seniority as the major criteria, inasmuch as it would operate automatically and mechanically.

Conclusion

We should not be dismissive of corporate HR-speak about 'people being our biggest asset'. On the contrary, we should take this as the definitive corporate agenda of late capitalism. The mobilization of commitment – *beyond* consent – *is* critical to the competitiveness of companies faced with the dilemma of simultaneously achieving step changes in efficiency and constant product innovation. And it is on this terrain, the cultural politics of production, that Foucault has most to offer. The categories of conventional labour process theory – job control, the effort bargain and job hierarchies – have little purchase on the meanings of work in team-based work regimes. In plants such as Pyramid there are no historic protocols derived from craft unionism; tasks are so broadly based and the labour process so fluid, that to focus on the technical division of labour risks obscuring the centrality of the cultural politics of production. That said, concepts such as 'mutual' or 'concertive' control and 'self-subordination' seriously overstate the reach and permanence of corporate ideologies of teamworking. Remember the unique setting of the 'factory of the future': an innovative microelectronics multinational establishing a greenfield site and using sophisticated psychometric techniques to select a 'team-oriented' workforce. There could be no more favourable setting for corporate ideology to colonize the psyche of their workforce. And yet, advanced HR practices have not enabled management to 'govern the soul' of its employees (Rose, 1990). Inside Pyramid, SiliCon has initiated a new *cultural* politics of production but has not constructed a form of shopfloor governance which has eliminated the control imperative or worker resistance. Here we should offer a word of caution. Teamworking remains a relatively new departure for Western managements breaking with a Fordist past. The techniques for monitoring teamworking remain primitive. It remains an open question just how far mutual control techniques can be developed as managerial devices without compromising the active consent necessary to sustain employee commitment to continuous innovation in work organization. That the cultural terrain of the corporation is being remade by both managers *and* workers is beyond doubt. We hope that we have demonstrated that this terrain remains contested.

References

SiliCon and Pyramid are pseudonyms. Our thanks to the managers and workforce of SiliCon whose words we report here. Many colleagues have helped to improve this paper: we thank them for their criticism and support.

Bowring, J. (ed.) (1838–43) *The Works of Jeremy Bentham*. Edinburgh/London: Simpkin Marshall.

Cressey, P., Eldridge, J. and MacInness, J. (1985) *Just Managing: Authority and Democracy in Industry*. Milton Keynes: Open University Press.

Cutrofello, A. (1994) *Discipline and Critique: Kant, Poststructuralism and the Problem of Resistance*. Albany, NY: State University of New York Press.

Dews, P. (1984) 'Power and subjectivity in Foucault', *New Left Review*, March–April: 72–95.

Fine, B. (1979) 'Struggles against discipline: the theory and politics of Michel Foucault', *Capital and Class*, 9: 75–95.

Foucault, M. (1979) *The History of Sexuality, Volume I*. Harmondsworth: Penguin.

Foucault, M. (1980) *Power/Knowledge: Selected Interviews and other Writings 1972–1977* (ed. Colin Gordon). Brighton: Harvester Wheatsheaf.

Foucault, M. (1989) *Foucault Live: Collected Interviews, 1961–1984* (ed S. Lotringer). New York: Semiotext(e).

Foucault, M. (1991) 'Questions of method', in G. Burchell, C. Gordon and P. Miller (eds), *The Foucault Effect: Studies in Governmentality*. London: Harvester Wheatsheaf. pp. 73–86.

Gane, M. (1991) *Baudrillard's Bestiary: Baudrillard and Culture*. London: Routledge.

Graham, L. (1995) *On the Line at Subaru-Isuzu: The Japanese System and the American Worker*. Ithaca, NY: ILR Press.

Grieco, M. (1987) *Keeping it in the Family: Social Networks and Employment Choice*. London: Tavistock.

Hacking, I. (1986) 'Self-improvement', in D.C. Hoy (ed.), *Foucault: A Critical Reader*. Oxford: Basil Blackwell. pp. 235–40.

Hirst, P. (1994) 'Foucault and architecture', *Architectural Association Files*, 26: 52–60.

Hochschild, A.R. (1983) *The Managed Heart: The Commercialization of Human Feeling*. Berkeley, CA: University of California Press.

Hodson, R. and Hagan, J. (1988) 'Skills and job commitment in high technology industries in the US', *New Technology, Work and Employment*, 3 (2): 112–24.

Hume, L.J. (1981) *Bentham and Bureaucracy*. Cambridge: Cambridge University Press.

Jameson, F. (1991) *Postmodernism, Or, the Cultural Logic of Late Capitalism.* London: Verso.

Kenney, M. and Florida, R. (1993) *Beyond Mass Production: The Japanese System and its Transfer to the US.* Oxford: Oxford University Press.

Knights, D. and Verdubakis, T. (1994) 'Foucault, power, resistance and all that', in J. Jermier, D. Knights and W. Nord (eds), *Resistance and Power in Organizations.* London: Routledge.

Kunda, G. (1992) *Engineering Culture: Control and Commitment in a High-Tech Corporation.* Philadelphia: Temple University Press.

Lyon, D. (1993) 'An electronic Panopticon? A sociological critique of surveillance theory', *Sociological Review*, 41 (4): 652–78.

McCarthy, T. (1994) 'The critique of impure reason: Foucault and the Frankfurt School', in M. Kelly (ed.), *Critique and Power: Recasting the Foucault/Habermas Debate.* Cambridge, MA: MIT Press. pp. 243–82.

McKinlay, A. and Starkey, K. (1988) 'Competitive strategies and organizational change', *Organization Studies*, 9 (4): 555–73.

McKinlay, A. and Taylor, P. (1996a) 'Power, surveillance and resistance: inside the "Factory of the future" ', in P. Ackers, C. Smith and P. Smith (eds), *The New Workplace and Trade Unionism.* London: Routledge. pp. 279–300.

McKinlay, A. and Taylor, P. (1996b) 'Commitment and conflict: worker resistance to HRM in the microelectronics industry', in B. Towers (ed.), *The Handbook of Human Resource Management*, Oxford: Basil Blackwell. pp. 467–87.

May, C. (1992) 'Individual care? Power and subjectivity in therapeutic relationships', *Sociology*, 26: 589–602.

Miller, P. and Rose, N. (1990) 'Governing economic life', *Economy and Society*, 19 (1): 1–31.

Offe, C. (1985) 'Two logics of collective action', in J. Keane (ed.), *Disorganized Capitalism: Contemporary Transformations of Work and Politics.* Cambridge: Polity.

Poster, M. (1990) 'Foucault and databases: participatory surveillance', in M. Poster (ed.), *Mode of Information: Poststructuralism and Social Context.* Cambridge: Polity. pp. 69–98.

Rose, N. (1990) *Governing the Soul: The Shaping of the Private Self.* London: Routledge.

Sayer, D. (1983) *Marx's Method: Ideology, Science and Critique in Capital.* Brighton: Harvester Wheatsheaf.

Scott, J.C. (1990) *Domination and the Art of Resistance: Hidden Transcripts.* New Haven, CT: Yale University Press.

Semple, J. (1993) *Bentham's Prison: A Study of the Panopticon Penitentiary.* Oxford: Clarendon.

Simons, J. (1995) *Foucault and the Political.* London: Routledge.

Sinclair, A. (1992) 'The tyranny of a team ideology', *Organization Studies*, 13 (4): 611–26.

Storey, J. (1992) *Developments in the Management of Human Resources.* Oxford: Basil Blackwell.

Thompson, P. and Ackroyd, S. (1995) 'All quiet on the workplace front? A critique of recent trends in British industrial sociology', *Sociology*, 29 (4): 615–33.

Townley, B. (1994) *Reframing Human Resource Management: Power, Ethics and the Subject at Work.* London: Sage.

Visker, R. (1995) *Michel Foucault: Genealogy as Critique.* London: Verso.

11

Beyond Good and Evil: Depth and Division in the Management of Human Resources

Barbara Townley

In this chapter I argue that Foucault's work re-orients our approach to analysing management strategies in human resource management (HRM). It does so by allowing us to take a perspective of depth, rather than being caught in binary oppositions which have typified our analyses of the management of the employment relationship. I begin by giving a very brief introduction to the binary oppositions which characterize HRM, suggest why these are prominent and then show how Foucault's alternative metaphor of depth can help us examine some of the most recent initiatives in HRM, as well as re-orient how we understand HRM in relation to other managerial disciplines.

Managing labour: a plethora of divisions

From the initial contrasts drawn between Taylorism and human relations, and their various derivatives – for example, theory X and theory Y – binary oppositions have been pervasive in theorizing about styles or approaches to the management of labour. Within mainstream industrial relations (IR) analysis has been posed in terms of an individualism/collectivism dichotomy. This was reflected in early distinctions between personnel management and industrial relations: personnel handling aspects of the employer–employee relationship; industrial relations concerned with trade-union–management concerns. This division was also overlaid with gendered interpretations of roles: the masculine concerns of bargaining, conflict and negotiation contrasted with the feminine, welfare aspect of personnel. Also within IR, Fox's (1974) early work on unitary and pluralist perspectives has been further elaborated into various typologies of managerial styles in industrial relations (Purcell and Sisson, 1983; Purcell and Gray, 1986). Binary oppositions also informed labour process analyses: Edwards's (1979) distinction between technical and bureaucratic control, Friedman's (1977) dichotomy between direct control and responsible autonomy. (For a detailed analysis of these, see Legge, 1995, Ch. 2.)

The most recent binary oppositions are prompted by an attempt to understand HRM and the extent to which it constitutes a new approach to managing labour. HRM is contrasted with traditional personnel management. The former is seen as being more pro-active, having implications for management at all levels, rather than being confined to a specialist staff position (Legge, 1989). Not only is HRM more strategic, it is usually associated with a range of personnel practices which indicate management's taking employees more seriously as a 'resource'. Thus, for example, HRM is associated with the commitment policies of the control/commitment dichotomy (Walton, 1985). Other oppositions contrast the old and the new IR; unitarist HRM with pluralist industrial relations (Guest, 1987, 1989); or HRM with IR/personnel, the latter blurring an earlier division (Storey, 1992).[1]

Within HRM itself there are also binary oppositions. Echoing Legge's (1989) distinction between deviant and conformist innovation in personnel management, Storey (1987) makes the distinction between 'hard' and 'soft' versions of HRM. The first is associated with treating employees as a resource, managing in a 'rational' way, focusing on the quantitative and the calculative. The second emphasizes the 'human' elements of production and stresses employee development, motivation and empowerment. This theme is also taken up and developed in Legge (1995), in which 'hard' corresponds to a utilitarian instrumentalism of strategic interventions designed to secure the full utilization of labour *resources*; and 'soft', a developmental humanism, designed to elicit commitment, adaptation and a concern with quality of *resourceful* humans.

These oppositions are problematic (Keenoy, 1990). In some, the detailed elements of the management of labour are not developed, whilst in others, the degree of coherence these oppositions assume, i.e. that certain types of practices will axiomatically be associated with others, fails to capture diversity and complexity (Hyman, 1987; Legge, 1989).[2] As a result these oppositions stimulate an ever elaborate typology of sub-divisions. Like Polonius in Hamlet, pontificating on the nature of drama 'Comedy, tragedy, history, pastoral . . . comical historical, tragedy historical . . .', the permutations grow. Whilst commentators have proposed modifications or reconstructions that might refine analysis, the basic binary oppositions still remain. The method of analysis has not been challenged. Foucault's work allows us to do this and suggests a different approach to understanding the management of labour.

A legacy of modernism

Analysis posed in terms of binary oppositions reflects a modernist approach to knowledge. The epistemology of the Enlightenment is premised on the dualism of a knowing subject gaining knowledge of a known object. The severing of the relationship between knowing and known which supports the subject/object dualism, characterizes the binary oppositions which pervade

Western thought: rational/emotional, mind/body, male/female, good/evil. In each, priority is given to one side of the opposition. One element of the dualism is privileged.

This subject/object dualism has influenced historiography. Explanations focus on a subject – a privileging either of individuals, institutions or class – and intentions – an intentional subject in history. Analyses focus on why. IR/HRM strategies are categorized with reference to managerial intentions, be they managerial strategies to secure control, or the response to the demands of efficiency. This historiography supports an analysis of power which, for Foucault, is problematic. Power is conceived as being a commodity. It is something held or possessed, located in a particular institution (class), or embodied in an individual or group (management), to be used for personal, organizational or class purposes. Power has a locus or origin – a centre. This supports a 'centralized', or descending, analysis of power. There is a search for origins, explanations in terms of the intentions of an occupational group or an identifiably coherent strategy on the part of a dominant class. But, as Weedon (1991: 124) writes, 'the failure to understand the multiplicity of power relations . . . will render an analysis blind to the range of points of resistance inherent in the network of power relations, a blindness which impedes political resistance'.

Foucault rejects the absolutes and the dichotomies of Enlightenment thought and has been critical of the historical method they support. His critique of conventional historical analysis is directed at its concepts of causality, its emphasis on totalizing explanations, the supremacy of subject and consciousness, and an implicit teleology (Foucault, 1972, 1980a, 1991a). There is some resistance to Foucault's work, in part stemming from his refusal to take established categories such as institutions, individuals, class or state as constituting his starting point for analysis. These are rejected in favour of concepts such as discourse, disciplines, governance, political rationalities and technologies. Foucault's method, however, allows for a de-centring of the subject, a focus on practices and an ascending analysis of power. Focusing on the 'how' of power, Foucault's concern is to capture 'ways of doing things', how certain actions and ways of thinking about objects become accepted at a certain historical period as being natural, self-evident and indispensable.

An important dimension of this focus is that it entails a modification of the normal negative connotations of power:

> We must cease once and for all to describe the effects of power in negative terms: it 'excludes', it 'represses', it 'censors', it 'abstracts', it 'masks', it 'conceals'. In fact, power produces: it produces reality; it produces domains of objects and rituals of truth. (Foucault, 1977: 194).

Power is *both* positive and negative, creative and repressive. This presentation of power informs Foucault's (1991b) understanding of governmentality: before a domain can be governed or managed it must first be rendered knowable in a particular way. Ways of thinking about or perceiving a domain render it visible and, through this visibility, open to intervention.

Analysis focuses on how, and with what effect, spheres or domains are rendered governable by being formulated in a particular conceptual way. For Foucault how, for example, 'madness', 'criminality', 'sexuality' have entered the domains of governmentality.

The creation of an exhaustively detailed knowledge of the 'reality' to be governed requires the exercise of discipline – 'an ensemble of minute technical inventions' (Foucault, 1977: 220).[3] Disciplines function through the political anatomy of detail. They capture events and phenomena to which government is to be applied, transcribing them in particular ways. Once captured or inscribed, knowledge about an arena may then be translated to other decision-making bodies, 'centres', enabling them to be governed at a distance (Latour, 1987). Disciplines simultaneously constitute a way of knowing, a system of knowledge; and an order, a system of power. They act as micro-technologies for producing a known and calculable arena, enhancing governability.

In studying the management of labour, a Foucauldian analysis would privilege neither the (alienated) individual nor managerial intentions and strategies of control; rather it focuses on practices which structure social relations. The practices of HR activity – job analysis, job evaluation, selection procedures and performance appraisal – so easily dismissed as merely technical procedures are implicated in strategies of power and knowledge. If we present the employment relationship as a 'space', the gap between promise and delivery, HRM represents one medium through which this space may be organized or disciplined (Townley, 1993). It represents the active creation or production of knowledge for the purposes of governance. It is a mechanism for the construction of a social order, the necessary prerequisite to coordinate and manage the 'rational' and 'efficient' deployment of a population.

There are three principal areas of knowledge which the management of personnel requires: knowledge of the 'body of labour' or the workforce generally; knowledge of the activity or labour to be undertaken; and knowledge of the individual. Ways of ordering populations, mechanisms for the supervision and administration of individuals and groups require the operation of disciplines. Technologies, or mechanisms of disciplinary power, establish an order through classifications (taxinomia) or through measurement (mathesis).[4] These technologies constitute systems of recording, classifying and measuring. They act as grids, configurations of knowledge which may be placed over a domain. Through a number of different mechanisms, personnel provides measurement of both physical and subjective dimensions of labour. It offers a technology which attempts to make individuals and their behaviour predictable and calculable, allowing the 'elimination of imprecise distributions, the uncontrolled disappearance of individuals, their diffuse circulation . . . to establish presences and absences' (Foucault, 1977: 143). It fixes individuals in conceptual space, orders or articulates the labour process, captures individuals within a form of visibility, a gaze, which serves to render actions, behaviour, and even thoughts, knowable.

The construction of knowledge through rules of classification, ordering and distribution, definitions of activities, fixing of scales, rules of procedure leads to the emergence of a distinct personnel discourse. Through the technologies of taxinomia, mathesis and a disciplinary matrix, HRM allows populations to be known in greater detail, at their depths (Townley, 1994). It 'disciplines' the interior of the organization, organizing time, space and movement within it. In so doing, personnel helps to bridge the gap between promise and performance, between labour power and labour, and organizes labour into a productive force.

Disciplinary power: the metaphor of depth

This Foucauldian reading of HRM has implications for our analysis of management of the employment relationship. It suggests that rather than pose analyses in terms of binary oppositions, we incorporate the metaphor of depth into our analysis (Marsden, 1993). Adopting this metaphor leads us to critically re-evaluate some of the central binary oppositions which have informed our understanding of managing labour. It undermines the contrast which is generally drawn between Taylorism and Human Relations, upon which many of our subsequent distinctions rest: the technical and the social; resource management and the 'human' side of the organization; direct control and responsible autonomy; control and commitment.

Hollway (1991: 73), for example, describes the move from Taylorism to human relations as a paradigm shift from the use of monopoly over knowledge to control the labour process to a social-psychological paradigm for understanding the individual at work. Human Relations represents a radical departure because of the way it constructs the individual, changing from a mechanical model of the employee, to a socio-emotional one, a shift from the body, 'hands', to the intervening variable of 'attitudes' between working conditions and work activity.[5] Hollway's distinction derives from a mind/body opposition which typifies the Enlightenment. The privileging of attitudes or 'sentiments' over physical characteristics is based on the nature or content of knowledge rather than its effects.

Analysis in terms of 'depth', however, introduces a different perspective. Under Taylor the reorganization of work was to optimize efficiency. First and foremost this requires the construction of knowledge. One of Taylor's principal concerns was the importance of placing order on what was viewed as a confused mass. He did this by constructing norms and standards. In essence, Taylorism was the application of disciplinary power to greater organizational depths. Human relations took this one stage further, finding out about the employee in depth. Measurement and performance were not downgraded in human relations but, rather, took different forms. The discourse of welfare and human relations clouds personnel's role in providing a nexus of disciplinary practices aimed at making employees' behaviour and performance predictable and calculable – in a word, 'manageable'.[6] Although the discourse became established in terms of motivation and

participation, essentially what was involved was the production of knowledge of the individual with the aim of rendering them manageable in the
domain of work. Aspects of human subjectivity were to be allied with
increased utility.

Equally, the distinctions drawn between technical (Tayloristic) and
bureaucratic control are rendered problematic. Bureaucratic control, the
specification of job tasks and formalized rules, has been understood as a
strategy of control that ensures a reduction in arbitrary authority and
favouritism through meritocratic allocation – the rule of law. In essence the
mechanism which ensures this is the development of taxinomia and
matheses. Taylor, using the same disciplinary mechanisms, also advocated
his ideas on the grounds that they constituted the rule of law and fact, and
that his method was based on procedure and science, rather than arbitrary
authority. 'Scientific management attempts to substitute . . . the government
of fact and law for the rule of force and opinion. It substitutes exact
knowledge for guesswork and seeks to establish a code of natural laws
equally binding on employers and workmen' (Hoxie quoted in Hollway,
1991: 21). In this sense both Taylorism and bureaucratic control are 'seekers
after consistency'.[7]

'Objective' standardized criteria for recruitment and promotion, another
element of bureaucratic control, are premised on the individual's being made
known in a particular way – skills, abilities, personality 'types', attitude – all
of which were prompted with the advent of human relations. Taylor had
advocated that individuals should be selected, trained and paid in accordance
with their ability to perform specific tasks. He also recognized that workers
had sentiments, particularly those which dissuaded them from working to
their utmost capacity. This was not elaborated in terms of the psychology of
individual differences, however, as this was poorly developed at the time of
his writing. In Taylorism, there is no lack of recognition of sentiments, but
rather the inability to make them the objects of knowledge – that is, to place
them in a matrix in which they could be known, and more importantly,
managed. Human relations and its construction of the dimensions of
individuality provided the basis for this.

An analysis in terms of 'depth' also helps us understand the significance
of some current developments in management practice which analyses in
terms of binary oppositions find hard to accommodate. Following, I illustrate
this with reference to two: total quality management and competencies. I
suggest that rather than see these in terms of an opposition between 'hard'
and 'soft' HRM, what both reflect is a deep commitment to the defining
characteristic of modernism – the will to knowledge at ever increasing
depths.

TQM

Total quality management (TQM) has several implications for plumbing the
depths of organizations. Clothed in broad statements about the importance of

creating a culture of quality, TQM can be considered as increasing the depth of organizational knowledge in several respects. If implemented correctly it is a total philosophy. Morgan and Murgatroyd (1994: 8, emphasis in the original) write, TQM 'assumes that quality is the outcome of *all* activities that take place within the organization; that all functions and *all* employees have to participate in the improvement process'. Because quality relies on continuous improvement, every single step or job process is open for review – 'all processes must be subject to the utmost scrutiny' (Morgan and Murgatroyd, 1994: 6). The foundation of TQM is to treat every task as a process. From this comes the need to 'define the process, monitor its performance and to forecast the required inputs and desired outputs' (Morgan and Murgatroyd, 1994: 18).

Although there may be decentralization, empowerment and autonomy, the corollary of changes in work reorganization and organizational restructuring is systematic measuring. TQM is a process of constant measurement and improvement in quality. One of its premises is that decision making should be based on data, detailed data. Hence a key emphasis on measurement tools and statistical process control. Error rates, cycle times, costs and quantities, the measurement of customer expectations and perceptions, become central concerns for the entire organization. The underlying principle is that actions and responses can be measured in a combination of cost, time, quantity, quality or human reaction (Fitz-Enz, 1993: 57). Measuring results will ensure that they are achieved – what gets measured, gets done. The mantras/clichés confirm this – 'if you don't measure results, you can't tell success from failure'; 'if you can't see success you can't reward it'; 'if you can't reward success you're probably rewarding failure'; 'if you can't see success you can't learn from it'.[8]

Benchmarking measures progress towards goals. The 'continuous process of measuring products, services, and practices against the toughest competitors or those companies recognised as industry leaders' (Camp, 1989: 10), may be either internal (measured against different areas of the organization); competitor based; functional; or generic (comparing organizations, regardless of industry). Individuals and organizations become surrounded by a calculus within which to measure themselves and others to see if they come up to the mark. 'It is not unusual to see walls covered in performance charts and achievement boards . . . nor is it unusual to see members of the [TQM] organization carrying data on performance indicators in their diaries – the idea of systematic measurement permeates the organization' (Morgan and Murgatroyd, 1994: 26).

Measures of activities and performance capture individuals, individual units and processes within a form of visibility, a gaze. Although there is an espousal of experimentation and ambiguity, a process of standardization underlies these practices. The identification of high-performing business units in bench marking essentially acts as a 'point of reference from which measurements may be made or something that serves as a standard' (Fitz-Enz, 1993: 26). The continuous process of measuring products and services against standards or leaders is a disciplinary process of examination, standardization and normalization. Establishing benchmarked performance criteria, essentially the introduction of comparative data, permits ranking and the construction of league tables – a disciplinary matrix of taxinomia and mathesis which allows for governance at a distance.

TQM and allied changes in business processes represent an attempt to render the organization more 'known' and concomitantly more manageable. Business Process Re-engineering (BPR), although presented as more strategic than the tactical concerns of TQM, and more radical in that it concentrates on core business processes rather than the continuous improvement of all processes, is in a similar vein. Hall et al. (1993: 119; their emphasis) state that 'redesign must penetrate to the company's core, fundamentally changing six crucial organizational elements or *depth levers*: role and responsibilities, measurements and incentives, organizational structure, information technology, shared values and skills'. Again a major component of BPR is a good tracking or performance-measurement system – a comprehensive system which can measure location-specific results and individual employee performance.

TQM and BPR are strategies of organizational governance relying on the relatively simple technologies of taxinomia, mathesis and examination. Taxinomia and mathesis attempt to capture a range of organizational phenomena and events within a verbal and numerical matrix, usually with the ultimate aim of translating these into their financial equivalent. These simple devices are disciplinary techniques, micro-technologies to enhance governmentality through constructing a more manageable and efficient entity. It is this construction of knowledge, through rules of classification, ordering and distribution, associated with concepts of rationality, measurement, grading, which reinforce the image of technicist knowledge, accuracy and objectivity, as though they are simple empirical mechanisms to access a pre-determined world. They are, however, disciplinary technologies, ordering a population and their activities, rendering them known in a particular way, thereby opening them to intervention and management.[9] They introduce more specific practices of taxinomia and mathesis, whilst at the same time incorporating subjective dimensions of empowerment or accountability, in the attempt to redefine the individuals' understanding of their own subjectivity in production.

Although one of the practices of government is the creation of an exhaustively detailed knowledge of the 'reality' to be governed, this achieves greatest effect when it extends or percolates down to individuals. 'The managing of a population not only concerns the collective mass of phenomena, the level of its aggregate effects, it also implies the management of a population in its depths and details. . . . Disciplines treat a body, 'en masse, "wholesale" as it were' but also individually, 'retail' (Foucault, 1977: 137). They operate simultaneously on the population and the individual, enabling both to be directed. The two are ineluctably linked. In the absence of a micro-technology for engaging the subjective force of labour, other disciplines are amenable to strategies of loose coupling. The disciplinary technologies which allow the individual to be known in depth and thereby rendered open to management are considered in the next section.

Technologies of the self

HRM has traditionally taken the individual as an essential identity, a self-evident entity, comprising personality, needs, attitudes, motivations and so on. A Foucauldian analysis reminds us that the individual is a product of power, irreducible to an internal core of meaning, continuously constituted and constructed. 'Certain bodies, certain gestures, certain discourses, certain desires come to be constituted as individuals. The individual . . . is I believe one of [power's] prime effects' (Foucault, 1980a: 98). In HRM, mechanisms designed to 'develop' human resources are an essential component of this process.

Foucault (1977: 193) writes, 'In a disciplinary regime . . . power becomes more anonymous and more functional, those on whom it is exercised tend to be more strongly individualised.' Technologies of the self are one of the mechanisms Foucault identifies for increasing this individualization. Technology is generally understood as that which enables the production, transformation and manipulation of things. Foucault's elaboration of this in technologies of the self serves to illustrate the ways in which individuals come to operate on their own bodies, thoughts, conduct and way of being, in order to change or transform themselves (Foucault, 1988). Technologies of the self are:

> technologies of power which determine the conduct of individuals and submit them to certain ends or domination, an objectivising of the subject . . . [They] . . . permit individuals to effect by their own means or with the help of others a certain number of operations on their own bodies and souls, thoughts, conduct and way of being, so as to transform themselves in order to attain a certain state of happiness, purity, wisdom, perfection or immortality. (Foucault, 1988: 18)

The technologies of the self which Foucault identifies revolve around the ambiguity in his work of the use of the terms subject and object. For Foucault, power operates on individuals in two ways. It objectivises them through making them objects of knowledge – that is, they become known 'objectively', and thereby able to be managed in a particular way – or they become subjectified. They are presented with an image of themselves, an identity, which then becomes the basis of their self-knowledge. Both provide the basis for individuals to modify or change their behaviour.

From Foucault it is possible to identify two principal practices or technologies of the self: the examination and the confession (Townley, 1994). Through their operation on bodies, thoughts and conduct, they enable individuals to be transformed, rendered more productive and in certain cases re-constituted. Their use can be seen in a range of HR practices, particularly performance appraisal (Townley, 1996), and management training and development (Townley, 1995a).

The examination is associated with the objectification of the individual. Allied with the demand to maximize the use of human resources within the organization, the examination tries to categorize the individual and components of individuality. It 'establishes over individuals a visibility through which one differentiates them and judges them' (Foucault, 1977: 184). Essentially a system of marking and classification, the simple device of questions and answers provides the basis for judgement and measurement. It allows individuals to be classified and managed, placed in a particular sequence, a hierarchy indicating quality or quantity. It is the fixing of 'scientific' differences. It locates individuals and their respective positions in populations and enables the calculation of 'gaps' between individuals. By referring individual actions to the 'population' it also allows 'norms' to be established. It makes possible the calculation of averages and the formation of categories. The worker becomes enmeshed in a series of calculative norms and standards. The examination enables individuals to become compartmentalized, measured, reported, inscribed and calculated, for the purpose of administrative decision making.

The confession constitutes the individual as a subject. In confessing, the self is tied to an identity, or 'inner reality' which has to be uncovered, 'by a conscience or self-knowledge', through prior self-examination. This 'truth' of the individual is premised on a belief that there is an authentic self which lies hidden within, which, with the aid of correct technologies, will reveal itself. It is a view which has a long genesis (Taylor, 1989). The confession enables the operation of what Foucault refers to as pastoral power – 'a form of power cannot be exercised without knowing the insides of people's minds, without exploring their souls, without making them reveal their innermost secrets. It implies a knowledge of the conscience and an ability to direct it' (Foucault, 1983: 214). The mind or the psyche is the key to gaining knowledge of performance; the self-directions of individuals are to be incorporated into the production process. As a result, technologies are required 'for self-reflection, self-knowledge, self-examination, for the deciphering of the self by oneself' (Foucault, 1988).

The confession, however, is more than 'taking stock', which is merely acting as one's own administrator for the purposes of becoming aware and attempting self-improvement, one's faults 'simply good intentions left undone' (Foucault, 1988: 33). The confession is judgemental; faults are the result of bad intentions. The individual's examination of self is with a view to penance, the renunciation of self, the routing out of inner impurity or evil:

> Each person has the duty to know who he is, that is, to know what is happening inside him, to acknowledge faults, to recognise temptations, to locate desires, and everyone is obliged to disclose these things either to God or to others in the community and hence to bear public or private witness against oneself. (Foucault, 1988: 40)

As Foucault (1988: 43) notes of this model, 'self-revelation is at the same time self-destruction'. Disclosure means renouncing. It goes beyond being tied to an identity through self-knowledge; it involves reconstituting the self. The transformation which is sought has oneself as object (Townley, 1995a).

Competencies

Personnel management offers a variety of micro-technologies for exploring, knowing and regulating the individual. Amongst the more recent initiatives is the focus on competencies. Their advent is part of the thrust of which TQM and BPR are a part. Within TQM, the individual, rather unidimensionally, is asked to constitute themselves as customer or supplier. With competencies, there is a far wider scope for 'creativity'. The need for more in-depth knowledge of the individual is stated by Hammer and Champy (1994: 71, their emphasis): 'it is no longer enough merely to look at prospective employees' education, training and skills; their *character* becomes an issue as well. Are they self-starting? Do they have self-discipline? Are they motivated to do what it takes to please a customer?' (cited in Marsden, 1994). Competencies are a mechanism for examining 'character'.

Competencies is a term associated with Boyatzis (1982), who drew upon the work of McClelland. Boyatzis (1982: 1) begins his work with the statement that organizations 'need competent managers to be able to reach . . . objectives both efficiently and effectively'. It is managers' competence that determines the return that organizations realize from their human capital. Boyatzis (1982) is critical of analyses which remain at the level of managerial tasks or functions, because they do not address the person in the job and therefore fail to establish a causal link between characteristics of people and performance in a job. Competencies examine 'the person in the job, not only the job' (Boyatzis, 1982: 43).

From an original question of what constitutes a competent manager, Boyatzis derives the concept of managerial competencies. Competencies are now dimensions of an individual. The general statement of the need to differentiate among competent managers has been elaborated into the competency model of management and the establishment of competencies *as a component of individuality*. Competencies are those characteristics or abilities which enable an individual to take appropriate actions. They are the capability that the individual brings to the job situation, 'an underlying characteristic of a person which results in effective and/or superior performance in a job' (Boyatzis, 1982: 21). In addition to a body of knowledge, competencies are composed of motives, traits, self image, social role, skills and behaviour, which may or *may not be known to the individual*. They are generic, apparent in many forms of behaviour or different actions. From this model, Boyatzis (1982) proposes that competencies form the basis of an integrated human resource management system. They are recommended as the basis of a selection and promotion system, performance appraisal, succession planning and career pathing, career planning and training, compensation and benefits. They are intended to inform the design of management jobs, organizational systems, policies, procedures, and pro-grammes. They are to be used to communicate to managers 'how they should act and what they should be doing' (Boyatzis, 1982: 1).

Competencies are arranged in clusters and involve the presentation of a set of images which the individual should strive to achieve. For example, within the goal and action cluster, individuals having this competency see 'the present and future . . . as a series of challenges and problems to be solved; events in life are viewed as opportunities to test themselves, accomplish something or take risks' (Boyatzis, 1982: 61). The person sees him or herself as someone who can do better. 'In social or organizational contexts, the person adopts the role of being an innovator. . . . These people express concerns about doing something better than it has been done previously. They may state this in terms of progress on an explicit standard of excellence, or a unique accomplishment' (Boyatzis, 1982: 62). Goals or deadlines they set are 'challenging but realistic'. Individuals see themselves as the originators of actions in their lives and believe themselves to be in control of their lives. They take first steps initiating action to accomplish things and readily accept responsibility for successes or failures. They 'collect objects of prestige, become officers in organizations to which they belong, and act assertively. They see themselves as important' (Boyatzis, 1982: 85). Not only this, 'they dress in a fashion considered desirable and attractive in their surroundings' (Boyatzis, 1982: 85).

And so it continues. In the leadership cluster (Boyatzis, 1982: Ch. 5, *passim*), individuals display self-confidence, know what they are doing and feel that they are doing it well. They express little ambivalence about decisions that have been made, have no reluctance in making a decision and living with it. They are forceful, unhesitating and impressive; 'they have a belief in the likelihood of their own success'. They demonstrate presence.

For each cluster, the individual is presented with various components of self – motives, traits, self-image (the perception of self and evaluation of the image), social role, skills and behaviour – which must be known, examined with or without the help of an 'expert', measured and acted upon. Perform-ance appraisal and competency assessments document competencies which have been demonstrated in a recent performance period, and identify competencies to be addressed in the next. They may be recorded on behaviourally anchored scales (the examination), or in a review of specific incidents (the confession). Training in competency acquisition involves, *inter alia*, self-assessment or instrumented feedback on the competency (examination and confession); experimentation with demonstrating the com-petency; to be followed by practice using the competency (re-constituting the self). Boyatzis (1982: 254) explains:

> once the image of how a superior-performing manager should think and act has been developed through the first two stages (i.e., an image of the ideal), people can determine where they stand on each competency through use of the self-assessment or assessment instruments specifically chosen to measure the com-petency . . . the integration of the information on how the superior-performing

> manager thinks and acts (i.e., the ideal) and how the potential manager stands on these competencies (i.e., the real) forms the beginning of a process of self-directed change. . . . It is through the realization of personal discrepancies between the ideal and the real on such competencies that people can perceive and feel a need for change.

It is self-directed change presented as teaching people about management. Other mechanisms for self-directed change include developmental assessment and mentoring or guidance. Increasingly forgotten in this is that Boyatzis's model of factors which influence competent management consists of three elements: the functions and demands of the management job; the organizational environment in which the job exists; and the competencies an individual brings to the job. These three elements *together* comprise effective job performance.

Technologies of the self are examples of the development of the subjective force of labour, capturing the individual within a form of visibility, a gaze, rendering the individuals' actions and thoughts knowable. The examination is not simply the neutral process of acquiring information, but provides the opportunity for establishing norms with which to measure difference. Neither is the confession simply a process of accessing knowledge of, or yielded up by a subject. It also acts to constitute the subject in terms of providing an aspect of identity. In both cases, knowledge *of* becomes knowledge *over*. Through rendering the individual more knowable, both technologies offer the promise of enhanced and more effective management.

The presentation of the 'power effects' of these technologies, however, is not to imply their production of a totally obedient subject. Their operation is informed by a concept of power which, as indicated earlier, is positive and productive as well as negative and repressive. These technologies do not simply act to constrain the individual. They are also positive. They offer procedures which confirm and sustain identity. They are productive in that individuals secure a sense of identity, a knowledge of their abilities and so on. The productive and positive aspects of knowledge which sharpen a sense of oneself and one's actions should not be underestimated or neglected (Roberts, 1991). However, there is an inherent ambiguity involved here. Identities which are constituted through power/knowledge are also made vulnerable. These technologies present an individual with a way of seeing themselves measured against a transitory ideal. Individuals face uncertainty and insecurity in the requirement to meet successful performance, instigating a search for constant reaffirmation of identity, to secure the acknowledgement, recognition and confirmation of self in practices confirmed by others as desirable.

The unities of discourse

The argument so far is that the metaphor of depth allows us to reconceptualize our approach to understanding strategies in the management of labour. In this section I wish to consider another dimension of this argument: HR's link with other disciplines. An interpretation of personnel influenced by its roots in welfare and the ideology of human relations, leads to the conventional interpretation that its concerns lie with the human or motivational aspects of organizations. This has led to a particular understanding of personnel management in relation to other academic and functional disciplines. Re-orienting our analysis to one informed by depth allows for a different analysis to be presented.

One benefit of Foucault's concepts is to decouple a body of knowledge from those who lay claim to it. The role of a body of knowledge, for example personnel, cannot be understood by restricting it to its common-sense use, as defined by a profession and maintained by professional and academic boundaries. Foucault offers the possibility of uncovering hidden unities – 'different types' of knowledge may be reassembled in new and sometimes illuminating ways. For Foucault (1972: 72), unity does not lie 'in visible, horizontal coherence of elements'; the coherence, for example, which is assumed in linking recruitment, appraisal, training and so on. Rather, unity for Foucault, again in keeping with the metaphor of depth, is vertical. It lies in a hierarchy of relations between institutions, economic and social practices, behavioural patterns, systems of norms, techniques, types of classification, modes of characterization and so on. In Foucault's terms, a unity is constituted if 'practices and statements constitute the same division of a perceptual field . . . presupposed on the same way of looking at things' (Foucault, 1972). This has implications for the way HRM may be understood in relation to other managerial disciplines.

Traditional interpretations of personnel, and indeed an enduring component of the binary oppositions in HRM, stress the 'human' side of the organization. As such, personnel is usually held to be in diametric opposition to the concerns of accountants and engineers. Armstrong (1989), for example, traces the relationship between personnel and 'rival' professions and argues that recent changes in personnel represent a deviation from an original trajectory, due to personnel's being appropriated by an accounting rationale. Armstrong's work follows the traditional analysis of a functional view of the organization – accounting, personnel, marketing and so on. Accounting's relationship with personnel is posed in terms of the relationship between the financial and the 'behavioural'. Questions then become phrased in terms of how the two (accounting and 'other than' accounting) relate to each other. There is an assumed antithesis; analysis is in terms of contrast and conflict. However, these constructions, reproducing the confines of established disciplines, are in danger of limiting our understanding of organizational practices for the control of the labour process.

Portraying personnel as the constitution of knowledge and order through a taxinomia, mathesis and the subjective technologies, illustrates its similarities to the other managerial disciplines as it participates in the disciplining of undisciplined domains. Equally, adopting a definition of accounting as the construction of a taxinomia and mathesis allows accounting's relationship with personnel management to be re-oriented from the traditional accounting/behavioural interface which has characterized its study (Townley, 1995b).[10]

These broader definitions of personnel and accounting provide a different complexion on the relationship between management disciplines. Both accounting and personnel provide an ordering of organizational activities. They reduce information about a whole variety of situations to a number of specific categories. Both offer an ordered account of organizational activities, structure meanings and orient actions. As systems of recording, classifying and measuring they offer a semblance of control, representing an arena as well-structured tasks and clearly measurable outputs. They organize time and space and prescribe and control work practices. They offer the prospect of enumeration – the possibility of assigning a measure at each point. By providing 'objectively' measurable characteristics of an organization, they both serve to render organizations calculable arenas. Both constitute processes of monitoring and observation that facilitate the functioning of a Panopticon, as information is relayed back to the centres of calculation. Both are calculative technologies which attempt to secure control of the labour process.

Accounting, however, is not a very precise technology of governance (Armstrong, 1994). Visibility is only partial, and accounting divisions leave a population distributed in groups with little further differentiation. The organization of productive effort requires a greater specificity of movement through time and space than is provided by accounting disciplines. The specificity of actions and of individuals often remains vague. Personnel technologies, however, render activities and individuals more visible. Through various techniques, tasks, behaviour and interactions are categorized and measured in an attempt to make individuals and their behaviour predictable and calculable. In this respect, personnel technologies, like some superior beers, reach the parts that others cannot reach. Personnel acts as an under-labourer providing a disciplinary framework of an organization, often providing the taxonomies and their mathematical representations for other disciplines (Townley, 1995b).

An obvious question which Foucault himself recognized in trying to identify the unity of a discourse was: 'Why proceed to dubious regroupings?, What new domains is one hoping to discover?, What hitherto obscure or implicit relations? In short, what descriptive efficacy can one accord to these new analyses?' (Foucault, 1972: 71). The answer again draws on Foucault: 'It's a method which seems to me to yield, I wouldn't say the maximum possible illumination but at least a fairly fruitful kind of intelligibility' (Foucault, 1981: 4). The interpretation of personnel and accounting offered here indicates that rather than their being seen as antithetical, they may establish a unified discourse. For example, recent developments in both the public and the private sectors with the introduction of performance management systems indicate that there may be a unity in the political rationality of 'accounting for performance'. Analysis of such a unity would illustrate how formal accounting procedures, performance indicators, and the technologies of the examination and the confession in individual performance appraisal, function at different levels to render a domain visible and governable, objectifying individuals and their activities (Townley, 1996).

For Foucault, it is disciplinary practices that make possible the 'disciplines' of accounting, personnel, engineering, management science. Disciplinary power can also be infinitely extended. As a result, it is important to understand the operation of *all* technologies of governance as they work to secure enhanced control over the labour process. Rather than debate being based on antithetical oppositions between the hard and calculative, and soft and behavioural, there is a need for an analysis of their interrelationship and reciprocal interaction. This requires analysis in terms of depth rather than division, complementarity rather than conflict. It also introduces the broader issue of the nature of academic and professional boundaries and whether the relationship with HRM and other managerial disciplines should not be located within a broader context of calculation and rationalization (Townley, 1995b; Marsden and Townley, 1996).

Conclusions: HRM – mapping the terrain

I have argued that binary oppositions which have typified our analysis of managerial strategies in HRM may be more fruitfully replaced by an analysis of depth. I suggest that we do not begin our analysis with an idealized model ('HRM') and go in search of practices, but rather the reverse: begin with an examination of the practices to see how they structure social relations. Because the individual and the organization are a product of the social techniques of power, analysis should be directed at what is involved in rendering the individual/arena knowable, how processes become established and used, and with what effects. This emphasizes the importance of studying in detail the actual practices which introduce the individual/ arena to enunciation and visibility, those mechanisms of inscription, recording and calculation which constitute the discursive practices that make knowledge of the individual/arena possible.

A useful metaphor when confronting depth in power/knowledge regimes is that of mapping. Santos (1987) suggests that the metaphor of mapping is an appropriate one for an analysis of regulation, and although Foucault did not extend his analysis to the discipline of 'geography', he acknowledges that it would be analogous (Foucault, 1980b). Maps differ according to whether they claim to represent (topography/terrain) or to orient (action). They may be either small scale or large scale. They also differ according to their chosen method of representation or symbolization (for example, accounting and personnel numbers). The study of HRM should focus on an analysis of the *topography* of employment systems according to the depth of knowledge produced and the areas in which this is concentrated. The maps produced may illustrate how arenas differ in terms of degree of detection (the extent to which they plumb the depths), or the extent to which they discriminate between areas. They would allow us to see how different maps become superimposed on an arena, and the extent to which they inter-penetrate. Such an analysis would allow binary oppositions to be replaced by diversity and multiplicity.

Interestingly, while arguing for the superiority of an analysis of manage-ment in terms of competencies, Boyatzis (1982: 258) concludes:

> if you are part of the scientific management tradition, you may view competencies as the specifications for the human machinery desired to provide maximum organizational efficiency and effectiveness. If you are part of the humanistic management tradition, you may view competencies as the key that unlocks the door to individuals in realizing their maximum potential, developing ethical organizational systems, and providing maximum growth opportunities of person-nel. If you are one of those people who work in organizations and/or one of the people who studies, thinks about, and tries to help organizations utilize their human resources effectively, the findings and model should provide needed relief from the eclectic cynicism or parochial optimism concerning management that many of us have developed.

Boyatzis argues that competencies provide an escape from analyses which are posed in terms of binary oppositions and their implicit connotations of good and evil. Equally, an analysis in terms of depth helps escape the essentialism ascribed to practices and the inherent privileging of binary oppositions.

There is an old saying 'the devil lies in the details'. In Hammer and Champy (1994: 25; the quote is not referenced) this has been reformulated, 'God is in the details', and attributed to the architect Mies van der Rohe. The accuracy is not pertinent here. Rather what is important is paying attention to the details of practices which bind our organizational lives. An analysis of the 'how' of power, practices rather than intentions, allows for a recognition of the negative *and* the positive in *all* practices and an evaluation of their effects. Through this we can begin to understand the simultaneous produc-tion of empowerment and repression, commitment and control. An analysis of practices that bury deep, not only into social spaces but into the individual, their notions of individuality and integrity, is the only basis on which we can begin to consider, and seriously debate, the ethical issues involved in such practices.

Notes

1 Storey (1992) offers a more elaborate dualism than others, identifying 25 key dimensions, considered under four headings of beliefs and assumptions, strategic aspects, line management and key levers.

2 As Legge (1989) points out, being strategic and commitment style polices need not coincide. Some business strategies, for example low-cost production, lead to policies not unlike the control perspective.

3 For Foucault, it was these methods of administering the accumulation of men, rather than the technological inventions of the period, which allowed for the accumulation of capital, industrialization and the development of capitalism.

4 Foucault identifies the disciplines of classification, codification, categorizing, precise calibration, tables and taxonomies as the basis of organizing human multiplicities – 'providing oneself with an instrument to cover it and to master it' (Foucault, 1977: 148). Their growth was allied to the population growth coinciding through the seventeenth and eighteenth centuries, which represented a change of a quantitative dimension in the scale of the population to be supervised. It is through organizing, clearing up confusion and establishing calculated distributions, that the particular utility of each element of a multiplicity is increased. Disciplines are designed to increase the utility of individuals, to enhance production, be this of health through treated patients, skills through educated pupils, or economic production.

5 Others have been more sceptical of a radical division. Braverman (1974: 87), for example, is more dismissive of 'styles' of economic exploitation: 'Taylorism dominates the world of production; the practitioners of "human relations" and "industrial psychology" are the maintenance crew for the human machinery.'

6 Equally the 'welfare' aspect of personnel suitably ignores the role of philanthropic middle-class women reconstructing the behaviour and lives of their working-class charges (Ross, 1992).

7 The phrase comes from Crichton (1968: 21), who describes personnel specialists as seekers after consistency through the establishment of policies and procedures.

8 These actually come from Osborne and Gaebler (1992). Public sector changes, however, reflect a similar emphasis to TQM. Osborne and Gaebler (1992), for example, emphasize the importance of results-oriented government which focuses on outcomes, not inputs, and stresses the importance of performance measures, periodic inspection and rating systems. Government policies are formulated in terms of goals, objectives and performance indicators, each linearly derived from the other. Control is ensured through measurement and the publication of performance indicators, which for schools might be test scores, satisfaction surveys, honours, drop out rates, placement rates and so on.

9 In keeping with the dual-sided nature of power these practices should not be understood in a deterministic way.

10 For example, research in personnel has focused on issues such as an increase in incentive payment schemes in organizations; the extent to which results oriented appraisal systems feature in managerial appraisal systems (Long, 1986); studies of how personnel departments evaluate and justify their activities in financial terms (Tyson and Fell, 1986). In terms of the influence of accounting on specific personnel policies, this is identified in the increasing use of profit-related incentive schemes and value-added payment systems, and the introduction of results-oriented appraisal systems based on budgetary measures.

References

Armstrong, P. (1989) 'Limits and possibilities for HRM in an age of management account-ancy', in J. Storey (ed.), *New Perspectives on Human Resource Management*. London: Routledge. pp. 154–166.

Armstrong, P. (1994) 'The influence of Michel Foucault on accounting research', *Critical Perspectives on Accounting*, 5 (1): 25–56.

Boyatzis, R. (1982) *The Competent Manager*. New York: Wiley.

Braverman, H. (1974) *Labour and Monopoly Capital*. New York: Monthly Review Press.

Camp, R. (1989) *Benchmarking: A Search for Industry Best Practices that Lead to Superior Performance*. Milwaukee, WI: ASQC Quality Press.

Crichton, A. (1968) *Personnel Management in Context*. London: Batsford.

Edwards, R. (1979) *Contested Terrain: The Transformation of the Workplace in the Twentieth Century*. New York: Basic Books.

Fitz-Enz, J. (1993) *Benchmarking Staff Performance*. San Francisco: Jossey-Bass.

Foucault, M. (1972) *The Archaeology of Knowledge*. London: Tavistock.

Foucault, M. (1977) *Discipline and Punish: The Birth of the Prison*. London: Allen Lane.

Foucault, M. (1980a) 'Two lectures', in C. Gordon (ed.), *Power/Knowledge*. Brighton: Harvester. pp. 78–108.

Foucault, M. (1980b) 'Questions on geography', in C. Gordon (ed.), *Power/Knowledge*. Brighton: Harvester. pp. 63–77.

Foucault, M. (1981) *The History of Sexuality, Volume 1: The Will to Knowledge*. London: Penguin.

Foucault, M. (1983) 'The subject and power', in H. Dreyfus and P. Rabinow (eds), *Michel Foucault: Beyond Structuralism and Hermeneutics*. Chicago: Chicago University Press. pp. 208–26.

Foucault, M. (1988) 'Technologies of the self', in L. Martin, H. Gutman and P.H. Hutton (eds), *Technologies of the Self*. London: Tavistock. pp. 16–49.

Foucault, M. (1991a) 'Questions of method', in G. Burchell, C. Gordon and P. Miller (eds), *The Foucault Effect*. Hemel Hempstead: Wheatsheaf. pp. 73–86.

Foucault, M. (1991b) 'Governmentality', in G. Burchell, C. Gordon and P. Miller (eds), *The Foucault Effect*. Hemel Hempstead: Wheatsheaf. pp. 87–104.

Fox, A. (1974) *Beyond Contract: Work, Power and Trust Relations*. London: Faber and Faber.

Friedman, A. (1977) *Industry and Labour*. London: Macmillan.

Guest, D. (1987) 'Human resource management and industrial relations', *Journal of Management Studies*, 24 (5): 503–21.

Guest, D. (1989) 'Human resource management: its implications for industrial relations and trade unions', in J. Storey (ed.), *New Perspectives on Human Resource Management*. London: Routledge. pp. 41–55.

Hall, G., Rosenthal, J. and Wade, J. (1993) 'How to make reengineering *really* work', *Harvard Business Review*, November–December, 119–31.

Hammer, M. and Champy, J. (1994) *Reengineering the Corporation*. New York: Harper Business.

Hollway, W. (1991) *Work Psychology and Organizational Behaviour*. London: Sage.

Hyman, R. (1987) 'Strategy or structure: capital, labour and control', *Work, Employment and Society*, 1 (2): 25–55.

Keenoy, T. (1990) 'HRM: a case of the wolf in sheep's clothing', *Personnel Review*, 19 (2): 3–9.

Latour, B. (1987) *Science in Action*. Cambridge, MA: Harvard University Press.

Legge, K. (1989) 'Human resource management: a critical analysis', in J. Storey (ed.), *New Perspectives in Human Resource Management*. London: Routledge. pp. 19–40.

Legge, K. (1995) *Human Resource Management: Rhetorics and Realities*. London: Macmillan.

Long, P. (1986) *Performance Appraisal Revisited*. London: IPM.

Miller, P. and O'Leary, T. (1987) 'Accounting and the construction of the governable person', *Accounting, Organizations and Society*, 12: 235–65.

Marsden, R. (1993) 'The politics of organizational analysis', *Organization Studies*, 14 (1): 93–124.

Marsden, R. (1994) *IRDL:317: Re-engineering the Organization*. Athabasca, Alberta: Athabasca University.

Marsden, R. and Townley, B. (1996) 'The owl of Minerva: reflections on theory in practice', in S. Clegg, C. Hardy and W. Nord (eds), *Handbook of Organization Studies*. London: Sage. pp. 659–75.

Morgan, C. and Murgatroyd, S. (1994) *Total Quality Management in the Public Sector*. Buckingham: Open University Press.

Osborne, D. and Gaebler, T. (1992) *Reinventing Government*. New York: Plume.

Purcell, J. and Gray, A. (1986) 'Corporate personnel departments and the management of industrial relations: two case studies in ambiguity', *Journal of Management Studies*, 23 (2): 205–23.

Purcell, J. and Sisson, K. (1983) 'Strategies and practice in the management of industrial relations', in G.S. Bain (ed.), *Industrial Relations in Britain*. Oxford: Blackwell. pp. 95–120.

Roberts, J. (1991) 'The possibilities of accountability', *Accounting, Organizations and Society*, 16 (4): 355–68.

Ross, E. (1992) 'Good and bad mothers: lady philanthropists and London housewives before World War I', in D. Helly and S. Reverby (eds), *Gendered Domains*. Ithaca, NY: Cornell University Press. pp. 199–216.

Santos, B. (1987) 'Law – a map of misreading: toward a postmodern conception of law', *Journal of Law and Society*, 14 (3): 279–302.

Storey, J. (1987) 'Developments in the management of human resources: an interim report', *Warwick Papers in Industrial Relations*, 17 (IRRU, University of Warwick).

Storey, J. (1992) *Developments in the Management of Human Resources*. Oxford: Blackwell.

Taylor, C. (1989) *Sources of the Self*. Cambridge, MA: Harvard University Press.

Townley, B. (1993) 'Foucault, power/knowledge and its relevance for human resource management', *Academy of Management Review*, 18 (3): 518–45.

Townley, B. (1994) *Reframing Human Resource Management: Power Ethics and the Subject at Work*. London: Sage.

Townley, B. (1995a) 'Know thyself: self-awareness, self-formation and managing', *Organization*, 2 (2): 271–89.

Townley, B. (1995b) 'Managing by numbers: accounting, personnel management and the creation of a mathesis', *Critical Perspectives on Accounting*, 6 (6): 555–75.

Townley, B. (1996) 'Accounting in detail: accounting for individual performance', *Critical Perspectives on Accounting*, 7 (5): 565–84.

Tyson, S. and Fell, A. (1986) *Evaluating the Personnel Function*. London: Hutchinson.

Walton, R. (1985) 'Towards a strategy of eliciting employee commitment based on policies of mutuality', in R. Walton and P. Lawrence (eds), *Human Resource Management, Trends and Challenges*. Boston: Harvard Business School Press. pp. 237–65.

Weedon, C. (1991) *Feminist Practice and Poststructuralist Theory*. Oxford: Basil Blackwell.

12

Re-framing Foucault: The Case of Performance Appraisal

Patricia Findlay and Tim Newton

In this chapter we aim both to explore the insights that derive from a Foucauldian perspective and to consider some of the limitations of this perspective. The chapter will start narrow and work broad. In order to focus our analysis, we will commence by examining a particular area of management, namely that of performance appraisal. Focusing in on one area allows us a particular scope in examining the benefits and constraints of a Foucauldian analysis. Further, performance appraisal is an area to which Foucault clearly speaks, and one which has already received some attention from writers on organizations applying Foucault (for example, Grey, 1994; Townley, 1994). Having used appraisal practice as a vehicle to close in on the constraints of Foucauldian work, we will then broaden our analysis to consider some issues raised by the wider developments in human resource management over the past decade. The final section of the chapter will address the theoretical limitations of Foucauldian analysis that our preceding work indicates.

We shall proceed by first presenting a brief introduction to appraisal, and then considering the broader relevance of Foucault to understanding appraisal. We will then consider difficulties that arise with a Foucauldian analysis of appraisal, through a critical evaluation of those applying Foucault (to appraisal), particularly Barbara Townley and Chris Grey. We will argue that a Foucauldian framework runs the danger of detracting from critical analysis, and we shall explore these issues more broadly by considering trends in the recent development of human resource management. We shall assert that, contrary to Foucault, monarchic power is not clearly on the wane (Newton, 1994; Newton et al., 1995), and that there are reasonable reasons why our 'representation of power has remained under the spell of monarchy' (Foucault, 1979: 88). We shall further suggest that the problem with detracting from the relevance of monarchic power is that it runs the risk of softening rather than sharpening critical analysis. Finally, we will argue that Foucauldian work has proved limited in its ability to address one of the central questions for sociology and organizational sociology, namely how we deal with the subject and human agency.

A brief introduction to appraisal

We wish to begin our discussion of the ideology of appraisal by presenting a brief outline of its central concepts and their post-war development.[1] Present work on appraisal remains situated within a neo-human-relations legacy, still employing many of the values and strategies of neo-human-relations writers such as McGregor, Likert, and Argyris. Although subsequent writers have not followed their arguments blindly, it remains neo-human-relations discourse which sets the terms of many current debates. A detailed review of this discourse is beyond the scope of this chapter, but we will illustrate its main assumptions as applied to performance appraisal.

In his oft-cited paper, McGregor (1957) laid out many of the concerns found in current papers and textbooks dealing with appraisal, including the problem of the conflicting roles of the appraiser as both a disciplinary 'judge', and yet a supposedly helpful 'counsellor':

> The modern emphasis upon the manager as a leader who strives to *help* his subordinates achieve both their own and the company's objectives is hardly consistent with the judicial role demanded by most appraisal plans. (1957: 90; emphasis added)

The judge/counsellor conflict still forms a feature of more recent debates about appraisal (for example, Fletcher and Williams, 1985; Latham, 1986), as do many of the other issues which McGregor examined, such as: the validity of appraisal technology and the need to place emphasis on appraisee job-related behaviour rather than personality; the resistance of appraisers to criticizing their subordinates; the argument that subordinates should formulate their own performance goals rather than having them dictated by their superiors; the idea that appraiser and appraisee discuss the appraisal draft report jointly; and the need to specify how performance goals will be achieved. Underlying all of these arguments is the neo-human-relations vision of the need 'to approach the whole subject of management from the point of view of basic social values' (McGregor, 1957: 91), drawing on 'our convictions about the worth and the dignity of the human personality' (1957: 90).

The support for the subordinate's participation in both the process of appraisal and the formulation of performance plans drew directly on this human relations imperative with its argument that the appraisee should become 'an active agent, not a passive "object"' (1957: 91). McGregor's arguments also incorporated the usual unitary approach of human and neo-human relations (Hollway, 1991), with its assumption that appraisal will automatically serve the supposedly common interest of employee and employer. 'Participative' appraisal meant that the employee

> can gain a genuine sense of satisfaction, for he [*sic*] is utilizing his own capabilities to achieve simultaneously both his objective and those of the organization. (1957: 92)

Because they are all working together, the appraiser in a participative appraisal process can be a true 'helper' rather than a judge.

> He [*sic*] is not telling, deciding, criticizing, or praising – not 'playing' God. He finds himself listening, using his own knowledge of the organization as a basis for advising, guiding, encouraging his subordinates to develop their own potentialities. Incidentally, this often leads the superior to important insights about himself and his impact on others. (1957: 92)

Appraisal is thus about people learning about themselves and working together to help themselves and the organization. In this caring, sharing world, 'a transfer or even a demotion can be worked out without the connotation of a "sentence by the judge"' (1957: 92).

It seems relatively easy now to criticize the organizational harmony that is supposed to follow from such neo-human-relations arguments. To take an obvious one, how can an appraisee view appraisal as a purely helping/ counselling exercise where they may 'confide' their job difficulties and anxieties, when there is often the possibility (even if not stated) that the appraisal 'data' will be used in assessing promotion, transfer, 'or even a demotion'? More generally, one must question the unitary perspective of human relations with its denial of any conflict of interest between employees and employers. Along with this unitarism goes an individualism that assumes that employees will want to take the responsibility for improving themselves through their 'active' participation in appraisal. There is no questioning of whether this should be viewed as a manipulation which places the burden of 'development' on the employee, and encourages them to see themselves as a resource which they must polish and refine according to their employer's needs (Salaman, 1979). And finally, there is little concern that developments in appraisal technology might represent new possibilities for the surveillance and discipline of employees.

In spite of such possible criticisms, most recent appraisal literature still conforms to the parameters set by neo-human-relations writers. For example, Fletcher and Williams ended their review of appraisal with a plea for a 'shift towards greater *participation/involvement* of individuals in their career planning and decision-making' (1985: 143; emphasis added), while textbooks such as that of Cascio make near-identical prescriptions to those of McGregor for the conduct of appraisals, such as the need to 'warm up and encourage subordinate participation, judge performance, not personality and mannerisms, be specific, be an active listener, avoid destructive criticism, set mutually agreeable goals for future performance' (1991: 102). Many writers appear to be largely unaware of the neo-human-relations discourse in which much of their text is situated. For example, Bowles and Coates argue that in appraisal 'an enlightened approach to the management of people must centre on empowerment, not judgement', where empowering employees means getting them involved in things such as 'making their own judgements of performance and identifying needs for development' (1993: 8). This is put forward as though it were a novel proclamation, whereas all it represents is a 1990s re-invocation of traditional neo-human-relations discourse.

In sum, appraisal discourse and supposed practice still appears to be set within neo-human-relations thinking, presenting the image of a progressive and participative practice geared to the mutual benefit of the appraisee, the appraiser, and the organization. However, from the mid to late 1980s onwards, this discourse has been subject to a small but growing volume of criticism. Much of this criticism has derived from those strongly influenced by Foucault, such as Wendy Hollway (1984, 1991) and Barbara Townley (1989, 1993a, 1994). In what follows below, we shall firstly present our own analysis of the way in which appraisal can easily be situated within a Foucauldian framework, relating this analysis to the brief discursive history of appraisal that we have given above. We will then critically analyse Foucauldian work on appraisal, and use this analysis to explore the limitations of a Foucauldian perspective.[2]

Foucault and appraisal

The emphasis upon discipline and surveillance in Foucault's earlier conceptualization of power (most especially in *Discipline and Punish*, 1979) finds an easy application in performance appraisal. Appraisal can be seen as epitomizing a desire for observation and surveillance, to make the employee a 'knowable, calculable and administrable object' (Miller and Rose, 1990: 5). It appears as one tactic working towards the notion of disciplinary power enshrined in Foucault's reference to Bentham's 'Panopticon', the model prison in which prisoners can always be seen, yet cannot see themselves. It is easy to see the panoptic power of appraisal in the plethora of appraisal measures, such as the use of Likert scales, graphic rating scales, critical incidents, mixed standard rating scales, behaviourally anchored rating scales and so on. All such measures are designed to refine the observational assessment of the appraisee, to provide an unfettered gaze upon their job performance and, particularly, to identify any inabilities they may have in meeting expected norms. At the same time, such techniques are not the only form of performance monitoring, since managers now have available a number of sophisticated 'electronic surveillance' possibilities, as illustrated by writers such as Zuboff (1988) and Sewell and Wilkinson (1992). However appraisal is about more than surveillance since it is not just about monitoring 'sub-standard' performance, but knowing why it occurred. Answering this question requires an ability to gaze upon the subjectivity of the worker, to know her feelings, anxieties, her identity and her consciousness (Newton et al., 1995). Only that kind of observation is really playing the kind of celestial power game envisaged in Foucault's symbolic use of the Panopticon, with its architectural metaphor of 'a mechanism of power reduced to its ideal form' (Foucault, 1979: 205).

A strong symbol of such thorough panopticism is provided by employee counselling, with its direct line to the 'soul' of the employee (following Foucault, 1979, counselling can be seen as the secular development of the

Christian confessional). Ever since the counselling programme at Western Electric's Hawthorne plant, the surveillance possibilities implicit in counselling have received some (limited) attention. For while the confidentiality of this counselling is generally assured, aggregate data about employee concerns, sentiments, grievances, and so on can be fed back to managers. In an article published in the *American Journal of Sociology* in 1951, one of the counsellors at Hawthorne, Jeane L. Wilensky, argued that 'Western Electric . . . has not only entered the worker's social life, his [*sic*] financial life, and his intellectual life, but now, through personnel counseling, his most intimate thoughts, deeds and desires may be laid bare to a representative of the company' (Wilensky and Wilensky, 1951: 266). Counselling can thus be seen as the most direct tactic for the appraisal of how the subjectivity of the worker relates to her job performance, with the potential of a panoptic capability far in excess of electronic surveillance (see Newton et al: 1995, for a review of the control implications of post-war counselling and employee assistance programmes). Rather than just monitoring job performance, it aims to reveal why workers are not working as hard as they might, through accessing their feelings about the job, their workmates, their managers, their home life, their anxieties and aspirations.

Performance appraisal can also be seen as having some similar effects to the deployment of employee counselling. Its rationale is the examination of the employee, and the 'learning' that can take place through the 'sharing' of difficulties. Yet, as we have seen, neo-human-relations writers such as McGregor were very aware of how this counselling role of appraisal was under threat because the appraiser is also a 'judge'. McGregor's concern was precisely to dissipate the notion of appraisal as involving a 'sentence by the judge' (1957: 92; see above). The kind of 'God' that the appraiser should personify was not one who is 'telling, deciding, criticizing', but rather one who 'finds himself listening, . . . advising, guiding, encouraging his subordinates to develop their own potentialities' (1957: 92). This participative vision of appraisal brings us close to the panoptic possibilities of counselling, of the 'God' who 'knows' and 'sees' and 'guides'. At the same time, it provides a remarkably neat example of Foucault's argument that modernity is characterized by a shift away from 'monarchic' and 'juridical' power towards other forms of power such as disciplinary, pastoral and 'biopower' (Foucault, 1979, 1981). Power is no longer exercised by right, or through judges who 'lay down the law'. Rather, for example, a disciplinary power can be seen to operate through observation and the ability

> to qualify, measure, appraise, hierarchize, rather than display itself in its *murderous splendour*: it does not have to draw the line that separates the enemies of the sovereign from his obedient subject; it effects distribution around the norm. (1981: 144; emphasis added)

The parallel to neo-human-relations prescriptions for performance appraisal is transparent. The appraiser is neither the sovereign nor the judge, but the observer (the 'listener') who must 'measure, appraise, hierarchize'. Appraisal technology uses the observational methods of personnel psychology to gauge where the appraisee 'stands', which can only be done with respect to some assessment of the average, the norm.

Appraisal can also be seen as providing an illustration of Foucault's argument that power is not simply repressive and negative, but is positive and productive through the constitution of the self in discourse. Neo-human-relations discourse can be seen as productively 'constituting' appraisers and appraisees in a discourse which emphasizes the 'learning' that can take place, through 'listening', 'sharing', through 'solving problems together'. Not only does it offer the promise of 'self-awareness' and a greater 'intelligibility' on the part of the appraisee or subordinate, but also, as McGregor noted, it 'often leads the superior to important insights about himself and his impact on others' (1957: 92). Following Foucault, a number of writers have argued against a straightforwardly negative view of power (e.g. Miller and Rose, 1990; Knights and Morgan, 1991; Rose and Miller, 1992; Townley, 1994). For example, Rose argues that modern discourses of the self such as those of self-growth and psychotherapy are subjectifying 'not because experts have colluded in the globalisation of political power, seeking to dominate and subjugate . . .', but because 'modern selves have become attached to the project of freedom, have come to live in terms of identity, and to search for means to enhance that autonomy through the application of expertise' (Rose, 1990: 258). Performance appraisal can be seen as one more example of a social science 'discursivity' tied to this same project, particularly through its neo-human-relations 'underwriters' and their desire for appraiser and appraisee to 'know themselves' through a participative dialogue. As Foucault argued, modernity can be seen as in part governed by 'bio-power', where discourses such as psychoanalysis, psychiatry, and education express the '"right" to life, . . . to the satisfaction of needs, . . . the "right" to discover what one is and all that one can be' (1979: 145). Such comments, albeit from a different perspective, could almost have been written by neo-human-relations writers such as McGregor and Maslow, who expressed a central concern with 'higher-order' need satisfaction and 'self-actualization'.

Appraisal can thus easily be read within a Foucauldian framework which stresses the productiveness of power/knowledge. Foucault directs us toward the assessment that lies at the heart of appraisal, but, contrary to the image created by some of those drawing on Foucault (e.g. Deetz, 1992), his work suggests that the disciplinary power so induced may be as positive as negative in its effects. One writer who has particularly stressed the positive aspects of the disciplinary power of appraisal is Barbara Townley, and we shall now turn to her work, and that of Chris Grey, in order to explore the difficulties of maintaining a positive image of power in the workplace, and to examine other constraints of the Foucauldian treatment of performance appraisal.

Foucauldians and appraisal

Barbara Townley has provided the most direct and detailed application of a Foucauldian framework to performance appraisal (e.g. Townley, 1992, 1993a, 1993b, 1993c, 1994). For this reason alone, her work is particularly relevant to our present concerns. For the sake of economy we shall particularly focus on her analysis of performance appraisal in 30 UK universities, which she based on a textual analysis of university appraisal documents (forms, notes of guidance, and so on; Townley, 1993a, 1993b). In this analysis, Townley appears concerned to maintain a view of power as 'positive and creative' (Townley, 1993a: 224, 1993b). However, this image is maintained in spite of descriptions of university appraisal practices which imply that, at least for those being appraised, the outcomes of appraisal can appear rather negative because of their potential to deliver increased employee discipline and control. For example, she notes how performance standards in one appraisal committee were moving towards being set around a 'model' work output. This arose through casual suggestions that the 'troops' might 'get some idea of what was required' if the appraisal record of an academic with 'a particularly successful publication record that year' were circulated to 'subsequent appraisees' (1993a: 232). Drawing on her Foucauldian account, Townley reads this as an example of how 'a "norm" becomes established' (1993a: 232). But, this is *not* Foucault's norm, since it is not the 'average' score implicit in Foucault's reference to norms and hierarchical assessment (Foucault, 1979). Instead, it is much closer to the 'outlier', to performance at the 'upper end of the scale', and as such, is reminiscent of Taylor's 'first class' worker. But of course, if you want to maximize employee output, you set outliers as your model performance, not norms. In sum, this example of Townley's appears to have much in common with more traditional views of power in the employment setting as negative and constraining.

Townley does acknowledge that the panoptic surveillance allowed by appraisal represents 'a method by which the powerful are helped to observe the less powerful but rarely, it must be noted, *vice versa*' (1993a: 233). But at the same time she ends this analysis by noting once again the 'productive role of power', and throughout she is careful to avoid any image of domination. Thus, following Foucault, she argues against the existence of a central controlling force, suggesting that power operates at a multiplicity of sites (1993a, 1993b). Yet this argument is to some extent contradicted by the textual analyses which she presents. For example, she notes how in some universities, appraisal is seen as 'a means of enabling "the VC to review the professors to see how they manage their staff"' (1993a: 233), whilst elsewhere she notes how appraisal can also ensure 'that the "centre" may strengthen its control' and how 'active management hierarchy becomes the organizing principle' (1993a: 234). Is this power operating through a multiplicity of sites and scattered locations? Is it really irrelevant to talk of a centre? Whilst this may not amount to the simple monistic domination by one omniscient group, her account does nevertheless suggest that the panopticism of appraisal may further aid and legitimate a centralization of knowledge and decision making. As Webster and Robins (1993) argue, rhetorics of delegation and decentralization may disguise enhanced surveillance processes which serve to concentrate power at the centre.

It is perhaps not surprising that there are some difficulties in continually maintaining an image of the positive potential of power in the workplace. After all, from a labour process perspective, issues such as job performance and its assessment are at the heart of the *control* of the labour process, critical to squeezing surplus value out of the worker. If one's concerns are centred away from the employment relationship (as for example, with the many modern discourses of the self such as self-growth and psychotherapy), it is perhaps easier to shy away from the negative image of discipline as control because there is no wage–labour relationship (e.g. in psychotherapy it is the client who pays the therapist, not the other way round; there is no dependency for economic livelihood, even though there may be a perception that 'psychological livelihood' is at stake). But once one is focusing on the wage–labour relationship it is hard to ignore the kind of monarchic/juridical power that Foucault was keen to dispel (Newton, 1994; Newton et al., 1995). Whilst, in the modern era, employers may no longer simply rule by right, with managers dictating exactly what employees will do, it can nevertheless be argued that the employer's *right* to punish and reward does create a lot of good-old-fashioned coercive possibilities. Though this quasi-monarchic power of right is only occasionally publicly displayed in all its 'murderous splendour' (Foucault, 1981: 144), it does still seem relevant to the way in which people toe the line, how they try to please and placate their superiors so that they may one day be granted favours just as kings and queens once rewarded their courtiers (Newton et al., 1995). And, of course, performance appraisal is an element in the granting of such favours (even if only indirectly linked to pay), in the presenting of oneself in the best possible light at the 'royal court'. There is a need for 'civility', and to not openly challenge the assumption that this is a participative exercise wherein the appraiser just happens to play an important role in the granting of favours (Elias, 1978, 1982; Newton, 1996a, 1997). To do so would be to ignore the coercive parameters of the exercise, and the fact that the conclusions of this very participative tribunal may affect one's present and future standing in the organization.

Chris Grey has recently provided an analysis which, though chiefly situated within a Foucauldian framework, can also be seen as providing a strong example of the need for courtly behaviour in performance management (Grey, 1994). One of us (Newton, 1996a) has presented a critical re-reading of Grey's work, and we draw on this analysis below. Grey's study addresses performance appraisal, but his central concern lies more broadly with the significance of people's *careers* in the *'realisation of [the] project of the self'* (1994: 484; original italics). Though his interest is therefore wider than the focus of the present chapter (on appraisal), his study is nevertheless worth examining in some depth, both in terms of its implications for appraisal, and in relation to the tensions it reveals in work drawing significantly on Foucault. Like Townley, Grey is at pains to stress that appraisal and career management should not just be seen as an example of 'negative' disciplinary power, since the 'techniques of disciplinary power become constructed as benevolent aids to career development' (1994: 494). Thus, in his study of career management among trainee and chartered accountants, Grey illustrates how the 'panoptic gaze' provided by recruitment interviews, appraisal ratings and professional examinations are not seen by trainee accountants as regulatory disciplinary devices, but as a means to assist them 'in the maximisation of [their] career prospects' (1994: 494). Yet what is most interesting about Grey's study is that his use of 'career' as a metaphor for 'productive' 'enabling' power almost becomes redundant if his data are *re-interpreted* from the angle of a quasi-monarchic power where aspiring novices continually need to maintain civility. For example, the 'royal court' provides a strong metaphor for Grey's analysis of the world of accountancy firms, where all those at lower levels of the hierarchy are continually begging favour from the managers and partners at the top of the hierarchy (Elias, 1978, 1982). The eventual goal of young accountants in their 'career' is to gain access to the inner elite of the 'accountancy court', the managers and partners who not only receive very good financial 'rewards' but who are also principally responsible for policing civil behaviour within the court. Thus all members may be criticized for inappropriate dress at the court such as 'having overly garish ties', whilst women 'universally wore skirts rather than trousers' (1994: 486). As very junior members of the court, trainee accountants are nevertheless 'expected to display *enthusiasm* and *commitment* at all times, regardless of the tediousness of the chores' (1994: 486; emphasis added). True aspiring members of the court will not see tedious mundane tasks as chores since 'through an (individualised) conception of career, their mundanity is transformed' (1994: 486).

Re-interpreting Grey's analysis, 'career' for these (very largely) white, male, middle-class courtiers becomes a metaphor for penetrating the inner circle of the accountancy court. Yet participation in court life is perilous. Not only are there the professional examinations to pass, but there is also 'the cull', whereby a number of the novitiates are sacked for reasons of business expediency. With the appropriate grace of courtly language, the sacking of employees is officially termed 'counselling out', since it is 'a supposedly mutual career decision for the employee to leave the firm' (1994: 489). Yet the effect remains the same; the new courtier is continually aware that his seniors may entertain their royal prerogative in all its 'murderous splendour', and in consequence 'an ingenious game is played between the employees and the personnel staff in which the former seek to identify those who are liable to be "culled"' (1994: 490). As Grey notes, there are a number of signs of one's standing in the court, chief of which is the salary level attained by the courtiers which 'is seen as a "sign of grace"' (1994:

490; differential salary levels are paid to employees in the same grade). The use of such language as 'grace' is remarkable if only because of its strong evocation of the sense of patronage, and attaining grace through civil and courtly behaviour (Elias, 1978). Performance appraisal in this context, though supposedly 'liberal' and participative, appears instead as the imposition of an almost 'royal decree'. First, it is directly linked to 'the cull' whereby those rated no better than 'satisfactory' are highly likely to be dismissed. Secondly, 'it is *not* a two way process' (1994: 491; original emphasis). Although invited to comment on their ratings, employees rarely do so since '"it wouldn't be very good for your career" (newly qualified accountant)' (1994: 491). The sensible courtier knows her place.

Thus, what is fascinating about Grey's analysis of performance appraisal and career management among accountants is that it can easily be (re)read as an example of *monarchic* discipline, *not* discursive discipline. Grey, however, interprets his data through the latter, seeing it as a neo-Foucauldian illustration of how 'work is a part of the entrepreneurial project of the self' (1994: 482; cf. Miller and Rose, 1990; Rose, 1990; Rose, 1991; Rose and Miller, 1992), whereby the organization of the self occurs 'through the self-discipline which is produced through [a] career' (1994: 482). Yet the question remains as to why this self-discipline comes about, and why this attachment to a career? Is it *just* because accountants in the 1980s and 1990s have become constituted in, say, the neo-liberal discourses associated with Thatcherism and Reaganomics (Rose and Miller, 1992), or embroiled in the 'psychologization' of work (Salaman, 1979; Rose, 1990). Or is it through a socialization in a much older kind of discipline, which comes about not so much through the government of the soul within modern discourse (Rose, 1990), as through the good-old-fashioned selling of the soul in the hope of both gaining traditional favours and rewards, and avoiding the 'murderous splendour' of our employers who may, in many instances, still be able to terminate our economic life?

Our criticism above of the work of Townley and Grey is not meant to imply that there are no insights to be gained from Foucauldian analysis. Such work both highlights the need to examine the way in which discourse has developed (such as that of human resource management and organizational psychology), and the kind of objects it creates in terms of, say, appraisers, appraisees, and appraisal practice. At the same time, we have no quarrel, in general, with a conceptualization of power as potentially positive, pleasurable and creative, nor with the argument that 'repression is not . . . fundamental and overriding' (Foucault, 1979: 73). However, it does seem to us that among *some* Foucauldians there is a tendency to attempt to continually rescue a positive image of power, whilst negating the difficulties of such a defence. In part, this problem may be seen to arise from an insufficient attention to the way in which discourse is 'established' (Newton et al., 1995). As Wetherell and Potter argue, 'discourse does take place in history, it feeds off the social landscape, the social groups, the material interests already constituted' (1992: 86). In the context of appraisal, this means that, as with any other organizational practice, we do need to look at appraisal discourse and practice as it is established within the power relations of the employment setting. In the employment relationship, we are still observing a quasi-monarchic exercise of employer power enshrined in labour contracts, and thus it seems likely to us that the terms of appraisal discourse and practice will be applied in a manner that is broadly convenient to management, and to the need to control the labour process – as shown by the unitary images of a consensus of interest between employer and employee contained in neo-human-relations discourse on appraisal. Thus, we must be attentive to the historical and social 'landscape' in which human resource management practices such as performance appraisal are situated. As Wilensky and Wilensky long ago noted of their experience at Hawthorne, counselling may mitigate against collective action or 'militancy' by helping to guard against 'grievances that might otherwise find expression in other [i.e. collective/union] channels' (1951: 276). Or as Lasch later put it, this kind of 'personnel management treats the grievance as a kind of sickness, curable by means of therapeutic intervention' (1977: 184). Whilst appraisal is less directly targeted on the employee 'confessional', its relevance to the gaining of consent and commitment is hard to ignore, because of its combination of a supposed participation between appraiser and appraisee (wherein if real 'learning/problem-solving' is to take place, problems must firstly be confessed), and because its focus is on individual rather than collective solutions to employee 'problems'.

Whilst noting that our quarrel is with the terms with which Foucault has been applied, we should, however, also note that a large part of the problem lies with Foucault himself. As we shall argue later on in this chapter, there is a major difficulty in accounting for how discourse and practice are played out in the context of local power relations, because of Foucault's neglect of the subject and human agency (Newton, 1994, 1996a). At the same time, this neglect means that a Foucauldian framework is also limited in analysing subjectivity in spite of the fact that the turn to Foucault amongst organizational writers was in large part prompted by a desire to tackle the issue of subjectivity (Newton, 1998). Before we consider this argument, however, we wish to firstly broaden from our analysis of appraisal to examine human resource management more generally, and its development over the last decade. In so doing we shall argue that the issues that we have so far examined are far from unique to the case of performance appraisal.

The rise and rise of human resource management

Most evaluations of both academic and popular management literature would suggest that managerial discourse has undergone a dramatic shift since the late 1970s, and it is no exaggeration to claim that discussions of human resource management have strongly influenced this discourse, despite major disagreements as to what constitutes human resource management and the extent to which it has been implemented (Storey, 1992). According to

Storey (1989), human resource management represents a shift away from a compliance-based model of employee management, based on proceduralism and joint regulation, towards a commitment-based model in which managerial policies (like appraisal, merit pay, and direct management communications) aim to elicit the active identification of all employees with the objectives of the organization. The language of commitment and self-regulation contained within discussions of human resource management fit well with the idea of disciplinary power enshrined in Foucault's analysis. Thus, it is worth considering the extent to which managerial discourse has changed in recent years, how far this has been reflected in managerial practice, and the impact of both discourse and practice on employees, in light of Foucault's claims of a move from monarchic toward disciplinary power.

There is considerable evidence of the existence of a new managerial language, built around the central tenets of human resource management. Storey (1992) refers to a major shift in managerial rhetoric, away from proceduralism and joint regulation, towards talk of competitive markets, the need for commitment, empowerment and so on. Keenoy and Anthony (1992) contend that the rhetoric of human resource management has meshed well with prevailing ideas on the predominance of the free market, the rise of entrepreneurialism, and the primacy of economic exchange over other social interactions. Central to most discussions of human resource management is the idea that for organizations to respond effectively to increasing organizational pressures of various sorts requires the active support rather than the passive compliance of employees. Thus, as Hollway (1991) suggests, the idea of commitment is about producing a self-regulated individual, thus avoiding bureaucratic and coercive measures which neither secure compliance nor accord with dominant social and political values. The link between the quest for employee commitment and disciplinary power is obvious, and thus, recent managerial rhetoric appears to support the increasing relevance of notions of disciplinary power.

In terms of general trends in managerial styles and the adoption of specific practices, Scott (1994) charts the decline since the late 1970s of informal employee relations practices based on negotiation, accommodation and the 'gentlemanly' industrial relations of the Donovan era, and their replacement with an overt and pro-active managerialism, with negative consequences both for trade union power and for the status and influence of the personnel function. Alongside this, according to Martinez and Weston (1994), existing worker's rights (both individual and collective) and interests have been re-articulated along managerial lines. In addition, both survey and case study data suggest a rise in the use of many of the practices associated with human resource management, such as performance appraisal, merit-related pay, quality initiatives, flexibility initiatives, more direct management communications, and employee involvement (e.g. Long, 1986; Townley, 1989; Geary, 1992; Sewell and Wilkinson, 1992; Marchington, 1994, 1995; Procter et al., 1994).

Thus, the idea that old-style employee management policies have been replaced has gained much ground. What, however, has replaced them? Here, it is interesting to note the (short) rise and fall of the macho-management thesis in the early 1980s. This suggested that the combined effects of Conservative government policies, extensive labour legislation and economic recession had resulted in the adoption of a 'macho-management' style and a 'new realism' in employee relations in Britain (Mackay, 1986). Thus, management, empowered by economic and political conditions, were adopting an increasingly assertive and aggressive stance towards labour, particularly organized labour. Employees, in their turn, aware of their weakened position in the labour market, were perceived to be 'keeping their heads down' and cooperating with management to a greater degree than previously. Managers were seen to have taken advantage of a climate more favourable to a strengthening of managerial control to restructure their relationships with employees, in the form of lower pay settlements, greater intensification of work, attacks on trade union demarcation lines and restrictive practices, and the bypassing of traditional trade union structures in order to forge a more direct link with their workforces, as well as to weaken plant trades unions. This thesis was criticized in two related ways: firstly, it was suggested that there was little evidence of macho management; and secondly, it was suggested that it may not be in management's interest to take advantage of its increased power relative to labour, since competitive conditions required a committed and adaptable labour force, rather than a strictly controlled and potentially hostile one (Terry, 1986; MacInnes, 1987). It is interesting that the macho-management thesis appears to have been almost entirely overtaken by the debate on human resource management, and is rarely referred to in current literature. Whilst this might be seen as a reflection of the waning of monarchic power, as managers and employees have become constituted in human resource management discourse, an alternative explanation is that the 'macho' practices of managers have become an established feature of organizational life in the 1990s, and thus merit little explicit acknowledgement. Thus, Cooper (1995) notes the existence of a number of studies where control systems are aimed directly at compliance rather than commitment (Edwards and Whitson, 1989; Knights and Morgan, 1990; Jones, 1992). In addition, Fernie et al. (1994) signal the existence of a large and rapidly growing sector of non-union workplaces which neither practise Donovan type proceduralism nor human resource management. These are referred to as the '"black hole" of modern employee relations', on which there is little available information, but which raise concerns among the authors that 'this unregulated vision of the future may be exploitative' (1994: 237). Such examples cast doubt both on the adoption of human resource management techniques, and on the argument that human resource management practice is chiefly situated within the disciplinary power of modern management discourse (or both). Rather they suggest that such practice still occurs within parameters that appear quasi-monarchic in their operation. This is hardly surprising, given the amount of discretion accorded to management within human resource management, and the value attached to informality and flexibility; such informality is likely to be coloured by broader power relations in specific organizations and in industry as a whole.

Not only are there significant examples of managerial approaches much at odds with the notion of disciplinary power; we would also argue that existing studies of employees raise scepticism over the notion that lower-level employees are constituted in managerial discourse (Morris et al., 1993; Cooper, 1995; Stewart and Garrahan, 1995). While Storey's 1992 case studies are neither extensive nor systematic in their consideration of employee response, anecdotal evidence therein suggests that employee behaviour has not shifted to the extent that management rhetoric would suggest. Similarly, Scott argues that 'modern attempts to manipulate workers' perception of status and responsibility have made little progress. Workers' perception of management authority has to date, continued relatively unaltered' (1994: 148). Scott further suggests that 'although managers have been experimenting with new approaches to industrial relations, they have not as yet discovered how to make them work on the shop floor' (1994: 149). He explains this partly in terms of a reluctance by managers to relinquish traditional (monarchic?) prerogatives, and to involve workers in a way acceptable to them, that is, by building real employee involvement through an independent representation of workers' views.

Of course, it can be argued that employees are constituted in human resource management discourse more by their resistance to it than by their acceptance of its logic and practice. Yet, we lack Foucauldian work which is attentive to such possibilities. In addition, many Foucauldian studies appear to theorize resistance inadequately, and overemphasize the significance of surveillance and of self-control. As has been argued elsewhere (Thompson and Ackroyd, 1994; Newton and Findlay, 1996), failure to accord sufficient attention to resistance, combined with a focus on discourse and text, can lead to a failure to acknowledge that managerial intentions are not always translated into their desired outcomes.

Part of the problem is that much of the work currently influenced by Foucault is insufficiently attentive to the way in which discourse may be differently read by individuals and groups, a problem which itself reflects a more general lack of attention to agency. For example, we contend that discourse may be read more directly by managers than by non-managerial employees, since the discourse is written in a managerial language, and generally advocates practices which can be seen to operate in management's favour. Similarly, human resource management discourse may be read differently among groups of managers: for example, in Barlow's study, the author notes the significantly differing responses of managers to the discourse surrounding appraisal (Barlow, 1989). We need, therefore, to look much more closely at the way in which management discourses differentially translate individuals and groups, and how such translation is affected by issues such as gender, race, and class (Newton, 1994, 1996b).

We have argued that quasi-monarchic power is still a central feature of the management–labour relationship. While a Foucauldian analysis might acknowledge the disciplinary potential of the panopticist practices associated with HRM, it is unlikely to see this as the whole picture. Implicit (or explicit) in a number of Foucauldian accounts is the view that people willingly enter into human resource management discourse because of a fragility of the self and the desire to confirm a precarious identity (Newton, 1998). People are supposedly constituted within the developing human resource management and organizational psychology discourse, either willingly through their search for identity, or less willingly through the panoptic observation that human resource management allows. However, if this is so, we might expect a more egalitarian and joint influence over human resource practices, since the language of human resource management still follows neo-human-relations ethics of participation, and the encouragement and utilization of employee's autonomy and creativity (McGregor, 1957; Likert, 1961). The labels may have changed slightly, with 'empowerment' replacing 'self-actualization', but the same sense of a 'growth of the individual to the benefit of the company' still remains. However, as we have suggested earlier, the evidence indicates that the reality is rather different. Given the continued relevance of a seeming quasi-monarchic power, and the disparity of power between management and employees in the recent economic and political environment, we would urge caution in explaining employee behaviour in terms of self-regulation and commitment, or in terms of an identity project (Newton, 1996a). Explanations of change solely in terms of people's acceptance or resistance to new managerial discourses do not seem sufficient. Rather, we need to examine in detail how new discourse and practice is played out in the context of local power relations. Further, as Thompson and Ackroyd (1995) suggest, we require an account which recognizes the specificity of the wage–effort bargain, a specificity which much of industrial sociology acknowledges.

At the same time, there is little in Foucault to explain local action. A Foucauldian framework does not give us insight into how the actions of organizational actors are constrained by operating within hierarchies that privilege certain actors – for example, senior over junior, line over personnel, (still more generally) men over women (Newton, 1996b). To take this further would require not only an acceptance that quasi-monarchic power continues to be relevant, but also a recognition that power relations in the workplace are far more complex than the concepts of either monarchic or disciplinary power would suggest. We accept the view put forward by Foucault and by many others, that power operates from a multiplicity of sites, but we would argue that the wage–effort bargain constitutes a primary defining feature affecting power relations in the workplace. Similarly, though we believe that Foucauldian analyses have been of major significance in drawing attention to the significance of power/knowledge relations, we nevertheless feel that many of these analyses remain limited by their lack of attention to human agency, and to the local power relations that surround the deployment of management discourse (Newton et al., 1995). We need theoretical frameworks which can, for example, account for the way in which personnel and line managers may (consciously or unconsciously) manipulate organizational psychology and equal opportunities discourse so as to legitimate personnel selection decisions that discriminate on grounds of class, gender, or race (Hollway, 1984; Newton, 1994). Similar arguments apply to other assessment practices, and to human resource management more generally. Until we can account theoretically for such aspects of agency and subjectivity, we are likely to remain limited in our ability to develop the work of Foucault within the context of organization analysis.

It may be argued that the above arguments run counter to the spirit of much of Foucault's work in its tendency to decentre from the subject. Yet we would contend that it is this very decentring which limits the otherwise insightful work of Foucauldian analyses of, say, performance appraisal, and human resource management. Following this argument, there remains a need for more 'socialized' accounts (Newton, 1996a) which relate agency and subjectivity to the way in which discourse is both established and deployed. The question that remains, however, is whether such accounts can be developed within what most people would recognize as a Foucauldian framework.

Notes

Pages 212–21 reproduce material previously published in an earlier paper: Newton, Tim and Findlay, Patricia, (1996) 'Playing God: the performance of appraisal', *Human Resource Management Journal*. The copyright for these pages is jointly held by Industrial Relations Services (18–20 Highbury Place, London N5 1QP) and Personnel Publications (17 Britton Street, London EC1M 5NQ).

1 This section of the paper could also be seen as presenting the beginnings of a genealogy of appraisal (in the Foucauldian sense). However, as one of us has argued elsewhere (Newton et al., 1995; Newton 1997), there are difficulties with the concept of genealogy. Whilst genealogical analysis has the advantage of not assuming that there is a linear (one historical building block upon another) development, it is not unique in this perspective (which, after all, would be shared by many modern historians). Neither is the denial of the legitimacy of 'the search for "origins"' (Foucault, 1984: 77) unique to genealogy. But more significantly from our perspective, we do not agree with a central plank of Foucault's advocacy of genealogy, namely that 'accidents . . . accompany every beginning' (Foucault, 1984: 80). 'History' may develop haphazardly with no great master plan, but that does not mean that it is a matter of accidents rather than strategies, or that there is no continuity. As Elias argues, there is unlikely to be any simple relation between a particular 'strategy' and a particular 'outcome', since within any historical development there is the 'interweaving of countless individual interests and intentions' (1994: 389). Yet there is a continuity between strategy and outcome in the sense that 'something comes into being that was planned and intended by none of these individuals, yet has *emerged nevertheless from their intentions and actions*' (Elias, 1994: 389; our italics). In sum, following Elias, we tend toward a non-linear 'patchwork' view of history whereby continuity is acknowledged.

2 Reference to 'Foucauldians' is not meant to imply that such writers are strict 'disciples' of Foucault. Rather we use the term to denote those writers whose analyses appear strongly conditioned by Foucault.

References

Barlow, G. (1989) 'Deficiencies and the perpetuation of power: latent functions in management appraisal', *Journal of Management Studies*, 26 (5): 499–518.

Bowles, M.L. and Coates, G. (1993) 'Image and substance: the management of performance as rhetoric or reality', *Personnel Review*, 22 (2): pp. 3–21.

Cascio, W.F. (1991) *Applied Psychology in Personnel Management* (4th edn). Englewood Cliffs, NJ: Prentice-Hall.

Cooper, John (1995) 'Managerial culture and the stillbirth of organisational commitment', *Human Resource Management Journal*, 5 (3): 56–76.

Deetz, Stanley (1992) 'Disciplinary power in the modern corporation', in Mats Alvesson and Hugh Willmott (eds), *Critical Management Studies*. London: Sage. pp. 21–45.

Edwards, P.K. and Whitson, C. (1989) 'Industrial discipline, the control of attendance, and the subordination of labour: towards an integrated analysis', *Work, Employment and Society*, 3 (1): 21–7.

Elias, N. (1978) *The Civilising Process*, vol. 1: *The History of Manners*. Oxford: Blackwell.

Elias, N. (1982) *The Civilising Process*, vol. 2: *State Formation and Civilization*. Oxford: Blackwell.

Elias, Norbert (1994) *The Civilizing Process: The History of Manners, and State Formation and Civilization*. Oxford: Blackwell.

Fernie, S., Metcalf, D. and Woodland, S. (1994) 'Lost Your Voice?', *New Economy*: 231–7.

Fletcher, C. and Williams, R. (1985) *Performance Appraisal and Career Development*. London: Hutchinson.

Foucault, M. (1979) *Discipline and Punish*. Harmondsworth: Penguin.

Foucault, M. (1981) *The History of Sexuality, Volume 1*. Harmondsworth: Penguin.

Foucault, Michel (1984) 'Nietzsche, genealogy, history', in Paul Rabinow (ed.), *The Foucault Reader*. Harmondsworth: Penguin. pp. 76–100.

Geary, J.F. (1992) 'Pay, control and commitment: linking appraisal and reward', *Human Resource Management Journal*, 2 (4): 36–54.

Grey, C. (1994) 'Career as a project of the self and labour process discipline'. *Sociology*, 28 (2): 479–98.

Hollway, W. (1984) 'Fitting work: psychological assessment in organizations', in J. Henriques, W. Hollway, C. Urwin, C. Venn and V. Walkerdine (eds), *Changing the Subject: Psychology, Social Regulation and Subjectivity*. London: Methuen. pp. 26–59.

Hollway, W. (1991) *Work Psychology and Organizational Behaviour*. London: Sage.

Jones, C.S. (1992) 'The attitude of owner-managers towards accounting control systems following management buyout', *Accounting, Organizations and Society*, 17 (2): 151–68.

Keenoy, Tom and Anthony, Peter (1992) 'HRM: metaphor, meaning and morality', in P. Blyton and P. Turnbull (eds), *Reassessing HRM*. London: Sage. pp. 233–55.

Knights, D. and Morgan, D. (1990) 'Management control in sales forces: a case study from the labour process of life insurance' *Work, Employment and Society*, 4 (3): 369–89.

Knights, D. and Morgan, G. (1991) 'Strategic discourse and subjectivity: towards a critical analysis of corporate strategy in organizations', *Organization Studies*, 12: 251–73.

Lasch, C. (1977) *Haven in a Heartless World: The Family Besieged*. New York: Basic Books.

Latham, G.P. (1986) 'Job performance and appraisal', in C.L. Cooper and I.T. Robertson (eds), *International Review of Industrial and Organizational Psychology*. Chichester: Wiley. pp. 117–55.

Likert, R. (1961) *New Patterns of Management*. New York: McGraw-Hill.

Long, P. (1986) *Performance Appraisal Revisited*. London: IPM.

MacInnes, J. (1987) *Thatcherism at Work: Industrial Relations and Economic Change*. Milton Keynes: Open University Press.

Mackay, L. (1986) 'The macho manager: it's no myth', *Personnel Management*, 18 (1): 25–7.

Marchington, M. (1994) 'Involvement and participation', in J. Storey (ed.) *Human Resource Management: A Critical Text*. London: Routledge. pp. 280–308.

Marchington, M. (1995) 'The dynamics of joint consultation', in K. Sisson (ed.) *Personnal Management* (2nd edn). Oxford: Blackwell. pp. 662–93.

Martinez, M. and Weston, S. (1994) 'New management practices in a multinational corporation: the restructuring of worker representation and rights?', *Industrial Relations Journal*, 25 (2): 110–21.

McGregor, D. (1957) 'An uneasy look at performance appraisal', *Harvard Business Review*, 35: 89–94.

Miller, P. and Rose, N. (1990) 'Governing economic life', *Economy and Society*, 19: 1–31.

Morris, T., Lydka, H. and O'Creevy, M.F. (1993) 'Can commitment be managed? A longitudinal analysis of employee commitment and human resource policies', *Human Resource Management Journal*, 3 (3): 21–42.

Newton, Tim (1994) 'Discourse and agency: the example of personnel psychology and "assessment centres"'. *Organization Studies*, 15 (6): 879–902.

Newton, Tim, Handy, Jocelyn and Fineman, Stephen (1995) *'Managing' Stress: Emotion and Power at Work*. London: Sage.

Newton, Tim (1996a) 'Resocialising the subject? A re-reading of Grey's "Career as a Project of the Self"'. *Sociology*, 30 (1): 137–44.

Newton, Tim (1996b) 'Agency and discourse: recruiting consultants in a life insurance company', *Sociology*, 30 (4): 717–39.

Newton, Tim (1997) 'An historical sociology of emotion?', in Gill Bendelow and Simon Williams (eds), *Emotions in Social Life: Social Theories and Contemporary Issues*. London: Routledge.

Newton, Tim (1998) 'Theorizing subjectivity in organizations: the failure of Foucauldian studies', *Organization Studies*.

Newton, T. and Findlay, P. (1996) 'Playing God? The performance of appraisal', *Human Resource Management Journal*, 6 (3) 42–58.

Procter, S.J., McArdle, L., Rowlinson, M., Forrester, P. and Hassard, J. (1994) 'Flexibility, politics and strategy: in defence of the model of the flexible firm', *Work, Employment and Society*, 8 (2): 221–42.

Rose, N. (1990) *Governing the Soul: The Shaping of the Private Self*. London: Routledge.

Rose, N. (1991) 'Governing the enterprising self', in P. Heelas and P. Morris (eds), *The Values of the Enterprise Culture – The Moral Debate*. London: Unwin Hyman. pp. 141–64.

Rose, N. and Miller, P. (1992) 'Political power beyond the state: problematics of government', *British Journal of Sociology*, 43: 173–205.

Salaman, G. (1979) *Work Organisations: Resistance and Control*. London: Longman.

Scott, A. (1994) *Willing Slaves? British Workers under HRM*. Cambridge: Cambridge University Press.

Sewell, G. and Wilkinson, B. (1992) 'Someone to watch over me: surveillance, discipline and the just-in-time labour process', *Sociology*, 26: 271–89.

Stewart, P. and Garrahan, P. (1995) 'Employee responses to new management techniques in the auto industry', *Work, Employment and Society*, 9 (3): 517–36.

Storey, J. (ed.) (1989) *New Perspectives on Human Resource Management*. London: Routledge.

Storey, J. (1992) *Developments in the Management of Human Resources*. Oxford: Blackwell.

Terry, M. (1986) 'How do we know if shop stewards are getting weaker?', *British Journal of Industrial Relations*, 24 (2).

Thompson, P. and Ackroyd, S. (1995) 'A critique of recent trends in British industrial sociology', *Sociology*, 29 (4): 615–33.

Townley, B. (1989) 'Selection and appraisal: reconstituting "social relations"', in J. Storey (ed.), *New Perspectives on Human Resource Management*. London: Routledge. pp. 92–108.

Townley, B. (1992) 'In the eye of the gaze: the constitutive role of performance appraisal', in P. Barrar and C. Cooper (eds), *Managing Organisations in 1992*. London: Routledge. pp. 185–202.

Townley, B. (1993a) 'Performance appraisal and the emergence of management', *Journal of Management Studies*, 30 (2): 27–44.

Townley, B. (1993b) 'Foucault, power/knowledge, and its relevance for human resource management', *Academy of Management Review*, 18 (3): 518–45.

Townley, B. (1993c) 'Accounting for performance: strategies of governance', revised version of paper presented at Critical Perspectives on Accounting, New York, April.

Townley, B. (1994) *Reframing Human Resource Management: Power, Ethics and the Subject at Work*. London: Sage.

Webster, F. and Robins, K. (1993) 'I'll be watching you: comment on Sewell and Wilkinson', *Sociology*, 27 (2): pp. 243–52.

Wetherell, M. and Potter, J. (1992) *Mapping the Language of Racism: Discourse and the Legitimation of Exploitation*. Hemel Hempstead: Harvester Wheatsheaf.

Wilensky, J.L. and Wilensky, H.L. (1951) 'Personnel counselling: the Hawthorne case', *American Journal of Sociology*, 17: 265–80

Zuboff, S. (1988) *In the Age of the Smart Machine*. Oxford: Heinemann.

13

Afterword: Deconstructing Organization – Discipline and Desire

Ken Starkey and Alan McKinlay

The main focus of the book has been the complicated workings of the power/knowledge nexus in the managerial search for effective forms of discipline. In the 'Afterword' we introduce another issue, one that Foucault paid increasing attention to in his later work – the relationship between discipline and desire. One of the issues Foucault struggled with was how to explain the apparent 'willing' involvement of subjects in systems of power that could be construed as working against their own best interests. What we are suggesting here is that we need to work on a deconstructive reading, particularly of Foucault's later work, that accommodates the tension between desire and discipline. In essence, what one is suggesting here is that a 'final' reading of Foucault – of course, any final reading is impossible – a reading that does ultimate justice to the complexity of the issues he was wrestling with in his later work, will focus upon more than the disciplinary concerns of his 'middle' period, but, of course, the work of the later period needs refracting through the middle period work and vice versa. What this view suggests is that one deconstructs the concern with discipline using the prism of its opposite, desire. Kilduff (1993: 15), drawing upon the work of Derrida (1978), captures the essence of the deconstructive gesture:

> A deconstructive reading opens up the text to renewed debate concerning the limits of the text and the relationship between the explicit and hidden textual levels. In investigating the limits of the text, the critic asks: . . . Why are certain themes never questioned, whereas other themes are condemned? Why, given a set of premises, are certain conclusions not reached? The aim of such questions is not to point out textual errors but to help the reader to understand the extent to which the text's obectivity and persuasiveness depend on a set of strategic exclusions.

A key concern of Foucault is with 'subjectification'. Individuals lose themselves in regimes of power but, paradoxically, are created as subjects/other-selves by these same regimes.

> This form of power [the *régime du savoir*] applies itself to immediate everyday life which categorizes the individual, marks him by his own individuality, attaches him to his own identity, imposes a law of truth on him which he must recognize and which others have to recognize in him. It is a form of power which makes individuals subjects. There are two meanings of the word *subject*: subject to someone ELSE by CONTROL and DEPENDENCE, and tied to his own identity

and conscience or self-knowledge. Both meanings suggest a form of power which subjugates and makes subject to. (Foucault, 1983: 212; original emphasis)

Towards the end of his life Foucault described his role thus: 'to show people that they are much freer than they feel, that people accept as truth, as evidence, some themes which have been built up at a certain moment during history, and that this so-called evidence can be criticized and destroyed' (Foucault, 1988a: 10). Foucault's later work continues his investigation into how things are 'known' and people are 'seen' (Foucault, 1980: 154) but in a manner in which his ongoing concern with the disciplinary power of knowledge is reframed in terms of an investigation of how self and desire are constituted. In the work of Foucault's middle period, in particular in *Discipline and Punish*, the emphasis is upon the creation of 'docile bodies', individuals constrained against their will *by* discipline embodied in technologies of domination (Foucault, 1988b: 19). In the later work his concern is with ways in which individuals create their own selves and realize their desires *through* discipline. The major focus is not how individuals are disciplined by others – that it is, what others do to subjects, – but how subjects (individuals/communities) create their own 'selves'. What Foucault suggests in his later work is that individuals/groups can free themselves from the overarching disciplinary power of knowledge and realize their own desires in a framework of self-discipline and self-knowledge of their own making.[1]

The legacy of Foucault's work for organization theory is not just a perspective on discipline, negatively construed. In the later work discipline is inextricably linked with the nature of desire and desire finds expression through forms of (self-) discipline freely created and embraced. Foucault himself saw this later work as a shift in emphasis. 'Perhaps I've insisted too much on the technology of domination and power. I am more and more interested in the interaction between oneself and others and in the technologies of individual domination, the history of how an individual acts upon himself, in the technology of the self' (Foucault, 1988b: 19). There is continuity with his earlier work in the ongoing concern with how we can escape an inherited/imposed relation to the self, but in the later work the escape is through the fashioning of our own selves out of our own desires. The first volume of *History of Sexuality* is a transitional work. The investigation of the techniques by which external authority manages the mind gives way to an analysis of techniques that enhance our capacity to assert power over our own behaviour of self-management and of how truth is created through self-management (Hutton, 1988: 132). The aim is to theorize the possibility of new ways of being that escape established forms of discipline, a political and ethical challenge (Privitera, 1995: 103–4). 'If the struggle with this modern power–knowledge–subjectivity formation is a politics of our selves, the key campaign in that struggle will be a new mode of fashioning an ethical way of being a self' (Bernauer, 1994: 63–4). This concern with the possibilities of, as well as the limits to freedom is latent in the unlikeliest of Foucault's works, *Discipline and Punish*, which, as Dumm

(1996: 78) comments, is about 'the practices of freedom and the conditions that bear upon those practices in the modern era. If we approach this book with this in mind, we might come to understand [it] as a preparatory text, a book that sets an agenda for uncovering not only the terms of our imprisonment but the conditions of our freedom.[1]

Although Foucault cautions against the explicit use of the concept of 'liberation', he does describe his later works as primarily interested in 'practices of freedom' (Foucault, 1984: 3). He contrasts these practices with 'states of domination, in which the relations of power, instead of being variable and allowing different partners a strategy which alters them, find themselves firmly set and congealed. When an individual or a social group manages to block a field of relations of power, to render them impassive and invariable and to prevent all reversibility of movement – by means of instruments which can be economic as well as political or military – we are facing what can be called a state of domination' (Foucault, 1984: 3). The practice of freedom is equated with the realization of desire through ethical behaviour in pleasurable relationships with others, and Foucault identifies morality with the 'deliberate' practice of liberty (Foucault, 1984: 4).

A major shift from his earlier work is in the concept of 'subjectification'. Previously, this was equated with 'subjection'. In the later work, subjectification is a process that involves the willing development and exercise of power and knowledge through the development of 'technologies of the self'. Foucault's earlier works study how human beings are 'made subjects'. The later work is dedicated to the principle of the formation and transformation of the self by the self and challenges us to reconsider discipline as perhaps the necessary price that we have to pay for realizing our desires. It is not that there is a radical break in the trajectory of Foucault's work. The later work elaborates his obsession with power–knowledge–discipline but from a perspective of self-creation through self-management in contexts where self-understanding is, as always, constructed in a matrix of social and discursive practices (Hoy, 1986: 18). The contexts examined in the later work are construed as 'allowing' space and time for self-development, and disciplinary practices are seen in a more benign, positive, self-enabling light.

Core themes reappear in the later work. In continuity with Foucault's earlier work, the unrelenting critique of modernist illusions about liberty and self-expression has lost none of its bite. Foucault is still implacably opposed to the Enlightenment heritage that is equated with thinking about 'what is not or is no longer indispensable for the constitution of ourselves as autonomous subjects' (Foucault, 1984: 42). The concern is with self-creation, not with self-discovery. 'I don't feel that it is necessary to know exactly what I am. The main interest in life and work is to become someone else that you were not in the beginning . . . All my analyses are against the idea of universal necessities in human existence. They show the arbitrariness of institutions and show which space of freedom we can still enjoy and how many changes can still be made' (Foucault, 1988b: 9, 11). Postmodern scepticism concerning the one true self remains, but the later work emphasizes human creativity, the ongoing re-creation of self in a quest for knowledge that is itself a form of self-care. The belief that the search for knowledge is liberating unites the ancient practitioners of the technologies of the self that Foucault examines in *History of Sexuality* and modern writers such as Freud. Human nature itself is in a constant process of reconstitution according to the forms of knowledge we create in the perpetual quest for meaning. For Foucault, it is in the creativity that we bring to this quest that our true power is revealed (Hutton, 1988: 140).

The later work challenges the criticism of Foucault's work, by, among others, Habermas (1986), Jameson (1991) and Giddens (1993), for its dystopian character. We need to contest the reading of Foucault's work as little more than an elaboration of Weber's 'iron cage' argument in which modern society and modernism are deconstructed as various expressions of a common theme – the generalization of panoptical or conformist forces in a unitary process of rationalization and normalization, as a result of which we all inhabit carceral archipelagos of one form or another. In *Discipline and Punish*, 'texts, practices and people struggle against each other' (Foucault, 1988a: 140) in contexts where power can seem irresistible, but in the later work the emphasis is different in that Foucault explicitly takes issue with the accusation that he thinks change is impossible. The impulse to 'excavate' our own culture is 'to open a free space for innovation and creativity' (Foucault, 1988d: 163).

> All my analyses are against the idea of universal necessities in human existence. They show the arbitrariness of institutions and show which space of freedom we can still enjoy and how many changes can still be made. (Foucault, 1988a: 11)

Technologies of the self

The Use of Pleasure (Volume Two of *The History of Sexuality*), addresses the following question: 'What were the games of truth by which human beings came to see themselves as desiring individuals?' (Foucault, 1986). The search for an answer to this question is driven 'not [by] the curiosity that seeks to assimilate what it is proper for one to know, but that which enables one to get free. . . . The object was to learn to what extent the effort to think one's own history can free thought from what it silently thinks, and so enable it to think differently' (Foucault, 1986: 8–9). In this text, the 'equilibrium' of Foucault's final work shifts from sex to the more general issue of the ways in which individuals and groups act upon themselves in a process of self-creation. The analysis of the problematization of sexual behaviour in antiquity is conceived by Foucault as one of the first chapters in a general history of 'techniques of self', also called 'arts of existence' in *The Use of Pleasure*, and later (Foucault, 1988b) 'technologies of the self'. The subject is no longer sex *per se* but modes of practice, developed and shared in communities and grounded in mutuality, whose goal is the pursuit of the good life. For example, one of the groups Foucault studies is the Epicureans.

Their '[t]eachings about everyday life were organized around taking care of oneself in order to help every member of the group with the mutual work of salvation' (Foucault, 1988b: 21).

Foucault defines 'techniques of self' as 'those intentional and voluntary actions by which men not only set themselves rules of conduct, but also seek to transform themselves, to change themselves in their singular being, and to make their life an *oeuvre* that carries certain aesthetic values and meets certain stylistic criteria' (Foucault, 1986: 10–11). Knowledge can serve to bind to an imposed discipline, but local knowledge can also provide a framework for self-creation and self-liberation that buffers individuals and groups from the normalizing and totalizing tendencies embodied in claims to universal knowledge. Individuals are not mere 'objects' in 'truth games'. They are self-referencing and self-creating 'subjects,' and the new concept of truth games is one based upon evolving relationships between truth, power and self, a genealogy of how the self constitutes itself as subject (Martin et al., 1988: 4). Technologies of the self are truth games that 'permit individuals to effect by their own means or with the help of others a certain number [and kind] of operations on their own bodies and souls, thoughts, conduct, and way of being, so as to transform themselves in order to attain a certain state of happiness, purity, wisdom, perfection, or immortality' (Foucault, 1988b: 18).

Through forms of self-definition and self-constraint – the *mode d'assujettissement*, 'the acceptance of obligations in a conscious way for the beauty or the glory of existence' (Foucault, 1991: 358) – people train themselves to become ethical persons. Ethical behaviour is the outcome of the shared understanding that comes from belonging to a particular community and from embracing the practice of being a good person according to the rules of that community (Hoy, 1986: 16). Subjectivization, here, is a 'process in which the individual delimits that part of himself that will form the object of his moral practice, defines his position relative to the precept he will follow, and decides on a certain mode of being that will serve as his moral goal. And this requires him to act upon himself, to monitor, test, improve, and transform himself' (Foucault, 1986: 28). Moral codes, therefore, should not be understood merely as an expression of a discipline geared to constraint. The codes of practice Foucault studies in *History of Sexuality* 'did not speak to men concerning behaviors presumably owing to a few interdictions that were universally recognized and solemnly recalled in codes, customs, and religious prescriptions. It spoke to them concerning precisely those conducts in which they were called upon to exercise their rights, their power, their authority, and their liberty: in the practices of pleasures that were not frowned upon' (Foucault, 1986: 23).

Self-creation requires self-sacrifice. Technologies of the self, as expounded in Foucault's analysis of the writings of the Stoics or the Epicureans, demand 'an ascetical practice, giving the word "ascetical" a very general meaning . . . not in the sense of abnegation but that of an exercise of self upon self by which one tries to work out, to transform one's self and to attain a certain mode of being' (Foucault, 1984: 2). In the case of sexuality, the 'quadri-thematics' of sexual austerity 'formed around and apropos of the life of the body, the institution of marriage, relations between men, and the existence of wisdom' (Foucault, 1986: 21). Sexual austerity, too, has liberating effects. It should be understood 'not as an expression of, or commentary on, deep and essential prohibitions, but as the elaboration and stylization of an activity in the exercise of its power and the practice of its liberty' (Foucault, 1986: 23).

Technologies of the self as practices of freedom are identified with an ethic of care for the self: 'an ethic was developing which was very explicitly oriented to the care of oneself, toward definite objectives such as retiring into oneself, reaching oneself, living with oneself, being sufficient to oneself, profiting by and enjoying oneself' (Foucault, 1991: 365). The practices of self-discipline include abstinences, memorizations, examinations of conscience, meditations, silence, and listening to others. Ethics is here construed as the knowledge and the practice of an 'aesthetics of existence'. Ethics and aesthetics are aligned in the notion of self-creation. 'From the idea that the self is not given to us, I think there is only one practical consequence: we have to create ourselves as a work of art' (Foucault, 1991: 351). Indeed the principal aim of this kind of ethics was aesthetic but its achievement is only deemed possible in specific circumstances. 'First, this kind of ethics was only a problem of personal choice. Second, it was reserved for a few people. . . . It was a personal choice for a small elite. The reason for making this choice was the will to live a beautiful life, and to leave to others memories of a beautiful existence. I don't think that we can say that this kind of ethics was an attempt to normalize the population' (Foucault, 1991: 341).

In the trajectory of Foucault's own work a concern with the 'history of ethical problematizations based on practices of the self' replaces the concern with 'a history of systems of morality based, hypothetically, on interdictions' (Foucault, 1986: 13). The production of truth is intimately involved with self governance 'without any relation with the juridical per se, with an authoritarian system, with a disciplinary structure' (Dreyfus and Rabinow, 1983: 235). Consequently there is a shift away from the interest in macrophenomena such as bio-power. In 1983 Foucault states emphatically that he no longer has time for a genealogy of bio-power in which the juridical and the disciplinary combine (Foucault, 1991: 344). Instead he turns his attention to communities in which individuals exercise power over themselves in the 'interstices of power'. Foucault uses this phrase in talking about the *juvenes* of the middle ages. These are male descendants without rights of inheritance, living on the margins of the 'linear genealogical successions which characterised the feudal system' (Foucault, 1980: 201–2). These originators of courtly literature addressed to the wives of landed lords were enmeshed in the 'very inverse of relations of power': 'a landless knight [troubadour] turning up at a chateau to seduce the lord of the manor's wife. So what one had here, engendered by the institutions themselves, was a sort of loosening of constraints, an acceptable unbridling, which yielded this real-fictive joust one finds in the themes of courtly love. It's a comedy around power relations which functions in the interstices of power but isn't itself a real power relation' (Foucault, 1980: 202). Foucault's concern has shifted from the normalization of populations to the choices that are possible in small groups ('elites') who band together to create their own modes of thinking and behaviour within their own communities.

Organization as discipline and desire

The dominant reading of Foucault focuses upon the negatives of disciplinary practice. For example, Townley (1993) examines HRM practices as 'mechanisms of registration, assessment and classification' and argues that they constitute 'a body of knowledge [which] operates to objectify those on whom it is applied. . . . Classification schemes, offered as techniques of simplification and clarification for the analysis of labour, both as effort and object, become inextricably tied to its disciplinary operation. . . . HRM employs disciplinary practices to create knowledge and power. These practices fix individuals in conceptual and geographical space, and they order or articulate the labour process. Processes of individualization and individuation create an industrial subject who is analyzable and describable' (Townley, 1993: 541).

Similarly, Barker (1993) situates Foucault in the line of organization theory that is concerned with control as a central issue, coupling him with Weber in the assumption that organizational life is increasingly rationalized, controlled and controlling, and reiterating Edwards's (1979) view that as control becomes less apparent it becomes more inclusive and powerful. Barker argues that entrapment in organization control is becoming more complete with the growth of 'concertive control', a powerful combination of rational rules and peer pressure in teamworking environments where team members are 'forced' to identify with the team's values and goals for the good of the group.

Neither Barker (1993) nor Townley (1993) consider that individuals might be willing to relinquish some of their desires for longer-term outcomes which satisfy, as Foucault suggests, other (deeper) forms of desire. On the level of explicit analysis, Foucault is turning his back on the world of work in the later concerns examined in this chapter. The problem is to discover a basis for ethical practice that a panopticon power cannot control, and he turns to collective practice between consenting adults in the 'moral, personal, private realm' (Foucault, 1986: 343). However, if one applies these ideas to the world of work and organizations, one can see that, implicitly, Foucault here reflects a growing concern in French social theory with pleasure in work, work as a means of self-realization – 'making work itself the territory of the social, the privileged space for the satisfaction of social need' (Donzelot, 1991: 5). Work involves 'games of truth through which the subject enters into its own formation' (Bevis et al., 1989: 339) but, contrary to Deetz (1992), who draws on Baudrillard (1975) to argue that the monopoly of existing 'codes' suppresses alternative representations, the implication of Foucault's later work is that society and organizations are potentially constituted of a range of discursive practices and are not irretrievably in thrall to any one unitary hegemonic power. It is undoubtedly true that organization 'has to be seen in relation to order and discipline if its power is to be understood' (Deetz, 1992: 37), but seeing organizations in this way is a necessary but insufficient perspective for full understanding. Beneath the veneer of formal organization there exist a variety of codes/ discursive practices which reflect the desires of the various groups that constitute an organization. One needs to consider organizations as the locus of a variety of desires of various groups to understand these codes/practices and the behaviours to which they give rise. Both discipline and desire are manifested in the organization of knowledge. Foucault challenges us to reconsider discipline as the price we have to pay for realizing desire.

Foucault's final emphasis is very much upon practice – taking care of rather than knowing the self (Foucault, 1988b: 22): 'care of oneself denotes a manner of living as well as self-knowledge of a quite different sort from the contemplative: it involves a practical proof, a testing of the manner of living and of truth-telling that yields a certain *form* to this rendering an account of oneself, a life-long examination that issues in a certain *style of existence*' (Flynn, 1994: 109; original emphasis). In modern times, ' "Know thyself" has obscured "Take care of yourself" because our morality, a morality of asceticism, insists that the self is that which one can reject' (Foucault, 1988b: 22). One of the central aims of the second and third volumes in the *History of Sexuality* is to 'investigate how individuals were led to practice, on themselves and on others, a hermeneutics of desire' and to 'analyze the practices by which individuals were led to focus their attention on themselves, to decipher, recognize, and acknowledge themselves as subjects of desire, bringing into play between themselves and themselves a certain relationship that allows them to discover, in desire, the truth of their being' (Foucault, 1986: 5).

Foucault's later concern with 'the constitution of ourselves as men [and women] of desire from Christian confessional practices through the Freudian hermeneutic of sexuality' (Dreyfus and Rabinow, 1986: 114, 117) also reflects his ongoing 'dialogue' with Lacan. Self-mastery is examined as the path to self-interpreting, autonomous, meaning-giving subjectivity in which desires are realized. According to Lacan, desire arises from the relationship between the subject and the other and is grounded in social relationships mediated by symbolic structures. Desire 'desires the recognition of another individual in order to know himself' (Leather, 1983: 109), and human motivation is driven by the unconscious attempt to remedy what is designated a sense of 'lack', of abandonment in the world. The attempt to overcome this sense of abandonment and lack focuses upon establishing symbolic relations with others. These relations structure the absence felt at the heart of individual existence. Being, therefore, is 'collective being-in-process' (Wilden, 1980: xx). The self is not some autonomous actor. Rather

> [d]esire is born of the fact that self-awareness is generated not through a perception of subjectivity, or myself, but through a perception of the Other, the non-me. The self is therefore never 'mine' so much as it is 'mine as given me by the Other'. We are, as it were, never fully in possession of our 'selves'. Rather, we are always seeking the Self from the Other. . . . Since, as Lacan (1977) points out, desire operates at this level of 'lack', what we desire is the Other that gives us our Self. In the Lacanian formula desire is the desire of the Other. . . . To say that we lack something at the center of our being is to say that we lack structure, the structure of an enframing hierarchy, a context which objectifies our being. (Leather, 1983: 109, 112, 116)

We 'find' ourselves in the mirror image of the other. 'The center of our "being" is a lack. We are continually trying to fill this lack through the mediation of the symbol, since that which we lack is our Self as given us by the other and it is the symbol which reconnects us with the Other' (Leather, 1983: 112). In Foucault's later work, communities of practice founded upon technologies of self create the contexts for filling the lack identified by Lacan through the creation of symbolic orders in which new versions of the self are experienced and practised (see Lash, 1985).

Conclusion

The fundamental argument of this chapter is that Foucault's later work opens up new spaces and challenges for discussion about organization. A major challenge concerns the nature of discipline in which the relationship between discipline and desire is a fundamental issue. The later work offers a different Foucault than the one emphasized in critical accounts of the corporate panopticon. In fully assessing Foucault's contribution to organization theory we need to devote more attention to the legacy of this later work and to the ways in which Foucault examines liberating practices as opposed to the constraints of discipline. In doing so we will be performing the important critical task of questioning the overwhelmingly negative view of discipline that has preoccupied critical organization theory.

In this light let us conclude by asking what this alternative Foucault legacy comprises.

1. Foucault's major contribution to social theory is his unrelenting attempt to deconstruct modern definitions of what it means to be a subject. In the later work, this project is construed as a 'political' task but the political manifests itself in an ethics of practice, in technologies of the self through which individuals and groups define themselves. Through these practices, individuals and groups embody forms of action that 'free' themselves from what they consider intolerable in their current situation and thus define their own new limits. Individuals and groups

create their own space in the interstices of power through the elaboration of technologies of the self, forms of self-discipline that are
willingly embraced (de Certeau, 1984). The practice of technologies of
the self provides an important topic for future organization analysis.

2. Foucault's concern is to create 'a historical ontology in relation to ethics
    through which we constitute ourselves as moral agents' (Foucault, 1991:
    351). Foucault advises us to create a critical ontology of our selves,
    which should be conceived not as a theory, doctrine or an accumulating
    permanent body of knowledge but as ethical practices. Such practices
    have as their goal 'the necessity of excavating our own culture in order
    to open a free space for innovation and creativity' (Foucault, 1988b:
    163). The critical ontology of ourselves 'has to be conceived as an
    attitude, an ethos, a philosophical life in which the critique of what we
    are is at once and the same time the historical analysis of the limits that
    are imposed on us and an experiment with the possibility of going
    beyond them' (Foucault, 1984: 50). A critical ontology of ourselves
    should be a major focus of organization analysis, aiming to examine
    both the limits of organization but also organization's potentially
    liberating qualities. Organizations bring individual selves into contact
    with others and allow, if we are willing, new definitions of the self and,
    therefore, of organization itself.

While acknowledging the reality of limits, organization theory needs to be
more concerned with how individuals/groups transcend limitations and
create forms of practice that reflect the pursuit of their own, not others',
desires. Here it is useful to consider organizations as communities of
practice (Brown and Duguid, 1991). In the gap between espoused and actual
practice a variety of communities pursue what the dominant culture would
perceive as non-canonical, developing and elaborating their own beliefs,
technologies, discipline and practices. We need to reconceive of organization as a community-of-communities, acknowledging in the process the
many non-canonical communities that exist in the interstices of formal
organization. Proponents of communities-of-practice argue that these dis-
sident communities must be allowed some latitude to shake themselves free
of received wisdom. 'A community of practice is an intrinsic condition for
the existence of knowledge, not least because it provides the interpretive
support necessary for making sense of its heritage. . . . The social structure
of this practice, its power relations, and its conditions for legitimacy define
possibilities for learning (i.e. legitimate peripheral participation)', (Lave and
Wenger, 1991: 98). Even where attempts are made to suppress such
'dissidence', alternative beliefs and practices survive and sometimes flour-
ish. Foucault's later work gives us a vital perspective on how discipline and
desire can be reconciled. Future research into organizational forms and
practice would do well to devote more attention to the way 'technologies of
the self' are developed to promote such a reconciliation.

Note

1 The major reference points in this chapter is volume two of *The History of Sexuality* (Foucault, 1986) and the collections of later interviews and seminars (Foucault, 1988a–d, 1994).

References

Barker, J.R. (1993) 'Tightening the iron cage: concertive control in self-managing teams', *Administrative Science Quarterly*, 38: 408–37.

Baudrillard, J. (1975) *The Mirror of Production*, St Louis, MO: Telos Press.

Bernauer, J.W. (1994) 'Michel Foucault's ecstatic thinking', in J.W. Bernauer and D. Rasmussen (eds), *The Final Foucault*. Cambridge, MA: MIT Press. pp. 45–82.

Bernauer, J.W. and Rasmussen, D. (eds) (1994) *The Final Foucault*. Cambridge, MA: MIT Press.

Bevis, P., Cohen, M. and Kendall, G. (1989) 'Archaeologizing genealogy: Michel Foucault and the economy of austerity', *Economy and Society*, 18 (3): 323–45.

Brown, J.S. and Duguid, P. (1991) 'Organizational learning and communities of practice: towards a unified view of working, learning, and innovation', *Organization Science*, 2: 40–57.

de Certeau, M. (1984) *The Practice of Everyday Life*. Berkeley, CA: University of California Press.

Deetz, S. (1992) 'Disciplinary power in the modern corporation', in M. Alvesson and H. Willmott (eds) *Critical Management Studies*. London: Sage. pp. 21–45.

Derrida, J. (1978) *Writing and Difference*. Chicago: University of Chicago Press.

Donzelot, J. (1991) 'Pleasure in work', in (eds), G. Burchell, C. Gordon and P. Miller, *The Foucault Effect: Studies in Governmentality*. London: Harvester Wheatsheaf. pp. 251–80.

Dreyfus, H.L. and Rabinow, P. (1983) *Michel Foucault: Beyond Structuralism and Hermeneutics*. Chicago: University of Chicago Press.

Dreyfus, H.L. and Rabinow, P. (1986) 'What is maturity? Habermas and Foucault on "What is Enlightenment?"' in D.C. Hoy (ed.), *Foucault: A Critical Reader*. Oxford: Blackwell. pp. 109–21.

Dumm, T.L. (1996) *Michel Foucault and the Politics of Freedom*. London: Sage.

Edwards, R. (1979) *Contested Terrain: The Transformation of the Workplace in the Twentieth Century*. New York: Basic Books.

Flynn, T. (1994) 'Foucault as parrhesiast: the last course at the College de France', in J. Bernauer and D. Rasmussen (eds), *The Final Foucault*. Cambridge, MA: MIT Press. pp. 102–18.

Foucault, M. (1980) 'The eye of power', in C. Gordon (ed.), *Michel Foucault: Power/ Knowledge*. London: Harvester. pp. 146–65.

Foucault, M. (1983) 'The subject and power', in H.L. Dreyfus and P. Rabinow (eds), *Michel Foucault: Beyond Structuralism and Hermeneutics*. Chicago: University of Chicago Press. pp. 208–26

Foucault, M. (1984) 'What is enlightenment?', in P. Rabinow (ed.), *The Foucault Reader*. London: Penguin. pp. 32–50.

Foucault, M. (1986) *A History of Sexuality, Volume 2: The Uses of Pleasure*. Harmondsworth: Viking.

Foucault, M. (1988a) 'Truth, power, self: an interview with Michel Foucault, October 25, 1982', in L.H. Martin, H. Gutman and P. Hutton (eds), *Technologies of the Self: A Seminar with Michel Foucault*. London: Tavistock. pp. 9–15.

Foucault, M. (1988b) 'Technologies of the self', in L.H. Martin, H. Gutman and P. Hutton (eds), *Technologies of the Self: A Seminar with Michel Foucault*. London: Tavistock. pp. 16–49.

Foucault, M. (1988c) 'The political technology of individuals', in L.H. Martin, H. Gutman and P. Hutton (eds), *Technologies of the Self: A Seminar with Michel Foucault*. London: Tavistock. pp. 145–62.

Foucault, M. (1988d) 'Afterword', in L.H. Martin, H. Gutman and P. Hutton (eds), *Technologies of the Self: A Seminar with Michel Foucault*. London: Tavistock Publications. p. 163.

Foucault, M. (1991) 'On the genealogy of ethics: an overview of work in progress', in P. Rabinow (ed.), *The Foucault Reader*. London: Penguin.

Foucault, M. (1994) 'The ethic of care for the self as a practice of freedom', an interview with Michel Foucault on 20 January 1984, conducted by R. Fornet-Betancourt, H. Becker and A. Gomez-Muller, translated by J.D. Gauthier, in J. Bernauer and D. Rasmussen (eds), *The Final Foucault*. Cambridge, MA: MIT Press. pp. 1–20.

Giddens, A. (1993) 'Critique of Foucault', in P. Cassell (ed.), *The Giddens Reader*. London: Macmillan. pp. 228–35.

Habermas, J. (1986) 'Taking aim at the heart of the present', in D.C. Hoy (ed.), *Foucault: A Critical Reader*. Oxford: Blackwell. pp. 103–8.

Hoy, D.C. (ed.) (1986) *Foucault: A Critical Reader*. Oxford: Basil Blackwell.

Hutton, P.H. (1988) 'Foucault, Freud and the technologies of the self', in L.H. Martin et al. (eds), *Technologies of the Self: A Seminar with Michel Foucault*. London: Tavistock. pp. 121–44.

Jameson, F. (1991) *Postmodernism, Or, the Cultural Logic of Late Capitalism*. London: Verso.

Kilduff, M. (1993) 'Deconstructing *Organizations*', *Academy of Management Review*, 18 (1): 13–31.

Lacan, J. (1977) *Écrits*. London: Tavistock.

Lash, S. (1985) 'Postmodernity and desire', *Theory and Society*, 14: 1–33.

Lave, J. and Wenger, E. (1991) *Situated Learning: Legitimate Peripheral Participation*. Cambridge: Cambridge University Press.

Leather, P. (1983) 'Desire: a structural model of motivation', *Human Relations*, 36: 109–22.

Martin, L.H., Gutman, H. and Hutton P.H. (eds) (1988) *Technologies of the Self: A Seminar with Michel Foucault*, London: Tavistock.

Privitera, W. (1995) *Problems of Style: Michel Foucault's Epistemology*. Albany, NY: State University of New York Press.

Townley, B. (1993) 'Foucault, power/knowledge, and its relevance for human resource management', *Academy of Management Review*, 18: 518–45.

Wilden, A. (1980) *System and Structure*. London: Tavistock.

Index